Discovering Your Vision and Voice

A Rhetoric and Reader

Fourth Edition

General Editors
Dr. Christopher Flavin
Dr. Maureen Johnson

D1231005

FOUNTAINHEAD
PRESS

Our green initiatives include:

Electronic Products
We deliver products in non-paper form whenever possible. This includes pdf downloadables, flash drives, & CDs.

Electronic Samples
We use Xample, a new electronic sampling system. Instructor samples are sent via a personalized web page that links to pdf downloads.

FSC Certified Printers
All of our printers are certified by the Forest Service Council which promotes environmentally and socially responsible management of the world's forests. This program allows consumer groups, individual consumers, and businesses to work together hand-in-hand to promote responsible use of the world's forests as a renewable and sustainable resource.

Recycled Paper
Most of our products are printed on a minimum of 30% post-consumer waste recycled paper.

Support of Green Causes
When we do print, we donate a portion of our revenue to green causes. Listed below are a few of the organizations that have received donations from Fountainhead Press. We welcome your feedback and suggestions for contributions, as we are always searching for worthy initiatives.
Rainforest 2 Reef
Environmental Working Group

Cover designer: Lori Bryan, Fountainhead Press
Design by Permafrost Publishing Services

Books may be purchased for educational purposes.

For information, please call or write:

1-800-586-0330
Fountainhead Press
Southlake, TX 76092
Web site: www.fountainheadpress.com
E-mail: customerservice@fountainheadpress.com

ISBN: 978-1-68036-945-8

Printed in the United States of America

Acknowledgements

The editors would like to acknowledge the ongoing support of the faculty and staff of the Department of Languages and Literature and the College of Liberal Arts at Northeastern State University in making it possible for us to put together another edition of this text that is usable and relevant to our students. We would also like to extend our thanks to Fountainhead Press for their professional support in finalizing the book and their responsiveness throughout the process of writing, editing, and design.

Introduction

The revised edition of *Discovering Your Vision and Voice* expands on the previous edition and refocuses the writing process to be more applicable across the curriculum and to emphasize the need for transferrable knowledge to write effectively, and to write well, throughout a student's university experience and beyond. The individual chapters in this book focus on the most common types of writing students are likely to encounter in an academic environment and are intended to prepare them for more advanced writing processes in Composition II and in upper division courses. Each of the chapters also presents critical skills that are transferrable to life outside the university, as they are necessary for effective writing under many different circumstances. The major chapters are:

Chapter One, "Active Reading, Writing, and Thinking," focuses on key concepts and skills. Critical reading, critical thinking, and engaged, accurate writing are the three skill sets that underlie all of the chapters and readings in this book. New to this edition is information related to effective note-taking and integration to help with retention and research. These are the most important skills for success in students' academic careers and are foundational skills for success after college. Year after year, employers, along with state and federal agencies, stress the need for clear writing and critical thinking as key factors in hiring decisions.

Chapter Two, "The Writing Process," introduces the processes for actually writing an essay. This chapter emphasizes the recursive nature of the process (as steps must often be repeated to write well), as well as the need for students to understand not only how they write, but why they make the choices they do when they write. Included in this chapter is a discussion of revising and editing as parts of the writing process, and writing the in-class essay (a survival guide).

Chapter Three, "Rhetoric and Argument," introduces foundational concepts of rhetoric and the concept of argument as a tool in writing. The need for students to understand not only what rhetoric is, but how it functions and how it can be applied across the curriculum, is critical to their success in academic writing generally and in writing beyond the university.

Chapter Four, "Writing, Logic, and the Rhetorical Modes," establishes the major modes of discourse, how they operate together and separately, and the need for clear logic and construction in student writing. Common problems with logic, such as the use of logical fallacies, are presented, along with reference materials for logical research and scholarly support.

Chapter Five, "Modern Models for Argument and Analysis," introduces some of the models for argument and analysis used in university and professional settings. The chapter outlines strategies for Toulmin and Rogerian argument as well as rhetorical and other forms of analysis.

Chapter Six, "Multimodal Composition," shifts the focus from traditional written essays onto the forms of argument and composition that use additional technologies and elements to build their case. This chapter presents the concepts of composition in other forms (non-written) as well as the ways in which elements translate, or do not, into other media including audio, visual, and online forms.

Chapter Seven, "Putting Writing in Perspective," expands on the concepts presented earlier and previews the kinds of work students will be expected to produce in Composition II and in other courses throughout the university, while contextualizing their work in this course in terms of writing beyond the university. While all academic writing can be seen as a form of argument, specifically argumentative essays have a number of distinct features that set them apart from the other forms discussed in this book.

The major chapters are sequenced so that they build on each other to show both the relationships between the kinds of writing students are expected to engage in and the connections between the forms of writing examined here and the larger needs of writers who apply what they have learned. The chapters, however, can function independently, presenting the student and the instructor with a toolbox of writing modes and methods that can be tailored to fit individual needs and teaching styles.

Likewise, the readings selected for this edition were chosen with a diverse audience in mind and the need for flexible, critical engagement as a fundamental part of university life. While the topics for individual readings range from current events, such as the ongoing military engagements around the world, to classical philosophy, each presents the student with a unique set of challenges and opportunities that reinforce the central ideas of the chapters presented in the rhetoric section.

This book, as is the case with all composition rhetorics and readers, represents a stage of an ongoing project to better prepare students for the expectations of academic writing and writing after college. Feedback, refinements, and suggestions are all welcome as we continue to improve on what we have done here to better serve the students and address the changes in university and workforce expectations.

Contents

Part 1: Rhetoric

Chapter One
Actively Reading, Writing, and Thinking

Writing well is a critical skill for both students and professionals. While it seems obvious that there will be a great deal of writing while you are in college, writing, and the other skills stressed in this course, will have a measurable impact on your life after graduation. Research by the McKinsey Global Institute shows that the average worker spends 2.5-3 hours *each day* engaged in some form of written communication, especially email. Other estimates suggest that, depending on the position, up to 60% of the average American's work day being spent in some form of written communication. What this means for students is that, regardless of your major, writing is likely going to be a major part of your academic and professional careers.

The writing styles, the modes, and the concerns outlined in this book are a starting point to becoming more effective readers and writers in the university and beyond. They are organized, in part, to help you integrate what you have already learned and experienced as a writer into a new framework and to develop the skills you will need moving forward. The concepts become more advanced as you work through the book, and new forms of writing are introduced. But, in the end, these are only starting points you can use to build more complex and nuanced texts of your own as you refine your skills and master the basics. No one is born a good writer, writing is a skill that can be learned and requires a great deal of practice to improve. As students develop, they refine the skills they have and continue to learn new skills and approaches to the material. This book presents some of the foundational information and approaches to make that possible.

Both inside and outside the university, to write effectively, you must be able to think and read critically, write clearly and effectively, and work independently. Each of these concepts are addressed later in this chapter, and each of the chapters in this book will show you how these elements build on other skills in various kinds of writing. While the focus in this course is on how these skills are applied specifically to the kinds of writing you will encounter in your academic work, these skills are transferrable not only to every other class you will take but to your future career and life.

Critical Reading and Critical Thinking

Reading and thinking critically is a process. Simply skimming the material, giving an opinion, and moving on to the next idea is insufficient. You must actively engage with the ideas you are trying to understand or express and show *how* and *why* these things are as they are. Critical thinking is often creative thinking, as it requires that you go beyond the obvious and ask additional questions to discover solutions and connections that are not immediately evident, but there is a method to the way this creativity is applied.

Critical thinking is grounded in fact and is problem driven. In many cases, the problem itself may be much more important than the facts and data you can apply to it. The process is what is most important. The Department of Labor shows the "real world" value of this ability by describing critical thinking this way:

> Problem solving and critical thinking refers to the ability to use knowledge, facts, and data to effectively solve problems. This doesn't mean you need to have an immediate answer; it means you have to be able to think on your feet, assess problems, and find solutions. The ability to develop a well thought out solution within a reasonable time frame, however, is a skill that employers value greatly.

This kind of thinking calls into question assumptions, habits, and the information given and turns them into action and engaged judgments.

Making engaged judgments and creating a plan of action requires prioritizing pieces of the problem at hand and being able to organize them to see how they relate. One model for this is Bloom's taxonomy. In the 1950s a team of academics led by Dr. Benjamin Bloom defined the processes they believe we go through in learning, be it intellectual, emotional, or physical. The culmination of this definition was called Bloom's Taxonomy.

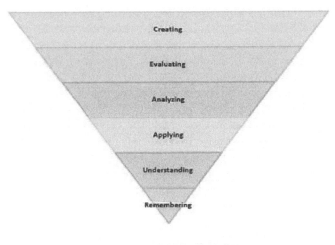

Creating

Evaluating

Analyzing

Applying

Understanding

Remembering

Revised edition by Lorin Anderson (a student of Bloom)

Bloom's Taxonomy of Learning Domains, www.bloomstaxonomy.org

Each of these terms represents a stage of critical thinking and how it can be applied in your writing here and elsewhere. Each of these is also used in a specific way in this book and in academic discourse in general.

- *Remembering*—involves recognizing and recalling information. Much of the work you've done previously in school focused on this first stage, memorizing and recalling, say, the dates and countries involved in World War I.

- *Understanding*—the ability to compare, classify, exemplify, infer, interpret, summarize, and tell or narrate information. Understanding means that you have integrated that remembered knowledge and can phrase it in your own words.
- *Applying*—using acquired knowledge in a new situation; to use facts or rules in a new way to solve a problem, to make predictions, or to act based on the information.
- *Analyzing*—breaking down information into parts, differentiating between and among; identifying motives or causes, and /or organizing information.
- *Evaluating*—checking and critiquing information, employing some type of criteria and explaining that criteria, establishing the merits or quality of the subject.
- *Creating*—synthesizing ideas and/or combining elements into a new pattern, something not there before; generating, planning, and producing new meaning or things.

Critical thinking goes beyond just reading and remembering what was said. To understand something, to engage with the ideas it presents, you must ask questions and look for answers that may not immediately be obvious. You must show that you understand an issue by being able to apply it to a specific event, which creates the opportunity to analyze the information and ideas in new ways or to reevaluate them in a new light. Each of these stages leads toward creating new meaning or new ideas, synthesizing what is read, said, or thought to move in new directions. Critical thinking is never binary (yes/no, black/white), and it requires you to be actively engaged in the process. This is not a hierarchy, it is an open process as individual stages interact and shift in response to different situations and needs. Bloom's Taxonomy is a guide to help understand what level of the process each piece of information or choice is functioning on. Higher level functions build on lower levels of thought, and knowing where you are in the process is an important step in reaching more complex and specific conclusions. Thinking in this way requires you to be aware of not only what you are engaging with, but also how you are doing so, and to be open to creative ways of restructuring your ideas to achieve the result you are seeking.

Robert Harris, in "Introduction to Creative Thinking," gives a good example of this by noting that creative insights can occur simply by changing direction or perspective:

> A classic example is that of the highway department trying to keep kids from skateboarding in a concrete-lined drainage ditch. The highway department put up a fence to keep the kids out; the kids went around it. The department then put up a longer fence; the kids cut a hole in it. The department then put up a stronger fence; it, too, was cut. The department then put a threatening sign on the fence; it was ignored. Finally, someone decided to change direction, and asked, "What really is the problem here? It's not that the kids keep getting through the barrier, but that they want to skateboard in the ditch. So how can we keep them from skateboarding in the ditch?" The solution was to remove their desire by pouring some concrete in the bottom of the ditch to remove the smooth curve. The sharp angle created by the concrete made skateboarding impossible and the activity stopped. No more skateboarding problems, no more fence problems.

This example reveals a critical truth in problem solving: **the goal is to solve the problem, not to implement a particular solution**. When one is not working, shift to another. There is no commitment to a particular path, only to a particular goal. Critical thinking then focuses on "exploring ideas, looking for many right answers rather than just one" (Harris).

The Active Reading Process

Critical thinking is closely tied to critical reading, as discussed below. As with critical thinking, simply reading for information is not enough, as you must be active and engaged in the reading in order to hone these skills.

Critical or active reading is not just reading to gather facts or information for a test. It is not skimming an essay to get an idea of what it argues, or quickly reading a short story to have a few points to contribute to the class discussion. It is an engaged process that connects your own views and opinions with those presented by a given work to come to rational, supported conclusions and to find new meanings and points of connection. This requires you to read slowly and with a purpose, paying attention to the details and to the larger ideas a piece may present. This is a process that gets easier with time and practice, and the strategies outlined here can help you begin to find the most effective ways for you to do this.

The most helpful thing a student can do before reading any text is to get in touch with what they already know about a topic and/or author. Research has demonstrated that it is easier to learn something new if you can connect the information with what you already know. Hence there are pre-reading strategies you can use to facilitate your reading comprehension and speed. In addition, there are things that can be done while you read that will also increase understanding and gather information you can use after reading. After reading a text, in most cases you will need to respond to the information in some way, applying or synthesizing what you have read to make it more immediately relevant or to help yourself better integrate the ideas it presents. There are several ways to do this, but active and rhetorical reading means being involved with not only what you read but how you are reading as you work through a text or assignment.

A pre-reading inventory may help you focus your reading and engage more with the text. Some pre-reading strategies that may help with this course, and across the university, include:

1. *Learn About the Author.* How does their life inform the text?
2. *Skim the Text.* What does the text say/do?
3. *Explore Your Own Knowledge and Beliefs on the Subject.* What do you think?

Many of us do this kind of inventory when we read without really thinking about it. We select the questions and supply our own answers without recognizing what we're doing as we begin reading. This part of the process can be made much more effective and efficient just by taking a few minutes to actively prepare to read a text. While this concept is discussed more later in the book, many students find it helpful to write down their pre-reading questions and their initial responses as part of their **reading notes**.

It may seem like an obvious thing to do, but many students do not make reading notes a part of their reading process. Formal note styles, such as Cornell notes or double-entry notes—like the sample notes at the end of this chapter—allow you to jot down key thoughts or ideas as you read and to come back to those points to develop them. The formatting for these kinds of notes allows you to develop your ideas in an organized way and helps you keep track of your points efficiently. This is particularly useful if you are doing research for an essay or studying for an exam as everything is in order and easy to find.

Some additional active reading strategies might be to:

1. *Annotate the Text.* Read the essay slowly, thinking about what meaning the author is trying to convey. It is a good idea to *annotate* (note or mark) as you read, particularly points that seem important and/or raise questions in your mind. If you don't want to write in your text, try photocopying assigned essays so you can annotate them.

2. *Outline.* An excellent way to distill the meaning of a text is *to create an informal outline* of the argument. If, as part of annotating the essay, you jot down the main subject of each paragraph in the margin, this will allow you to see the organization of the essay and outline it easily.

Outlining may seem to be very close, in some ways, to Cornell notes or other notes systems, but there are a few key differences. The outline method is useful for checking your own comprehension of the material and for finding key points or terms, but not for developing these thoughts or deeper engagement. Think of outlining as a key for finding information in your notes or as a memory aid rather than a substitute for good notes.

Even after reading the text, particularly a long essay or chapter, some post-reading activities may help lock in the important parts for you and help get more from the reading.

3. *Freewrite About the Text After Reading.* Another way to distill the meaning of a text after you have read it carefully is to lay the essay aside and freewrite *for a few minutes about the content and purpose of the essay.* Freewriting is an easy way to gauge your understanding of a text.

4. *Summarize the Text.* Write a summary of what you consider to be the primary meaning of the text and compare it to the original text. This can also serve as the basis for some of the prewriting and brainstorming activities discussed in the next chapter.

To write a clear summary, you must understand the essay. Test your understanding by reading the essay again and deciding whether your summary is accurate. Writing summaries helps you understand your assignments. In addition, you will be asked to write *summary-analysis-response* papers based on the text you read and summarized in many other classes.

5. *Analyze and Evaluate.* Once you have written an accurate summary of the text as presented, analyze and evaluate the thesis statement (or claim), the support points provided, and the conclusion.

These strategies are suggestions, steps in a process, and not a strict system or sequence. For example, you could practice annotation as a reading strategy or study skill only for a given text. Another example would be to survey read and make predictions about a text to gain preliminary information as to whether this is useful information for your assigned task. Each of us has unique habits and approaches that will make some methods more valuable than others; be flexible but keep in mind that it is often necessary to approach different texts in various ways to achieve the best possible results.

Actively Writing

Every field has its own expectations of what it means to write effectively. When you write in a certain course, for a certain professor, or on a specific topic, one of the expectations across the university is that you will adhere to the discourse conventions (the specific ways language is used; how things are said and done) for that course, professor, or topic. A composition course cannot cover all of the possible discourse conventions, but there are a number of concepts that are considered to be traits of effective writing in all the disciplines on campus, and are also valuable in the world outside of the university. Here, we will discuss a few of the most important features and divide them into three broad categories: style, mechanics, and usage.

Style

As writers, we each prefer certain styles. Many times, we will write something the way we might say it in conversation. In many cases, this does not meet all of the conventions for a specific discourse community. A few general guidelines for the appropriate style would include:

Keep your tone professional. This seems obvious, but it is very easy to use inappropriate contractions, shorthands, or local turns of phrase that would be perfectly acceptable in a conversation with your friends, but could turn into a problem in a memo to your boss, in an essay for class, or in other contexts.

Keep the audience in mind. This is closely related to the previous point. Who are you directing your writing toward? Is it your boss, your professor, your coach? Each audience requires slightly different approaches, even if you are providing them with the same information. This is covered in depth in later chapters.

Keep your form in mind. Several different kinds of writing, in terms of purpose and form, are discussed in this book, and more are introduced in Composition II. The kind of essay or response you have been asked to write, or the kind of letter you need to send, has a considerable impact on not only what you write but how you write it.

Be clear and direct. Every word in a sentence should work toward showing the reader something important. This point is discussed in Chapter Two and is mentioned elsewhere throughout this book. Lazy or muddled sentences, or jumbled ideas, alienate your reader and tend to lose their strength. The reader will only have your words on the page to give them your argument, and the more direct and clear you can be the stronger your writing becomes. Simply being direct, professional, and to the point is often the correct choice.

Mechanics

Many students assume that grammar, spelling, and punctuation only matter in English classes. This could not be further from the truth. Regardless of what you write, or to whom you are writing, all of these issues do count. An essay may contain great ideas, but if the reader cannot figure out where one sentence ends and another begins they will not invest the time and energy needed to uncover those thoughts. In a broader context, a poorly-written business letter loaded with misspelled words and awkward phrases will often cost you business (if not your job).

Proofread Carefully. This is discussed in the next chapter of this book, but you should always proofread your work line-by-line for simple mechanical errors. This takes time, but if fifteen minutes means the difference between a B and a D on an essay, or the difference between saving and spending money in the world outside the academy, it is worth it.

Learn the Rules. Some punctuation, such as commas, and the required citation style for a particular class or field can be difficult to master. While it may be tempting to trust the grammar checker on your computer or to use the citation generator, software is only as good as the information you put in and will increase the number of errors you make in most cases. Simply learning the rules can save you a great deal of time and a number of headaches later.

Using the handbook to clear up issues you are having can go a long way toward solving some common problems in writing. You should also visit the writing center or use the available tutoring services to help you focus on specific mechanical issues you are having; the more specific you are regarding the problems you're having the more help these resources can provide. Also, every citation style (MLA, APA, Chicago) has slightly different rules as to where some punctuation is used or how some of the mechanical elements of a sentence work.

Control Your Sentences. Run-on sentences and fragments are often mechanical problems. These are usually easy to fix, but they can do a considerable amount of damage to your work if they are not corrected.

Use

The way we use words in our writing is important. Some of this is stylistic, as was discussed above, and some of it is mechanical, but the words you choose make a difference. The right word makes all the difference. Some problems, such as problems with pronouns, vague wording, or improperly used terms can be difficult to identify. A few quick rules for effective writing might be:

Right Words, Right Places. Use the language appropriate for the subject, including specialized terms or jargon, and use them in the correct way. If you are not certain that a word is right in context, it probably isn't. Similarly, if the reader does not know a word and cannot figure out its meaning from context, you probably want a different word.

No "Fluff." Get rid of excessive language within a sentence. Say what you mean, mean what you say, and be direct. Overly poetic language, circumlocutions (talking around something, i.e., "passed away" instead of "died"), and unnecessarily complicated syntax distract the reader and add nothing to your work.

This Word May Not Mean to the Reader What It Means to You. Every word has a connotative and denotative meaning. The denotative definition of any word, the dictionary definition, may have several options to choose from. The connotation of the word, what it means in a specific context, lets you know which of the possible denotative meanings is intended. Just because a word means one thing where you live does not guarantee that your reader has all of the same connotations for the term. While this is related to the first point about "right words," be aware of any local color or odd uses that may creep into your writing. When in doubt, use a different word that will be clearer to someone outside your region.

Each of these categories is closely related to the others. As you will see in Chapter Two (The Writing Process), and in the other chapters, all of the elements of effective writing overlap and depend on each other to move ideas forward. Writing uses critical thinking, critical reading, and effective use, but good writing is always more than the sum of the pieces that it brings together.

Students often assume that good writers are simply talented at writing. Writing is actually a skill. The distinction between *talent* and *skill* is important because we can learn to master skills. It doesn't take any particular talent to figure out how to summarize an essay or where a comma goes. Writing involves many different elements, some of which are complex and even complicated, but anyone can learn to write well if they apply themselves. In addition, even good writers can improve their skills to become better writers. And, if you are lucky enough to have some talent at writing, a little work on improving critical skills will yield huge results and help you to be a better writer.

Taking Effective Notes

Academic reading assignments, which range from textbook chapters to peer-reviewed academic articles, require time, patience, and concentration. These denser texts, which often contain unfamiliar technical or discipline-specific language, can take 2-3 times as long to read as a more casual article of the same length. Some might panic, while others may simply scan the text to get the main idea; neither strategy will lead to a solid understanding of the text. Similarly, it is essential to note that reading for test-worthy details (names, dates, and definitions) is a very simplistic approach that does not allow for the in-depth, analytical reading habits necessary to perform research, to write solid argumentative essays, and to fully understand more demanding texts.

Strong note-taking skills improve attentiveness and reading comprehension, which can significantly reduce stress when studying for examinations and writing essays. Many readers struggle to remain focused when the text is less pleasurable and compelling than what they would personally choose. If these same readers would actively take notes whenever they are reading for class, they will likely find it easier to remain focused, to remember what they have read, and to better organize what they have learned, when asked to deliver a speech or to provide a written response. Passive reading leads to a superficial understanding of the text, at best.

In this section, we will explore several different approaches to taking reading notes, and you will have the opportunity to practice these strategies, using Barbara Tuchman's "The Historian as Artist" as a demonstration and practice text.

SQ3R or SQRRR (Survey, Question, Read, Recite, Review)

SQ3R is a reading technique developed by Francis Pleasant Robinson and published in his 1946 text, *Effective Study*. Robinson's goal was to empower students to read critically and accurately, and his technique is particularly effective for reading and understanding college-level textbooks, but the steps can be adapted for other genres. While many students learned this strategy in their primary or secondary schools, others were not taught explicitly how to use this technique. SQ3R is the "grandparent" of many note-taking and reading comprehension strategies developed over the past few decades, so we will focus first on this strategy.

Survey: Skim the text you are to read, focusing on titles, introductory materials, headings, subheadings, graphs and charts, boxed text, highlighted vocabulary words, and summary notes.

Question: Write a set of pre-reading questions, based on what you discovered while surveying the text. If subheadings and headings are used, you could convert those into questions. While this stage will likely only take a few minutes, these questions are essential because they help readers maintain their focus while working through the text.

Read: Assisted now by a quick survey and a series of pre-reading questions, it is time to actively read the text to see how it addresses your pre-reading questions. You can take reading notes on the same paper you used to record your questions.

Recite: After you have finished reading the text, close your book, turn your paper over, and, using your own words, write down the major ideas and answers to the pre-reading questions you drafted.

Review: Check your recitation against the actual text and your notes to verify that you have accurately recalled the material you just read. Re-read and revise your notes, as necessary.

Let us look now to our example text, "The Historian as Artist," which comes from Barbara Tuchman's collection of essays, *Practicing History* (1981). This essay does not follow the readerly expectations one might have of a textbook because her audience is more open to the general reading public. Thus, she does not provide the introductory or concluding materials many rely on to help understand textbook discourse and information: summaries, outlines, word banks, comprehension questions, and subheadings. SQ3R may seem less workable than other options, but it can be adapted, in part, to understand this excerpt.

Survey: Beginning with the title, "The Historian as Artist," we understand that she will demonstrate how a historian is, or can be, an artist; we do not know how she will make that connection, or what she means by it, but we have a two-word start: "historian" and "artist." We can also skim the text to see if any words are in *italics* or **boldface**, and there are quite a few. Beginning on the first page and continuing throughout, Tuchman uses italics to emphasize words; in other cases, she presents a variety of other resources to us, and as they are book titles, they appear in italics.

Question: Sample questions might include: What does Tuchman mean when she uses the word "artist?" Does she argue that history writers are artists? What is the significance of the book titles she references?

Read: An attentive reader discovers that Tuchman argues that history writers should and can be creative writers because they should engage the general public in the stories found in history by being both clear and interesting. She uses the term "artist" as more of a description of the work a historian does, rather than as some lofty title bestowed upon classic artists. She refers to a wide range of books, including one of her own titles (*The Proud Tower*), as well as widely-known authors and characters from novels, because she wants to demonstrate the similarities between literary fiction and creative nonfiction.

Recitation and Review would follow next, prompting you to re-read with greater attention to detail and to meaning.

Cornell Notes

We imagine that most students will be familiar with Cornell notes, a system developed in the 1950s by Walter Pauk, a professor at Cornell University, and which appeared in his book *How to Study in College.* Not all students will find this method helpful, nor does it suit every subject or note-taking situation well, but it does help many students recall concepts, connections, models, theories, and other more abstract concepts. Students might find this method particularly suited to the synthesis writing you will do this semester.

The general format for the Cornell notes system includes two columns, the left much narrower than the right, as well as a text box below for summary. Students should use the larger column to record notes, whether from class discussions or from reading assignments, then return to these notes within the next 24 hours. The second step is to review the notes and to reflect on the material to see where possible test questions or connections to other materials might be made, and then record these questions and connections in the left-hand column. The summary box is for students to record a summary, in their own words, regarding the material on that page. Using Cornell notes to record a class discussion or lecture is a slightly different approach, given that shorthand and key words are emphasized when taking class notes, whereas the system would need to be tweaked when using the concept for taking reading notes.

Below is an example of how Cornell notes can be applied to reading Barbara Tuchman's "The Historian as Artist" (in the *Readings* portion of this book).

Date:	Citation: Tuchman, Barbara. "The Historian As Artist." *Discovering Your Vision and Voice.* Ed. Christopher Flavin. Fountainhead Press, 2014. 139-143. Print.
Questions, Comments, Connections	**Notes and Quotes**
Why does Tuchman use the word "artist" to describe the work of a historian?	p. 139 reports that Trevelyan said "that ideally history should be the exposition of facts about the past, 'in their full emotional and intellectual value to a wide public by the difficult art of literature.'" p. 140–141 notes that historians must work to understand the evidence and use imagination to make connections, fill in missing pieces, and understand how and why X happened
Why is she talking about "real estate" in this piece?	p. 140 "real estate" refers to the idea that historians are brokers of fact, truth, and reality ... writers of reality ... historians are thus realtors ... and "real estate" describes the genre they are writing
What are the three parts to the creative process? *Similar to the canons of rhetoric: vision=invention, memory, delivery; medium = style; design or structure = arrangement, memory	p. 141 "first, the extra vision with which the artist perceives a truth and conveys it by suggestion. Second, medium of expression: language for writers, paint for painters, clay or stone for sculptors, sound expressed in musical notes for composers. Third, design or structure."
Her examples for the three parts of the creative process	p. 140–141: qtd. from Trevelyan: "the largest intellect, the warmest human sympathy and the highest imaginative powers" p. 141–142 "clarity, interest, and aesthetic pleasure" "my own form is narrative, which is not every historian's"
What challenges do "realtors" face in their writing?	p. 142–143 "structure is chiefly a problem of selection" "how to explain background and yet keep the story moving" "how to create suspense and sustain interest in a narrative of which the outcome (like who won the war) is [. . .] known"
Ouch!	p. 143 slams Truman Capote for deeming himself an original, when historians have been doing what he's been doing since Herodotus
Historians rely on imagination and moral sympathy to fill in the blanks between what is known about a person or event, and this reliance is part of why Tuchman refers to historians as artists: their task is far more creative than many realize.	

Double-Entry Notes

Some students prefer a less scripted approach to note-taking; double-entry notes are also beneficial for many because they help distinguish between what the text says and how the reader responds. This approach can be particularly beneficial when reading sources for research and other writing because most students work hard to avoid academic dishonesty, but struggle with the opposite problem: finding ways to integrate sources into their writing.

Double-entry notes can be divided into two columns on a page, with the textual information on one side (i.e., brief quotes, definitions, theories, interpretations, etc.) and the reader's response on the other. Some prefer to jot down a brief note or quotes from the text, followed by their own response. The reader's response might include questions about what something means or how this particular source connects to another source. Other response notes might identify where the text provides solid evidence to support the reader's interpretations and arguments. Regardless, it is important to distinguish between fact and opinion, between what one person said and how another interprets the same issue. You also want to find a way to clarify where *your* thoughts begin and end so that all work is properly attributed.

Here is a brief example of how double-entry notes might compare to the Cornell notes example laid out previously.

Tuchman, Barbara. "The Historian as Artist." *Discovering Your Vision and Voice*. Ed. Christopher Flavin. Fountainhead Press, 2014. 139–143. Print.

a.   p. 140–141 Trevelyan notes that historians must work to understand the evidence and use imagination to make connections, fill in missing pieces, and understand how and why X happened

*Similar to what I just read in Shannon Swearingen's interview with Jason Bittel, in creativity in science writing. Bittel said: "I read scientific papers every day; they're the foundation upon which my craft is built, but I can tell you right now that you will not like the way they taste. They're thick, they're dry, and they're full of words you will have to Google. That's why I see it as my job to take all of those raw ingredients—facts, figures, and interviews—and turn them into something palatable. A spoonful of creative writing helps the science go down."

re: "The Line Between Science and Writing: An Interview with Jason Bittel."

Creative Nonfiction. n.d. https://www.creativenonfiction.org/online-reading/line-between-science-and-writing

---

The double-entry note-taking system provides more space for the reader to make meaningful connections, to point out where something is unclear or contradicts other sources, and to offer alternatives to the author's interpretations. Thus, using double-entry notes might well prove more meaningful for many students, particularly those who have less experience responding to texts and using these texts as evidence for their own ideas. Many students who use this technique state that they use the double-entry system as a form of prewriting to help them discover what they want to say before they begin drafting.

Regardless of which style of note-taking you prefer, taking good notes is key to the kind of active reading you will need in order to both remember the major points of what you read and be able to use the information effectively in your own writing. Good notes and active reading make research much easier and help you better organize your thoughts *before you sit down to write*. As noted earlier in this chapter, this seems like common sense but many students either have not been shown how to take effective notes or don't really understand why good notes are so important. Finding a note style that works for you, the material you are studying, and your field, can require a little trial and error, so being aware of several different formats for taking notes can also be very helpful.

Conclusion

No one is born a good writer; good writing comes from practice and being engaged with the material, and writing is a major component in most professional fields today. Being able to recognize not only what you are doing as you attempt to solve problems, form arguments, or engage with new ideas often means being able to put your thoughts in order (Bloom's taxonomy, for example) and being able to think critically and clearly about the issue and to see it from different perspectives. This process of critical thinking extends to critical reading, being able to really engage with problems in writing and in your research in order to write about it effectively. Taking good notes and being able to apply critical thought are key elements of active reading. All of the points raised in this chapter are part of the process of becoming an effective professional in your field and a successful academic writer in your classes. Another part of the process of developing as a writer is being aware of your writing process and how to overcome problems you find in your own writing, which is the topic of the next chapter.

Chapter Two

The Writing Process

Just as active reading and critical thinking are processes, effective and engaged writing is a process with several steps involved. The more aware you are of your writing process, the steps involved, and how you most effectively work through that process, the easier it is to write clearly and effectively for a variety of purposes. The writing process itself can be broken down into a few clear stages for students in a composition course:

- *Prewriting:* Generating ideas
- *Drafting:* Translating those ideas into words on paper or screen
- *Revising:* Looking at what has been written and making changes
- *Editing:* Correcting typos or errors to polish the final piece

Any form of writing involves a process of discovery: through the writing process, we clarify our ideas and feelings on a topic. Clarifying our ideas is useful when we know what we want to say but cannot find the right words, when we are faced with the fear of a blank computer screen, or when we are exploring what we know about a topic. Even when we have a list of ideas or notes, the writing process helps us determine *what* to do with this information: how to organize it, how to establish connections among ideas, or how to see where we might need to do more reading or research to support our ideas. In short, writing goes hand-in-hand with thinking. The writing process is a vehicle that connects us to discovery and meaning-making rather than strolling through the aisles of thought looking for perfectly prepackaged ideas to fill an empty shopping cart of form.

A lot of planning and work goes into a piece of writing throughout its development, and "behind the scenes of a finished product is a messy process of exploratory writing, conversation, discarded drafts, and midnight agony" (Sachs). By understanding your own writing process, you can improve both the quality of your writing process and the finished essay you produce (Coe viii).

Writing is messy, even though the stages of the writing process may suggest it as a sequence of linear steps:

> Prewriting → Drafting → Revising → Editing

As you read about the stages of the writing process and reflect on your own writing experiences, though, you should be able to see that the process isn't linear; it is recursive and closer to "the forward motion of a wheel, the leading edge breaking new ground but then doubling back on itself" (Lindemann 24):

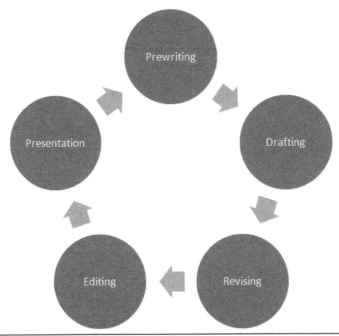

Stages of the Writing Process

In addition to being recursive (a continuous cycle), the writing process is highly individualized: no two writers' process look exactly alike. Your age, experience as a writer, and your writing task can also change your writing process (Lindemann 22). Chapter One introduced the fundamentals of active reading and academic writing. The strategies in this chapter will help you become an effective writer by teaching you how to become more aware of your writing process and how the process impacts the final written product.

Prewriting

From the moment we get a writing task, we are frequently thinking about it at some level, working out a lot of the preliminary exploration, idea generation, and organization of the topic. Invention techniques can help you generate information and are also a great way to develop and explore ideas rather than simply repeating them. Five common invention techniques are **brainstorming, clustering, freewriting, journals**, and **heuristics**. Try to practice with several of these options and challenge yourself to vary the techniques you rely on. Some invention techniques might be more natural for a writer's personality and style; some invention techniques might suit an academic discipline or assignment better than others.

Brainstorming is a form of free association where you write whatever comes to mind about a topic, no matter how obvious or strange the ideas might be. The more ideas and material you can generate in your brainstorming, the more useful it will be, and you might even be delighted to see interesting details and patterns that emerge. What details jump out at you? In what ways can the details be grouped? What patterns have emerged in the list? You can brainstorm by yourself, or you can bounce ideas off of friends or classmates.

Example

Topic: Things that annoy you

- *Bad drivers: changing lanes/too slow or too fast/aggressive drivers/distracted drivers (cell phones)*
- *People who use cell phones in bathrooms (or don't wash their hands after using bathroom)*
- *Bad hygiene habits: Like bathroom? Sneezing on their hands? Coughing or sneezing without covering mouth? Bad during cold and flu season!*
- *Talking during movies—anything distracting during movies: cell phones again! Bright screens in dark theaters! What about bringing a toddler to an R-rated movie? High ticket prices. Every movie is 3-D now.*

Clustering, also called "mapping" or "webbing," can be used as its own strategy or can be used to organize items from a brainstorming list. To use this technique, put a word, phrase, or sentence in a circle at the center of your page. Then, put every new idea in a circle and show its relationship to a previous thought by drawing a connecting line. Clustering helps you explore the many possible ways to organize your material. Clustering also shows you the relationships among topics, subtopics, and supporting examples.

From the brainstorming list above, an idea emerged from the last item on the brainstorm list: movie annoyances. Let's take that idea as a new topic and cluster it, putting the main topic in the center bubble and the supporting points around it, like spokes of a wheel:

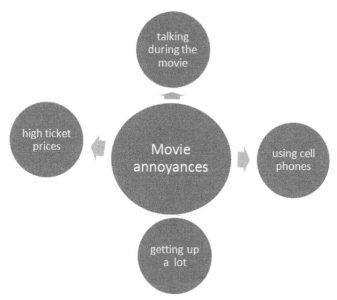

Freewriting can help you discover what you want to say, and, similar to brainstorming, is a form of free association. To freewrite, write for 10-20 minutes, without stopping, about anything that comes into your head: What are you seeing, feeling, touching, or thinking? Do you have nothing to say? Say so. Recopy the sentence you just wrote—the crucial thing is to keep writing, even if you feel like you have nothing to say. Your freewriting might even look something like this:

> I have to write this paper about what annoys me, but so many things annoy me. Am I a bad person? I notice how often cell phones annoy me—I wonder why? I decided on movie annoyances. I think my list is not very good. I worry that I will sound like a grouchy old lady instead of someone convincing and rational. But I still think this is important to talk about—maybe I could merge cell phones and movie annoyances since cell phones seem to be their own movie annoyances. It's like cell phones bring out a whole other level of rudeness in people than we've seen before, and combined with the darkness of a movie theater, people feel more anonymous and brave—maybe? I like the idea of darkness providing cover, kind of like how people can be ruder on the internet because no one knows who they are. I read things online that make me sad with their rudeness and anger—would people really talk like that to someone in person? Is that why even when people are on their phones in the movie no one confronts them but they make comments under their breath? I am starting to wonder about this.

At the end of your freewriting time, look at what you've written. There might be a lot of filler or unusable thoughts, but you might also be surprised at discoveries or insights you produced. Find words or phrases that jump out at you. Put these words or phrases at the top of a second page and start freewriting again, letting your thoughts take shape around the emerging ideas.

Journals provide a place for you to write without the fear of making mistakes or facing criticism for what you've written. It is similar to freewriting, but with a journal, you have more of a sense of writing *to* someone, such as yourself or your teacher. A journal can be a space to record your thoughts and feelings, write down your dreams, favorite quotes, funny jokes, or song lyrics; respond to reading assignments, record questions for class discussions; or make lists; the possibilities are endless.

Heuristics prompt thinking by means of questions. Most of you are familiar with the heuristic questions journalists use: Who? What? Where? When? How? Why? Heuristic questions do not have right or wrong answers, but they do encourage you to explore different points of view or produce thoughts or details useful to your writing assignments. Here is an example of using direct questions to generate ideas for the topic movie annoyances:

Who: *Who goes to movies? [People of all ages: friends, couples, families, parents]*
       Who commits these annoyances? [Anyone with a cell phone, which is most everyone these days]

What: *What happens? [People talk or text during the movie]*
       What do the guilty parties do? [Use phones when they're supposed to be quiet]

What do the rest of the moviegoers do?[Tell the cell phone users to be quiet or stop, or they sigh, mutter under their breath, or kick the person's chair]

Where: *Where does this take place? [Inside the specific theater where a movie is playing]*

When: *When does this happen? [At the beginning of the movie, or throughout]*

How: *How are these behaviors annoying? [The light from the phone screen and the sound of talking distract others from watching the movie; they may not be able to hear dialogue or miss important scenes of the movie]*

Why: *Why do they happen? [Increasing reliance on cell phones; being connected all the time; sometimes there could be practical reasons, like an emergency or a sick child at home.]*

To use heuristics as an invention technique, write each question on a sheet of paper, leaving space between them. Then write phrases or sentences to answer each question as it relates to your topic. Look over your answers. You might discover that you had more to say about one or two of the questions, or that your answers were all fairly balanced, or that you were not able to answer a question. How might this awareness help you decide on a thesis? How might it reveal where you need more information, either through library research, reading, or examples? For example, the heuristic questions for "movie annoyances" reveal that the writer has a lot more to say about the "how" and "why" something happens rather than the "when" or "where." How might you use this lack of balance to direct your research or to shape your paper?

Do not wait until you are in the middle of your paper to try to figure out what you want to discuss. Find and explore topics before you begin the paper, which will make writing the paper much less stressful and much more effective. Try using several invention techniques in order to help you determine the order of your ideas in your essay. For example, use brainstorming to generate ideas and use clustering to organize the information from the brainstorming list, show relationships among ideas, and create an informal outline of the order of your response.

Your next step is to consider **audience, purpose,** and **form** (or genre). Your writing assignments will often tell you who your audience should be and what the purpose and form of the assignment should be (Flachmann and Flachmann 23). The first feature, **audience**, identifies the person or the group of people you will address in your essay. What does your audience already know, think, or feel about your topic? The second feature, **purpose**, is your reason for writing the essay: Is your goal to entertain? To inform? To speculate? To argue? This usually takes the form of a **thesis statement**, the controlling idea of your essay. The third feature, **form** (or genre), determines the format of the written product. A financial analysis for an investment class looks different than a literary analysis in a Shakespeare class; a research proposal for a graduate course in educational research looks different than a treatment plan in a counseling class. Because of these differences, knowing what format or genre is required helps you make decisions about the design, the organization, and the style of your paper.

Together, knowing your audience, purpose, and form helps you make many decisions about the writing process: what types of sentences you use, what words you choose, what you want to say, what you need to say, or even what you *can* say.

Drafting

In the drafting stage of the writing process, you use your information from the prewriting material to write a draft of your paper. Your assignment and your prewriting should have helped you make important preliminary decisions about your topic, purpose, and audience, so the drafting should follow as a natural next step (Flachmann and Flachmann 23). In most cases, depending on your assignment or writing task, the purpose of your paper is to **solve a problem** or to **answer a question**.

For example, imagine that your Comp I instructor asks you to write a 3-4 page **rhetorical analysis** of what good writing in your chosen major looks like and how you can write effectively in that field. The problem or question is posed in the assignment (identifying what good writing in your major looks like), another question is posed by your research (how does good writing in your field work), and the solution or answer will be provided in your essay (by analyzing both the form and content rhetorically).

When you sit down to write your paper, remember that your drafting stage should help you generate plenty of raw material. As tempting as it may be to read and re-read every sentence, focus on developing your ideas before you worry about correctness or how your audience will react to them. *Use your knowledge of the writing process as a recursive process, not a linear one, while you write a draft of your essay.* Have you written everything you wanted to say, but the paper is too short? Go back to your invention techniques to explore your topic from other avenues. Have you read through what you've written so far and don't feel like you've given enough supporting examples to justify your reading? Brainstorm more examples, or try asking "how" or "why" after your main points to see if any additional questions arise. Are you stuck on what to say next and getting stressed about finishing your paper? Freewrite for 15 minutes to quiet your inner critic or to flex your writing muscle so that you can continue with your assigned paper topic.

During the drafting stage, do not hesitate to experiment with different ways of organizing your material. If you were given a cause-and-effect analysis essay prompt, there are several ways to organize the response: the writer could explore all relevant causes and effects, progressing either from the least to most influential or the most to least influential; the writer could discuss multiple causes that created a single effect; or the writer could analyze how multiple effects traced back to a single cause. Most kinds of writing you are likely to encounter in the university classroom are just as flexible. In many cases, there is no one *right* way to structure your essay but there are *better* ways to present your thoughts depending on audience, purpose, and the expected form the writing will take.

The Revision Process

The revision stage of the writing process involves more than correcting grammar or fixing sentences; it is crucial to your writing. The revision process can be stressful, whether you are a student or a professional writer. We invest much of ourselves—time, energy, intellect, and passion—in the writing process. To have our writing returned to us with multiple directives and a note that says, "Revise!" may very well send us into a tailspin. Student writers should be heartened to know that instructors, as well as other writing professionals, have to revise all of the time, whether they are writing an essay, a course design, a letter to the Dean, a quarterly report, or an email to a colleague. Understanding how revision works is *not* a simple process; just as we cannot rely on a set of rules to help us write beautifully and clearly in each and every rhetorical situation, we cannot rely on a set "how-to" list when it comes to revision. This chapter, however, will provide preliminary strategies for a solid revision foundation.

Before we begin, we must define several commonly used terms: global revision, local revision, editing, and proofreading.

Global Revision: This step involves the most work, but is sometimes absolutely necessary. If you misunderstood the assignment, you must rewrite the majority of the essay. Global revision also can include reworking a thesis and argumentative structure, using new and different forms of evidence, addressing a different audience, rewriting the essay in a different voice (i.e., the difference between a social letter and an academic essay), and redefining terms and reestablishing ideas.

Local Revision: You may discover that certain parts of the essay are in need of revision, such as the introduction or the conclusion. Perhaps the way one source is incorporated into the essay is a problem. Another very common error is that many students rely on passive voice and on second-person voice; others believe that they must frame all of their ideas as "I think," "I feel," and "I believe" statements. Thus, the student focuses on these limited-scale revisions, *but also must review the entire essay to be sure that the new elements work.*

Editing: Until we review our writing, we have no idea how easily our sentences can become mangled between our brains and the page. Some examples of this process are editing sentences to reduce the use of jargon, editing to avoid wordiness, and editing to avoid repeating the same sentence structure over and over (where inappropriate, rhetorically).

Proofreading: Most think of proofreading when they hear the word "revision." Proofreading *is* important, but it is not the same activity as the previous three. Proofreading requires diligent attention to each and every word, phrase, and sentence in an essay. You must attend to subject/verb agreement issues, punctuation problems, citation errors, formatting errors, and homonym errors, such as confusing its/it's, your/you're, there/their/they're, witch/which, our/hour, etc.

This list is not intended to overwhelm writers; certainly, the more we grow as writers, the more natural and instinctive our revision habits become. The rest of this chapter will focus on strategies you can use to help revise, edit, and proofread your essays.

Global Revision

While global revision may entail rewriting an entire essay, this is rarely the case. Usually, writers need to sit down and examine the different components of their essays, especially those related to their readers' and instructors' comments. For example, an instructor might say, "Your sources are not appropriate for this assignment, and your citations are not well-integrated into your essay. In addition, your voice is not appropriate for an academic audience. I suggest that you work to find scholarly resources and to rewrite your sentences so that they sound more professional, more scholarly."

At first glance, it may seem that the writer will have to start all over; however, the thesis or controlling purpose may well be sound, as might be the introduction and conclusion paragraphs. The overall argument might be well-reasoned, and the writing may progress logically from Point A to Point B. If the teacher or your other readers have not addressed other key components in your writing, do *not* assume that all is well. And do *not* assume that you will only have to do one revision to "fix your mistakes." We recommend that you work to address the immediate and most pressing concerns, as identified by your instructor and other readers, leaving yourself a few extra days, at least, to continue to revise, edit, and proofread. Read the example below to see one example of a poorly integrated source:

> Howard M. Spiro, a doctor, says:
>
> Empathy helps us to know who we are and what we feel. Nowhere is the old saw, 'if you don't use it, you lose it,' truer. During medical education, we first teach the students science, and then we teach them detachment. To these barriers to human understanding, they later add the armor of pride and the fortress of a desk between themselves and their patients. (8-9)
>
> Spiro goes on to say that undergraduates are really passionate about medicine, but later become too focused on disease to the point where they don't care about the patient.

Perhaps you wonder what the problem is with the above example. After all, the quote is cited, and the writer does use his own words to discuss Spiro's essay. The problem is that the writer barely exists in this paragraph. This is nothing more than an account of what someone else has thought and has written. The long block quote is an excellent sign that the writer is having trouble developing his own ideas, or perhaps understanding the research well enough to write confidently. The student has not, therefore, posed an argument; he has merely told us what somebody else has already said. Here is an example of how Spiro's thoughts might be better integrated into an essay:

> Many real-life physicians, such as Howard M. Spiro, persistently worry about the damage done to the medical student, both in the classroom and in the teaching hospital. He notes the physical distance between physician and patient, maintained

by a large, official desk; **presumably, this distance-creating desk is also employed when training medical students, in order to physically and visually reinforce the distinctions between student-status and expert-status.** That students begin learning on dead bodies before practicing with live ones further reinforces these lessons in detachment, and does not allow for empathy to flourish. **Although the training that medical students receive is both excellent and rigorous,** Spiro argues that if knowledge is honored at the expense of empathy, then physicians face possible burn-out, substance abuse problems, and eventually lose the ability to maintain their strongest diagnostic tool: listening.

The writer still relies a little too much on Spiro's ideas in this example, but he has improved dramatically by using his own words to discuss Spiro's ideas *and* by incorporating more of his own interpretation. The bold text represents the student's own interpretation and analysis.

What Is A Thesis?

While some of this information has been covered in the first chapter, it is worth reviewing the purpose of a thesis, its function in your essay, and how your thesis can be clarified and refined to improve your essay. This section is a quick review of what a thesis is, and also what a good thesis is not, in academic writing.

A thesis may be contained in one or two sentences, or it may appear more as a controlling purpose that organizes the inquiry (research + argument) in your essay.

A thesis may make a claim:

"Princess Culture," while often disparaged, may provide models of strength and intelligence to young girls, not mere visions of passive virtue dressed in fancy gowns.

A thesis may organize your analysis and research:

My project is to explore the nuances of physician-patient relations as they appear in popular television series such as *Grey's Anatomy, House, M.D.,* and *Private Practice.*

If your thesis looks like any of the following examples, it is time to completely revamp your essay.

A thesis does not announce the essay's topic:

In this essay, I will discuss abortion in American society.

A thesis does not state that the essay will explore the pros and cons of a particular behavior:

This essay explores the pros and cons of attending a university.

A thesis is not a statement of fact:

A lot of dangerous chemicals are used to make meth.

How do you begin to develop your thesis? Let's start at the most basic point. What is the purpose of your essay? How long must it be? Who is the audience? Does the assignment require research? How many sources must be scholarly? Review your assignment prompt, review your handbook, and make absolutely certain that you understand the requirements.

Let us begin with a typical example. Alison wants to write about how advertisers often portray men as incompetent. She has heard her father sigh with disgust while they watch television together, and has noticed that men in advertising are different from the men she knows in real life, including her father, her classmates, her boss, and her teachers. She begins with a basic sentence:

I want to explore how advertisers treat men.

Next, Alison frames the declarative sentence as an interrogative sentence:

How do advertisers portray men?

Her question prompts her to pay attention to television, magazine, newspaper, and Internet advertisements. She writes down eighteen examples that caught her eye. For each example, she writes a few notes about what she saw in the advertisement. For some, she noticed that the men were portrayed almost as helpless as children, while in others, they were likened to dogs. She divides her research up, and discovers that she found more examples of television ads that portrayed men as imbeciles, so she decides to focus purely on television ads. This leads her to more analysis: the ads typically appear during women's programming or on women's channels, they portray men as incapable of performing simple household tasks, portray the children as having contempt for their fathers, and portray men who are incapable even of creating pointless work for their wives.

Alison's professor requires mostly scholarly sources for this research paper, so she heads to the library to see if she can find four or five solid articles, book chapters, or books that focus on misandry—hatred of men—in the media. She hypothesizes that she will learn more particulars about the kinds of advertisements that appear, and that insights from sociologists, psychologists, and others will help her understand how she feels about the advertisements. Alison knows that she feels uncomfortable while viewing them, especially with her father, but does not quite understand how she can talk about this discomfort. She finds more sources than she can read, which means that this might well be a good research topic. After reading a number of the sources, she then composes a working thesis:

Although a number of media critics claim that male-as-buffoon advertisements are merely humorous and not hurtful, the truth is that they not only harm male dignity, but female as well.

See how that happened? Alison formed her working thesis throughout the early stages of inquiry. Her thesis evolved as her knowledge evolved: this is natural and beneficial. Paying attention to these matters early in the process will mean less pain later on. Fewer revisions will be needed because you will be more confident while conducting research, while forming an argument, while formulating paragraphs and sentences, and while revising.

Local Revision

As stated earlier, local revision involves problems that are limited to portions of the essay, or to particular issues with voice. Many students struggle to write effective introduction and conclusion sentences, largely because they have not properly established a thesis, nor have they performed the research necessary to construct an engaging argument. Issues with voice will also more easily be resolved once students are confident in their topics and in their research. Thus, local revision *cannot* constructively begin until a sound global revision has been performed.

Introductions and Conclusions

Part of the reason it can be so difficult to write powerful, engaging introductions and conclusions is that we simply do not understand what they are or how to write them. We may also have a limited or incorrect understanding as to what they are.

Introduction paragraphs provide a first impression for the reader. Your job here is to introduce your thesis, and to make certain that your reader understands why your thesis is important. You might say that this paragraph answers the question: "Who cares?" Additional concerns addressed in an introduction paragraph deal with approaches and interpretations, as well as any briefly stated background information or context that your reader will need. *Note that these concerns are common to the humanities, the social sciences, and the natural sciences.* Introduction paragraphs for academic essays should NOT:

- simply list one fact after another, nor should they begin with a definition from Dictionary.com;
- begin with a rhetorical question;
- resemble the "hook" techniques employed by journalists in magazines, newspapers, and blogs;
- begin too broadly, with statements such as, "In today's society, there are many problems faced by young people;"
- announce the basic structure of the essay, unless students are writing a lengthier piece, in which case students should familiarize themselves with procedural introductions.

The introduction to a procedural essay, such as lab reports or a chemistry essay, has different concerns than the introductions to other forms of academic writing. The concern, here, is when students simply write, "In this paper, I will discuss the implications of World War II. First, I will discuss how it began. Second, I will discuss the tragedies people faced. Third, I will discuss how it ended." A better opening would establish something more along the lines of:

> In this paper, I will first discuss the misunderstandings regarding how the United States came to be involved in World War II. I will then examine several cases of direct involvement in Western Europe, such as Operation Cobra and the Battle of the Bulge, to establish how U.S. forces worked with other Allied forces. Finally, I will challenge the need for a formalized United Nations, given that the nations were already working together, either one-on-one, or en masse.

Other types of procedural introductions are intended for more technical pieces of writing, such as a memorandum or a summative report. In these cases, writers need to be sensitive to their audience's needs, which often require accuracy, brevity, and clarity. A procedural introduction allows readers to see exactly what will be discussed, how it will be discussed, and what is at stake. Unlike a number of the other kinds of academic writing discussed in this book, the procedural essay introduction sets out a very precise timeline for the essay, which makes it more difficult to write effectively.

Conclusion paragraphs are the last chance the writer has to answer the question "So what?" Here, you might consider comparing what you have discussed to other, similar situations. You also might raise an interesting question, pose a challenge, or issue a warning, depending on your topic, your audience, and the assignment itself. Many excellent opportunities are lost because writers use techniques they simply should NOT use:

- repeating, word for word, exactly what the introduction paragraph stated. Writers should *synthesize* the essay, using sentences that *reflect* what has already been said, not simply repeat the thesis sentence and the topic sentences of each paragraph;
- rhetorical questions. An example of this might be: "Whose business is it, whether or not teenagers smoke cigarettes?" Instead, you could say, "The question here is whether or not the research thus far indicates any way to help teenagers understand the health concerns their smoking causes."

Finally, you should apply this analysis to your own writing. Select an early or later draft of an essay for one of your classes, and analyze your introduction and conclusion to see whether you have provided a well-developed response to the question "So what?" Open a new computer file, and copy and paste *only* the body paragraphs into this new file. Then, write a new introduction and conclusion based on what we have discussed in this revision chapter. Read these two versions of your essay, and if you have trouble deciding which works better, bring both copies to your instructor and to the Writing Center for further assistance.

Voice and Tone

When we write letters or emails to friends and family, we use a different tone than we would use were we to address the President of the United States or the hiring manager of a company. Academic writing has its own rules and writers should avoid using familiar language in their writing. Students often see the second-person voice used in magazines or opinion pieces, and believe that it sounds catchy and engaging. The second-person voice might work for a number of general interest publications, but it should be avoided in academic writing. Not sure what the second-person voice is? Check out these examples:

1) Dear Grandma,

   I am really looking forward to Winter Break. Will you be in town, or will you be visiting Irma?

   Love,

   Maria

2) You're alone in the computer lab, writing your final paper, and you realize that the lab is closing in ten minutes. What do you do?

Neither example is *wrong*, really—just wrong for academic language. Another problem often seen in academic writing is when writers continually frame their ideas this way: "I think that this solution would be best," "I believe that the evidence is reliable," or, "I feel that any other interpretation of the book is unfair." Clearly, if your name is on the essay, the reader may assume that it contains your thoughts, beliefs, and feelings. Your job as a writer is to convey these thoughts, beliefs, and feelings in a professional manner, not to continually draw the reader's attention to the fact that these are your personal feelings. Such a tone reduces the authority with which you write; You can undermine an effective argument and sound evidence by introducing your personal feelings. It may be helpful to use a checklist like the one below to help organize your thoughts and address common problems as you revise your writing.

Revising Checklist

Have I answered the question or task as fully as possible?

☐ What is my thesis/main assertion/central position?

☐ Have I given background information or provided the context for my topic?

☐ Have I explained important terms/concepts that I will discuss?

☐ Is the focus/purpose of my paper clear?

☐ Does my introduction prepare the reader for what follows?

Is my paper clearly structured?

☐ Does my paper have a clear introduction, body, and conclusion?

☐ Does my paper advance in logical stages?

☐ Are the major points connected and relationship between them explained clearly?

☐ Do all major points relate to the topic and contribute to answering the question or assignment?

Are my paragraphs clearly connected and coherent?

☐ Does each paragraph begin with a topic sentence?

☐ Do sentences flow smoothly and logically from one to the other? Does each sentence clearly follow from the one before?

☐ Is each paragraph clear and complete; do any need more evidence and detail?

☐ Are there adequate transitions between paragraphs? Are they varied or all the same kind?

☐ Are all examples and quotes relevant to and illustrative of my main points?

Have I fully referenced my sources of information?

☐ Have I cited all ideas, quotes, and sources of information in my paper?

☐ Have I used a consistent referencing style?

- ☐ Are quotations properly introduced? Are they accurate? Are they formatted correctly?
- ☐ Is there a clear distinction between my thoughts and words and those of the author(s) whom I've cited?
- ☐ Do quotations add evidence or provide an authoritative voice, or am I letting the author(s) speak for me? Would writing the ideas in my own words be more effective?

Editing and Proofreading

The final stages of revision involve editing sentences to be certain they are grammatically and rhetorically correct, and proofreading for simpler mistakes. What follows is a checklist of the most common writing mistakes, including those that student writers often do not understand. Read through the list, and then read through a few of your essays to see if you can find the errors patterns. Regardless, all writers can use an outside reader. You should take one or two essays to one of the tutors at the Writing Center *and* to your instructors so they can assist you in finding and fixing your errors. The checklists provided here are basic questions that can help you more effectively revise and edit your work at each stage of development.

Editing Checklist

Grammar

- ☐ Have I written complete sentences throughout the essay?
- ☐ Do I avoid run-on sentences?
- ☐ Do all my subjects and verbs agree?
- ☐ Are my pronoun references clear?
- ☐ Do all of my pronouns and their antecedents agree?
- ☐ Do I avoid shifting voice?
- ☐ Do I avoid sexist language and use gender-neutral language?
- ☐ Do I keep a consistent verb tense throughout the essay?
- ☐ Are my modifiers as close as possible to the words they modify?

Punctuation

- ☐ Does each sentence contain end punctuation?
- ☐ Have I used commas correctly?
- ☐ Have I used semicolons, colons, and dashes effectively and correctly?
- ☐ Have I used quotation marks correctly?

Mechanics

- ☐ Is the first word of each sentence capitalized?
- ☐ Are all proper nouns capitalized?
- ☐ Have I followed conventional rules for underlining, abbreviating, and using numbers?
- ☐ Have I used italics and boldface type correctly?

Words

- ☐ Are all of my words spelled correctly?
- ☐ Do I avoid unnecessary or "dead" words?
- ☐ Is my word choice correct?

Is my paper well presented?

- ☐ Does my paper follow guidelines set by my teacher or department (font, margins, line spacing, and cover page)?

Writing the In-Class Essay

One of the most common, and possibly most stressful, writing experiences for many college students is the in-class essay or a timed essay exam. This kind of writing makes it difficult to fully apply the stages of the writing process as discussed above due to the time limits on the writing and the available materials. However, your writing process knowledge can help you writing an in-class essay or an essay exam. The writing process provides a strategy for writing an essay from start to finish:

In-Class Essay or Essay Exam Suggestions:

1. **Take your time and use it well.** Rushing and skipping steps can often have a negative effect on your writing, and your grade. Plan to use the available time in blocks: at the beginning to read the assignment and plan, time at the end to proofread and correct any errors, and the remaining time broken into units to help you manage your writing more effectively.
2. **Read the directions and all the questions.** Make sure you understand what the assignment is asking you to do. Pay close attention to your instructor's requirements as stated in the directions.
3. **Make notes for your answer.** Use invention strategies to generate information, and find and explore topics before you begin writing. Craft a strong thesis.
4. **Support your answer** with examples that fit the question or assignment, making sure to explain their significance. Support general statements with concrete, specific examples that are clearly relevant to the point you are making.
5. **Avoid using your opinion** unless instructed to do so. Avoid editorializing, taking issue with, or complaining about the question or assignment in the

body of your paper. Remain businesslike; imagine you are having a polite, intelligent conversation over a cup of coffee with your favorite professor.

6. **Use a recognizable organizational pattern.**
7. **Use transitions.**
8. **End with a summary sentence or conclusion.**
9. **Save time at the end for proofreading.** Often, you do not realize that you've missed a crucial point or need to explain a point more until you have already moved on in the exam or essay. Planning to use ten percent of the time for the exam to proofread and correct your work can go a long way toward catching omissions and errors.

There are some commonly used words associated with essay exams and timed writing as well. The table below presents some of the most common ones and contextualizes them a bit. Every field uses them slightly differently, but the general sense of each is the same.

Commonly Used Essay Exam Words[1]:

STATE: Explain precisely.	**CONTRAST:** Show differences. Set in opposition.
COMPARE: Examine two or more things. Identify similarities and differences. Comparisons generally ask for similarities more than differences.	**CRITICIZE:** Make judgments. Evaluate comparative worth. Criticism often involves analysis.
DEFINE: Give the meaning; usually a meaning specific to the course of subject. Determine the precise limits of the term to be defined. Explain the exact meaning. Definitions are usually short.	**DESCRIBE:** Give a detailed account. Make a picture with words. List characteristics, qualities and parts.
DISCUSS: Consider and debate or argue the pros and cons of an issue. Write about any conflict. Compare and contrast.	**INTERPRET:** Comment upon, give examples, describe relationships. Explain the meaning. Describe, then evaluate.
EVALUATE: Give your opinion or cite the opinion of an expert. Include evidence to support the evaluation.	**ILLUSTRATE:** Give concrete examples. Explain clearly by using comparisons or examples.
ENUMERATE: List several ideas, aspects, events, things, qualities, reasons, etc.	**OUTLINE:** Describe main ideas, characteristics, or events.
PROVE: Support with facts (especially facts presented in class or in the test).	**ANALYZE:** Break into separate parts and discuss, examine, or interpret each part.
SUMMARIZE: Give a brief, condensed account. Include conclusions. Avoid unnecessary details.	**TRACE:** Show the order of events or progress of a subject or event.

---

1   Adapted from DeLeon, Joy. "How to P.L.A.E. Until the End of the Semester." Beloit, WI: Beloit College, 2013. Web. 15 Apr. 2012.

Conclusion

Writing is a messy, recursive process that takes work to master and requires you to be aware not only of what you are writing, but *how* you write and *why* you are doing it that way. There is no one right answer for any stage of the writing process, every writer has different habits and preferences. The common factor is that effective writers in all fields and professions are aware of their writing process and can use that knowledge to their advantage. Changing seemingly minor parts of your writing process, such as mapping rather than outlining or taking better reading notes as you study and do research, can often help you overcome problems in your writing and keep you more engaged in both your writing and your writing process. Every step of the process is important, as skipping steps or not fully addressing them can seriously impact the quality of your writing and create problems for both you and your readers. Being aware of your writing process can also help you be more aware of the rhetoric used in your writing, which is discussed in the next chapter.

Works Cited

Coe, Richard. *Process, Form, and Substance: A Rhetoric for Advanced Writers.* London: Longman Publishing, 1990. Print.

Flachmann, Kim, and Michael Flachmann. *The Prose Reader: Essays for Thinking, Reading, and Writing* (8th ed.). Upper Saddle River, NJ: Pearson Education, 2008. Print.

Lindemann, Erika. *A Rhetoric for Writing Teachers* (3rd ed.). New York: Oxford University Press, 1995. Print.

Sachs, Andrew. "The Link between Writing and Critical Thinking." *Buffalo.edu*. The University at Buffalo. 2004. Web. 14 Oct. 2013.

Chapter Three

Rhetoric and Argument

In casual conversation, we often use the word *argument* to mean that people are quarreling or fighting over some disagreement. In an academic context, however, we use the word in a more limited, specialized sense. An **argument** is a set of statements that support a claim with evidence and reasoning. Of course, some arguments are better than others, and our goal in this chapter is to help you to write sound, reasonable, and effective academic arguments. Academic arguments are usually persuasive on some level, which means they apply various kinds of rhetoric to add weight and force to the points being raised. Contrary to popular use, rhetoric is not just empty talk or a way to discuss something. Plato described rhetoric as "the art of winning the soul," while his student Aristotle claimed that it is "the faculty of discovering in any particular case all of the available means of persuasion." Aristotle's definition is in many ways more clearly aligned with how rhetoric is discussed in writing courses today, and Thomas B. Farrell takes this a step further. Farrell describes rhetoric, as we use the term today as "an acquired competency, a manner of thinking that *invents* possibilities for persuasion, conviction, action, and judgments."[1] Rhetoric is both the tool set for inventing argument and the force behind the argument in Farrell's definition, and is essential for argument and persuasion.

Rhetoric, as the means of persuasion your argument carries, is as important in many cases as your thesis and the actual argument you put forth. To use these tools effectively, you need to know how rhetoric works in different environments and how to engage with the ideas. We will first examine the rhetorical situation: who composes the argument (the writer), who attends to it (the audience), and what the vehicle for the argument is (the text). Then we will look at two concepts from classical rhetoric, *kairos* and *stasis*, before discussing the canons of rhetoric (the broad functions of rhetoric) and how these elements work in arguments today.

The Rhetorical Situation

The rhetorical situation is often called the communication triangle. This model provides a visual representation of the dynamic relationship between the key elements of communication. Different disciplines will use different language for the elements, such as encoder, decoder, and signal, but for our purposes we will label the three corners of the triangle as writer, text, and audience (Figure 1). This relationship may seem obvious on the surface because texts must have writers

---

1   *The Norms of Rhetorical Culture*, 1993.

and readers, but a closer look at the rhetorical situation provides some useful insights for writers who want to construct meaningful and effective arguments.

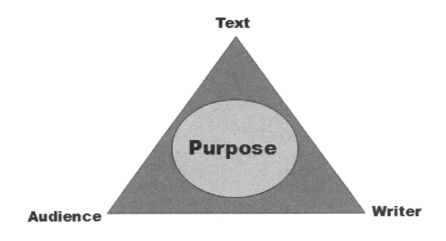

Figure 1. The Rhetorical Situation

The Writer

Most of us write in our own voices. We use words and phrases that are natural to us. We should recognize, however, that we also adjust readily to different arenas and audiences. The language and style of a text message to a friend is not the language and style of a business letter, which is not the language and style of an academic argument in a particular discipline. Remember that the academic community has conventions and expectations, and that you want to position yourself so that your writing will be accepted as part of a dialogue in an academic context. On one level, these conventions include proper grammar, mechanics, and usage. On another, perhaps more important, level, these conventions include the appropriate handling of information, the proper use of sources, and the disciplined approach to particular subjects.

While conventions will vary from one discipline to another, writers generally aim to exhibit three traits: (1) to be honest and trustworthy; (2) to have good intentions and goodwill for the audience; and (3) to have expertise on their subject matter. These three traits correspond to the three corners of the communication triangle (writer, reader, and text), and together constitute what is called the writer's *ethos*, a term often treated as being equal to the credibility of the writer. These three characteristics are essential to the writer because readers will be slow (or refuse entirely) to accept an argument from someone they deem untrustworthy, dishonest, ill-willed, ignorant, or incompetent. The character of the writer permeates the whole text and operates in the background of the argument, so writers who want to be persuasive and effective should attend to their *ethos*.

Still, as essential as it is, the projection of the writer's character really is not the centerpiece of any academic argument because most of the time the writer's personality and identity are secondary issues in objective, well-reasoned arguments. At the same time, anything in the text that calls into question or raises concerns about the writer's lack of honesty, goodwill, or expertise will quickly undermine an argument. Ultimately, our goal is to construct arguments that accurately reflect reality in such a way that the reader will be moved to consider or accept our argument. Being a good person who reasons well, as it is put in the classical formulation of the writer's *ethos*, is necessary to accomplish that goal.

So, the identity of the writer is you, but it is the best *you* that you can present. Unlike music, fiction, or poetry, where writers routinely adopt fictional personae to deliver a song, a story, or a poem, writers of argument are who they are. That does not mean, however, that the writer settles for being uninformed, ill-willed, or disingenuous. A small-town resident who wants to argue something about the fashion industry must immerse him- or herself fully in the knowledge and workings of that industry. A big-city resident who wants to argue something about rural life must likewise become an expert in rural life. Writers owe it to their readers to say something worthwhile. The only way to do so is to put in the work to become a writer who has something worth saying. You want the reader to believe that you are qualified to make the argument you are making.

The Audience

In academic writing, the audience is in some ways easier to define than it is outside the university. Students sometimes think of their instructor or professor as their only audience, particularly when they think about who grades their essays and papers. Including faculty members in the audience is legitimate and useful because it pushes students to make stronger arguments, to strengthen their reasoning, to expand and solidify their evidence, and to write more clearly and with more sophistication. Making your instructor the only member of the audience, however, is detrimental because it often leads to an overly-inflated style and motivates writers to overreach in their efforts. Of course writers should strive to improve, and doing so sometimes leads to errors. We all have misused a word, misunderstood a concept, or misrepresented what we thought we understood. That is part of thinking and writing about a complex world. But, those errors should not be what defines a text. All writers (students and professionals) develop over time. This development happens best when it is natural, as the writer learns and experiences new things, as the writer builds a larger set of skills and tools.

We can safely assume some common characteristics for these readers: they are typically inquisitive and want to know things; they are usually fairly well-educated, even if they do not know the specific area under discussion in your argument; they are often as busy and stretched for time as anyone, and they will appreciate clear, concise arguments; they are often willing to entertain ideas for the sake of doing so, but they are also likely to dismiss unsound or unfair arguments quickly. Beyond that, though, we should consider carefully what, if any, preconceptions, predispositions, and biases an audience brings to the text. These preconceived ideas may stem from shared values of a particular community, from political or social affiliations, from regional or geographical connections, or any number of other relationships that exert influence or create bias. Identifying these preconceptions as they relate to a particular argument will help you formulate and structure your argument in a way that is more likely to convince your reader of your point.

The Text

On the most basic level, the text is simply the vehicle for your meaning; the collection of words, sentences, and paragraphs that constitute your argument. Most students tend to think of formal guidelines for essays and assignments as arbitrary or unnecessary rules. They are essentially arbitrary: nobody really cares whether your margin is 1" or 1¼", except that some prevailing authority, such as the Modern Language Association (MLA), has declared that it will be this way versus that way. On many points, though, the prevailing authorities disagree because no absolute virtue resides in a particular size of a margin. The key is to follow the prevailing authority for the conventions that govern your text. In English, MLA rules. In Psychology, APA does. Whatever your discipline, know the style sheet and conventions that members of that community accept. Then meet those expectations in your text. When you use standard form, mechanics, and grammar in your text, you allow the reader to focus attention where it belongs—on the substance of your argument. The reader wants to investigate your claims, to consider the evidence and reasoning that support your claims, and to entertain the significance of your argument. When your text violates conventions, however, the errors become distracting and undermine your efforts.

On a deeper level, the text is the entirety of your argument: the content, its substance, and its structure. It encompasses essential elements, such as the focus, the coherence, and the purpose of your writing. Just as using the wrong form for citing a source may distract a reader, slips in application—such as a loss of focus, a flaw in organization, an irrelevant digression, or faulty reasoning—rupture the unity and purpose of your essay and undermine your effort to advance a compelling argument.

The goal for your text is to make your message as clear, concise, and compelling as you can. Doing so allows your reader to focus on what really matters: the argument at hand.

Purpose

The writer writes a text. The reader reads the text. The point of this transaction is to communicate something. In real life, the text may be the note to say that someone will be late for dinner or that someone needs to restock the milk before breakfast tomorrow. It may be an email or text to wish someone well. But in academic argument, the purpose is most often to persuade the reader to think about something in a different way, to consider information that might not have been considered before, to change the way something is done, or to act in a way that improves this or that situation. On the most general level, the purpose that ought to motivate every writer is the desire to say something meaningful about a subject in a way that influences the reader to understand and act accordingly. It may be something practical such as where to invest money for retirement or where to shop for groceries. It may be something philosophical about quantum physics, art, literature, or life. It may be somewhere in between. The assumption that drives academic writing is that the writer has something significant to say and wants to engage readers in the argument, even if they ultimately choose not to accept it. For a writer, then, the glue that holds the rhetorical situation together is purpose.

Although we have talked individually about the writer, the reader, the text, and purpose, these elements work together and exist as a whole, not in parts, and the interactions between them shape and define the choices we make as we construct arguments. The relationship is dynamic and changes as the writer moves through the writing process. Good writers usually define each of these elements at the beginning of the writing process and then reassess and refine those definitions during the drafting and revising of the essay.

Kairos

The Greeks had two conceptions of time. *Chronos* is linear time, the time we use on clocks and calendars to mark our passage through days, weeks, and life. *Kairos* is closer to what we mean by opportunity, the opportune moment or right time for something. A writer may formulate an excellent argument, but if the time and place of the argument is not the right time and place, the argument may fail in spite of how well argued, how reasonable, and how sound it is.

Many times, the opportune moment arises due to external circumstances that have little or nothing to do with the writer, or, at least, circumstances that the writer does not or cannot control. At the risk of oversimplifying the issue and the historical record, we might consider arguments surrounding slavery in the United States. The various arguments for and against slavery resonated long before the Civil War, but ultimately they led to a division of entrenched opposition, eventually to a rupture in the agreement between and among the states to be bound by a single constitution. The events surrounding the Civil War in the United States and the victory of the Union over the Confederacy creates an opportunity for the argument to outlaw slavery, most prominently voiced in the Emancipation Proclamation. In this example, the external circumstances (the division of entrenched opposition) created an urgency to address certain topics (slavery). These circumstances made the argument more compelling and persuasive.

Other times, however, the writer constructs the sense of urgency. For instance, if you examine essays and speeches by Martin Luther King, Jr., you will find him exerting much effort to create an awareness of *kairos*. In his famous *Letter from Birmingham Jail*, King addresses his fellow clergymen in a response to their accusation that his efforts in Birmingham were "unwise and untimely." His letter repeatedly underscores the urgency and timeliness of his efforts to overcome racial injustice and oppression. Indeed, one way to read his letter is to see it as an argument to establish *kairos* so that his audience would perceive the need for change now, not at some undefined future point.

Complex realities surround any given argument. A writer obviously cannot attend to all of the complexities at once. But good writers will take stock of matters that shape perceptions and values related to the issue. They will consider ways of heightening a sense of urgency, so that their readers will consider their argument reasonable and sound. They will make the most of their opportunity to create a moment when their argument—and their audience's willingness to accept it—makes sense.

Stasis

The term *stasis* comes from the Greek word meaning "a stand." The term comes into Latin as *status* or *constitutio*, the latter word literally meaning "standing together." These terms are at the heart of English words such as *status*, *station*, *stationary*, and even *constitution*. *Stasis* refers to a position or place to stand, that is, literally a place where a speaker stands to deliver an argument, and figuratively the position that one stakes out in an argument. The Latin term *constitutio*, however, is perhaps more useful for our purposes, because it refers to a number of people who come together and stand together in agreement. Thus, a constitution declares terms that bind a group together through their agreement. In rhetorical terms, *stasis* is the point at which individuals agree to disagree. That is, given different people who hold differing opinions about a particular subject, the *stasis* is the central issue at the heart of the disagreement.

In classical rhetoric, the Sophists and later Cicero devised a model to help a rhetorician identify the stasis of an argument. In more advanced rhetoric classes, you are likely to encounter "stasis theory," which focuses on developing arguments based on questions that help a writer to develop a systematic approach to particular issues. These questions fall in four categories: questions of fact or conjecture, questions of definition, questions of quality and degree, and questions of policy.

Questions of Fact/Conjecture:	Did some event occur?
	Does something happen?
	Does something exist?
	What are its origins and where did it come from?
Questions of Definition:	What kind of thing or event is it?
	What kind of problem or issue does it present?
	Does it belong to a larger class of events of things?
	What are its parts and how do they relate to each other?

Questions of Quality/Degree:	Is it something good or bad? Right or wrong? Honorable or dishonorable? etc.
	How serious is the problem or issue?
	Is there potential for it to get better or worse?
	What are the qualities of this thing or event relative to similar things or events?
Questions of Policy:	Should some action be taken?
	What should be done?
	Who should act?
	What policies can be implemented to resolve the issue, solve the problem, or address the issue?
	How will proposed policies and actions affect the situation? Will they make things better or worse? How and in what way?

You may find it useful to consider these or similar questions early in the discovery process. They can help you focus your attention on the heart of the issue in an argument. At the very least, they will prompt you to think through matters that will clarify the issue.

Determining the stasis, the central point of contention, in an argument sounds easier than it often is. If you think of contemporary arguments that seem to be nearly unresolvable—arguments in which advocates for different perspectives seem to argue continually without much hope that the issue will be decided now or in the future—those arguments have probably failed to establish stasis so that the interested parties can agree to examine the issue in a productive way. Historically, the presence of slavery in the United States generated that sort of problem. Was slavery an economic necessity? Was slavery a violation of human dignity and rights? Was there reason to allow precedence to justify future policy? Did the federal government have a compelling interest to establish a law that applied to all states, or were states granted authority to determine what path to take regarding slavery? Probably the core disagreement concerned the definition of the problem as an issue of economics or as an issue of human rights. Until the Civil War, the differing perspectives failed to come to a real agreement about the issue. Once the different interested parties agreed or were forced to agree that the issue was, in fact, a human rights issue, the arguments about how to proceed were possible. In more recent times, arguments about abortion, capital punishment, gun control, and many other controversial topics exhibit similar patterns. Opposing views are voiced loudly, but if you listen closely you will realize that many or even most of the views fail to recognize that their argument has little or nothing to do with the opposing viewpoints precisely because there is no agreement about what the stasis is or what it should be.

Understanding the concepts of *kairos* and *stasis* helps explain the ways the rhetorical canons further help you shape your argument. The **canons of rhetoric** are categories designed to take you through the various steps involved in crafting an effective or persuasive speech or piece of writing. To summarize briefly, the five canons of rhetoric are:

- **invention**, which involves considering all the strategies for planning your work, such as finding an interesting topic, deciding who your audience will be, and making use of prewriting activities;
- **arrangement**, which asks you to consider how you will organize information to make it more appealing based on cultural expectations (that is why our argumentative essays tend to repeat the pattern of introduction, thesis statement, presentation of proofs, refutation of opposing viewpoints, and conclusion);
- **style**, you must consider what tone is more appropriate in a given context (for example, casual speech while chatting with friends vs. formal language when writing a short story analysis);
- **memory**, which encompasses everything from the use of mnemonic devices to remember a speech for delivery to the inclusion of memorable imagery in a story so that readers will not easily forget your work; and
- **delivery**, which requires that you seriously consider which medium is more appropriate to your message and more likely to bring your message to the attention of your chosen audiences. (Lanham 1991)

These canons function in and through the broader argument you are staging in your essay or in a conversation. Being more aware of the canons and how using them effectively can improve your overall argument is important to your writing, as all the reader will be able to access about what you know about the issue and what it means is what you have chosen to include. This is closely related to the "right words, right places" point raised in Chapter One, the right use of the right rhetorical elements where appropriate in your essay makes your points both more memorable to the reader and more effective in their ability to persuade the reader. This comes down to how you use the available language in argument.

The Language of Argument

When it comes to the language used in an argument, James Berlin divides rhetoric three distinct categories. The language chosen by an arguer could determine the method of interpretation used by the reader or audience.

- **Objective rhetoric** is neutral language used by an author to present information in a way that does not involve or overwhelm the audience with their own personal views or emotions. The purpose is to gather data and arrive at generalizations based on that data. The reader or writer has the role of abandoning any personal views or preconceptions to remain neutral.
- **Subjective rhetoric** is based on the individual's perception of the data. This rhetoric involves emotion of the reader or writer and the bias that comes from it.
- **Transactional rhetoric** is based on the subject, object, audience and language operating simultaneously. This rhetoric is used less when writing; it is more likely used by an audience or reader to understand a text or argument.

Effective argument is not just being able to support your thesis and support your claims, but also being able to identify the variables of audience, time, purpose, and the persuasive goals of your argument. Persuasion means motivating the reader to say, do, think, feel, or believe something in a particular way, to get the audience to *believe* your argument and not just agree with individual points This is why the canons, how you are developing and staging the rhetoric of your argument, and the kinds of rhetoric you are engaging in are so important. This is much more the case in written arguments, such as essays, as the way you present and structure your argument is the only chance you have to persuade your reader.

Classical Logical Argument

The classical forms of argument stem from classical oratory, which dates back to the Greeks but is still very relevant today. This form of argument is driven by logic and by the structuring and sequencing of the points. In many ways, it is the foundation for legal arguments, debates, and the written arguments in many fields you are likely to encounter. To use this form effectively, it is necessary to understand both its forms and the underlying appeals which are used to motivate the argument itself. Some of the points discussed in this section are equally relevant in using the modern models for argument discussed in Chapter Five and elsewhere in this book.

Every argument that is well structured should have the six parts of classical organization. Each aspect of an essay should be evident, regardless of the length of each section. Without these elements of structure, certain areas of your argument could be lacking and possibly ineffective. In the classical tradition, each of these elements was given a unique name which not only indicated its role in the argument but how it functioned. These elements are as follows.

The Exordium: The exordium or **introduction** makes the subject and purpose clear. This establishes the validity of the argument, its purpose, and its function. This is also a means of establishing common grounds with the audience and the parameters for the argument.

The Narratio: The narratio or **narration** provides background about the subject and the events, why the subject is important, and gives the author an opportunity to establish *ethos* by citing reasons for an interest in the subject and qualifications for writing about it.

The Partitio: The partitio or the **statement of preposition and division** states the claim of the argument. It also sometimes names the major points of argument so that it is easier for readers to follow along (also known as the thesis statement).

The Confirmatio: The confirmatio or **confirmation** offers the proof of the argument. It provides reasons and evidence that are acceptable to the audience to prove the proposition or claim.

The Refutatio: The refutatio or **refutation** allows the author to engage with any opposing positions. According to Aristotle, if the opposition has a lot of objections to your position, it is better to remove these objections early, before you give your reasons. The refutatio also allows for the further development of specific points of your argument and refining the focus.

The Peroratorio: The peroratorio is **the conclusion and a restatement of the argument**. As a conclusion, it emphasizes the most important point and reminds the audience of the other important points that were covered in the argument.

Several of these elements, such as the refutation, can be moved to different points within the argument as long as they are present in some way. It is not uncommon for smaller arguments to be embedded as part of a larger argument, using the central three or four elements to break down major points even further and to add depth to the argument. While it seems highly structured, the classical model is very flexible in some ways. Which is why it is one of the major structural models for argument used today.

More modern models for argument, such as those discussed in Chapter Five, use the elements of the classical model for argument as their basic units. This is due, in part, to the ways in which these logical structures have become "hard wired" into many aspects of modern life. Legal arguments usually follow the classical oratory model, as do many academic forms of writing, so the underlying logical structures make sense to us when we see them used in other environments, and the recursive structure feels normal to us. In terms of writing well inside and outside of the academy, the classical model is adaptable to a number of purposes and is a good foundational approach to argument.

Conclusion

Rhetoric, the awareness of all possible means of persuasion, is at the heart of academic writing and writing well in general. Being more aware of the canons of rhetoric, the different kinds of rhetoric, and the forms of argument that stem from traditional rhetorics give you the basis for most kinds of writing you are likely to encounter in the university and in your career. Being able to understand the rhetorical situation and to see through the argument being presented and engage with its individual elements builds on the critical reading skills discussed elsewhere in this book and makes it easier for you to both create your own arguments and to refute or support the arguments of others. As demonstrated in later chapters, argument is flexible and is the basis for most writing, everything is an argument after all. While classical rhetoric is the foundation of modern argument, it must be presented to the reader using modes they can easily understand, which is the focus of the next chapter.

Chapter Four
Writing, Logic, and the
Rhetorical Modes

While there are as many kinds of writing as there are writers, each of us uses elements of the different forms of writing for specific effect every time we set pen to paper or start typing. There are, however, a few key rhetorical modes—also called **modes of discourse**—which broadly define what kind of writing you are attempting or what the conventions, purpose, and effect of the writing might be. The rhetorical modes are different than genre, as genre is an effect of mode and not the other way around and one mode might be used in a number of genres. The four most commonly encountered rhetorical modes are *narrative, description, exposition,* and *argumentation.* Each of these modes is discussed in this chapter, as is the need for clear, logical presentation of your ideas. When logic fails in writing, particularly in argument, you run the risk of engaging in *fallacies.* Finally, regardless of the rhetorical mode most prominent in the writing, academic writing relies heavily on valid research to support your claims and analysis, as discussed toward the end of the chapter.

The Rhetorical Modes

Narrative

The desire to order our human experience through the process of storytelling seems an innate and unique trait. Today, we live in a world saturated with narrative: facts arranged to form a coherent story. From the founding of a nation to the early struggles and eventual triumph of a championship team, from the story of the flood to the pregnancy of a reality TV star, from the growing pains of a young wizard to the failings of a presidential campaign, we look to stories for entertainment, instruction, and sense in the disparate moments of life.

Narrative writing at its heart is simply telling a story. When you hear a story, what are the parts that catch your attention? What are the parts that move you? What are the parts that make you laugh? Narrative writing, like any writing, should have a point—your narrative needs to go somewhere. Of course, how you get there is just as important. Novels, short stories, plays, biographies, and profiles all tend to use narrative writing as a dominant style. Many fields of study, including history, art, journalism, and social sciences like sociology and anthropology, use narrative as a major element of writing in the field.

Many of the narratives we pay attention to every day are first given shape, or exist entirely, in a written form. Novels and narrative non-fiction books, and even most of the media we consume through TV and film—news stories, superhero movies, documentaries, financial reports, sitcoms—begin as narrative, either as source material or as a script. If it is not immediately narrative, like stock information or statistics, a story is fashioned out of it for the audience, moving from raw data to the narrative of the falling fortunes of a company or the rise of a popular political movement. The ability to tell a story, and tell it well, is one of our most ancient skills and one that dominates our world today.

Narrative writing is usually organized around an arc—the story begins before an important event or conflict, builds to that event or conflict, and then shows what has changed afterwards. Within that arc, the most important rule of narrative writing is "show, don't tell." In essence, this means that you describe scenes rather than stating facts directly.

This is important in academic and professional writing, as being able to tell the audience the story behind the logical argument you are making is what makes them invest in your writing and pay attention to it. The more engaged your reader is with the narrative, the easier it is for them to interpret and assimilate the facts you are presenting.

Exposition

Expository writing tells the audience facts. Often seen in such sources as newspaper articles, textbooks, manuals, and research papers, expository writing attempts to inform the audience about a particular topic. Because it is used to impart information to the reader, expository writing should strive for clarity. After finishing the text, a reader should be able to recall all the key points of your subject.

We use expository writing in narrative for a number of reasons. First, it gets information across much more efficiently than descriptive writing. Rather than show the scene in a creatively narrative way, the writer delivers information clearly and directly to get to the heart of the story.

Expository writing also gets across information in narrative that cannot be reliably shown in another way, such as larger abstractions that might not manifest in reality, or manifest in broad ways. When transmitting to the reader these larger abstractions—the decline of the steel industry in Ohio, for example—exposition communicates that large, vague fact in clear terms. Like all expository writing, it tells the reader in straightforward fashion what they need to know to better understand the critical elements of the argument.

Finally, expository writing can be used to clarify ideas related to the argument that are not part of the immediate discussion. If you explain the meaning behind the issue, the ones that lie just outside your claim and still influence your argument, you are using expository writing. In these cases, the expository writing is less driven by an attempt to make the elements clearer than it is by your desire to make clear the related or larger issues that surround the argument: its relevance to the audience, its construction, its importance to you as the writer.

Descriptive Writing

Unlike exposition's telling, descriptive writing shows the reader what's going on. Descriptive writing uses words to paint a scene for the reader. Unlike expository writing, which helps us to understand, descriptive writing makes us feel what we're reading. One of the most powerful elements of descriptive writing is its ability to make the reader, however briefly, forget who they are and experience reality through the viewpoint of someone else. When you read a novel and you get tense during a scene when a character declares her love or fights in the final battle, that is the power of descriptive writing (usually with expository writing mixed in to keep the context clear).

This is done by dramatizing, by capturing the external world in language, by showing. Sensory details are key to strong descriptive writing, as they make the story vivid to the reader. Just as the senses serve as our means of interacting with the exterior world, so are sensory details a primary means for bringing the narrative world to life and making it concrete. Engaging a reader's senses—through the growl of a dog, the smell of an open sore, the look of a long, menacing shadow—makes a story resonate beyond the bare facts. You don't have to engage all the senses, of course (the taste of the dog probably isn't a detail that makes much sense to include).

Also important to descriptive writing is strong word usage, particularly the use of active verbs. Passive verbs, forms of *to be* (is, was, were, shall be, etc.) can be acceptable in expository writing, as expository writing attempts to explain and clarify. While often not ideal, because passive verbs tend to make the writing less interesting or vivid, they do serve a purpose in direct explanation. Descriptive writing, on the other hand, attempts to depict the kinetic world, and nothing mimics action in writing so concisely as an active verb—slunk, tore, vomited, embraced, united. Many teachers will require that your writing in general, and your descriptive writing in particular, be as full of active verbs as possible, with much of the descriptive writing in present tense to make the actions even more vivid to the reader.

Persuasion

Whether an essay is more expository or descriptive, almost all forms of writing involve some form of persuasion. You are creating a narrative structure that not only provides facts and information (the "show" element) and places the facts in a broader context for the reader (the "tell"), but also makes those pieces work toward a defined purpose. This involves developing a firm, reasonable stance on a debatable issue and then supporting that stance through both internal (reasoning, examples) and external (sources) support. Though it has many of the same elements as other kinds of writing, persuasive writing goes one step further to convince the reader of a particular point of view.

The most important element of persuasive writing is a clear, concise, and reasonable thesis or claim. The thesis is your stance on the topic. It should be clear, so that the audience knows after reading it what you will be arguing for or against. Also, for persuasive writing to be effective, it must be both arguable and worth arguing. Claims that are either purely subjective ("Blue is the best color.") or not directly related to either the issues you are discussing or based on simple, inarguable observations ("The sky is often blue.") do not work in persuasive writing. Finally, like descriptive writing, it needs to carefully use language to affect the reader.

Detail

While one can go overboard with unnecessary detail, in both expository and descriptive writing detail is vital to helping the reader understand and experience the story. Whenever possible, make your language as specific as possible. It wasn't a town, it was a subdivision outside of Akron. It wasn't a dog, it was a half-starving Rottweiler. The car in the driveway wasn't an old car, it was a red 1955 Chevy.

This need for detail works toward two goals. First, as stated above, it helps the reader. It helps the reader to see the story more clearly, to understand the context of what's going on, and ultimately to be more affected by the writing.

Second, it helps the writer. By forcing yourself to include detail in your story, you'll ensure that you know and see it clearly as well. When a writer isn't sure of the details, the writing becomes vague and broad. Vague, broad writing has little effect on a reader beyond boring them. The consistent use of detail is an aspect of writing that goes beyond narrative. Throughout your academic career, you should constantly strive to keep your writing as precise and detailed as possible.

One qualifying note: not all detail is necessary detail. You might be precise and rich in your detail, and still be describing something that has little relevance or importance to the narrative as a whole.

This sort of detail, while precise, is unnecessary and tends to distract the reader and slow the story down. Be as specific as you can with your detail, but also make sure your use of detail is in service to the larger, central aspects of the story.

Purpose

All writing, especially academic writing, is organized and structured for a specific purpose. The first step in determining what kind of writing is appropriate for a given assignment, a particular job, or even to convince a particular person of a specific fact is to establish for yourself if the writing needs to inform, to persuade, or to entertain—or even all of these. You next need to determine your audience.

Students often make the mistake of assuming that their instructor is the audience. Expand your horizons and ask yourself who will be reading your paper beyond your instructor. Your audience for any assignment might actually consist of other students in your peer group, the diverse community of your university, or the community beyond your college or university—the town or city in which it resides. Most essays will include several styles of writing. You will often start in an expository style, exposing certain facts, before moving into narrative and descriptive styles as you show how you relate, through your senses, to the topic, or what other factors are involved. You may even employ persuasive styles as you motivate your readers into a course of action. Good writing is fluid; it shifts and moves as it develops and responds to the issues at hand. What ties the possibilities together is the overall purpose behind the writing and what you need to convey to the reader.

Fallacies

Good writing, good argument, and proper use of rhetoric depends largely on being honest with the reader and transparent. As discussed earlier in this book, being aware of the possible means of persuasion (rhetoric) carries with it an ethical obligation to be honest about how those tools are being used (including *ethos* in the rhetorical situation). However, writers sometimes stray into fallacious arguments, as discussed below, by error or by choice. Sometimes the logic of the argument as it is presented simply does not work correctly or rhetorical choices are made that complicate the transparency of the argument, and weaken it in the process.

People sometimes use the term "fallacy" or "fallacious" to mean that a statement is false or dishonest. In writing, particularly in rhetoric, the terms are more specialized and technical, and indicate that an argument contains a breakdown in logic. Some fallacies follow common patterns because people tend to make similar types of mistakes in their thinking.

In honest, academic argument, writers avoid the use of fallacies as part of their arguments because we want the validity and strength of the argument to be determined by reason and logic. In real writing, however, one encounters fallacies fairly regularly. Writers may use them because they do not know any better and fail to recognize the error in their reasoning, or they may employ fallacies intentionally in an effort to persuade the reader. Fallacies can, in fact, be effective at swaying audiences to accept arguments that they ought to reject as unreasonable, but an educated and trained person will be able to recognize the fallacy for what it is.

You will encounter fallacies in advertisements, visuals, newspapers, and even academic writing. Because they are so common, you need to be able to recognize them, understand the type of error in reasoning that they show, and know how to counter them with sound reasoning. As a writer, you should also know that it is best to avoid using them if you are advancing a well-reasoned argument.

A Brief List of Fallacies

A complete list of fallacies and a careful discussion of the errors in reasoning would require a book-length discussion. Following is a list of some of the major fallacies, and each has a brief description or definition, an example (if appropriate), and a short explanation of the way it works.

Fallacies of Misused Information

Begging the Question. Begging the question (also known as *petitio principii* or circular reasoning) is embedding the desired conclusion in the argument as a premise for that conclusion. At its most basic level, such an argument amounts to, "X is the way it ought to be because X is the way it ought to be." For instance, a student might protest a grade by saying, "I am a graduating senior. The class is required, and I must pass it." It begs the question, "Are you, in fact, a graduating senior (if you aren't passing a class required to graduate)?"

Complex Question. A complex question is really two simple questions that are embedded and posed as a single question. The famous example is "So, Mr. Smith, when did you stop beating your wife?" Of course, the two questions are obvious: (1) Mr. Smith, do you beat your wife? (2) When did you stop? The problem is equally obvious: it assumes the conclusion that Mr. Smith is a wife-beater. In that sense, it is similar to begging the question.

Cherry Picking. Good arguments depend upon the reliability of the supporting evidence and data. Unfairly excluding relevant data by filtering the evidence, stacking the deck, or stacking the evidence to ensure that only supportive data comes to light is dishonest logic (**cherry picking**).

Hasty or Sweeping Generalizations. Most arguments depend on accumulating enough data to support the claim and to lead convincingly to a conclusion. Figuring out how much data is enough is difficult, and many students simply stop too soon. When they do so, good readers and instructors will frequently comment on the hasty generalization. Unfair stereotypes and prejudices are often the product of this sort of error, jumping to conclusions about whole classes of experiences and people based on too little evidence and too few examples.

Fallacies based on irrelevant information. Good arguments are unified and focused. They exclude irrelevant information. Weaker arguments often do include irrelevant and unnecessary information. This both weakens the argument being presented and distracts the reader from the issue being discussed. While this is frequently accidental, it is a logical problem.

Red Herring. One of the most common fallacies. A red herring is the knowing inclusion of irrelevant material that distracts the audience or reader from the real argument. Sidebar information used to distract the reader from the issue at hand or weaknesses in the argument can be red herrings.

Bandwagon. Bandwagon (*argumentum ad populum*, meaning argument to the people) is an argument that contends the rightness of an argument based on the number of people who believe it. "Everyone knows…," or "It is common knowledge that…," are common signs that you are about to encounter a bandwagon.

Ad hominem. Also called mud-slinging, name-calling, and poisoning the well (*argumentum ad hominem*, literally "argument to the man," i.e., attacking the person) call into question the character of an opponent rather than the argument at hand.

Guilt by Association. A form of *ad hominem* is guilt by association. In this case, the argument is mostly implied and is carried by shared values. If society has determined that a group of individuals are mean, wrong, or evil, linking a particular person to that group implies that the individual is equally mean, wrong, or evil.

Appeal to Authority. The question of relevance is similarly at the heart of arguments that appeal to authority and tradition. Celebrities, sports stars, and politicians regularly convince us that they are experts in the best foods, cars, and beer. We know better, but we accept these fallacious appeals to authority anyway. In academic argument, we strive to do better and to avoid appeals to illegitimate authority.

Appeal to Tradition. Similar to the appeal to authority (or the fallacy involving a faulty appeal to authority), the appeal to tradition may or may not be fallacious. Precedent or the way things have always been done may, in fact, be a good reason for doing something a particular way. The rhetorical questions, then, become whether the appeal to tradition is relevant to a given context and whether the merit of the argument is sound on its own terms.

Straw Man. A straw man seems relatively simple on the surface (and in most textbook definitions): attributing an argument to an opponent (an argument that the opponent does not actually make) and making sure the argument is easy to defeat so that your own argument can prevail. Almost always, the misrepresentation is an effort to make the opponent's argument more extreme and rarely contains even a hint of truth. As such, it involves fear-mongering and scare tactics, which can be effective in spite of their fallacious nature.

False Analogy. False analogy attempts to draw a connection between two situations, events, or actions, arguing that they are similar, when in reality they are not. For an analogy to be legitimate, the similarities must reveal meaningful insight into the situation.

Appeal to Pity. Pulling on the heart strings of an audience (*argumentum ad misericordiam*, literally "argument to the heart pain," i.e., appeal to pity) may be effective, and the conclusions may even be the correct one, but playing on people's emotions is not an accepted form of sound argument.

Fallacies of Faulty Assertion

Post hoc, ergo propter hoc. *Post hoc, ergo propter hoc* is Latin and means "after this, therefore because of this." This fallacy mistakes a chronological relationship for a causal relationship, that because Y happened X *must* have happened earlier. In other words, just because something happens before another does not mean that it necessarily causes the other to happen. The key is to recognize that a cause must precede an effect, but timing alone is not enough to establish causality.

Slippery Slope. Sometimes referred to as the domino effect or the hell-in-a-handbasket argument. The basic structure of the argument is that if one thing occurs (A), it will put in motion a series of results (B, C, D...) that inevitably lead to some disastrous final outcome (Z). The metaphor of the slippery slope is meaningful if you picture yourself stepping off the peak of an icy hill. The inevitable result is a slide to the bottom and a bruised ego at the very least. These sorts of arguments are common in areas of policy and policy-making.

Additional Fallacies

False Dilemmas, Either/Or, and Black-and-White. False dilemmas, either/or arguments, and black-and-white thinking are a type of fallacy that results from oversimplification, by imposing two-valued thinking onto something complex.

Argumentum ad ignorantiam. Literally "argument to ignorance" or appeal to ignorance, i.e., argument from ignorance, this is a common tactic in arguments involving conspiracy. in essence, the argument boils down to a ridiculous assertion: "I don't know X, so I know Y is true." In reality, the only logical conclusion is to say, "I don't know, so I don't know."

Correcting fallacies in your research material or even in your argument is easy to do if you also understand approaches to solid argument. Though you will learn about various approaches and argument styles in later chapters, it's important to understand that there are basic elements in any type of argument, and once you learn how to correctly use these basic tools, constructing an effective argument becomes easier. Other potential issues in writing are discussed later in this book where they are relevant.

Research and Writing

The modes used to convey your argument are important, having sufficient research to support your argument is also important, as is honesty in argument and avoiding the fallacies discussed above and presenting valid logic to support your claims. Research is another critical element of writing, as it provides both the context for your argument and the support it needs to persuade your reader.

Research is a critical part of academic writing, and is useful in many forms of writing outside the university. Valid research provides connections to broader discussions and shows connections for your argument. People do research every day, even common activities like checking the calories on a carton of yogurt while on a diet or figuring out how much money they can spend on a birthday present. The information gathering performed for an essay or assignment simply means looking for different kinds of information and in different places. Using research to build credibility as a writer allows you to develop knowledge acquired from everyday experiences by incorporating research about the topic to make your argument more relevant and meaningful.

Credible Research is Key

In doing academic research, one factor to keep in mind is the credibility of each chosen source. Peer-reviewed journals and books published by reputable publishers are examples of credible sources. Information from news magazines has more weight than that from popular magazines. Many instructors forbid the use of Wikipedia as a source, not because all the information is inaccurate, but because unlike other credible sources, it is created by volunteers, not by experts in the field. The reader has to evaluate Wikipedia articles to determine if the article is authoritative rather than having a reputable editor and publisher determine the accuracy of the information. Even then, the information on Wikipedia is continuously being edited and re-edited which makes it problematic at best.

The general guidelines for establishing the credibility of a source can be as straightforward as asking how much scrutiny the work has been subjected to and how many experts in the field have reviewed it for accuracy and specificity.

Types of Research

Primary Research

Primary research refers to original pieces that do not provide an interpretation of anything else or another's work. This can include:

Interviews—Interviews with experts in the field are valuable in many areas because they provide a specialized insight into the issue and a unique perspective. In some cases, students are required to conduct interviews to build discipline-specific skills. Many forms of argument also lend themselves well to the use of interviews as a primary method for information gathering.

Observation—Close observation of descriptive detail can enhance almost any topic. Some academic fields, such as the sciences, use observation as one of the primary means of research because there are some changes and responses that must first be observed to be understood. This is not simply looking at the thing in question and writing about it, though that can certainly be part of it, but rather engaging with the subject over time to look for changes and effects.

Original Texts—In some fields, such as English and history, the original source at the heart of an argument, such as a novel, the U.S. Constitution, a painting, or a film, are referred to as the primary text or primary source.

Secondary Research

This kind of research is the first thing many students associate with the word "research." **Secondary research** is locating additional information about a subject using secondary sources. These sources provide interpretations, analysis, or studies about primary sources. Book reviews, film reviews, literary criticisms, biographies, and histories are all examples of secondary sources. Generally speaking, some forms of secondary research are more valid or valuable than others in most cases. A list of secondary sources, from the most to least valid, might look something like this:

Books—Many books, particularly scholarly works, also provide ample citations and other resources that can show connections to other arguments and ideas that cannot be discussed sufficiently in journal articles or popular media.

Scholarly journals—These articles offer criticism, evaluation, and research, and are sometimes more current than books. These articles and essays have been peer-reviewed, meaning they have been reviewed by professionals for reliability and relevance before being published.

Government documents—Government documents present a wealth of information for statistics and many contemporary events and issues. In many cases, these documents have been written by experts or for experts in the field to use.

Major magazines and newspapers—These publications feature stories, reports and news articles, written by journalists, based on actual observation of events and interviews with experts, and also present informed editorial opinions. Example publications are *Time, Newsweek,* and *U.S. News & World Report;* newspapers, such as the *New York Times,* the *Boston Globe,* the *Wall Street Journal,* and the *Washington Post.* Because they are written for a general audience, they are not held to the same standards for review and accuracy that scholarly sources are and, occasionally, these sources may be incorrect or much more biased.

Internet—Information from websites must be carefully evaluated as to author, publishing organization, and other criteria to establish how reliable the information actually is. Resources provided by colleges and universities (.edu), government agencies (.gov), state agencies, and a number of nonprofit groups (.org) can be valid sources when properly used. Even these sources can have problems, and every Internet source should be used with caution.

Time is another factor to consider when citing information. Depending on the topic, information published within the last three years is generally more relevant than information published ten years ago. Information has a "shelf life" in many fields, especially in fields like science and medicine which see major changes in a very short time. This is especially true today as information is being generated at an incredible pace. Each kind of source plays a specialized role in this process, as it develops and refines the information over time and through intense discussion and review in a field.

Evaluating Sources

Many people tend to believe what they see in print. They may think that if information is in a book or a news magazine, it must be true. If you read critically, however, you know that all sources must be evaluated. With the Internet, perhaps even more than with print texts, it is important to evaluate your sources. Here are some guidelines to consider when evaluating sources.

Who is the author?

This question is equally important whether the source in question is a book, a magazine, or a website. The author's academic credentials and university affiliation, what previous books the author has published, and other information can all be used to establish what qualifies the author to have written this particular argument.

For which audience is the text written?

The same information can be presented in a number of ways for different audiences. The more academic the intended audience, the more valid the source usually is as academic writing requires much more support and detail than a general presentation of facts. Is it written for general knowledge or for experts?

Does the author use in-text citation?

If you are working with an academic text, the sources should be clearly cited in the text, whether it is MLA or APA or a different citation style format. If it is a more popular book or article, sources are acknowledged less formally; however, a credible author will still make an effort to credit sources. For example, an article might say, "According to the March, 2009, issue of the *New England Journal of Medicine...*"

Does the text have an obvious bias?

Ask yourself if the argument is logical and if sources are mentioned for any statistics or other evidence. Are any opposing viewpoints discussed fairly? Does the author engage in name calling, a clear sign of bias? Are there obvious holes or contradictions in the argument?

This is not an exhaustive list of research questions and problems, but almost everything you write will require some form of research both in classes and outside of the university. Knowing the basics can go a long way toward succeeding in any form of writing for any audience.

Problems in writing

Beyond research, there are some common problems in writing, particularly in writing for classes at the university. As noted earlier in this book, academic writing is logical, organized, and effective. However, there are a number of issues that can appear in writing, not just academic writing but in other forms of persuasion as well, that need to be discussed. By recognizing not only what the problems are, but why they are problems, it becomes easier for you to avoid these issues in your own work.

A Note on Plagiarism

Plagiarism is as "to steal or purloin and pass off as one's own the ideas, words, or artistic production of another; to use without credit the ideas, expressions, or productions of another." Simply, plagiarism is the theft of ideas and attempting to pass them as original. It is, however, important to realize that the unintentional use of others' words is also considered plagiarism. This is handled at length in your handbook, as well as how to avoid plagiarism in your own work.

Conclusion

There are a number of potential kinds of writing for every purpose both in the university and beyond. Part of the challenge in writing well is determining what the writing at hand needs to accomplish and how to best meet those goals, which helps determine what kind of writing it will generally be. As discussed here, you will find yourselves combining these modes and forms as you write to better position your ideas for the reader and make them more persuasive and effective. This is part of writing well, knowing not only when to use the different forms but also how to combine them for the right effect. This depends on logical organization, appropriate use of the other elements, and other factors, but errors can (and do) happen to everyone. By being aware of fallacies and other common problems, it is easier to avoid them as you are building your skills and engaging with other forms of argument, which are discussed in the next chapter.

Chapter Five
Modern Models for
Argument and Analysis

There are a number of different models that can be used to understand and create arguments today. As discussed in Chapter Three, the classical model is only one form argument can take. Others include models based on the work of Stephen Toulmin (1922-2009) and Carl Rogers (1902-1987). The classical, Toulmin, and Rogerian models of argument represent some of the forms of argument, but they also function as tools of analysis. Analysis is a form of argument that breaks apart an artifact (such as a book or an article) into pieces in order to develop an insight. Analysis searches for hidden meanings behind artifacts by finding the artifact's persuasive elements. This chapter will show the elements of the Toulmin and Rogerian models of argument as well as forms of analysis, including rhetorical, Toulmin, Rogerian, and other types.

Models of Argument

The Toulmin Model

Claim: the main point of an argument

Qualifier: limits or restrictions on various elements in the argument

Data: evidence that supports the claim

Warrant: reasoning or assumptions that must be true for the data to support the claim

Backing: material that supports the warrant

Rebuttal: demonstrating weakness(es) of opposing or alternative claims

Figure 1. Elements of the Toulmin Model of Argument

British philosopher Stephen Toulmin published *The Uses of Argument* in 1958, which outlines an influential model used in both communication and rhetoric. Toulmin's approach to argument provides a flexible and practical model for analyzing the structures of arguments and for composing our own arguments. The model breaks down argument into different elements, which often go by slightly different names. For this discussion, Toulmin's elements will be called: claims, qualifier, data, warrants, backing, and rebuttals.

- **Claim**—The claim of an argument is the assertion that controls the development of the whole argument. People often refer to the major claim of an argument as the thesis. From a writer's perspective, the claim is the main point that you are trying to convince your audience to accept (or at least to consider) in your argument. It is the conclusion that you would like your audience to accept as a result of your argument. In academic writing, a claim remains the central focus of the essay (the thesis statement) and is supported by a series of subclaims, which are related to the main claim of the argument. As writers build academic essays, they are structured around subclaims, which often become the topic sentences. Claims and subclaims should not be confused with evidence; instead evidence should be used to back the claims.

- **Qualifier**—Qualifiers limit the scope of the statements and narrow the parameters of the argument to a specific context. Good writers restrict their arguments to specific contexts and avoid sweeping generalizations. No argument can address every aspect of an issue. Qualifiers make arguments more effective by limiting their context. Qualifiers may restrict the subject in terms of space or time—to a particular location, area, region, state, country, or to a particular season, year, decade, or century. They may restrict the subject in terms of frequency (often, sometimes, periodically, occasionally, rarely). They may restrict the subject in terms of likelihood (probably, possibly, improbably, unlikely). They may restrict the subject in terms of other considerations or events. They may spell out certain exclusions or exceptions to the argument.

- **Data**—In Toulmin argument, data (sometimes called evidence) is material used to support the claim. Data may be anecdotal evidence, personal experience, testimonials, reports of authorities, observable or factual evidence, experimental or statistical data, and so on. In academic contexts, data will tend to be verifiable, factual evidence. Given a claim, the data offers the grounds for accepting the claim. Data supports the claim by offering evidence and examples, providing a foundation for the claim.

- **Warrant**—The warrant is the reasoning that connects the data to the claim. More simply put, the warrant is what the audience knows or needs to know to accept the claim. Implicit warrants represent material audiences already know and do not need to be directly stated. Conversely, explicit warrants require an explanation from the writer. Warrants directly relate to the audience for a text; some audiences know the pertinent background information and some do not. The writer needs to carefully analyze the audience to determine what information needs to be explained.

- **Backing**—Slightly different than data, backing is material that supports explicit warrants. Oftentimes when a warrant requires explanation, there needs to be evidence to support that explanation. When a warrant is obvious, it rarely needs further support because the reader is likely to accept it as providing a legitimate bridge between the data and the claim.

- **Rebuttal**—This often goes by names such as acknowledgment or counterclaim, but rebuttals are addressing alternative points of view to a claim. Writers frequently consider opposing or alternative viewpoints in their arguments, typically to demonstrate the shortcomings or errors of the other views. Rhetorically this is a sound strategy because, if handled effectively, it weakens competing claims and bolsters the writer's point in the original argument. In the rebuttal of other arguments, writers must be fair and represent the opposing views accurately or the audience is likely to lose faith in the writer. If, in your discovery and invention process, you encounter an opposing argument that you simply cannot rebut or accommodate, you probably need to consider modifying or changing your claim.

The Toulmin model can help in the invention process. To use it as an invention method, consider these questions:

Claim: What is my point? What am I trying to convince the audience to think, to believe, to accept, to consider, or to do if they accept my argument?

Qualifier: Do I need to limit the scope of my argument to avoid overstating my case or to avoid implications that I do not intend?

Data: What sort of evidence is required for me to build a strong argument? What is my burden of proof to make a compelling argument? How much data is necessary to make this argument effective for a reasonable reader?

Warrants: What underlying assumption or reasoning explains the way the data supports the claim? What must be true in order for the data to provide adequate support of the claim?

Backing: What support is necessary for the warrants to be reasonable and sound?

Rebuttal: Are there opposing arguments that the audience might find attractive? Can I explain why those arguments should not be considered good alternatives to my argument?

This approach could be applied to a topic, such as parking. Starting with a claim, the approach should be an arguable claim. That means a claim that can be argued from more than one position or stance by reasonable people. For example, if your claim is "I need a parking space," that is not an arguable claim. It is simply a fact that your car needs to be parked. On the other hand, if you say, "The university should provide more parking for students," that is an arguable claim. Some may argue there is enough parking; others may argue the university cannot afford to build more lots. The claim about the university building can be argued from one than one perspective, thus it makes for a stronger academic argument. Additionally, this claim functioned as a qualifier. The argument started with the topic of parking, but the claim narrowed the context of the parking to student parking at the university. This qualifier narrowed the topic to a more manageable and local topic.

To support this claim, effective data might include a range of items, including:

- anecdotal testimony of students who have encountered difficulties finding parking
- results from a survey of staff members, faculty members, students, and visitors about their experience with parking on campus
- a statistical analysis of available parking and the number of drivers who compete for those spaces
- findings from specialists and planners who have studied parking needs in similar situations and would be able to provide relevant ratios of parking spaces for the number of users

It would also probably require some cost analysis to demonstrate that the need to construct parking is worth the investment to the institution. Ultimately, any material that supports and provides grounds for accepting the claim is data.

Now that there is a claim, qualifier, and data, the writer should consider the warrant. For this assignment, like many composition assignments, the audience will be classmates, the instructor, and the writer. One implicit warrant is that the audience understands the importance of campus parking. Some explicit warrants, that may require backing, include: (1) a person should not need to search so long for a parking space that it makes them late; (2) it is unfair to expect a person to search so long in order to attend required activities on campus; or (3), the university has an obligation to its students and faculty to provide adequate parking to accommodate their busy schedules. These warrants may require some backing. For example, an anecdotal story about a student who searched 45 minutes for a parking space may work to support the first warrant.

To make this argument most effective, one last element needs to be added: rebuttals. For this parking argument one differing point of view could be that the university lacks the space or money to build a parking lot. An effective rebuttal could be the cost analysis information that was gathered. The argument could be made to increase parking sticker costs. As for space, many universities add parking garages which offer more parking on the same piece of land. Acknowledging these alternative points of view and then providing evidence that makes them less effective makes the overall argument stronger.

The Rogerian Model

Toulmin's model is only one model for arguments. Another common model used in academic argument is the Rogerian model, developed by Carl Rogers in the 1950s, which focuses on a "common ground" approach for presenting arguments.

Rogerian argument, based on psychologist Carl Rogers's belief that it is important to see things from the point of view of others, advocates an empathic response to disagreement rather than the adversarial one frequently characteristic of traditional approaches. Rogerian argument presents differing perspectives fairly in order to find common ground or position(s) within an issue with which all can agree to some extent.

A Rogerian argument structure recognizes the importance of each position before attempting to change people's minds. An introduction to the problem is presented; this is followed by a statement that illustrates the opposing position(s) is understood, and the contexts in which that position is valid. The writer then presents his/her position and the contexts in which it is valid. The next move is to show how the opposing position might be strengthened by adopting some of the elements of the writer's position. If the two positions can be shown to complement, rather than oppose one another, an ideal situation for resolution of the disagreement exists.

A major difference between traditional argument and the Rogerian approach is that the first step is to seek a clear understanding of the viewpoint of the other person or group not for purposes of refuting it per se, but rather for gaining an empathic understanding of why people think and feel as they do. This approach calls for "walking a mile in someone else's shoes" in that one needs to experience the context—the frame of reference—which results in the "expressed idea and attitude" on a problem or issue.

Once this understanding is clear, the next step is to determine under what circumstances or in what context is the person's or group's position valid. This investigation is essential; if you cannot find evidence that the position has validity somewhere within the issue, there is no point in going further. If, however, you determine there is validity for the position in some circumstances or context, you are ready to move forward.

A major characteristic of Rogerian argument is that it reflects understanding and, perhaps more importantly, respect for the opinion, position, and feelings of others. In turn, it asks them to respond in kind with understanding and respect for the writer's position. With this as a starting point, communication barriers are removed and active discussion of problem resolution can occur.

Much like with the Toulmin method, Rogerian argument offers a tool for invention. This involves looking at an issue and evaluating the points to be raised by your argument in the following ways.

- **Objective Analysis**—Is the object or central point of the argument evaluated fairly and objectively? Is it clear and concise? Are there specific points which need to be foregrounded to show an objective position here?
- **Opposing Positions**—This in some ways mirrors the refutation in the classical model, as it means engaging with the possible objections or refutations of the argument you are staging. Some key questions might include: Have the objections to the argument been given a fair and objective evaluation? Are the major objections represented, or are there points which should be added? What are the major problems with the argument at hand and how are they usually raised?
- **Positioning the Argument**—What is the position taken in this argument? What is the context for the argument? When and where are these points valid and both arguable and worth arguing?
- **Common Ground**—Where are both sides of the argument in agreement? How does each side of the argument support the other? Where are the points of agreement, and in what context? How can both sides benefit from the argument being staged here?

To return to the university parking example addressed above, a Rogerian analysis would carefully consider both the students' and university's position on the parking issue. The objective analysis acknowledges that parking is an issue at the university. This analysis could address how many spaces are available, cost of parking, and university expenditures on parking. Keep in mind this should remain a neutral positioning of the argument. Unlike Toulmin, this is not saying there should be more parking, but rather that parking is an issue.

The next step would be to outline the opposing issues. This is an opportunity to present what each side says about the issue. To effectively address these opposing issues, use a topical approach. For example, what does each side say about the cost of parking? What does each side say about the available spaces? What solutions does each side propose?

After outlining what each side says, it is helpful to position the argument by addressing the areas of the argument that are worth arguing. For the parking issue, both sides agree that space is an issue and that more parking is needed. This positioning can then lead to the common ground. A common ground argument could focus on how the university could build a parking garage. But unlike the Toulmin argument, the Rogerian approach would argue that a parking garage would provide a common ground between the opposing sides on this issue.

Types of Analysis

Just as you can formulate arguments using rhetorical, Toulmin, and Rogerian methods, you can also use those methods, and others, for analysis. As mentioned at the beginning of this chapter, analysis is a tool for breaking an artifact into pieces in order to gain an insight. Good analysis highlights the parts that make up the whole in order to show something that cannot be seen by looking at the whole. Analysis is a tool used in everyday life, but it often remains unrecognized. For example, you use analysis to decide what path to take to class. Experience tells you that some paths are shorter or less crowded than others. You use that experience for considering all of the paths to determine the pros and cons of each and decide which path to take.

In academic settings, particularly in composition classes, analysis more often takes the form of breaking down arguments in order to better understand them. You may read an argument and agree with it, but you are unsure as to *why* you agree with it. Analysis helps understand the why. Academic analysis often highlights the good and bad of artifacts. Rarely does analysis point out that an artifact does everything right, rather it shows the effective and ineffective elements of arguments.

Academic analysis requires careful reading of texts (both written and visual) in order to understand the material. For any analysis project, expect to read and/or view the text multiple times in order to understand the multiple layers of meanings. Additionally, writers need to understand the context of the artifact being analyzed. That means recognizing when it was created as well as any public reaction to the text. If it is an older text, analysis should address the long-standing impact of a text. For example, if you were to analyze Leonardo da Vinci's *Mona*

Lisa, then you should address the painting's long-standing cultural impact. Here are some forms of analysis that can be used in academic settings.

Rhetorical Analysis

As discussed in Chapter Three, there are three rhetorical appeals: *ethos*, *logos*, and *pathos*. Scholars more recently have added *purpose* to these three appeals. Rhetorical analysis breaks down a text using those rhetorical appeals. Most often in rhetorical analysis, breaking apart the artifact by showing its *ethos*, *logos*, and *pathos* often makes the purpose of the text clearer. When doing rhetorical analysis, keep in mind that *ethos*, *logos*, *pathos*, and purpose are part of every artifact. You cannot have *ethos*, but not *logos*, or no *ethos* but *pathos*. All of these elements always exist together. When you think maybe one isn't there, it is likely that the one of the elements is being done poorly. For example, someone may have a poor *ethos* in making an argument or use ineffective or unreliable data for the *logos*. These are areas to discuss in writing an analysis. While it may seem like a simple task to break down these appeals, effective rhetorical analysis talks about each of these in detail. Here are some ways to talk about each with more depth:

- **Ethos:** Too often *ethos* becomes simplified to mean speaker or ethics. Defining *ethos* as speaker or ethics oversimplifies this rhetorical appeal. *Ethos* represents multiple qualities at once. Just to name a few items to consider, *ethos* is the speaker, the speaker's credibility, the credibility of the argument being made, and the voice or tone used in the argument. When writing an analysis, the writer should address all of these qualities in discussing the *ethos* of the analyzed artifact. Oftentimes, writing about *ethos* in analysis papers requires some level of research. Students may need to do some research to determine who the author is. For example, are they a professor at a university? Which one? What is their research specialty? Rhetorical analysis should offer good detail about the author's experience and credibility and then address how the author presents their argument. Oftentimes the tone of the argument shows a bias or lack of credibility. For example, if you were reading an academic article and you came across excessive profanity, it would affect how you view the credibility of the author. By the same token, if a professional journalist seems to be presenting a neutral tone, you may find language that shows the journalist leans toward supporting one side of an argument. All of these elements can be discussed in a rhetorical analysis.
- **Logos:** Simply put, *logos* is the message or information provided. Oftentimes, *logos* becomes simplified into just logic, but *logos* is much more complicated. It is related to logic, but again it is not solely logical. Texts do not have to use logical thought to persuade. To bring this back to the Toulmin argument elements you read earlier in this chapter, *logos* is the data. *Logos* provides the foundation for the argument being made. To analyze *logos*, you must determine the quality of the data or information being provided. Is the research used reliable (refer to Chapter Four for advice on this)? How effectively does the author present the research? Is the data easy to understand? Keep in mind, that because *logos* is always connected to *ethos*, *pathos*, and purpose, effective

data also contributes to the *ethos* of an author. If the author uses only unreliable sources, it affects both their *ethos* and their *logos*.

· **Pathos:** The last of the traditional rhetorical appeals is *pathos*, which is the audience. Again, this appeal becomes simplified to represent emotion, but *pathos* is more than emotion. *Pathos* represents the intended audience for an artifact, audiences beyond the intended audience, how the artifact affects the audience (emotionally is just one example of this), and the language and format used to reach specific audiences. Analysis should consider all of these elements in determining the effectiveness of the *pathos* of an artifact. Again, *pathos* remains tied closely to *ethos*, *logos*, and purpose. If someone uses childlike language to speak to an audience of adults, it shows a poor understanding of *ethos*, *logos*, and *pathos*.

· **Purpose:** The newer addition to the rhetorical appeals, purpose represents the reason why an artifact was created. A simple way to consider purpose is to consider it the "so what?" question. As you analyze an artifact consider its importance and relevance. Often in doing rhetorical analysis the purpose becomes clear and becomes the insight you gain by breaking apart the artifact. Thus, many times the purpose can become the thesis of the rhetorical analysis paper.

The preceding discussion presents the traditional approach to rhetorical analysis. This analysis can be applied in different ways. You can take the same rhetorical analysis format and apply it to visual elements. For example, apply *ethos*, *logos*, *pathos*, and purpose to a piece of art or a billboard. Groups, such as the Center for Media Literacy, offer a slightly altered version of rhetorical analysis. The Center suggests analyzing texts for authorship, format, audience, content, and purpose. You can see those are basically rhetorical analysis with the addition of format.

Toulmin Analysis

Much like rhetorical analysis breaks apart the elements of a text to show its *ethos*, *logos*, *pathos*, and purpose, Toulmin analysis breaks apart a text by the elements of Toulmin analysis: claim, qualifier, data, warrant, backing, and rebuttal. Again like rhetorical analysis, an argument may do an ineffective job of one or more of these elements, which just provides more material to write about in the Toulmin analysis. Much as in rhetorical analysis, a Toulmin analysis of an artifact requires an in-depth discussion of these elements. It is more than just identifying the claim, but also arguing whether the claim is effective.

The Rogerian Model of Analysis

Just like in argument, the Rogerian model of analysis is about finding the common ground. Unlike the rhetorical and Toulmin models, the Rogerian model often takes a more structured form. The general structure of a Rogerian argument is as follows:

1. A Rogerian analysis begins with an objective description of the issue and the problem(s) to be solved.
2. This is followed with an analytical, neutral, and objective description of the opposing position. When writing this, avoid any type of judgmental or evaluative statements. Your goal is to illustrate you understand not only the opposing position, but also the reasons for it and the contexts in which it is valid. Additionally, this section is more effective if organized by topics. Focus on the areas where the two sides can be in conversation with each other.
3. Next, provide an analytical description of your position in a neutral and objective manner, and once again, avoid any moralizing or evaluative statements. State the contexts in which this position is valid. This section is critical in that solid evidence must be given that illustrates fair-mindedness on your part. Otherwise, the argument will not be convincing.
4. Find common ground by analyzing and stating what the two positions have in common; in doing this, consider shared goals and values as well as facts.
5. State how the opposing position could benefit by incorporating elements of your position into it.
6. Offer a resolution that recognizes and includes the best of both positions.

These elements make it easy to follow the general structure of the argument and to pick out specific points in context. The emphasis on common grounds and reciprocal understanding also make it an inviting model for staging possibly problematic arguments in a lower threat environment.

Some incorrectly summarize the Rogerian model as a "win-win" situation in which each party gets something they want out of the argument. This is a gross oversimplification of what Rogers really intends in his model, which is logical argument from common ground with mutual communication.

Other Forms of Analysis

This chapter cannot address every form of analysis. Here is a quick explanation of some other forms of analysis that you may use or read.

Process—These analyses can either explain how something is done (instructional) or explain how something works (Informational).

Causal—This type of analysis considers both an event happened as well as the impact of the event.

Compare and contrast—This form of analysis compares two elements to determine the areas of similarity and difference. Similar to a Rogerian analysis, this form considers the key claims of the argument, the values of the author(s), worldviews/ideologies, ideas/ideals, concerns/fears, and goals/priorities.

Data—This analysis looks at a set of data, either quantitative (numerical) or qualitative (not numerical), to determine what that information means.

Literature—A Literature analysis does a close reading of a literary artifact, addressing issues such as character, point of view, plot, setting, theme, and artifact's impact.

Visual—This type of analysis looks at the components of a visual and determines their individual meanings and then determines how all of those meanings come together to determine the visual's message.

Conclusion

The Toulmin Model, the Rogerian Model, and the classical model are only a few of the concepts that students need to know as they develop their skill at constructing sound, reasonable, and effective arguments. In the end, these models are just that: *models* for providing the basic structure of the argument you are writing and not explicit blueprints for your work. Similarly, these models provide tools for breaking down other people's arguments that you encounter so you can understand them more fully (the types of analysis section shown above). Throughout the writing process, from discovery and invention, drafting, revising, and editing, these concepts will prompt you to think carefully and deeply about what you are trying to accomplish with your arguments.

While written arguments are the most common forms in the university, in the university and beyond you will likely encounter arguments that use multiple modes (text, visuals, audio, and more) to accomplish their goals, and it is this kind of multimodal argument that is discussed in the next chapter.

Chapter Six

Multimodal Composition

In its simplest form, **multimodal composition** refers to any text that assembles information presented in different rhetorical modes (as discussed in Chapter Four) and arranges them in effective ways. We often think of traditional modes of discourse (like narrative) as written texts, often called alphabetic texts. Multimodal composition reconsiders traditional modes of discourse and puts them into new formats, often combining alphabetic texts and visual or auditory elements (such as graphs, charts, pictures, podcasts, videos). While it may seem like these texts do not fit in all academic disciplines, multimodality functions across college curriculums. For example, business and science courses often require the use of charts and graphs to present blocks of information visually. The use of photos and layout elements are part of the regular curriculum in the humanities, the social sciences, and education classes. Similarly, these kinds of multimodal composition are everyday occurrences in the working world outside of the university. Teachers regularly design visual collages and other texts for students and parents; professionals compile reports and other documents that use graphs and charts; journalists and other writers often use images or illustrations to enhance their work and to help clarify specific points for the reader.

The concept of multimodality is not new. For example, Charles Dickens's novels often contained illustrations, which made them multimodal. Also, movies in the silent era combined visuals and texts. These books and films exist on a physical plane, or rather they are objects that can be touched. Conversely, in the twenty-first century many multimodal compositions exist in virtual or digital environments. We engage in digital multimodality every day therefore understanding the creation process as well as its meanings are critical to our engagement with the world.

Multimodal digital assignments are becoming increasingly common in university classrooms and, more importantly, in the world outside the university as a whole. Social and professional media has changed the way many people, both students and professionals, think about writing and argument on a daily basis. You are likely to encounter a number of multimodal writing assignments during your coursework that are intended to help prepare you for the changing professional world, therefore it is an important part of the discussion of writing and arguing effectively.

What Is Multimodal Digital Composition?

Digital technology affects how and where we communicate with one another. Social and professional media have created new locations for interaction where people can come together virtually, and we can now access more information than we could possibly process at the push of a button or the click of a link. Because they allow messages to be conveyed easily and extensively, and permit the mixing of different forms of communication, these media call for new forms of literacy and composition. That is, digital spaces require that we redefine basic terms like "reading" and "writing," terms that we often take for granted. Most of the time when we talk about reading, we assume that the information read is being presented in linguistic form, but pictures and other visual texts must also be "read" so that we may decipher their meaning. When it comes to the word "writing," the image that is conjured is ordinarily one of setting pen to paper to write out a traditional essay or short story, although we might replace the image of the pen with a keyboard. However, composing in and for digital spaces means that we must consider more than a basic switch in the tools that we use to assemble our messages. We must also think about the arrangement of information within a message, and consider which mode of delivery might be better suited to advance particular elements of a message and why. We must pay close attention to how messages are framed and delivered through existing technology to appeal to previously unanticipated audiences, and how we may combine different appeals to craft effective multimodal compositions.

Digital spaces tend to be characterized by their use of nonlinear logic and by greater flexibility in arrangement in comparison to standard print or visual media. They allow us to bring together different kinds of information presented in diverse forms that cannot be accommodated by earlier media, and to do so in new and exciting ways. A newspaper can impart information using words and images, but you cannot embed a video or link to another website in an article unless that newspaper is published online. Because of the Internet's capacity for bringing together different forms of communication, discussions of multimodal composition are often associated with the use of digital technology. Digital technology provides a new means of engaging in multimodality, but, as noted earlier, they are not the only form of multimodal composition. In fact, you may not realize that many of the texts you encounter on a daily basis are actually multimodal because they combine diverse kinds of appeals.

When a message brings together a variety of these strategies to support a specific claim or set of claims, we describe it as **multimodal**, meaning that an argument is being advanced using a combination of modes in various media, such as a mix of videos, music, and words. Modes are not the same thing as media, although we tend to associate the use of certain media with particular modes of communication. *Modes* usually correspond to the *senses* that we wish to engage, while *media* are the *means* we create to make that possible. Painting and video are distinct media that both employ the visual mode; a speech and a symphony are both considered texts in the aural mode. It is important to make this distinction because the real focus of multimodal composition is the use of diverse modes, not just diverse media; it aims to appeal to as many of the human senses as necessary to make as complete a connection between the message and the audience as possible.

Thus, multimodal means compositions that are created using multiple modes or media. For example, a movie and video games are multimodal because they include video, audio, and, oftentimes, text. Similarly, an essay combining images and graphics could be considered multimodal. As with every composition, these texts require a careful consideration of audience. The format or media you choose to use in a composition should be relevant to the content of the composition as well as the audience for the text. For example, for an audience of kindergarten students, you may want to create a picture book. Conversely, for an audience of college students, a video may be more appropriate. Just like all forms of rhetoric, multimodality provides new means for communicating with an audience, and, ultimately, more tools for persuasion.

The Advantages of Digital Multimodal Composition

Multimodal composition has come to be regarded as synonymous with composition using digital technology since more and more, communication venues are moving into the realm of cyberspace. The seemingly endless combinations of media and modalities that computers make possible ensure that multimodal composition is often aimed at digital spaces. As this technology was emerging, scholars dubbed it "new media," a term designed to encompass the wide array of digital options. More recent scholarship recognizes that new media is largely a matter of perspective; at some point in time all media was deemed new, even those that may now seem old-fashioned (Palmeri 2012). Whether discussing old or new media, technology always alters the way we create and perceive texts. Much like the typewriter changed the way we can read and create texts, digital technologies provide new opportunities to develop interactive texts that encourage audiences to take actions or participate in the text. Audience members become active participants rather than passive consumers of information.

One example of this would be advertisers choosing to incorporate elements of actual gameplay into an ad for a new video game, allowing gamers feel the sensory rush that they will experience if they purchase the full game. This kind of multimodal appeal is more effective since they can anticipate whether they will enjoy playing the game for hours on end based on what they see *and* feel. Crafting successful multimodal texts requires that writers learn how to make smart use of all existing media and modes while remaining attentive to the persuasive possibilities that accompany the production of new technologies.

Another major characteristic of multimodal composition is its capacity for **repurposing**, or making use of older modes of communication in innovative ways through the formation of inventive combinations. One example of repurposing is the use of film clips in a blog-based analysis as proof of the claims being made about a movie; the clips may have been intended originally to provide entertainment for fans of the film or to convince people to watch it, but now they are being used as an essential component of an argument. In addition to repurposing, digital technology makes **remixing** a possibility. Remixing is taking two or more elements and putting them together to make something new. One example would be taking film clips of people dancing in several old movies and placing an audio of a more contemporary song. This remixing makes it appear as if a dancer from another time is dancing to the more current song.

The idea of repurposing or remixing makes it seem as if it is eliminating previous modes of communication, but that is not the case. Just as radio allowed audiences who could not read a newspaper to receive news reports aurally, the invention of television meant that audiences could see as well as hear the people talking to them. Today, we can surf the Internet for news at any time without having to wait for regularly scheduled broadcasts, but we still read, watch, or listen to the news even though it is presented online. The development of new technologies does not mean that "old" technologies and modes go away, only that they can now be used differently than they had been to achieve previously unforeseen effects.

Another advantage of multimodal composition is that it highlights and makes use of our dependence on **hypertextuality**, or the connections we draw between texts that help us to create meaning. For example, a print magazine intended for auto mechanics may assume its readership has a basic knowledge of car parts and how they work, and may leave out basic descriptions to save money on printing. In contrast, a website for mechanics can feature definitions of parts, system schematics, and photographs at no additional cost. Hyperlinks leading to separate pages that feature descriptions or diagrams of car parts would let novice mechanics access much-needed information easily without distracting those who do not need this additional data.

While webpage hyperlinks represent the most familiar example of our reliance on hypertextuality, these connections do not have to be computer-based. Our ability to interpret one text's meaning usually relies on our knowledge of other texts, even when connections to additional texts exist only in our memory. For instance, when a novel you are reading alludes to another narrative with a similar theme, the allusion adds to the significance of the novel without distracting you from the story at hand. However, you must be familiar with both stories for the allusion to work. Multimodal composition increases our ability to create these hypertextual connections by linking associated texts even though they are presented in different modes, ensuring that these connections do not go undetected; it also allows us to arrange these texts, making each text more accessible to the audience, adding to the persuasive effect of their combination.

Drawbacks of Digital Multimodal Composition

So far, we have seen some of the very useful features of multimodal composition. However, digital forms of multimodal composition also present disadvantages. Being aware of these possible drawbacks can help us to become more careful planners and composers. It is important not to alienate the audience, and yet that is something that can easily happen when texts stand in for us in cyberspace.

The most notable drawbacks associated with digital multimodal composition involve the issue of **accessibility**, or how certain combinations of modes include or exclude particular demographics. Digital technology's design flexibility means that now we can easily tell stories through sets of carefully arranged images or compose arguments in ways that combine print and video. However, even as we take these media for granted as part of our everyday existence, not everyone experiences media in the same way or necessarily knows how to "read" media the same way we might. We must consider ways that will allow us to help audiences appreciate how the different modes we use work together.

The most obvious form of exclusion is based on an audience's **physical access to digital technology**. Computers may be important features of everyday life for a lot of people, but that does not mean that everyone has constant access to a computer or the Internet. Think of it this way: while smaller businesses may only advertise online to save money, larger companies still use aural ads via radio and visual ads via television because it is good business to try to reach as many people as possible.

Also, we must be conscious that people's **abilities and disabilities** may affect how different modes are received. Someone with limited vision may better appreciate your work if you include brief aural descriptions of the images in a PowerPoint presentation. A person who is experiencing hearing loss may depend on closed captioning to follow the argument in your video. We all have different ways of learning, and learn better when information is presented to us in modes that appeal to our particular preferences and strengths. Scholars in the fields of composition and disability studies suggest that we make use of Universal Design principles as much as possible (Dolmage 2005). Universal Design is a set of aims and practices that focuses on making everything from buildings to documents as accessible as possible to everyone, whether or not they may experience some form of disability. As students of multimodal composition, we should strive to bring together diverse modes and media in thoughtful ways that consider disabilities among members of our prospective audiences and that appeal to different audiences' preferred modes of reception in order to leave a positive lasting impression.

Lastly, an accessibility issue that is often overlooked is our own **preconceived notions of background knowledge**. That is, we often take for granted what audiences may or may not know about the topic based on our own experiences with texts and multimodality. As in the example of the different skill levels of mechanics used earlier in this chapter, a simple hyperlink that connects the main text to additional helpful images and videos is immediately more inclusive of those who do not know enough about cars to make full use of the website. Even when making a multimodal presentation for class, the right combination of modes can help you to prevent this problem; you may have already accounted for this by providing your classmates with a handout that lists key terms and definitions while giving a speech, or projecting images of famous people so they know who you are talking about during your oral report. A bit of preplanning regarding multimodal components can go a very long way, but failing to do so can also send out the wrong kind of a message—that you are not concerned with appealing to certain kinds of audiences.

We should always try to anticipate how our uses of different modes will affect the reception of what we have to say by as many people as possible—especially when using digital technology. While giving a multimodal presentation in person, you might more easily accommodate your audience's needs by providing supplementary information in another mode that works. In the depersonalized environment of cyberspace, you might not have the same timely opportunity to correct any oversights until well after you may have already lost or even caused offense to a significant portion of your audience. It is vital that during the various stages of composition, we give serious thought to ways by which we may unintentionally limit people's access to our work and seek to prevent these issues ahead of time.

The Language of Multimodality

Just like with many forms of composition, there is a language to creating multimodal compositions. While each of these categories has hundreds of terms related to them, here is a brief guide to some key terms to help you create and analyze multimodal design.

Video terms
- **Point of view:** The perspective from which a video is shot. For example, first person video games often are shown from the point of view of the player's chosen character or avatar.
- **Cinematography:** This addresses the lighting and camera angles chosen for a scene.
- **Shots:** These are the way in which a moment on a video is filmed. There are three basic types: a **closeup**, which is a shot focusing tightly on the person or thing being filmed; a **medium shot**, which shows more of the background of what is being shot; and a **long shot,** which shows a scene from a further distance. Most movies, television shows, and professional videos employ a variety of these shots within scenes.

Sound terms
- **Sound editing:** Recordings often contain multiple layers of sounds. Sound editing is deciding on what key sounds are needed and removing unwanted sounds.
- **Sound mixing**: Although related to editing, sound mixing focuses more on bringing together multiple sounds, from the original recording to the addition of non-dialogue elements called **sound effects**.
- **Background noise:** Oftentimes when trying to record a specific sound, other sounds (like traffic or weather) can be recorded as well. Background noise are those other sounds. Sound editing can lessen the effect of those sounds.

Design terms
- **Layout:** The design layout is the placement of elements (words, photos, graphics) on the page. The layout addresses where specific elements are placed.
- **Visual hierarchy:** In western culture, we tend to read images much like we read books or other texts. Visual theorists Gunther Kress and Theo

van Leeuwen stress that we tend to put the highest priority on what is in the top left corner and the lowest priority to elements in the lower right corner. Thus, in design, elements at the top of page are considered the most important.

- **Typography:** Typography is simply how words and letters are presented on a page. Typography involves the **font** (type of text used), as well as size and position of the text. When reading texts, words in larger type are considered more important, or higher in the visual hierarchy.
- **Contrast:** An important design element, contrast represents the difference in two elements, whether that difference be in size, color, or shade.
- **Repetition:** Design elements often repeat on a page. For example, good design tends to limit the use of fonts to one or two and repeats those one or two fonts across the layout.
- **Alignment:** Designs tend to line up materials along invisible horizontal or vertical lines. One example, would be a website, where the page generally has an invisible line on the left side where the page's elements line up.
- **Proximity:** Related design elements should be placed close to one another. How close an element is to another element suggests they are related.

Conclusion

Multimodal composition requires writers to make informed choices about how best to adapt and combine media in different modes to reach wider and more diverse audiences. As more opportunities for composition are found online, we must learn how to effectively employ digital technology to create original multimodal texts. However, we should be aware that these computer-based texts nonetheless make use of older media and more traditional modes. It is only by understanding that much of the communication within our everyday cultures already happens multimodally, and by recognizing the potential advantages and drawbacks of specific multimodal combinations that we will find ourselves in a better position to make such informed choices. We may then craft texts that make use of already established expectations and preferences and avoid those multimodal patterns that inadvertently send the wrong message.

Works Cited

Amsler, Mark. "Affective Literacy: Gestures of Reading in the Later Middle Ages." *Essays in Medieval Studies* 18 (2001): 83–110.

Clark, Christine, and Paul Gorski. "Multicultural Education and the Digital Divide: Focus on Socioeconomic Class Background." *Multicultural Perspectives* 4.3 (2002): 25–36.

Dolmage, Jay. "Disability Studies Pedagogy, Usability and Universal Design." *Disability Studies Quarterly* 25.4 (2005): n.p.

Haas, Angela M. "Wampum as Hypertext: An American Indian Intellectual Tradition of Multimedia Theory and Practice." *Studies in American Indian Literatures* 19.4 (2007): 77–100.

Lanham, Richard A. *A Handlist of Rhetorical Terms*. 2nd ed. Berkeley: U of California P, 1991.

Palmeri, Jason. *Remixing Composition: A History of Multimodal Writing Pedagogy*. Carbondale: Southern Illinois UP, 2012.

Reynolds, Garr. "The Big Four: Contrast, Repetition, Alignment, Proximity." *Presentation Zen: Simple Ideas on Presentation Design,* New Riders, 2012.

Selber, Stuart A. *Multiliteracies for a Digital Age*. Carbondale: SIUP, 2004.

Sirc, Geoffrey. "Serial Composition." *Rhetorics and Technologies: New Directions in Writing and Communication*. Columbia: U of South Carolina P, 2010. 56–73. Print.

Suggested Readings

Bickmore, Lisa, and Ron Christiansen. "Who Will Be the Inventors? Why Not Us? Multimodal Composition in the Two-Year College Classroom." *Teaching English in the Two-Year College* 37.3 (2010): 230–242.

Meyer, A. and Rose, D. "Universal Design for Individual Differences." *Educational Leadership* 58:3 (2000) 39–43.

Mietlicki, Connie. "Multimodal Literacies for the Critical-Thinking Needs of Learners in the 21st Century." *Talking Points* 21.1 (2009): 11–18.

Yancey, Kathleen Blake. "Made Not Only in Words: Composition in a New Key." *College Composition and Communication* 56.2 (2004): 297–328.

Chapter Seven
Putting Writing in Perspective

One of the most frequently asked questions in a composition class is "how will this help me?" Some students mean in regard to their other classes, many mean in the world outside of the university. As was emphasized in Chapter One, writing well and being able to respond to a number of different kinds of writing as part of the normal course of business is one of the skills many employers look for in an employee. One example of how important effective, clear writing is in every profession would be Tina Fields and Jeffrey Hatala's survey of workplace writing.[1] Fields and Hatala state the issue plainly based on ten years of research:

> According to Collins & Bissell (2004), employers expect people who have graduated from college to have a basic understanding of grammar. However, Quible (2008) found many employers were dissatisfied with the writing skills of their employees. This parallels a survey of 120 American corporations, employing 8 million people, which found that about two-thirds of the salaried employees had some writing responsibility, yet over 40% of the firms had to provide training/retraining in writing skills (National Commission on Writing, 2004). Since writing is a "threshold skill," the emphasis on good writing skills is crucial to the viability of an organization, as organization functions that are most dependent on communication (i.e., customer contact and research and development) are least likely to be outsourced (National Commission on Writing, 2004, p. 8). Many companies see writing as a "marker" that is associated with high-skill, high-wage, professional work (Quible & Griffin, 2007). Thus, people who communicate in a clear manner are more likely to be hired and to be considered for promotion. This is substantiated by a survey that found approximately 50% of all companies consider writing abilities when making promotion decisions (National Commission on Writing, 2004). (4-5)

As was noted in this book, writing is a valuable skill and one that employers both expect and demand in employees who are going to last in every field. The same is true in every discipline in the university, effective, clear, and professional writing is both expected and demanded from the students who are going to do well in their courses and develop the additional skills and knowledge they need to succeed after they graduate.

Fields and Hatala, along with most researchers of the issue, also agree—as does this book—that effective writing is a transferrable skill that can be learned. That is the real value of an effective composition course, showing you how to develop the critical active reading and writing skills that are useful across the curriculum and beyond and, perhaps more importantly, practicing those skills so you can develop them efficiently.

---

1   Fields, Tina L., and Jeffrey J. Hatala. "That, That, But Not That...Using a Cafeteria Plan to Enhance Writing Skills." *Administrative Issues Journal* 4.2 (2014): 3-11.

How Did We Do This?

Looking back across the semester, think about the work you have done for this class. As was likely discussed several times during the course, the major and minor writing assignments—the major essays, the in-class writings, and even the essay exams—each emphasized specific forms of writing, specific approaches to writing, reading, and thinking critically in order to build a defined set of skills and approaches to prepare you for more frequent, and often more sustained, writing than you had been used to doing in high school. The variety of assignments, the length of the essays, the active responses to other people's writing (both your peers' work and the readings in this book), and other kinds of writing help build and sharpen the skills you need to succeed. Your instructor likely asked the class on a few occasions if they had already seen similar assignments in other classes, and if they had seen changes in their writing in non-Composition classes. This is part of demonstrating how important and transferrable these skills are. The philosophy behind this approach is often called Writing Across the Curriculum (WAC). WAC is not a new idea, in fact the oldest integrated WAC programs in the United States adopted this approach in the 1970s. The WAC approach tries to coordinate writing across all the courses in the university so that students receive constant feedback on their writing and continue to develop their writing skills throughout their academic careers—in order to prepare them as well as possible for their professional careers.

This is also part of the logic in the way the composition courses are sequenced. No class can help you fully develop these skills in sixteen weeks, and even with two composition courses you will continue to develop them in your own major and minors. We can, however, give you the tools and the awareness of your writing process to keep developing your writing long after your last composition class. Turning back to Fields and Hatala, they also provide some important information as to the "why" of this approach:

> Many students tend to think of writing as a "talent" or a "gift" and thus do not consider how extensive practice could enhance their abilities (Ericsson, 2006). They fail to realize that composing good text requires self-regulation (Lovett, Lewandowski, Berger, & Gathje, 2010). This is because writing requires many self-regulatory mechanisms such as planning, evaluating, and revising (Graham & Harris, 2000). In order to self-regulate, students need to control their environment, behavior, and personal processes (Graham & Harris, 2000). Only after students become comfortable in setting goals and planning for a task, seeking the necessary information, organizing information, and putting information into their own words can they become better writers (Graham & Harris, 2000). Students tend to become more self-regulating with age and schooling (Graham & Harris, 2000), whether this is based on maturation or having had greater opportunities to practice the skill. (5)

If you reflect on the specific issues raised in each of the chapters here, you will see that process, practice, revision, goals and planning, and making your argument your own are exactly what we have been working on since the class began. These are the skills that make effective writing possible in the first place, not "talent" or a "gift." The textbook provides the background information you need, the assignments allow you to apply these concepts and internalize them in a variety of ways.

It may be helpful to review how each chapter has built on your previous writing experience and added new layers to your approach to writing in general. The emphasis throughout this book has been on approaches and skills that are transferrable to a number of disciplines and careers, in addition to being important elements to writing well in general. The first chapter introduced the key concepts for the class as a whole, **active reading, critical reading**, and **active writing**. This chapter also emphasized that it is your approach and engagement that makes for good writing, not innate skill or a natural gift. Instead, these are skills that can be developed and applied outside the classroom.

The second chapter discussed the writing process, specifically that writing itself is a process with a number of discrete steps. Writing takes time, and establishing the time for writing is critical to being a successful writer in any environment. This chapter also emphasized the need for proofreading and revision as a part of the writing process. Without allowing sufficient time and space for **proofreading**, **editing**, and **revision**, even the best idea will not be as successful as it could or would be otherwise. You have to be aware of your writing process and what you can change if something is not working as it should. Not every writing project has the same flow, the same needs, or even the same time allowed to do it in, knowing how to manage your time and writing process effectively are key to writing well and being effective in your argument.

Chapter Three presented a brief overview of rhetoric and the rhetorical situation. A major part of the writing process, and knowing when to change up your process or approach, is being aware of the **rhetorical situation**, the audience, and the goal you have in writing in a particular mode. **Rhetoric** is a flexible concept, as we have discussed here, and depending on what kind of rhetoric a specific piece of writing calls for your approach will have to change to do it well.

The fourth chapter presented the modes of writing, some of which may have been familiar but some were likely new. In the end, almost every kind of writing you will compose in the university and in professional life will use several of the **modes**, and possibly be **multimodal** (as discussed in Chapter Six). There is not one "right" mode of writing for a specific situation, but being aware of what the major modes are, and being aware of the rhetorical situation, can help you make the best possible decisions in how to compose your work or to respond to a given situation.

Chapter Four also presented two critical issues: **logical fallacies** and **good research**. The value of being aware of the logical fallacies should be clear, they illustrate how and why the logic of an argument can (and sometimes will) fail and how to avoid those traps. If you know that something is, or can be seen by the audience as being, fallacious, you can avoid those logical traps in your own writing and improve your work overall. Research is critical not only in academic writing but in the professional world as well. There is a reason the sources cited in this book include government documents, professional research, and traditional academic research, valid research is used in almost every field to justify claims and to bolster arguments. There is no escape from doing research, and being able to establish what the best possible support for your claims could be is important in growing as a writer and being more effective in your writing.

Similarly, the fifth chapter provides some of the most common models for building arguments and analysis. As discussed in that chapter, the Toulmin Model or the Rogerian approach can provide helpful starting points for argumentative papers as well as analytical papers. Additionally, several forms of analysis can provide tools for understanding arguments. Critical engagement and a flexible approach to writing are key to success, regardless of your field, and being able to respond to your audience on their own terms and using their own logic makes you a better and more efficient writer.

Chapter Six, **multimodal argument**, may have initially seemed a bit out of place in a Comp I book. However, most disciplines use some form of multimodal composition—charts, graphs, images, or other visuals in addition to the text of the argument—and being aware of how and why multimodal approaches are effective and how they can go awry is important in deciding how to present your points to the audience and what points may be more effectively conveyed visually or in another mode.

The key here is you, as a student, being aware of your writing process and discovering what does and does not work for you in terms of writing effectively. As you have likely discovered, while you have some key writing habits, you often need to adjust your specific approach to individual kinds of writing or assignments. Being aware of your writing process and having alternative approaches to apply is, in itself, a transferrable skill. Add to that the practices of revision, proofreading, and active engagement developed in this class and you can almost immediately see why understanding not just *what* you write but *why and how* you write, points frequently raised in this class, is so important. Taking ownership of your writing is an important first step to writing well regardless of the situation.

What Comes Next?

That, beyond a certain point, depends on you. Composition I takes a WAC approach, while Composition II often takes a WID (Writing in Discipline) approach that helps you more directly apply these skills to arguments in your major (therefore in your future career field). The essential skills you learned in this class will be expanded on and refined to help you prepare for the other kinds of writing you will encounter in the university and the professional world. Many majors also require that you take a professional writing course or a course devoted to writing in your chosen field, which will continue to build these skills and make you a more effective, efficient writer overall.

In terms of this book, the readings which make up the last half of the text are also models for successful writing. All of them have been published, and each does specific things particularly well (as you likely discussed when you read them for class). Having models for good writing is a useful resource as it gives you examples of what has worked in the past and how you might approach any given discussion in writing. The readings also help you to further sharpen your critical reading skills and engage on different levels with a variety of arguments.

Final Thoughts

The purpose of this book has been to introduce you to a variety of forms, approaches, and concepts in writing that you can use not only here but throughout your academic career and into your professional life. Good writing, writing that is clear, effective, and efficient, is writing that not only appeals to your audience but also demonstrates your skill as a writer in a number of ways. Each of the chapters here has given you valuable insight into how writing works, how your writing process should flow for you to write effectively, and how writing sometimes goes wrong. Being aware of who you are as a writer, how you write most effectively, and how you can approach your writing differently to improve your work are all part of being critically engaged with your writing and your writing process. No one is born a good writer; all good writers become better writers through practice, awareness of their own writing and writing process, and work.

Part 2: Reader

Values and Culture

Somewhere Sequoyah is Weeping

Thelma Moton

Thelma Moton (1927–2015): Born Thelma Faye Rogers, Thelma Moton married her husband Dale shortly after World War II. She has two children, Gale and Darrel, and one granddaughter, Karen. She has spent most of her life working with Native American children. Her selection in this anthology is taken from her memoirs of the battle against Sequoyah Fuels, *Somewhere Sequoyah is Weeping*.

This oral history was edited by Joseph M. Faulds, Ph.D. Faulds taught literature and composition, Classical Latin, Biblical Greek, and Native American Studies for 29 years in the Languages and Literature Department and the Honors Program of Northeastern State University in Tahlequah, Oklahoma, where he currently teaches part-time as Professor Emeritus. He has served as a permanent deacon in the parish of St. Brigid in the Tulsa diocese of the Catholic Church for the past 21 years. He is the author of several published works, including *Conversations With Kid Cougar and Lim Hang High, The Seasons of Their Love,* and *Dream of a Holy Woman: the Kateri Chantings.*

Salus populi suprema lex. From 1970 to 1993, near Gore, Oklahoma, Sequoyah Fuels Corporation (SFC) operated a facility for uranium conversion which produced radioactive waste. Though the plant was finally shut down, contaminated matter remains a serious concern in the buildings, equipment, sludge, ground, and groundwater. Thelma Moton's memoir of the struggle to counter the facility and the ill effects of its presence in the surrounding area presents a poignant remembrance of human suffering and quietly heroic striving to save the people and the earth from the terrible side effects of nuclear injury. In Thelma Moton's words: "I guess this is the end of my story. I know there will be many more cancer deaths in this area for years to come. I have done all I can to inform and help the people. Now it is in God's hands as always." As for me, I have done nothing more here than edit this text, but I sometimes wonder if in some holy place of God's keeping the great Cherokee Sequoyah is weeping for the people of the county which preserves his dwelling and bears his name.

—Mitakuye Oyasin (All My Relations) Joseph Faulds / Editor

Thelma Moton: This is my story of living in hell instead of enjoying a quiet retirement, and of the most sorrowful of homecomings. In 1962 my husband and I bought over two acres of land near Lake Tenkiller in Sequoyah County, Oklahoma. Since we both were born in this county, we assumed we would retire here. We live about nine miles north of Gore, Oklahoma. After my husband retired in 1982 we moved as planned to our property. But we soon noticed there were no birds on our land. The birds were missing. I asked some of our relatives about that absence and they could not give me any answer.

We also noticed a yellow dust on everything. When I asked—what is it?—I was told it was pollen. But I had never seen pollen in the fall and winter. We had been gone from the area for several years because my husband worked for the government. We only came through here going to other places during our working years. So finally I asked my youngest sister, Wanda—what is that yellow dust?

She said we did not have that yellow dust until a plant called Sequoyah Fuels Corporation moved to the Gore area in 1968. She told me that the yellow dust was so bad that when her daughter went by there to Connors College that yellow dust got on her car and she had to use the windshield wipers to see how to drive, and that it eats the paint off her car and ruins the windshield. They had to paint her car and put in a new windshield. I then learned that SFC painted and replaced the windshields on their employees' cars, too.

I kept asking—what do they make there? Wanda said, "I really do not know, but there sure are lots of people that have cancer and are dying." Several of her neighbors had died with cancer. She said many strange looking weather balloons were floating over her house. She was of the opinion someone was testing the air current in this area. There had never been any cancer in our families until Sequoyah Fuels moved to this area. I asked my sister if she had ever heard of a Karen Silkwood, and she said, "Oh, yes, but do not mention her name around here." She said that people who worked at that plant knew what is going on and were afraid if they said anything they would lose their jobs. No one wants to lose the means of family support.

Sequoyah County has been a welfare area since there has been welfare, due to a scarcity of jobs and the cycle of low expectations, so if you have a dirty and dangerous plant, what better place to bring it but to Sequoyah County, where people are in need of jobs and are desperate for economic development? You can prey on the needs of the poor.

Jessie Deerinwater lived in Vian, Oklahoma, near the SFC plant, and she worked as a hairdresser. She began to hold meetings in her home or anywhere she could to express her fears and anger. She lost her job for speaking out. Jessie Deerinwater founded an environmental group called Native Americans for a Clean Environment (NACE). She had no money to run the group so she had bake sales, car washes, any way to raise funds to help alert the people in this county to what was going on.

My sister Wanda and I attended some of Jessie's meetings. This is where I finally learned what was being made at the SFC plant. It was manufacturing uranium hexaflouride, an intermediary product in the production of nuclear reactor fuel. It was called yellow cake, hence the yellow dust all over this area. I became very concerned about our health and the health of others who lived in this region. My husband noticed some lesions on his chest and he went to a doctor who took one look at it and said, "You have cancer." He had surgery to remove it. Two of my cousins died with cancer and four people I had known all my life died of cancer. My brother-in-law's brother died of cancer. My sister Wanda was not feeling good, nor was my brother-in-law. Then he was told he had lung cancer. Our cousin who was a school teacher died with kidney cancer. My husband had more cancer surgery. Cancer was everywhere. I was running from one hospital to the other, and to the funeral homes. We lost eleven members of our family from 1984 to 1987. Eleven human beings we loved were gone in about three years.

My brother-in-law died. Wanda was going from one hospital to the clinics to try to find out what was wrong with her. She had always been so robust and jolly and now she could hardly move her feet and was so pale, and she could not sleep nights; five clinics in this area and Ft. Smith, Arkansas, could not tell her what was wrong. I knew something was terribly wrong, and I was so scared it was cancer.

Finally, she had to be hospitalized. They ran all kinds of tests and still could not come up with an answer. I asked a nurse if a bone marrow test had been done. She said no. I said, "You had better do that." I asked Wanda to tell her doctor to do that test. They did and found she had multiple myeloma bone cancer. She needed nine pints of blood fast. She was in a Ft. Smith, Arkansas, hospital and the round trip from my home is 130 miles. My husband was well enough I could leave him at home and drive to see Wanda every day because I knew of no one who had ever recovered from that type of cancer. She and I were so angry at all the people who were over the SFC plant, who were not doing their jobs to protect our health.

Can you imagine the helpless rage you begin to feel watching your family die because of someone's greed and negligence?

I began to write and call all of our elected officials. I asked for a cancer survey to be done door to door. I was in hopes someone would notice the large numbers of cancer deaths in this area. But the way a cancer survey is done in Oklahoma is by death certificates, and the majority of the people who had cancer went to Ft. Smith, Arkansas for medical help. They died in the hospitals there, so, though they were buried in Oklahoma, there is no record of their deaths in Oklahoma.

I received form letters and platitudes from everyone I wrote to for help, except the one from the Director of the Oklahoma State Health Department. He informed me that a cancer health survey had been done here by death certificates in 1984 and he was not going to use their money for a door to door survey, since such a survey would be unscientific and flawed. How he could figure that his survey was not flawed is beyond me!

Wanda was allowed to come home from the hospital and she had to go to a clinic and take chemotherapy. She was able to write, so she wrote to all our elected leaders and got the same answers as I had. She placed an ad in the local newspaper asking for anyone who had cancer or had lost a loved one to cancer to call or write her. She received lots of calls and mail. She got some push pins and put them on the map by the people's names; red for dead, green for terminal, and yellow for still fighting the cancer. The map of this county was not large enough for all the cancer victims' names; they spilled over into the counties around us. Jessie's group had done a partial cancer survey in the Gore area. She gave those names to Wanda to put on the map.

The Nuclear Regulatory Commission sent an administrative judge to hold a meeting in Sallisaw on a hearing to expand the Sequoyah Fuels plant to make UF4; UF4 was to be used to make a product for armor piercing bullets. The plant already produced UF6. My sister Wanda called the Nuclear Regulatory Commission office in Texas and asked if she could appear before the judge at this hearing. She was told that she could. She was just barely able to go to the meeting and she had written out a statement she wanted to read. When she told who she was, SFC employees at this meeting tried to keep her from being allowed to speak. She told them she was dying from cancer and she was there to speak on behalf of all the sick children who were not allowed to speak up.

She said "I am Wanda J. Kelley of Marble City, Oklahoma. On May 27, 1986, I was diagnosed as having multiple myeloma and 75% kidney failure. Then again the lump I've had over my eyebrow for a year was diagnosed as Basal Cell Epithelioma, which will require surgery to remove and correct the scar. So now I have two kinds of malignant cancer. I have lost so many friends, neighbors, and loved ones recently to cancer, and have many more, who, like myself, are fighting for life, and all of us live in Sequoyah County.

"I began to suspect something was frightfully wrong with the Arkansas River two years ago because too many of the fish we caught had sores on them, so I quit fishing and knowingly eating fish from any waters in Sequoyah County.

"My suspicions of something being wrong with our environment were rekindled when I was told I had cancer. I was the first member of our lineage to get cancer. So after a lengthy stay in St. Edward's Hospital for testing, six months of chemotherapy in IVs, push injections, many pills, weekly visits to outpatient clinics, losing my hair, spending $8,000, and all the long drives to and from Ft. Smith, and a poor prognosis, I decided to do something constructive. I decided on one of the few days that I was able during October that I would make a few random phone calls to see if my fear about a cancer epidemic in Sequoyah County was warranted; apparently cancer is something the EPA, the Oklahoma State Health, and the County Health departments don't want to acknowledge. They remind me of those three monkeys who see no evil, hear no evil, and speak no evil.

"I know that there is indeed a cancer epidemic in Sequoyah County, because when I made only 17 phone calls, I acquired the names of 79 cancer victims in the county, most of whom have developed cancer within the last ten years. I had been sent a copy of NACE's health list for people who lived within a 10 mile radius of Sequoyah Fuels, and of those who had cancer, severe ailments, multiple miscarriages, birth deformities within the past ten years, I took only the names of the cancer victims from their list and from mine, and transposed all 300 of them onto a Sequoyah County map, which clearly showed a high concentration of cancer and death rates in close relation to the location of Sequoyah Fuels.

"It's too late for me and late for many other cancer victims in Sequoyah County, but with the last of my strength I implore you for the sake of our children to close the doors of Sequoyah Fuels permanently. They have no one's interest at heart but their own greed."

That trip set her back for days. And it did not matter how many spoke out against that plant, the NRC allowed them to expand to produce the UF4 product. Every time the people who lived here spoke out against the plant, the NRC ignored our pleas, as did the Environmental Protection Agency, as did every elected official in Oklahoma. It got so bad we began to refer to the NRC as the Nobody Really Cares Agency. I blame them for the many cancer deaths in this area. They lied to us, ignored us, and didn't do their job. They should be investigated by Congress for not doing their job and lying to the public. To whose benefit was all this incompetence and falsehood? I want to know.

My husband had more cancer surgery, and his nephew also was having skin cancer removed from his face. The nephew had visited several of our relatives with cancer. He said, "If my doctor ever tells me I have cancer inside and I need surgery or chemotherapy or radiation, I will not have it. There's an easier way out of all that suffering." A few months later he killed himself by putting a shotgun to his head and pulling the trigger. We assumed his doctor had told him he had internal cancer. I don't think that's the right way to deal with it.

So many lives have been lost to cancer, so much suffering, so many huge medical bills, and so many funerals for so few jobs, 150 jobs, at the most 300 people employed at that plant. A lot of their employees or their family members have died with cancer. None of the presidents or higher supervisors of SFC would live in Sequoyah County. When we would ask: Why? They said: "No housing, and the schools are no good." Well, one of these "no good" school buildings became too contaminated to use! We told them they lied because they knew the danger of living here. The people in this area were subjected to chronic radiation doses ever since SFC was in production, and it is my opinion this is the cause of so much cancer death.

Consider raffinate. Raffinate is a liquid by-product of the SFC uranium refining operation; in reality it is a low level radiation sludge that has actually been used as a fertilizer. What sort of insanity is that? Someone described raffinate at a meeting in Oklahoma City as the greatest fertilizer around today. The NRC approved the spraying of raffinate as a fertilizer in 1982. In 1992, ten test wells approved by the EPA were filled along the Illinois and Arkansas rivers bend adjacent to the SFC plant. Test results indicated higher than normal levels for heavy metals and water samples taken from half the underground wells showed that contamination exceeded existing and proposed national drinking water standards. This test was only for radioactive contaminants.

One local family was paying for a beautiful brick home for 13 years. Their home, lawn, and private property were sprayed with raffinate. It killed their parrot that was on their porch. The trees in their yard died and they had to move out of their home. I saw their property title auctioned off on the courthouse steps in Sallisaw. Pushing the use of radioactive sludge as fertilizer goes beyond the boundaries of reason. One woman told me they had their own well dug but also had running water in their home; she said her husband was the only member of their family to drink the well water and he died of cancer. She stated her belief that the well water was contaminated from SFC. Is that an unscientific conclusion? Please excuse me. But multiply this story by many victims and remember their souls.

My dear sister Wanda passed away on December 13, 1987. She had three types of cancer by then, multiple myeloma, clear cell sarcoma, and lung cancer. I was so tired I didn't think I could go on. I just kept praying day and night for the strength to carry on. It is the people of this poor county in Oklahoma who have suffered and who will continue to pay the terrible human cost of uranium conversion for the profit and the power of those in governments and corporations who will never come to live here, and whose families I hope will never be contaminated by their radioactive waste, or should I say their radioactive greed?

This past week was another sad time for this family. We lost the 15th member of our family to cancer. She herself had lost her son a year ago to kidney cancer. Another neighbor who retired here passed away recently with cancer, and a woman who lives nearby is dying with cancer. I admired her working in her garden all summer long as she gathered her harvest of vegetables, looking so healthy, but she has terminal lung cancer. She and her courage will be missed by all of us, as so many others are missed.

And I ask you—can such an injustice ever be disremembered? May God have mercy on the victims.

Epilogue

Thelma Moton's narrative of the impact of Sequoya Fuels was first published nearly two decades ago, but the story of Sequoya Fuels continued until late in 2018. Moton herself remained active in the effort to have Sequoya Fuels and the Nuclear Regulatory Commission address the health concerns and residual contamination at the Gore processing plant until her death in 2015. It was not until November, 2018 that the Cherokee Nation and the State of Oklahoma announced that Sequoya Fuels had finally removed the raffinate dust and hexafluoride acid that had remained on site at the decommissioned plant since its final closure in 1993.

Under legal pressure from the Cherokee Nation and the State of Oklahoma's environmental agency, Sequoya Fuels initially agreed in 2007 to pay for the removal but when more than 10,000 tons of contaminated materials had been collected in 2016, with additional materials likely to be discovered, the company attempted to minimize their financial exposure by enclosing the raffinate and other radioactive materials in concrete and burying it on the site at the junctions of the Illinois and Arkansas rivers. This plan would have created what Cherokee Nation Secretary of Natural Resources Sara Hill described in an interview with the Tahlequah Daily Press as "a time bomb waiting to go off, because "that material would be radioactive for millions of years." Additional lawsuits were filed before the company agreed to comply with the initial court order and to pay to have the materials taken to Utah for proper processing and disposal, the cost of which will exceed the $3.5 million initial judgement. The agreement was announced by the Cherokee Nation at a meeting in Gore on November 29, 2018. While the site and the surrounding area continue to be concerns for the residents of Gore and the other communities impacted by the plant's contamination over the years due to lingering background radiation, Moton's mission to correct as many of the ills her family and community as possible has finally come to an end.

Sources

Poindexter, Kim. "Sequoyah Fuels radioactive material leaves state." *Tahlequah Daily Press,* November 30, 2018.

How to Slowly Kill Yourself and Others in America: A Remembrance

Kiese Laymon

Kiese Laymon is an essayist and social commentator in addition to being an Associate Professor of English and the co-director of Africana Studies at Vassar College. This version of his essay was originally published on his blog, *Cold Drank,* in 2012.

I've had guns pulled on me by four people under Central Mississippi skies— once by a white undercover cop, once by a young brother trying to rob me for the leftovers of a weak work-study check, once by my mother and twice by myself. Not sure how or if I've helped many folks say yes to life but I've definitely aided in few folks dying slowly in America, all without the aid of a gun.

***

I'm 17, five years younger than Rekia Boyd will be when she is shot in the head by an off duty police officer in Chicago. It's the summer after I graduated high school and my teammate, Troy, is back in Jackson, Mississippi. Troy, who plays college ball in Florida, asks me if I want to go to McDonald's on I-55.

As Troy, Cleta, Leighton and I walk out of McDonald's, that Filet-o-Fish grease straight cradling my lips, I hold the door open for a tiny, scruffy-faced white man with a green John Deere hat on.

"Thanks, partner," he says.

A few minutes later, we're driving down I-55 when John Deere drives up and rolls his window down. I figure that he wants to say something funny since we'd had a cordial moment at McDonald's. As soon as I roll my window down, the man screams, "Nigger lovers!" and speeds off.

On I-55, we pull up beside John Deere and I'm throwing finger-signs, calling John Deere all kinds of clever "motherfuckers." The dude slows down and gets behind us. I turn around, hoping he pulls over.

Nope.

John Deere pulls out a police siren and places it on top of his car. Troy is cussing my ass out and frantically trying to drive his Mama's Lincoln away from John Deere. My heart is pounding out of my chest, not out of fear, but because I want a chance to choke the shit out of John Deere. I can't think of any other way of making him feel what we felt.

Troy drives into his apartment complex and parks his Mama's long Lincoln under some kind of shed. Everyone in the car is slumped down at this point. Around 20 seconds after we park, here comes the red, white and blue of the siren.

We hear a car door slam, then a loud knock on the back window. John Deere has a gun in one hand and a badge in the other. He's telling me to get out of the car. My lips still smell like Filet-o-Fish.

"Only you," he says to me. "You going to jail tonight." He's got the gun to my chest.

"Fuck you," I tell him and suck my teeth. "I ain't going nowhere." I don't know what's wrong with me.

Cleta is up front trying to reason with the man through her window when all of a sudden, in a scene straight out of Boyz n the Hood, a black cop approaches the car and accuses us of doing something wrong. Minutes later, a white cop tells us that John Deere has been drinking too much and he lets us go.

16 months later, I'm 18, three years older than Edward Evans will be when he is shot in the head behind an abandoned home in Jackson.

Shonda and I are walking from Subway back to Millsaps College with two of her white friends. It's nighttime. We turn off of North State Street and walk halfway past the cemetery when a red Corolla filled with brothers stops in front of us. All of the brothers have blue rags covering their noses and mouths. One of the brothers, a kid at least two years younger than me with the birdest of bird chests, gets out of the car clutching a shiny silver gun.

He comes towards Shonda and me.

"Me," I say to him. "Me. Me." I hold my hands up encouraging him to do whatever he needs to do. If he shoots me, well, I guess bullets enter and hopefully exit my chest, but if the young Nigga thinks I'm getting pistol whupped in front of a cemetery and my girlfriend off of State Street, I'm convinced I'm going to take the gun and beat him into a burnt cinnamon roll.

The boy places his gun on my chest and keeps looking back and forth to the car.

I feel a strange calm, an uncanny resolve. I don't know what's wrong with me. He's patting me down for money that I don't have since we hadn't gotten our work-study checks yet and I just spent my last little money on two veggie subs from Subway and two of those large Chocolate Chip cookies.

The young brother keeps looking back to the car, unsure what he's supposed to do. Shonda and her friends are screaming when he takes the gun off my chest and trots goofily back to the car.

I don't know what's wrong with him but a few months later, I have a gun.

A partner of mine hooks me up with a partner of his who lets me hold something. I get the gun not only to defend myself from goofy brothers in red Corollas trying to rob folks for work-study money. I guess I'm working on becoming a black writer in Mississippi and some folks around Millsaps College don't like the essays I'm writing in the school newspaper.

A few weeks earlier, George Harmon, the President of Millsaps, shuts down the campus paper in response to a satirical essay I wrote on communal masturbation and sends a letter to over 12,000 overwhelmingly white Millsaps students, friends and alumnae. The letter states that the "Key Essay in question was written by Kiese Laymon, a controversial writer who consistently editorializes on race issues."

After the President's letter goes out, my life kinda hurts.

I receive a sweet letter in the mail with the burnt up ashes of my essays. The letter says that if I don't stop writing and give myself "over to right," my life would end up like the ashes of my writing.

The tires of my Mama's car are slashed when her car was left on campus. I'm given a single room after the Dean of Students thinks it's too dangerous for me to have a roommate. Finally, Greg Miller, an English Professor, writes an essay about how and why a student in his Liberal Studies class says, "Kiese should be killed for what he's writing." I feel a lot when I read those words, but mainly I wonder what's wrong with me.

It's bid day at Millsaps.

Shonda and I are headed to our jobs at Ton-o-Fun, a fake ass Chuck E. Cheese behind Northpark Mall. We're wearing royal blue shirts with a strange smiling animal and Ton-o-Fun on the left titty. The shirts of the other boy workers at Ton-o-Fun fit them better than mine. My shirt is tight in the wrong places and slightly less royal blue. I like to add a taste of bleach so I don't stank.

As we walk out to the parking lot of my dorm, the Kappa Alpha and Kappa Sigma fraternities are in front of our dorm receiving their new members. They've been up drinking all night. Some of them have on black face and others have on Afro wigs and Confederate capes.

We get close to Shonda's Saturn and one of the men says, "Kiese, write about this!" Then another voice calls me a "Nigger" and Shonda, a "Nigger bitch." I think and feel a lot but mostly I feel that I can't do anything to make the boys feel like they've made us feel right there, so I go back to my dorm room to get something.

On the way there, Shonda picks up a glass bottle out of the trash. I tell her to wait outside the room. I open the bottom drawer and look at the hoodies balled up on the top of my gun. I pick up my gun and think about my Grandma. I think not only about what she'd feel if I went back out there with a gun. I think about how if Grandma walked out of that room with a gun in hand, she'd use it. No question.

I am her grandson.

I throw the gun back on top of the clothes, close the drawer, go in my closet and pick up a wooden T-ball bat.

Some of the KA's and Sigs keep calling us names as we approach them. I step, throw down the bat and tell them I don't need a bat to fuck them up. I don't know what's wrong with me. My fists are balled up and the only thing I want in the world is to swing back over and over again. Shonda feels the same, I think. She's right in the mix, yelling, crying, fighting as best she can. After security and a Dean break up the mess, the frats go back to receiving their new pledges and Shonda and I go to work at Ton-o-Fun in our dirty blue shirts.

I stank.

On our first break at work, we decide that we should call a local news station so the rest of Jackson can see what's happening at Millsaps on a Saturday morning. We meet the camera crew at school. Some of boys go after the reporter and cameraman. The camera gets a few students in Afros, black face and Confederate capes. They also get footage of "another altercation."

A few weeks pass and George Harmon, the President of the college, doesn't like that footage of his college is now on television and in newspapers all across the country. The college decides that two individual fraternity members, Shonda and I will be put on disciplinary probation for using "racially insensitive language" and the two fraternities involved get their party privileges taken away for a semester. If there was racially insensitive language Shonda and I could have used to make those boys feel like we felt, we would have never stepped to them in the first place. Millsaps is trying to prove to the nation that it is post-race(ist) institution and to its alums that all the Bid Day stuff is the work of an "adroit entrepreneur of racial conflict."

A few months later, Mama and I sit in President George Harmon's office. The table is an oblong mix of mahogany and ice water. All the men at the table are smiling, flipping through papers and twirling pens in their hands except for me. I am still 19, two years older than Trayvon Martin will be when he swings back.

President Harmon and his lawyers don't look me in the eye. They zero in on the eyes of Mama, as Harmon tells her that I am being suspended from Millsaps for at least a year for taking and returning *Red Badge of Courage* from the library without formally checking it out.

He ain't lying.

I took the book out of the library for Shonda's brother without checking it out and returned the book the next day. I looked right at the camera when I did it, too. I did all of this knowing I was on parole, but not believing any college in America, even one in Mississippi, would kick a student out for a year, for taking and returning a library book without properly checking it out.

I should have believed.

George Harmon tells me, while looking at my mother, that I will be allowed to come back to Millsaps College in a year only after having attended therapy sessions for racial insensitivity. We are told he has given my writing to a local psychologist and the shrink believes I need help. Even if I am admitted back as a student, I will remain formally on parole for the rest of my undergrad career, which means that I will be expelled from Millsaps College unless I'm perfect.

19-year-old black boys cannot be perfect in America. Neither can 61-year-old white boys named George.

Before going on the ride home with Mama, I go to my room, put the gun in my backpack and get in her car.

On the way home, Mama stops by the zoo to talk about what just happened in George Harmon's office. She's crying and asking me over and over again why I took and returned the gotdamn book knowing they were watching me. Like a black mother of black boy, Mama starts blaming Shonda for asking me to check the book out in the first place. I don't know what to say other than I know it wasn't Shonda's fault and I left my ID and I wanted to swing back, so I keep walking and say nothing. She says that Grandma is going to be so disappointed in me. "Heartbroken," is the word she uses.

There.

I feel this toxic miasma unlike anything I've ever felt not just in my body but in my blood. I remember the wobbly way my Grandma twitches her eyes at my Uncle Jimmy and I imagine being at the end of that twitch for the rest of my life. For the first time in almost two years, I hide my face, grit my crooked teeth and sob.

I don't stop for weeks.

The NAACP and lawyers get involved in filing a lawsuit against Millsaps on my behalf. Whenever the NAACP folks talk to me or the paper, they talk about how ironic it is that a black boy who is trying to read a book gets kicked out of college. I appreciate their work but I don't think the irony lies where they think it does. If I'd never read a book in my life, I shouldn't have been punished for taking and bringing back a library book, not when kids are smoking that good stuff, drinking themselves unconscious and doing some of everything imaginable to nonconsenting bodies.

That's what I tell all the newspapers and television reporters who ask. To my friends, I say that after stealing all those Lucky Charms, Funyons, loaves of light bread and over a hundred cold dranks out of the cafeteria in two years, how in the fuck do I get suspended for taking and returning the gotdamn *Red Badge of Courage*.

The day that I'm awarded the Benjamin Brown award, named after a 21-year-old truck driver shot in the back by police officers during a student protest near Jackson State in 1967, I take the bullets out of my gun, throw it in the Ross Barnett Reservoir and avoid my Grandma for a long, long time.

I enroll at Jackson State University in the Spring semester, where my mother teaches Political Science. Even though, I'm not really living at home, everyday Mama and I fight over my job at Cutco and her staying with her boyfriend and her not letting me use the car to get to my second job at an HIV hospice since my license is suspended. Really, we're fighting because she raised me to never ever forget I was on parole, which means no black hoodies in wrong neighborhoods, no jogging at night, hands in plain sight at all times in public, no intimate relationships with white women, never driving over the speed limit or doing those rolling stops at stop signs, always speaking the king's English in the presence of white folks, never being outperformed in school or in public by white students and most importantly, always remembering that no matter what, white folks will do anything to get you.

Mama's antidote to being born a black boy on parole in Central Mississippi is not for us to seek freedom; it's to insist on excellence at all times. Mama takes it personal when she realizes that I realize she is wrong. There ain't no antidote to life, I tell her. How free can you be if you really accept that white folks are the traffic cops of your life? Mama tells me that she is not talking about freedom. She says that she is talking about survival.

One blue night my mother tells me that I need to type the rest of my application to Oberlin College after I've already hand-written the personal essay. I tell her that it doesn't matter whether I type it or not since Millsaps is sending a Dean's report attached to my transcript. I say some other truthful things I should never say to my mother. Mama goes into her room, lifts up her pillow and comes out with her gun.

It's raggedy, small, heavy and black. I always imagine the gun as an old dead crow. I'd held it a few times before with Mama hiding behind me.

Mama points the gun at me and tells me to get the fuck out of her house. I look right at the muzzle pointed at my face and smile the same way I did at the library camera at Millsaps. I don't know what's wrong with me.

"You gonna pull a gun on me over some college application?" I ask her.

"You don't listen until it's too late," she tells me. "Get out of my house and don't ever come back."

I leave the house, chuckling, shaking my head, cussing under my breath. I go sit in a shallow ditch. Outside, I wander in the topsy turvy understanding that Mama's life does not revolve around me and I'm not doing anything to make her life more joyful, spacious or happy. I'm an ungrateful burden, an obese weight on her already terrifying life. I sit there in the ditch, knowing that other things are happening in my mother's life but I also know that Mama never imagined needing to pull a gun on the child she carried on her back as a sophomore at Jackson State University. I'm playing with pine needles, wishing I had headphones—but I'm mostly regretting throwing my gun into the reservoir.

When Mama leaves for work in the morning, I break back in her house, go under her pillow and get her gun. Mama and I haven't paid the phone or the light bill so it's dark, hot and lonely in that house, even in the morning. I lie in a bathtub of cold water, still sweating and singing love songs to myself. I put the gun to my head and cock it.

I think of my Grandma and remember that old feeling of being so in love that nothing matters except seeing and being seen by her. I drop the gun to my chest. I'm so sad and I can't really see a way out of what I'm feeling but I'm leaning on memory for help. Faster. Slower. I think I want to hurt myself more than I'm already hurting. I'm not the smartest boy in the world by a long shot, but even in my funk I know that easy remedies like eating your way out of sad, or fucking your way out of sad, or lying your way out of sad, or slanging your way out of sad, or robbing your way out of sad, or gambling your way out of sad, or shooting your way out of sad, are just slower, more acceptable ways for desperate folks, and especially paroled black boys in our country, to kill ourselves and others close to us in America.

I start to spend more time at home over the next few weeks since Mama is out of town with her boyfriend. Mama and I still haven't paid the phone bill so I'm running down to the pay phone everyday, calling one of the admissions counselors at Oberlin College. He won't tell me whether they'll accept me or not, but he does say that Oberlin might want me because of, not in spite of, what happened at Millsaps.

A month passes and I haven't heard from Oberlin. I'm eating too much and dry humping a woman just as desperate as me and lying like its my first job and daring people to fuck with me more than I have in a long time. I'm writing lots of words, too, but I'm not reckoning. I'm wasting ink on bullshit political analysis and short stories and vacant poems that I never imagine being read or felt by anyone like me. I'm a waste of writing's time.

The only really joyful times in life come from playing basketball and talking shit with O.G. Raymond "Gunn" Murph, my best friend. Gunn is trying to stop himself from slowly killing himself and others, after a smoldering break up with V., his girlfriend of eight years. Some days, Gunn and I save each other's lives just by telling and listening to each other's odd-shaped truth.

One black night, Ray is destroying me in Madden and talking all that shit when we hear a woman moaning for help outside of his apartment on Capitol Street. We go downstairs and find a naked woman with open wounds, blood and bruises all over her black body. She can barely walk or talk through shivering teeth but we ask her if she wants to come upstairs while we call the ambulance. Gunn and I have taken no Sexual Assault classes and we listen to way too much The Diary and Ready to Die, but right there, we know not to get too close to the woman and just let her know we're there to do whatever she needs.

She slowly makes her way into the apartment because she's afraid the men might come back. Blood is gushing down the back of her thighs and her scalp. She tells us the three men had one gun. When she makes it up to the apartment, we give the woman a towel to sit on and something to wrap herself in. Blood seeps through both and even though she looks so scared and hurt, she also looks so embarrassed. Gunn keeps saying things like, "It's gonna be okay, sweetheart," and I just sit there weakly nodding my head, running from her eyes and getting her more glasses of water. When Gunn goes in his room to take his gun in his waistband, I look at her and know that no one man could have done this much damage to another human being. That's what I need to tell myself.

Eventually, the ambulance and police arrive. They ask her a lot of questions and keep looking at us. She tells them that we helped her after she was beaten and raped by a three black men in a Monte Carlo. One of the men, she tells the police, was her boyfriend. She refuses to say his name to the police. Gunn looks at me and drops his head. Without saying anything, we know that whatever is in the boys in that car, has to also be in us. We know that whatever is encouraging them to kill themselves slowly by knowingly mangling the body and spirit of this shivering black girl, is probably the most powerful thing in our lives. We also know that whatever is in us that has been slowly encouraging us to kill ourselves and those around us slowly, is also in the heart and mind of this black girl on the couch.

A few weeks later, I get a letter saying I've been accepted to Oberlin College and they're giving me a boatload of financial aid. Gunn agrees to drive me up to Oberlin and I feel like the luckiest boy on earth, not because I got into Oberlin, but because I survived long enough to remember saying yes to life and "no" or at least "slow down" to a slow death.

My saying yes to life meant accepting the beauty of growing up black, on parole, in Mississippi. It also meant accepting that George Harmon, parts of Millsaps College, parts of my state, much of my country, my heart and mostly my own reflection, had beaten the dog shit out of me. I still don't know what all this means but I know it's true.

This isn't an essay or simply a woe-is-we narrative about how hard it is to be a black boy in America. This is a lame attempt at remembering the contours of slow death and life in America for one black American teenager under Central

Mississippi skies. I wish I could get my Yoda on right now and surmise all this shit into a clean sociopolitical pull-quote that shows supreme knowledge and absolute emotional transformation, but I don't want to lie.

I want to say and mean that remembering starts not with predictable punditry, or bullshit blogs, or slick art that really ask nothing of us; I want to say that it starts with all of us willing ourselves to remember, tell and accept those complicated, muffled truths of our lives and deaths and the lives and deaths of folks all around us over and over again.

Then I want to say and mean that I am who my Grandma thinks I am.

I am not.

I'm a walking regret, a truth-teller, a liar, a survivor, a frowning ellipsis, a witness, a dreamer, a teacher, a student, a joker, a writer whose eyes stay red, and I'm a child of this nation.

I know that as I've gotten deeper into my late twenties and thirties, I have managed to continue killing myself and other folks who loved me in spite of me. I know that I've been slowly killed by folks who were as feverishly in need of life and death as I am. The really confusing part is that a few of those folk who have nudged me closer to slow death have also helped me say yes to life when I most needed it. Usually, I didn't accept it. Lots of times, we've taken turns killing ourselves slowly, before trying to bring each other back to life. Maybe that's the necessary stank of love, or maybe—like Frank Ocean says—it's all just bad religion, just tasty watered down cyanide in a styrofoam cup.

I don't even know.

I know that by the time I left Mississippi, I was 20 years old, three years older than Trayvon Martin will be when he is murdered for wearing a hoodie and swinging back in the wrong American neighborhood. Four months after I leave Mississippi, San Berry, a 20-year-old partner of mine who went to Millsaps College with Gunn and me, would be convicted for taking Pam McGill, a social worker, in the woods and shooting her in the head.

San confessed to kidnapping Ms. McGill, driving her to some woods, making her fall to her knees and pulling the trigger while a 17-year-old black boy named Azikiwe waited for him in the car. San says Azikiwe encouraged him to do it. Even today, journalists, activists and folks in Mississippi wonder what really happen with San, Azikiwe and Pam McGill that day. Was San trying to swing back? Were there mental health issues left unattended? Had Ms. McGill, San and Azikiwe talked to each other before the day? Why was Azikiwe left in the car when the murder took place?

I can't front, though. I don't wonder about any of that shit, not today.

I wonder what all three of those children of our nation really remember about how to slowly kill themselves and other folks in America the day before parts of them definitely died under the blue-black sky in Central Mississippi.

Doing What's Best for the Tribe

Marcia Zug

Marcia Zug is professor of law at the University of South Carolina who specializes in family law and American Indian Law. She is a frequent contributor to *Slate* and other online publications, and her writing focuses on the law and culture. This article first appeared on *Slate* on August 23, 2012.

Two-year-old "Baby Veronica" was ripped from the only home she's known. The court made the right decision.

On July 26, the South Carolina Supreme Court issued a decision affirming the return of Veronica, an adopted 2-year-old Cherokee child, to her biological father, Dusten Brown. The court's decision was devastating for her adoptive parents, Melanie and Matt Capobianco, who had been raising the child since her birth after her biological mother willingly gave her up for adoption. "I'll always remember her crying when we had to—we had to walk out of that office and leave her there," said Melanie Capobianco referring to Veronica's reunification with Brown. "We're kind of reeling from it, and reliving having to hand her over in our minds constantly is painful," the couple added.

Since Veronica's reunification with Brown in January, the Capobiancos have been fighting ceaselessly for her return. Veronica's case has garnered national attention and unprecedented support. For months, pictures of the smiling toddler with her adoptive parents have been splashed across South Carolina papers and featured on CNN and in the *Weekly Standard*. Moreover, these news stories about "Baby Veronica" almost uniformly support the Capobiancos, with articles and commentary expressing outrage at the fact that although South Carolina law supports terminating Brown's parental rights due to his lack of involvement and financial support before and after Veronica's birth, this state law is superseded by an "obscure law" or "federal loophole" known as the Indian Child Welfare Act (ICWA).

ICWA is a federal statute that regulates the custody and placement of American Indian children. Brown is an enrolled member of the Cherokee tribe, and Veronica is also eligible for membership. As a result, ICWA applies to Veronica's adoption, supersedes state law, and mandates her reunification with Brown. Many Native American law scholars and advocates believe that ICWA is the most important American Indian law ever enacted, but its application in this case has caused fury. More than 20,000 people have signed the "Save Veronica" petition, which calls for an amendment to ICWA to prevent the return of children like Veronica. However,

ICWA is no "loophole." The act specifically contemplated situations like Veronica's, and in this case, ICWA operated exactly as it was intended to.

ICWA was enacted in 1978 "to protect the best interests of Indian children and to promote the stability and security of Indian tribes and families." It was also a federal recognition of the long history of forced removal of American Indian children from their families and tribes by nontribal public and private agencies. Beginning in 1869, the United States removed thousands of American Indian children from their families and tribes and sent them to government boarding schools. In these schools, American Indian children were given European names, forbidden to speak their own language, barred from practicing their religion or culture, and prevented from seeing their families. Hundreds (some say thousands) of American Indian children never returned and were lost to their families and tribes. Eventually, the boarding schools were shut down, but they were replaced with an equally devastating policy of nonnative adoption. Between 1958 and 1967, the Indian Adoption Act was used to remove hundreds of Native American children from their homes and place them with adoptive families who were not American Indians. The purpose of these policies was assimilation—the extinction of the tribes as separate entities.

Although it has been decades since these policies of forced assimilation ended, the effects continue to be felt. A century of removing American Indian children wreaked havoc on Native American families and tribes. Even after the passage of ICWA, the percentage of American Indian children in foster care and placed for adoption remains astonishingly high. American Indian families and tribes are struggling to recover from the devastating history of forced removal, but such recovery is impossible if they continue to lose their children. Congress recognized this struggle and intentionally drafted ICWA to cover both the involuntary removal of American Indian children from American Indian families and the voluntary placement of American Indian children outside of American Indian families. Congress understood that in order to ensure a tribe's control over its children and its future, ICWA must also apply to voluntary placements.

Under ICWA, Veronica is a Native American child, and her Native American heritage was neither a secret nor a surprise. Everyone involved in Veronica's adoption was aware she was American Indian and that this could complicate the adoption, even though it was voluntary. The U.S. Supreme Court affirmed this understanding of ICWA in 1989 in *Mississippi Band of Choctaw v. Holyfield*, its first and only ICWA decision. *Holyfield* involved a pregnant Choctaw mother who wished to place her unborn twins with a non-Native American couple. Although the mother lived on the Choctaw reservation, she specifically left the reservation to give birth in the hope that this move would make ICWA inapplicable to her children's adoption. Despite the mother's significant efforts to avoid tribal jurisdiction and control her children's adoptive placement, the court held that the placement decision remained the tribe's. The decision further explained that the tribe's right to its children and an American Indian child's right to grow up American Indian outweighed individual tribal members' rights to place their children for adoption outside the tribe. The court understood that permitting voluntary adoptions to bypass ICWA's requirements could defeat the entire purpose of the act.

As the *Holyfield* decision made clear, even in voluntary placements, the child's tribe must be notified and ICWA's placement preferences followed. Thus, when an American Indian child is available for adoption, preference is first given to a member of the child's extended family, second to other members of the child's tribe, and third to other Native American families. Only after such placement preferences have been exhausted may nonnative adoption be considered. This process did not happen in Veronica's case, so her adoption was a clear violation of ICWA. It should never have happened, but the situation is heart-wrenching because despite the inappropriateness of her adoption, placement did occur and lasted for two years. Nonetheless, if the passage of time were enough to defeat ICWA, then the requirements of the act could simply be avoided by delay and obfuscation.

The Capobiancos are now hoping to petition the U.S. Supreme Court and Congress to amend ICWA, and as parents, their actions are understandable. However, the remedy they seek would be disastrous for American Indian tribes. Through congressional amendment or Supreme Court decision, the Capobiancos hope to reduce tribal control over American Indian child adoptions and revive the "existing Indian family exception" to ICWA. This doctrine is a judicially created exception that courts have used to avoid the application of ICWA in cases where the court determines the child is not part of a sufficiently American Indian family. The idea behind the exception is that in cases involving American Indian children who have never been part of an American Indian home, such as children placed for adoption at birth, ICWA should not apply because there is no "Indian family" being destroyed by the adoption. The problem with this exception is that it ignores the fact that ICWA was passed not simply to preserve specific American Indian families but to protect the tribe's interest in the adoption of American Indian children as well. As the court held in *Holyfield*, ICWA is "a means of protecting not only individual Indian children and their families, but also of the tribes themselves." Although this exception, first introduced in 1982, was initially embraced by many states, the doctrine has now been almost universally rejected. Courts rejecting the exception understand that without ICWA, the future of American Indian tribes is imperiled.

Veronica's case is deeply troubling, and our hearts should go out to all involved, but the problems it highlights are not problems with ICWA. Rather, her case reveals the problems with ignoring ICWA. This case agonizingly demonstrates the importance of observing ICWA's placement and termination procedures in order to prevent impermissible adoptions from occurring and then being invalidated later. Everyone involved in Veronica's adoption knew she was an American Indian child, and if the ICWA requirements had been followed, Veronica would not have been placed with the Capobiancos in the first place. It was because of this mistake that Veronica was 2 years old rather than an infant when she was reunited with her father. The lesson from Veronica's case is not that ICWA is some obscure loophole that should be closed. Rather, the ongoing court battle demonstrates that ICWA is a pivotal piece of American Indian legislation that cannot be ignored without traumatic consequences.

The Third Thing

Donald Hall

Donald Hall (b. 1928) is an American poet, editor and critic who has written over 50 books. His poetry tends to focus on everyday events and commonplace voices in nature. His essays are similarly focused on common events and histories of rural life. Hall served as the Poet Laureate of the United States for one year (2006), and this essay appeared in *Poetry* in October, 2005.

Jane Kenyon and I were married for twenty-three years. For two decades we inhabited the double solitude of my family farmhouse in New Hampshire, writing poems, loving the countryside. She was forty-seven when she died. If anyone had asked us, "Which year was the best, of your lives together?" we could have agreed on an answer: "the one we remember least." There were sorrowful years—the death of her father, my cancers, her depressions—and there were also years of adventure: a trip to China and Japan, two trips to India; years when my children married; years when the grandchildren were born; years of triumph as Jane began her public life in poetry: her first book, her first poem in the *New Yorker*. The best moment of our lives was one quiet repeated day of work in our house. Not everyone understood. Visitors, especially from New York, would spend a weekend with us and say as they left: "It's really pretty here" ("in Vermont," many added) "with your house, the pond, the hills, but . . . but . . . but . . . *what do you do?*"

What we did: we got up early in the morning. I brought Jane coffee in bed. She walked the dog as I started writing, then climbed the stairs to work at her own desk on her own poems. We had lunch. We lay down together. We rose and worked at secondary things. I read aloud to Jane; we played scoreless ping-pong; we read the mail; we worked again. We ate supper, talked, read books sitting across from each other in the living room, and went to sleep. If we were lucky the phone didn't ring all day. In January Jane dreamed of flowers, planning expansion and refinement of the garden. From late March into October she spent hours digging, applying fifty-year-old Holstein manure from under the barn, planting, transplanting, and weeding. Sometimes I went off for two nights to read my poems, essential to the economy, and Jane wrote a poem called "Alone for a Week." Later Jane flew away for readings and I loathed being the one left behind. (I filled out coupons from magazines and ordered useless objects.) We traveled south sometimes in cold weather: to Key West in December, a February week in Barbados, to Florida during baseball's spring training, to Bermuda. Rarely we flew to England or Italy for two weeks. Three hundred and thirty days a year we inhabited this old house and the same day's adventurous routine.

What we did: love. We did not spend our days gazing into each other's eyes. We did that gazing when we made love or when one of us was in trouble, but most of the time our gazes met and entwined as they looked at a third thing. Third things are essential to marriages, objects or practices or habits or arts or institutions or games or human beings that provide a site of joint rapture or contentment. Each member of a couple is separate; the two come together in double attention. Lovemaking is not a third thing but two-in-one. John Keats can be a third thing, or the Boston Symphony Orchestra, or Dutch interiors, or Monopoly. For many couples, children are a third thing. Jane and I had no children of our own; we had our cats and dog to fuss and exclaim over—and later my five grandchildren from an earlier marriage. We had our summer afternoons at the pond, which for ten years made a third thing. After naps we loaded up books and blankets and walked across Route 4 and the old railroad to the steep slippery bank that led down to our private beach on Eagle Pond. Soft moss underfoot sent little red flowers up. Ghost birches leaned over water with wild strawberry plants growing under them. Over our heads white pines reared high, and oaks that warned us of summer's end late in August by dropping green metallic acorns. Sometimes a mink scooted among ferns. After we acquired Gus he joined the pond ecstasy, chewing on stones. Jane dozed in the sun as I sat in the shade reading and occasionally taking a note in a blank book. From time to time we swam and dried in the heat. Then, one summer, leakage from the Danbury landfill turned the pond orange. It stank. The water was not hazardous but it was ruined. A few years later the pond came back but we seldom returned to our afternoons there. Sometimes you lose a third thing.

The South Danbury Christian Church became large in our lives. We were both deacons and Jane was treasurer for a dozen years, utter miscasting and a source of annual anxiety when the treasurer's report was due. I collected the offering; Jane counted and banked it. Once a month she prepared communion and I distributed it. For the Church Fair we both cooked and I helped with the auction. Besides the Church itself, building and community, there was Christianity, the Gospels, and the work of theologians and mystics. Typically we divided our attentions: I read Meister Eckhart while Jane studied Julian of Norwich. I read the Old Testament aloud to her, and the New. If it wasn't the Bible, I was reading aloud late Henry James or Mark Twain or Edith Wharton or Wordworth's *Prelude*. Reading aloud was a daily connection. When I first pronounced *The Ambassadors,* Jane had never read it, and I peeked at her flabbergasted face as the boat bearing Chad and Mme. de Vionnet rounded the bend toward Lambert Strether. Three years later, when I had acquired a New York Edition of Henry James, she asked me to read her *The Ambassadors* again. Late James is the best prose for reading aloud. Saying one of his interminable sentences, the voice must drop pitch every time he interrupts his syntax with periphrasis, and drop again when periphrasis interrupts periphrasis, and again, and then step the pitch up, like climbing stairs in the dark, until the original tone concludes the sentence. One's larynx could write a doctoral dissertation on James's syntax.

Literature in general was a constant. Often at the end of the day Jane would speak about what she had been reading, her latest intense and obsessive absorption in an author: Keats for two years, Chekhov, Elizabeth Bishop. In reading and in everything else, we made clear boundaries, dividing our literary territories. I did not go back to Keats until she had done with him. By and large Jane read intensively while I read extensively. Like a male, I lusted to acquire all the great books of the world and add them to my life list. One day I would realize: I've never read Darwin! Adam Smith! Gibbon! Gibbon became an obsession with me, then his sources, then all ancient history, then all narrative history. For a few years I concentrated on Henry Adams, even reading six massive volumes of letters.

But there was also ping-pong. When we added a new bedroom, we extended the rootcellar enough to set a ping-pong table into it, and for years we played every afternoon. Jane was assiduous, determined, vicious, and her reach was not so wide as mine. When she couldn't reach a shot I called her "Stubbsy," and her next slam would smash me in the groin, rage combined with harmlessness. We rallied half an hour without keeping score. Another trait we shared was hating to lose. Through bouts of ping-pong and Henry James and the church, we kept to one innovation: with rare exceptions, we remained aware of each other's feelings. It took me half my life, more than half, to discover with Jane's guidance that two people could live together and remain kind. When one of us felt grumpy we both shut up until it went away. We did not give in to sarcasm. Once every three years we had a fight—the way some couples fight three times a day—and because fights were few the aftermath of a fight was a dreadful gloom. "We have done harm," said Jane in a poem after a quarrel. What was *that* fight about? I wonder if she remembered, a month after writing the poem.

Of course: the third thing that brought us together, and shone at the center of our lives and our house, was poetry—both our love for the art and the passion and frustration of trying to write it. When we moved to the farm, away from teaching and Jane's family, we threw ourselves into the life of writing poetry as if we jumped from a bridge and swam to survive. I kept the earliest hours of the day for poetry. Jane worked on poems virtually every day; there were dry spells. In the first years of our marriage, I sometimes feared that she would find the project of poetry intimidating, and withdraw or give up or diminish the intensity of her commitment. I remember talking with her one morning early in New Hampshire, maybe in 1976, when the burden felt too heavy. She talked of her singing with the Michigan Chorale, as if music were something she might turn to. She spoke of drawing as another art she could perform, and showed me an old pencil rendering she had made, acorns I think, meticulous and well-made and nothing more. She was saying, "I don't *have* to give myself to poetry"—and I knew enough not to argue.

However, from year to year she gave more of herself to her art. When she studied Keats, she read all his poems, all his letters, the best three or four biographies; then she read and reread the poems and the letters again. No one will find in her poems clear fingerprints of John Keats, but Jane's ear became more luscious with her love for Keats; her lines became more dense, rifts loaded with ore. Coming from a family for whom ambition was dangerous, in which work was best taken lightly, it was not easy for Jane to wager her life on one number. She lived with someone who had made that choice, but also with someone nineteen years older who wrote all day and published frequently. Her first book of poems came out as I published my fifth. I could have been an inhibitor as easily as I was an encourager—if she had not been brave and stubborn. I watched in gratified pleasure as her poems became better and better. From being promising she became accomplished and professional; then—with the later poems of *The Boat of Quiet Hours,* with "Twilight: After Haying," with "Briefly It Enters," with "Things," she turned into the extraordinary and permanent poet of *Otherwise.*

People asked us—people still ask me—about competition between us. We never spoke of it, but it had to be there—and it remained benign. When Jane wrote a poem that dazzled me, I wanted to write a poem that would dazzle her. Boundaries helped. We belonged to different generations. Through Jane I got to be friends with poets of her generation, as she did with my friends born in the 1920s. We avoided situations which would subject us to comparison. During the first years of our marriage, when Jane was just beginning to publish, we were asked several times to read our poems together. The people who asked us knew and respected Jane's poems, but the occasions turned ghastly. Once we were introduced by someone we had just met who was happy to welcome Joan Kenyon. Always someone, generally a male English professor, managed to let us know that it was sweet, that Jane wrote poems too. One head of a department asked her if she felt dwarfed. When Jane was condescended to she was furious, and it was only on these occasions that we felt anything unpleasant between us. Jane decided that we would no longer read together.

When places later asked us both to read, we agreed to come but stipulated that we read separately, maybe a day apart. As she published more widely we were more frequently approached. Late in the 1980s, after reading on different days at one university, we did a joint question-and-answer session with writing students. Three quarters of the questions addressed Jane, not me, and afterwards she said, "Perkins, I think we can read together now." So, in our last years together, we did many joint readings. When two poets read on the same program, the first reader is the warm-up band, the second the featured act. We read in fifteen-minute segments, ABAB, and switched A and B positions with each reading. In 1993 we read on a Friday in Trivandrum, at the southern tip of India, and three days later in Hanover, New Hampshire. Exhausted as we were, we remembered who had gone first thousands of miles away.

There were days when each of us received word from the same magazine; the same editor had taken a poem by one of us just as he/she rejected the other of us. One of us felt constrained in pleasure. The need for boundaries even extended to style. As Jane's work got better and better—and readers noticed—my language and structure departed from its old habits and veered away from the kind of lyric that Jane was writing, toward irony and an apothegmatic style. My diction became more Latinate and polysyllabic, as well as syntactically complex. I was reading Gibbon, learning to use a vocabulary and sentence structure as engines of discrimination. Unconsciously, I was choosing to be as unlike Jane as I could. Still, her poetry influenced and enhanced my own. Her stubborn and unflagging commitment turned its power upon me and exhorted me. My poems got better in this house. When my *Old and New Poems* came out in 1990, the positive reviews included something like this sentence: "Hall began publishing early . . . but it was not until he left his teaching job and returned to the family farm in New Hampshire with his second wife the poet Jane Kenyon that . . ." I published *Kicking the Leaves* in 1978 when Jane published *From Room to Room.* It was eight years before we published our next books: her *The Boat of Quiet Hours,* my *The Happy Man.* (When I told Jane my title her reaction was true Jane: "Sounds too depressed.") I had also been working on drafts of *The One Day,* maybe my best book. Then Jane wrote *Let Evening Come, Constance,* and the twenty late poems that begin *Otherwise.* Two years after her death, a review of Jane began with a sentence I had been expecting. It was uttered in respect, without a sneer, and said that for years we had known of Jane Kenyon as Donald Hall's wife but from now on we will know of Donald Hall as Jane Kenyon's husband.

We did not show each other early drafts. (It's a bad habit. The comments of another become attached to the words of a poem, steering it or preventing it from following its own way.) But when we had worked over a poem in solitude for a long time, our first reader was the other. I felt anxious about showing Jane new poems, and often invented reasons for delay. Usually, each of us saved up three or four poems before showing them to the other. One day I would say, "I left some stuff on your footstool," or Jane would tell me, "Perkins, there are some things on your desk." Waiting for a response, each of us already knew some of what the other would say. If ever I repeated a word—a habit acquired from Yeats—I knew that Jane would cross it out. Whenever she used verbal auxiliaries she knew I would simplify, and "it was raining" would become "it rained." By and large we ignored the predicted advice, which we had already heard in our heads and dismissed. Jane kept her work clear of dead metaphor, knowing my crankiness on the subject, and she would exult when she found one in my drafts: "Perkins! Here's a dead metaphor!" These encounters were important but not easy. Sometimes we turned polite with each other: "Oh, really! I thought that was the best part . . ." (False laugh.) Jane told others—people questioned us about how we worked together—that I approached her holding a sheaf of her new poems saying, "These are going to be *good!*" to which she would say, "Going to be, eh?" She told people that she would climb back to her study, carrying the poems covered with my illegible comments, thinking, "Perkins just doesn't get it. And then," she would continue, "I'd do everything he said."

Neither of us did everything the other said. Reading *Otherwise* I find words I wanted her to change, and sometimes I still think I was right. But we helped each other greatly. She saved me a thousand gaffes, cut my wordiness and straightened out my syntax. She seldom told me that anything was *good.* "This is almost done," she'd say, "but you've got to do this in two lines not three." Or, "You've brought this a long way, Perkins"—without telling me if I had brought it to a good place. Sometimes her praise expressed its own limits. "You've taken this as far as the intellect can take it." When she said, "It's finished. Don't change a word," I would ask, "But is it any *good? Do you like* it?" I pined for her praise, and seldom got it. I remember one evening in 1992 when we sat in the living room and she read through the manuscript of *The Museum of Clear Ideas.* Earlier she had seen only a few poems at a time, and she had not been enthusiastic. I watched her dark face as she turned the pages. Finally she looked over at me and tears started from her eyes. "Perkins, I don't *like* it!" Tears came to my eyes too, and I said, rapidly, "That's okay. That's okay." (That book was anti-Jane in its manner, or most of it was, dependant on syntax and irony, a little like Augustan poetry, more than on images.) When we looked over each other's work, it was essential that we never lie to each other. Even when Jane was depressed, I never praised a poem unless I meant it; I never withheld blame. If either of us had felt that the other was pulling punches, it would have ruined what was so essential to our house.

We were each other's readers but we could not be each other's only readers. I mostly consulted friends and editors by mail, so many helpers that I will not try to list them, poets from my generation and poets Jane's age and even younger. Jane worked regularly, the last dozen years of her life, with the poet Joyce Peseroff and the novelist Alice Mattison. The three of them worked wonderfully together, each supplying things that the other lacked. They fought, they laughed, they rewrote and cut and rearranged. Jane would return from a workshop exhausted yet unable to keep away from her desk, working with wild excitement to follow suggestions. The three women were not only being literary critics for each other. Each had grown up knowing that it was not permitted for females to be as aggressive as males, and all were ambitious in their art, and encouraged each other in their ambition. I felt close to Alice and Joyce, my friends as well as Jane's, but I did not stick my nose into their deliberations. If I had tried to, I would have lost a nose. Even when they met at our house, I was careful to stay apart. They met often at Joyce's in Massachusetts, because it was half way between Jane and Alice. They met in New Haven at Alice's. When I was recovering from an operation, and Jane and I didn't want to be separated, there were workshops at the Lord Jeffrey Inn in Amherst. We four ate together and made pilgrimages to Emily Dickinson's house and grave, but while they worked together I wrote alone in an adjacent room. This three-part friendship was essential to Jane's poetry.

Meantime we lived in the house of poetry, which was also the house of love and grief; the house of solitude and art; the house of Jane's depression and my cancers and Jane's leukemia. When someone died whom we loved, we went back to the poets of grief and outrage, as far back as *Gilgamesh;* often I read aloud Henry King's "The Exequy," written in the seventeenth century after the death of his young wife. Poetry gives the griever not release from grief but companionship in grief. Poetry embodies the complexities of feeling at their most intense and entangled, and therefore offers (over centuries, or over no time at all) the company of tears. As I sat beside Jane in her pain and weakness I wrote about pain and weakness. Once in a hospital I noticed that the leaves were turning. I realized that I had not noticed that they had come to the trees. It was a year without seasons, a year without punctuation. I began to write "Without" to embody the sensations of lives under dreary, monotonous assault. After I had drafted it many times I read it aloud to Jane. "That's it, Perkins," she said. "You've got it. That's it." Even in this poem written at her mortal bedside there was companionship.

Shooting an Elephant

George Orwell

George Orwell was the pen name for Eric Arthur Blair (1903-1950), an English novelist, essayist, and critic. Best known for his novel *1984*, Orwell's short essays often give a unique insight into life in the British Empire in the early 20th century. This essay was originally published in *New Writing* in 1936.

In Moulmein, in lower Burma, I was hated by large numbers of people—the only time in my life that I have been important enough for this to happen to me. I was sub-divisional police officer of the town, and in an aimless, petty kind of way anti-European feeling was very bitter. No one had the guts to raise a riot, but if a European woman went through the bazaars alone somebody would probably spit betel juice over her dress. As a police officer I was an obvious target and was baited whenever it seemed safe to do so. When a nimble Burman tripped me up on the football field and the referee (another Burman) looked the other way, the crowd yelled with hideous laughter. This happened more than once. In the end the sneering yellow faces of young men that met me everywhere, the insults hooted after me when I was at a safe distance, got badly on my nerves. The young Buddhist priests were the worst of all. There were several thousands of them in the town and none of them seemed to have anything to do except stand on street corners and jeer at Europeans.

All this was perplexing and upsetting. For at that time I had already made up my mind that imperialism was an evil thing and the sooner I chucked up my job and got out of it the better. Theoretically—and secretly, of course—I was all for the Burmese and all against their oppressors, the British. As for the job I was doing, I hated it more bitterly than I can perhaps make clear. In a job like that you see the dirty work of Empire at close quarters. The wretched prisoners huddling in the stinking cages of the lock-ups, the grey, cowed faces of the long-term convicts, the scarred buttocks of the men who had been flogged with bamboos—all these oppressed me with an intolerable sense of guilt. But I could get nothing into perspective. I was young and ill-educated and I had had to think out my problems in the utter silence that is imposed on every Englishman in the East. I did not even know that the British Empire is dying, still less did I know that it is a great deal better than the younger empires that are going to supplant it. All I knew was that I was stuck between my hatred of the empire I served and my rage against the evil-spirited little beasts who tried to make my job impossible. With one part of my mind I thought of the British Raj as an unbreakable tyranny, as something clamped down, in saecula saeculorum, upon the will of prostrate peoples; with another part I thought that the greatest joy in the world would be to drive a bayonet into a Buddhist priest's guts. Feelings like these are the normal by-products of imperialism; ask any Anglo-Indian official, if you can catch him off duty.

One day something happened which in a roundabout way was enlightening. It was a tiny incident in itself, but it gave me a better glimpse than I had had before of the real nature of imperialism—the real motives for which despotic governments act. Early one morning the sub-inspector at a police station the other end of the town rang me up on the phone and said that an elephant was ravaging the bazaar. Would I please come and do something about it? I did not know what I could do, but I wanted to see what was happening and I got on to a pony and started out. I took my rifle, an old 44 Winchester and much too small to kill an elephant, but I thought the noise might be useful in terrorem. Various Burmans stopped me on the way and told me about the elephant's doings. It was not, of course, a wild elephant, but a tame one which had gone "must." It had been chained up, as tame elephants always are when their attack of "must" is due, but on the previous night it had broken its chain and escaped. Its mahout, the only person who could manage it when it was in that state, had set out in pursuit, but had taken the wrong direction and was now twelve hours' journey away, and in the morning the elephant had suddenly reappeared in the town. The Burmese population had no weapons and were quite helpless against it. It had already destroyed somebody's bamboo hut, killed a cow and raided some fruit-stalls and devoured the stock; also it had met the municipal rubbish van and, when the driver jumped out and took to his heels, had turned the van over and inflicted violences upon it.

The Burmese sub-inspector and some Indian constables were waiting for me in the quarter where the elephant had been seen. It was a very poor quarter, a labyrinth of squalid bamboo huts, thatched with palmleaf, winding all over a steep hillside. I remember that it was a cloudy, stuffy morning at the beginning of the rains. We began questioning the people as to where the elephant had gone and, as usual, failed to get any definite information. That is invariably the case in the East; a story always sounds clear enough at a distance, but the nearer you get to the scene of events the vaguer it becomes. Some of the people said that the elephant had gone in one direction, some said that he had gone in another, some professed not even to have heard of any elephant. I had almost made up my mind that the whole story was a pack of lies, when we heard yells a little distance away. There was a loud, scandalized cry of "Go away, child! Go away this instant!" and an old woman with a switch in her hand came round the corner of a hut, violently shooing away a crowd of naked children. Some more women followed, clicking their tongues and exclaiming; evidently there was something that the children ought not to have seen. I rounded the hut and saw a man's dead body sprawling in the mud. He was an Indian, a black Dravidian coolie, almost naked, and he could not have been dead many minutes. The people said that the elephant had come suddenly upon him round the corner of the hut, caught him with its trunk, put its foot on his back and ground him into the earth. This was the rainy season and the ground was soft, and his face had scored a trench a foot deep and a couple of yards long. He was lying on his belly with arms crucified and head sharply twisted to one side. His face was coated with mud, the eyes wide open, the teeth bared and grinning with an expression of unendurable agony. (Never tell me, by the way, that the dead look peaceful. Most of the corpses I have seen looked devilish.) The friction of the great beast's foot had stripped the skin from his back as neatly as one skins a rabbit. As soon as I saw the dead man I sent an orderly to a friend's house nearby to borrow an elephant rifle. I had already sent back the pony, not wanting it to go mad with fright and throw me if it smelt the elephant.

The orderly came back in a few minutes with a rifle and five cartridges, and meanwhile some Burmans had arrived and told us that the elephant was in the paddy fields below, only a few hundred yards away. As I started forward practically the whole population of the quarter flocked out of the houses and followed me. They had seen the rifle and were all shouting excitedly that I was going to shoot the elephant. They had not shown much interest in the elephant when he was merely ravaging their homes, but it was different now that he was going to be shot. It was a bit of fun to them, as it would be to an English crowd; besides they wanted the meat. It made me vaguely uneasy. I had no intention of shooting the elephant—I had merely sent for the rifle to defend myself if necessary—and it is always unnerving to have a crowd following you. I marched down the hill, looking and feeling a fool, with the rifle over my shoulder and an ever-growing army of people jostling at my heels. At the bottom, when you got away from the huts, there was a metalled road and beyond that a miry waste of paddy fields a thousand yards across, not yet ploughed but soggy from the first rains and dotted with coarse grass. The elephant was standing eight yards from the road, his left side towards us. He took not the slightest notice of the crowd's approach. He was tearing up bunches of grass, beating them against his knees to clean them and stuffing them into his mouth.

I had halted on the road. As soon as I saw the elephant I knew with perfect certainty that I ought not to shoot him. It is a serious matter to shoot a working elephant—it is comparable to destroying a huge and costly piece of machinery—and obviously one ought not to do it if it can possibly be avoided. And at that distance, peacefully eating, the elephant looked no more dangerous than a cow. I thought then and I think now that his attack of "must" was already passing off; in which case he would merely wander harmlessly about until the mahout came back and caught him. Moreover, I did not in the least want to shoot him. I decided that I would watch him for a little while to make sure that he did not turn savage again, and then go home.

But at that moment I glanced round at the crowd that had followed me. It was an immense crowd, two thousand at the least and growing every minute. It blocked the road for a long distance on either side. I looked at the sea of yellow faces above the garish clothes—faces all happy and excited over this bit of fun, all certain that the elephant was going to be shot. They were watching me as they would watch a conjurer about to perform a trick. They did not like me, but with the magical rifle in my hands I was momentarily worth watching. And suddenly I realized that I should have to shoot the elephant after all. The people expected it of me and I had got to do it; I could feel their two thousand wills pressing me forward, irresistibly. And it was at this moment, as I stood there with the rifle in my hands, that I first grasped the hollowness, the futility of the white man's dominion in the East. Here was I, the white man with his gun, standing in front of the unarmed native crowd—seemingly the leading actor of the piece; but in reality I was only an absurd puppet pushed to and fro by the will of those yellow faces behind. I perceived in this moment that when the white man turns tyrant it is his own freedom that he destroys. He becomes a sort of hollow, posing dummy, the conventionalized figure of a sahib. For it is the condition of his rule that he shall spend his life in trying to impress the "natives," and so in every crisis he has got to do what the "natives" expect of him. He wears a mask, and his face grows to fit it. I had got to shoot the elephant. I had committed myself to doing it when I sent for the rifle. A sahib has got to act like a sahib; he has got to appear resolute, to know his own mind and do definite things. To come all that way, rifle in hand, with two thousand people marching at my heels, and then to trail feebly away, having done nothing—no, that was impossible. The crowd would laugh at me. And my whole life, every white man's life in the East, was one long struggle not to be laughed at.

But I did not want to shoot the elephant. I watched him beating his bunch of grass against his knees, with that preoccupied grandmotherly air that elephants have. It seemed to me that it would be murder to shoot him. At that age I was not squeamish about killing animals, but I had never shot an elephant and never wanted to. (Somehow it always seems worse to kill a large animal.) Besides, there was the beast's owner to be considered. Alive, the elephant was worth at least a hundred pounds; dead, he would only be worth the value of his tusks, five pounds, possibly. But I had got to act quickly. I turned to some experienced-looking Burmans who had been there when we arrived, and asked them how the elephant had been behaving. They all said the same thing: he took no notice of you if you left him alone, but he might charge if you went too close to him.

It was perfectly clear to me what I ought to do. I ought to walk up to within, say, twenty-five yards of the elephant and test his behavior. If he charged, I could shoot; if he took no notice of me, it would be safe to leave him until the mahout came back. But also I knew that I was going to do no such thing. I was a poor shot with a rifle and the ground was soft mud into which one would sink at every step. If the elephant charged and I missed him, I should have about as much chance as a toad under a steam-roller. But even then I was not thinking particularly of my own skin, only of the watchful yellow faces behind. For at that moment, with the crowd watching me, I was not afraid in the ordinary sense, as I would have been if I had been alone. A white man mustn't be frightened in front of "natives"; and so, in general, he isn't frightened. The sole thought in my mind was that if anything went wrong those two thousand Burmans would see me pursued, caught, trampled on and reduced to a grinning corpse like that Indian up the hill. And if that happened it was quite probable that some of them would laugh. That would never do.

There was only one alternative. I shoved the cartridges into the magazine and lay down on the road to get a better aim. The crowd grew very still, and a deep, low, happy sigh, as of people who see the theatre curtain go up at last, breathed from innumerable throats. They were going to have their bit of fun after all. The rifle was a beautiful German thing with cross-hair sights. I did not then know that in shooting an elephant one would shoot to cut an imaginary bar running from ear-hole to ear-hole. I ought, therefore, as the elephant was sideways on, to have aimed straight at his ear-hole, actually I aimed several inches in front of this, thinking the brain would be further forward.

When I pulled the trigger I did not hear the bang or feel the kick—one never does when a shot goes home—but I heard the devilish roar of glee that went up from the crowd. In that instant, in too short a time, one would have thought, even for the bullet to get there, a mysterious, terrible change had come over the elephant. He neither stirred nor fell, but every line of his body had altered. He looked suddenly stricken, shrunken, immensely old, as though the frightful impact of the bullet had paralysed him without knocking him down. At last, after what seemed a long time—it might have been five seconds, I dare say—he sagged flabbily to his knees. His mouth slobbered. An enormous senility seemed to have settled upon him. One could have imagined him thousands of years old. I fired again into the same spot. At the second shot he did not collapse but climbed with desperate slowness to his feet and stood weakly upright, with legs sagging and head drooping. I fired a third time. That was the shot that did for him. You could see the agony of it jolt his whole body and knock the last remnant of strength from his legs. But in falling he seemed for a moment to rise, for as his hind legs collapsed beneath him he seemed to tower upward like a huge rock toppling, his trunk reaching skyward like a tree. He trumpeted, for the first and only time. And then down he came, his belly towards me, with a crash that seemed to shake the ground even where I lay.

I got up. The Burmans were already racing past me across the mud. It was obvious that the elephant would never rise again, but he was not dead. He was breathing very rhythmically with long rattling gasps, his great mound of a side painfully rising and falling. His mouth was wide open—I could see far down into caverns of pale pink throat. I waited a long time for him to die, but his breathing did not weaken. Finally I fired my two remaining shots into the spot where I thought his heart must be. The thick blood welled out of him like red velvet, but still he did not die. His body did not even jerk when the shots hit him, the tortured breathing continued without a pause. He was dying, very slowly and in great agony, but in some world remote from me where not even a bullet could damage him further. I felt that I had got to put an end to that dreadful noise. It seemed dreadful to see the great beast Lying there, powerless to move and yet powerless to die, and not even to be able to finish him. I sent back for my small rifle and poured shot after shot into his heart and down his throat. They seemed to make no impression. The tortured gasps continued as steadily as the ticking of a clock.

In the end I could not stand it any longer and went away. I heard later that it took him half an hour to die. Burmans were bringing dash and baskets even before I left, and I was told they had stripped his body almost to the bones by the afternoon.

Afterwards, of course, there were endless discussions about the shooting of the elephant. The owner was furious, but he was only an Indian and could do nothing. Besides, legally I had done the right thing, for a mad elephant has to be killed, like a mad dog, if its owner fails to control it. Among the Europeans opinion was divided. The older men said I was right, the younger men said it was a damn shame to shoot an elephant for killing a coolie, because an elephant was worth more than any damn Coringhee coolie. And afterwards I was very glad that the coolie had been killed; it put me legally in the right and it gave me a sufficient pretext for shooting the elephant. I often wondered whether any of the others grasped that I had done it solely to avoid looking a fool.

On Being a Cripple

Nancy Mairs

Nancy Mairs (1943-2016) was an American author, essayist, disability advocate, and educator. The author of three volumes of fiction, several volumes of essays, and an audio CD of her work, Mairs became a self-described "cripple" after being diagnosed with MS at the age of 28. Many of her essays focus on the experiences of those with disabilities trying to make it in the "normal" world. This essay was originally published in her book *Plaintext* in 1986.

The other day I was thinking of writing an essay on being a cripple. I was thinking hard in one of the stalls of the women's room in my office building, as I was shoving my shirt into my jeans and tugging up my zipper. Preoccupied, I flushed, picked up my book bag, took my cane down from the hook, and unlatched the door. So many movements unbalanced me, and as I pulled the door open I fell over backward, landing fully clothed on the toilet seat with my legs splayed in front of me: the old beetle-on-its-back routine. Saturday afternoon, the building deserted, I was free to laugh aloud as I wriggled back to my feet, my voice bouncing off the yellowish tiles from all directions. Had anyone been there with me, I'd have been still and faint and hot with chagrin. I decided that it was high time to write the essay.

First, the matter of semantics. I am a cripple. I choose this word to name me. I choose from among several possibilities, the most common of which are "handicapped" and "disabled." I made the choice a number of years ago, without thinking, unaware of my motives for doing so. Even now, I'm not sure what those motives are, but I recognize that they are complex and not entirely flattering. People—crippled or not—wince at the word "cripple," as they do not at "handicapped" or "disabled." Perhaps I want them to wince. I want them to see me as a tough customer, one to whom the fates/gods/viruses have not been kind, but who can face the brutal truth of her existence squarely. As a cripple, I swagger.

But, to be fair to myself, a certain amount of honesty underlies my choice. "Cripple" seems to me a clean word, straightforward and precise. It has an honorable history, having made its first appearance in the Lindisfarne Gospel in the tenth century. As a lover of words, I like the accuracy with which it describes my condition: I have lost the full use of my limbs. "Disabled," by contrast, suggests any incapacity, physical or mental. And I certainly don't like "handicapped," which implies that I have deliberately been put at a disadvantage, by whom I can't imagine (my God is not a Handicapper General), in order to equalize chances in the great race of life. These words seem to me to be moving away from my condition, to be widening the gap between word and reality. Most remote is the recently coined euphemism "differently abled," which partakes of the same semantic hopefulness that transformed countries from "undeveloped" to "underdeveloped," then to "less developed," and finally to "developing" nations. People have continued to starve in those countries during the shift. Some realities do not obey the dictates of language.

Mine is one of them. Whatever you call me, I remain crippled. But I don't care what you call me, so long as it isn't "differently abled," which strikes me as pure verbal garbage designed, by its ability to describe anyone, to describe no one. I subscribe to George Orwell's thesis that "the slovenliness of our language makes it easier for us to have foolish thoughts." And I refuse to participate in the degeneration of the language to the extent that I deny that I have lost anything in the course of this calamitous disease; I refuse to pretend that the only differences between you and me are the various ordinary ones that distinguish any one person from another. But call me "disabled" or "handicapped" if you like. I have long since grown accustomed to them; and if they are vague, at least they hint at the truth. Moreover, I use them myself. Society is no readier to accept crippledness than to accept death, war, sex, sweat, or wrinkles. I would never refer to another person as a cripple. It is the word I use to name only myself.

I haven't always been crippled, a fact for which I am soundly grateful. To be whole of limb is, I know from experience, infinitely more pleasant and useful than to be crippled; and if that knowledge leaves me open to bitterness at MY loss, the physical soundness I once enjoyed (though I did not enjoy it half enough) is well worth the occasional stab of regret. Though never any good at sports, I was a normally active child and young adult. I climbed trees, played hopscotch, jumped rope, skated, swam, rode my bicycle, sailed. I despised team sports, spending some of the wretchedest afternoons of my life, sweaty and humiliated, behind a field-hockey stick and under a basketball hoop. I tramped alone for miles along the bridle paths that webbed the woods behind the house I grew up in. I swayed through countless dim hours in the arms of one man or another under the scattered shot of light from mirrored balls, and gyrated through countless more as Tab Hunter and Johnny Mathis gave way to the Rolling Stones, Creedence Clearwater Revival, Cream. I walked down the aisle. I pushed baby carriages, changed tires in the rain, marched for peace.

When I was twenty-eight I started to trip and drop things. What at first seemed my natural clumsiness soon became too pronounced to shrug off. I consulted a neurologist, who told me that I had a brain tumor. A battery of tests, increasingly disagreeable, revealed no tumor. About a year and a half later I developed a blurred spot in one eye. I had, at last, the episodes "disseminated in space and time" requisite for a diagnosis: multiple sclerosis. I have never been sorry for the doctor's initial misdiagnosis, however. For almost a week, until the negative results of the tests were in, I thought that I was going to die right away. Every day for the past nearly ten years, then, has been a kind of gift. I accept all gifts.

Multiple sclerosis is a chronic degenerative disease of the central nervous system, in which the myelin that sheathes the nerves is somehow eaten away and scar tissue forms in its place, interrupting the nerves' signals. During its course, which is unpredictable and uncontrollable, one may lose vision, hearing, speech, the ability to walk, control of bladder and/or bowels, strength in any or all extremities, sensitivity to touch, vibration, and/or pain, potency, coordination of movements—the list of possibilities is lengthy and, yes, horrifying. One may also lose one's sense of humor. That's the easiest to lose and the hardest to survive without.

In the past ten years, I have sustained some of these losses. Characteristic of MS are sudden attacks, called exacerbations, followed by remissions, and these I have not had. Instead, my disease has been slowly progressive. My left leg is now so weak that I walk with the aid of a brace and a cane; and for distances I use an Amigo, a variation on the electric wheelchair that looks rather like an electrified kiddie car. I no longer have much use of my left hand. Now my right side is weakening as well. I still have the blurred spot in my right eye. Overall, though, I've been lucky so far. My world has, of necessity, been circumscribed by my losses, but the terrain left me has been ample enough for me to continue many of the activities that absorb me: writing, teaching, raising children and cats and plants and snakes, reading, speaking publicly about MS and depression, even playing bridge with people patient and honorable enough to let me scatter cards every which way without sneaking a peek.

Lest I begin to sound like Pollyanna, however, let me say that I don't like having MS. I hate it. My life holds realities—harsh ones, some of them—that no right-minded human being ought to accept without grumbling. One of them is fatigue. I know of no one with MS who does not complain of bone-weariness; in a disease that presents an astonishing variety of symptoms, fatigue seems to be a common factor. I wake up in the morning feeling the way most people do at the end of a bad day, and I take it from there. As a result, I spend a lot of time in extremis and, impatient with limitation, I tend to ignore my fatigue until my body breaks down in some way and forces rest. Then I miss picnics, dinner parties, poetry readings, the brief visits of old friends from out of town. The offspring of a puritanical tradition of exceptional venerability, I cannot view these lapses without shame. My life often seems a series of small failures to do as I ought.

I lead, on the whole, an ordinary life, probably rather like the one I would have led had I not had MS. I am lucky that my predilections were already solitary, sedentary, and bookish—unlike the world-famous French cellist I have read about, or the young woman I talked with one long afternoon who wanted only to be a jockey. I had just begun graduate school when I found out something was wrong with me, and I have remained, interminably, a graduate student. Perhaps I would not have if I'd thought I had the stamina to return to a full-time job as a technical editor; but I've enjoyed my studies.

In addition to studying, I teach writing courses. I also teach medical students how to give neurological examinations. I pick up freelance editing jobs here and there. I have raised a foster son and sent him into the world, where he has made me two grandbabies, and I am still escorting my daughter and son through adolescence. I go to Mass every Saturday. I am a superb, if messy, cook. I am also an enthusiastic laundress, capable of sorting a hamper full of clothes into five subtly differentiated piles, but a terrible housekeeper. I can do italic writing and, in an emergency, bathe an oil-soaked cat. I play a fiendish game of Scrabble. When I have the time and the money, I like to sit on my front steps with my husband, drinking Amaretto and smoking a cigar, as we imagine our counterparts in Leningrad and make sure that the sun gets down once more behind the sharp childish scrawl of the Tucson Mountains.

This lively plenty has its bleak complement, of course, in all the things I can no longer do. I will never run again, except in dreams, and one day I may have to write that I will never walk again. I like to go camping, but I can't follow George and the children along the trails that wander out of a campsite through the desert or into the mountains. In fact, even on the level I've learned never to check the weather or try to hold a coherent conversation: I need all my attention for my wayward feet. Of late, I have begun to catch myself wondering how people can propel themselves without canes. With only one usable hand, I have to select my clothing with care not so much for style as for ease of ingress and egress, and even so, dressing can be laborious. I can no longer do fine stitchery, pick up babies, play the piano, braid my hair. I am immobilized by acute attacks of depression, which may or may not be physiologically related to MS but are certainly its logical concomitant.

These two elements, the plenty and the privation, are never pure, nor are the delight and wretchedness that accompany them. Almost every pickle that I get into as a result of my weakness and clumsiness—and I get into plenty—is funny as well as maddening and sometimes painful. I recall one May afternoon when a friend and I were going out for a drink after finishing up at school. As we were climbing into opposite sides of my car, chatting, I tripped and fell, flat and hard, onto the asphalt parking lot, my abrupt departure interrupting him in mid-sentence. "Where'd you go?" he called as he came around the back of the car to find me hauling myself up by the door frame. "Are you all right?" Yes, I told him, I was fine, just a bit rattly, and we drove off to find a shady patio and some beer. When I got home an hour or so later, my daughter greeted me with "What have you done to yourself?" I looked down. One elbow of my white turtleneck with the green froggies, one knee of my white trousers, one white kneesock were blood-soaked. We peeled off the clothes and inspected the damage, which was nasty enough but not alarming. That part wasn't funny: The abrasions took a long time to heal, and one got a little infected. Even so, when I think of my friend talking earnestly, suddenly, to the hot thin air while I dropped from his view as though through a trap door, I find the image as silly as something from a Marx Brothers movie.

I may find it easier than other cripples to amuse myself because I live propped by the acceptance and the assistance and, sometimes, the amusement of those around me. Grocery clerks tear my checks out of my checkbook for me, and sales clerks find chairs to put into dressing rooms when I want to try on clothes. The people I work with make sure I teach at times when I am least likely to be fatigued, in places I can get to, with the materials I need. My students, with one anonymous exception (in an end-of-the-semester evaluation), have been unperturbed by my disability. Some even like it. One was immensely cheered by the information that I paint my own fingernails; she decided, she told me, that if I could go to such trouble over fine details, she could keep on writing essays. I suppose I became some sort of bright-fingered muse. She wrote good essays, too.

The most important struts in the framework of my existence, of course, are my husband and children. Dismayingly few marriages survive the MS test, and why should they? Most twenty-two- and nine-teen-year-olds, like George and me, can vow in clear conscience, after a childhood of chicken pox and summer colds, to keep one another in sickness and in health so long as they both shall live. Not many are equipped for catastrophe: the dismay, the depression, the extra work, the boredom that a degenerative disease can insinuate into a relationship. And our society, with its emphasis on fun and its association of fun with physical performance, offers little encouragement for a whole spouse to stay with a crippled partner. Children experience similar stresses when faced with a crippled parent, and they are more helpless, since parents and children can't usually get divorced. They hate, of course, to be different from their peers, and the child whose mother is tacking down the aisle of a school auditorium packed with proud parents like a Cape Cod dinghy in a stiff breeze jolly well stands out in a crowd. Deprived of legal divorce, the child can at least deny the mother's disability, even her existence, forgetting to tell her about recitals and PTA meetings, refusing to accompany her to stores or church or the movies, never inviting friends to the house. Many do.

But I've been limping along for ten years now, and so far George and the children are still at my left elbow, holding tight. Anne and Matthew vacuum floors and dust furniture and haul trash and rake up dog droppings and button my cuffs and bake lasagna and Toll House cookies with just enough grumbling so I know that they don't have brain fever. And far from hiding me, they're forever dragging me by racks of fancy clothes or through teeming school corridors, or welcoming gaggles of friends while I'm wandering through the house in Anne's filmy pink babydoll pajamas. George generally calls before he brings someone home, but he does just as many dumb thankless chores as the children. And they all yell at me, laugh at some of my jokes, write me funny letters when we're apart-in short, treat me as an ordinary human being for whom they have some use. I think they like me. Unless they're faking....

Faking. There's the rub. Tugging at the fringes of my consciousness always is the terror that people are kind to me only because I'm a cripple. My mother almost shattered me once, with that instinct mothers have—blind, I think, in this case, but unerring nonetheless—for striking blows along the fault-lines of their children's hearts, by telling me, in an attack on my selfishness, "We all have to make allowances for you, of course, because of the way you are." From the distance of a couple of years, I have to admit that I haven't any idea just what she meant, and I'm not sure that she knew either. She was awfully angry. But at the time, as the words thudded home, I felt my worst fear, suddenly realized. I could bear being called selfish: I am. But I couldn't bear the corroboration that those around me were doing in fact what I'd always suspected them of doing, professing fondness while silently putting up with me because of the way I am. A cripple. I've been a little cracked ever since.

Along with this fear that people are secretly accepting shoddy goods comes a relentless pressure to please—to prove myself worth the burdens I impose, I guess, or to build a substantial account of goodwill against which I may write drafts in times of need. Part of the pressure arises from social expectations. In our society, anyone who deviates from the norm had better find some way to compensate. Like fat people, who are expected to be jolly, cripples must bear their lot meekly and cheerfully. A grumpy cripple isn't playing by the rules. And much of the pressure is self-generated. Early on I vowed that, if I had to have MS, by God I was going to do it well. This is a class act, ladies and gentlemen. No tears, no recriminations, no faint-heartedness.

One way and another, then, I wind up feeling like Tiny Tim, peering over the edge of the table at the Christmas goose, waving my crutch, piping down God's blessing on us all. Only sometimes I don't want to play Tiny Tim. I'd rather be Caliban, a most scurvy monster. Fortunately, at home no one much cares whether I'm a good cripple or a bad cripple as long as I make vichyssoise with fair regularity. One evening several years ago, Anne was reading at the dining-room table while I cooked dinner. As I opened a can of tomatoes, the can slipped in my left hand and juice spattered me and the counter with bloody spots. Fatigued and infuriated, I bellowed, "I'm so sick of being crippled!" Anne glanced at me over the top of her book. "There now," she said, "do you feel better?" "Yes," I said, "yes, I do." She went back to her reading. I felt better. That's about all the attention my scurviness ever gets.

Because I hate being crippled, I sometimes hate myself for being a cripple. Over the years I have come to expect—even accept—attacks of violent self-loathing. Luckily, in general our society no longer connects deformity and disease directly with evil (though a charismatic once told me that I have MS because a devil is in me) and so I'm allowed to move largely at will, even among small children. But I'm not sure that this revision of attitude has been particularly helpful. Physical imperfection, even freed of moral disapprobation, still defies and violates the ideal, especially for women, whose confinement in their bodies as objects of desire is far from over. Each age, of course, has its ideal, and I doubt that ours is any better or worse than any other. Today's ideal woman, who lives on the glossy pages of dozens of magazines, seems to be between the ages of eighteen and twenty-five; her hair has body, her teeth flash white, her breath smells minty, her underarms are dry; she has a career but is still a fabulous cook, especially of meals that take less than twenty minutes to prepare; she does not ordinarily appear to have a husband or children; she is trim and deeply tanned; she jogs, swims, plays tennis, rides a bicycle, sails, but does not bowl; she travels widely, even to out-of-the-way places like Finland and Samoa, always in the company of the ideal man, who possesses a nearly identical set of characteristics. There are a few exceptions. Though usually white and often blonde, she may be black, Hispanic, Asian, or Native American, so long as she is unusually sleek. She may be old, provided she is selling a laxative or is Lauren Bacall. If she is selling a detergent, she may be married and have a flock of strikingly messy children. But she is never a cripple.

Like many women I know, I have always had an uneasy relationship with my body. I was not a popular child, largely, I think now, because I was peculiar:

intelligent, intense, moody, shy, given to unexpected actions and inexplicable notions and emotions. But as I entered adolescence, I believed myself unpopular because I was homely: my breasts too flat, my mouth too wide, my hips too narrow, my clothing never quite right in fit or style. I was not, in fact, particularly ugly, old photographs inform me, though I was well off the ideal; but I carried this sense of self-alienation with me into adulthood, where it regenerated in response to the depredations of MS. Even with my brace I walk with a limp so pronounced that, seeing myself on the videotape of a television program on the disabled, I couldn't believe that anything but an inchworm could make progress humping along like that. My shoulders droop and my pelvis thrusts forward as I try to balance myself upright, throwing my frame into a bony S. As a result of contractures, one shoulder is higher than the other and I carry one arm bent in front of me, the fingers curled into a claw. My left arm and leg have wasted into pipe-stems, and I try always to keep them covered. When I think about how my body must look to others, especially to men, to whom I have been trained to display myself, I feel ludicrous, even loathsome.

At my age, however, I don't spend much time thinking about my appearance. The burning egocentricity of adolescence, which assures one that all the world is looking all the time, has passed, thank God, and I'm generally too caught up in what I'm doing to step back, as I used to, and watch myself as though upon a stage. I'm also too old to believe in the accuracy of self-image. I know that I'm not a hideous crone, that in fact, when I'm rested, well dressed, and well made up, I look fine. The self-loathing I feel is neither physically nor intellectually substantial. What I hate is not me but a disease.

I am not a disease.

And a disease is not—at least not single-handedly—going to determine who I am, though at first it seemed to be going to. Adjusting to a chronic incurable illness, I have moved through a process similar to that outlined by Elizabeth Kubler-Ross in *On Death and Dying*. The major difference—and it is far more significant than most people recognize—is that I can't be sure of the outcome, as the terminally ill cancer patient can. Research studies indicate that, with proper medical care, I may achieve a "normal" life span. And in our society, with its vision of death as the ultimate evil, worse even than decrepitude, the response to such news is, "Oh well, at least you're not going to die." Are there worse things than dying? I think that there may be.

I think of two women I know, both with MS, both enough older than I to have served me as models. One took to her bed several years ago and has been there ever since. Although she can sit in a high-backed wheelchair, because she is incontinent she refuses to go out at all, even though incontinence pants, which are readily available at any pharmacy, could protect her from embarrassment. Instead, she stays at home and insists that her husband, a small quiet man, a retired civil servant, stay there with her except for a quick weekly foray to the supermarket. The other woman, whose illness was diagnosed when she was eighteen, a nursing student engaged to a young doctor, finished her training, married her doctor, accompanied him to Germany when he was in the service, bore three sons and a daughter, now grown and gone. When she can, she travels with her husband; she plays bridge, embroiders, swims regularly; she works, like me, as a symptomatic-patient instructor of medical students in neurology. Guess which woman I hope to be.

At the beginning, I thought about having MS almost incessantly. And because of the unpredictable course of the disease, my thoughts were always terrified. Each night I'd get into bed wondering whether I'd get out again the next morning, whether I'd be able to see, to speak, to hold a pen between my fingers. Knowing that the day might come when I'd be physically incapable of killing myself, I thought perhaps I ought to do so right away, while I still had the strength. Gradually I came to understand that the Nancy who might one day lie inert under a bedsheet, arms and legs paralyzed, unable to feed or bathe herself, unable to reach out for a gun, a bottle of pills, was not the Nancy I was at present, and that I could not presume to make decisions for that future Nancy, who might well not want in the least to die. Now the only provision I've made for the future Nancy is that when the time comes—and it is likely to come in the form of pneumonia, friend to the weak and the old—I am not to be treated with machines and medications. If she is unable to communicate by then, I hope she will be satisfied with these terms.

Thinking all the time about having MS grew tiresome and intrusive, especially in the large and tragic mode in which I was accustomed to considering my plight. Months and even years went by without catastrophe (at least without one related to MS), and really I was awfully busy, what with George and children and snakes and students and poems, and I hadn't the time, let alone the inclination, to devote myself to being a disease. Too, the richer my life became, the funnier it seemed, as though there were some connection between largesse and laughter, and so my tragic stance began to waver until, even with the aid of a brace and a cane, I couldn't hold it for very long at a time.

After several years I was satisfied with my adjustment. I had suffered my grief and fury and terror, I thought, but now I was at ease with my lot. Then one summer day I set out with George and the children across the desert for a vacation in California. Part way to Yuma I became aware that my right leg felt funny. "I think I've had an exacerbation," I told George. "What shall we do?" he asked. "I think we'd better get the hell to California," I said, "because I don't know whether I'll ever make it again." So we went on to San Diego and then to Orange, up the Pacific Coast Highway to Santa Cruz, across to Yosemite, down to Sequoia and Joshua Tree, and so back over the desert to home. It was a fine two-week trip, filled with friends and fair weather, and I wouldn't have missed it for the world, though I did in fact make it back to California two years later. Nor would there have been any point in missing it, since in MS, once the symptoms have appeared, the neurological damage has been done, and there's no way to predict or prevent that damage.

The incident spoiled my self-satisfaction, however. It renewed my grief and fury and terror, and I learned that one never finishes adjusting to MS. I don't know now why I thought one would. One does not, after all, finish adjusting to life, and MS is simply a fact of my life—not my favorite fact, of course—but as ordinary as my nose and my tropical fish and my yellow Mazda station wagon. It may at any time get worse, but no amount of worry or anticipation can prepare me for a new loss. My life is a lesson in losses. I learn one at a time.

And I had best be patient in the learning, since I'll have to do it like it or not. As any rock fan knows, you can't always get what you want. Particularly when you have MS. You can't, for example, get cured. In recent years researchers and the organizations that fund research have started to pay MS some attention even though it isn't fatal; perhaps they have begun to see that life is something other than a quantitative phenomenon, that one may be very much alive for a very long time in a life that isn't worth living. The researchers have made some progress toward understanding the mechanism of the disease: It may well be an autoimmune reaction triggered by a slow-acting virus. But they are nowhere near its prevention, control, or cure. And most of us want to be cured. Some, unable to accept incurability, grasp at one treatment after another; no matter how bizarre: megavitamin therapy, gluten-free diet, injections of cobra venom, hypothermal suits, lymphocytapheresis, hyperbaric chambers. Many treatments are probably harmless enough, but none are curative.

The absence of a cure often makes MS patients bitter toward their doctors. Doctors are, after all, the priests of modern society, the new shamans, whose business is to heal, and many an MS patient roves from one to another, searching for the "good" doctor who will make him well. Doctors too think of themselves as healers, and for this reason many have trouble dealing with MS patients, whose disease in its intransigence defeats their aims and mocks their skills. Too few doctors, it is true, treat their patients as whole human beings, but the reverse is also true. I have always tried to be gentle with my doctors, who often have more at stake in terms of ego than I do. I may be frustrated, maddened, depressed by the incurability of my disease, but I am not diminished by it, and they are. When I push myself up from my seat in the waiting room and stumble toward them, I incarnate the limitation of their powers. The least I can do is refuse to press on their tenderest spots.

This gentleness is part of the reason that I'm not sorry to be a cripple. I didn't have it before. Perhaps I'd have developed it anyway—how could I know such a thing?—and I wish I had more of it, but I'm glad of what I have. It has opened and enriched my life enormously. This sense that my frailty and need must be mirrored in others, that in searching for and shaping a stable core in a life wrenched by change and loss, change and loss, I must recognize the same process, under individual conditions, in the lives around me. I do not deprecate such knowledge, however I've come by it.

All the same, if a cure were found, would I take it? In a minute. I may be a cripple, but I'm only occasionally a loony and never a saint. Anyway, in my brand of theology God doesn't give bonus points for a limp. I'd take a cure; I just don't need one. A friend who also has MS startled me once by asking, "Do you ever say to yourself, 'Why me, Lord?'" "No, Michael, I don't," I told him, "because whenever I try, the only response I can think of is 'Why not?'" If I could make a cosmic deal, whom would I put in my place? What in my life would I give up in exchange for sound limbs and a thrilling rush of energy? No one. Nothing. I might as well do the job myself. Now that I'm getting the hang of it.

12 Ways Airports are Secretly Manipulating You

Jessica Hullinger

Jessica Hullinger is a freelance journalist who writes for publications such as Fast Company and FORTUNE. This essay appeared on the online website mental_floss on July 22, 2017.

Over the years, airports have evolved from bare-bones transportation hubs for select travelers to bustling retail centers for millions. They're being designed to both complement and influence human behavior. Everything from the architecture and lighting to the trinkets on sale in the gift shops is strategic. Here are a few tricks airports use to help travelers relax, get to their gates safely and on time, and hopefully spend some money along the way.

1. They make sure you can see the tarmac

One key to a successful airport is easy navigation. Travelers should be able to get from security to their gate without getting lost, with help from subtle design cues nudging them in the right direction. In design lingo, this process is called wayfinding. "I tell my staff that signage is an admission of failure," says Stanis Smith, executive vice president and leader of the airports sector at consulting firm Stantec. "Obviously one needs signs, but the best thing for designers to do is look for ways you can assist with wayfinding that are subtle."

For example, in many new airports, passengers can see through to the tarmac immediately after they leave security, or sooner. "More important than anything is a view directly out to airside and you see the tails of all the aircraft," says Robert Chicas, Director of Aviation and Transportation at HOK, the architectural firm that helped redesign the Indianapolis International Airport. "Does it matter whether it's your aircraft? Probably not. It gives you an orientation so you know generally that's the direction you need to head in."

2. The signs send subliminal messages

"Very, very little in the style of an airport sign is arbitrary," writes David Zweig, author of *Invisibles: The Power of Anonymous Work in an Age of Relentless Self-Promotion.* Take the font, for example. In 75% of all airports, you'll find one of three typefaces: Helvetica, Frutiger, and Clearview. All three are sans serif because it's easier to read at a distance. The unofficial rule for size, according to the Transportation Research Board's guide to wayfinding, is that every inch of letter height adds 40 feet of viewing distance (so a "3 inch tall letter would be legible from 120 feet"). Sometimes different terminals will have their own distinct signature sign design—like rounded edges or a specific color. "If you are ever in an airport or campus or hospital or other complex environment and suddenly something feels off, you sense you are going the wrong way, there's a good chance it's not just magic or some brilliant internal directional sense," Zweig writes, "but rather you may be responding to a subconscious cue like the change of shape from one sign system to another."

3.   They lighten the mood

Newer airports incorporate as many windows as possible, even in stores. "There's a trend that the shops face the tarmac. Passengers tend to walk more into shops that have direct access to the sunlight," says Julian Lukaszewicz, lecturer in aviation management at Buckinghamshire New University. "If they're closed off with artificial light passengers feel they are too dark and avoid them."

4.   They herd you with art

That big sculpture in your terminal isn't just there to look pretty. It's another tool to help travelers navigate. "We like to use things like artwork as kind of place markers that create points of reference through an airport terminal," says Smith. "For example, in Vancouver International Airport we have a spectacular 16-foot high sculpture at the center of the pre-security retail area. People say, 'Meet you at the sculpture.' It acts as a point of orientation."

Art also serves to create a sense of place, transforming the airport from a sterile people-mover to a unique atmosphere where people want to spend time (and money!). In one survey, 56% of participants said "a more culturally sensitive and authentic experience tied to the location" is something they'd like to see more in airports by 2025.

5.   They use carpeting

In many airports, the long walk from check-in to gate is paved in linoleum (or some other hard surface). But you'll notice that the gate waiting area is carpeted. This is an attempt to make holding areas more relaxing by giving them a soft, cozy feeling, like you might find in your own living room. Happy, relaxed travelers spend 7% more money on average on retail and 10% more on Duty Free items. And it doesn't stop with a layer of carpeting. Yoga rooms, spas, and even airport therapy dogs are becoming more common as airports look for new ways to relax travelers and encourage spending.

6.   The "golden hour" is key for profit

In airport manager lingo, the time between when a passenger clears security and boards their plane is called "dwell time." This is when, as the *Telegraph* puts it, "passengers are at a loose end and most likely to spend." Especially crucial is the "golden hour," the first 60 minutes spent beyond security, when passengers are "in a self-indulgent mood." Display boards listing flight information are there in part to keep you updated on your flight, but also to reassure you that you still have plenty of time to wander and shop. Similarly, some airports are installing "time to gate" signs that display how far you are from your destination. And because 40% of us would prefer to avoid human interaction when we shop, self-service kiosks are becoming more common in airport terminals. According to the Airports Council International, 50% of American airports now have robo-retailers.

7. They're increasing dwell time

The "golden hour" is great, but two golden hours are even better. "One hour more at an airport is around $7 more spent per passenger," says Lukaszewicz. Anything that's automated, from check-in to bag drop, is meant to speed things up. And it works. Research suggests automated check-in kiosks are 25% faster than humans. "A lot of airports, especially in Japan and New Zealand, are now doing this, where you don't actually get any assistance from any staff member from check-in," says Lukaszewicz. "You print your own baggage tag. You put it on the bag on the belt. You go through auto-security and immigration where there is no one. At the boarding gate you just touch your barcode and they open a gate and you walk onto the plane without any interaction." One study found that for every 10 minutes a passenger spends in the security line, they spend 30% less money on retail items. Last year, the TSA announced it would give $15,000 to the person who comes up with the best idea for speeding up security.

8. Shops are strategically placed

Most airport spending is done on impulse (no one really *needs* a giant pack of Toblerone), so the key is getting the goods out where they can be seen by as many people as possible. Shops are located where airport footfall is highest. Some airports force passengers to wander through Duty Free to get to the gates. And the more twists and turns, the better. According to one report from consulting company Intervistas, Duty-Free shops with "serpentine walk-through" designs have 60% more sales "because 100% of customers are exposed."

Shops and restaurants are often clustered to evoke a Main Street feel, because people tend to shop in bustling environments. "It's no different than if you're in a town in Europe or in Manhattan," Smith says. "Retail succeeds when it has a critical mass."

9. They go local

Airport shops are packed with souvenirs and trinkets that reflect the local culture because that's what travelers want to buy. For example, more than 20 years after its release, "Sleepless in Seattle" shirts are still a top-selling item at Seattle-Tacoma International Airport. In the Phoenix Sky Harbor Airport, shoppers go wild for potted cactus plants. "Local brands, local services, reinforce this idea of place, and that you are in a special place on your way to the rest of the world," says Ripley Rasmus, senior design principal at HOK.

10. Walkways curve to the left

The majority of humans are right-handed, and according to Intervistas, this influences airport design. "More sales are generated if a walkway curves from right to left with more merchandise and space on the right side because passengers are looking right while (perhaps unconsciously) walking left," says one report.

11. A single queue puts us at ease

While the line for check-in and security may seem absurdly long, a single queue actually lowers stress levels by increasing the perceived sense of fairness, according to Lukaszewicz. No one worries the other line is going faster than theirs, because there is no other line. "If you implement a one-queue system for check-in, or for security, so one long line and then you go just to the next available counter, passengers perceive it as more fair because each person is standing in the same line," he says. "It's strange but true because you always think the queue next to you moves quicker."

12. The security officers get conversational

Since 2007, the TSA has been pouring $200 million a year into agents trained to spot suspicious behavior in passengers. The program, called Screening of Passengers by Observation Techniques (SPOT), was developed by a psychology professor at the University of California Medical School in San Francisco named Paul Ekman. It involves a list of 94 signs of anxiety and fear, like lack of eye contact or sweating. But one report found that SPOT is ineffective because "the human ability to accurately identify deceptive behavior based on behavioral indicators is the same as or slightly better than chance."

Another method of screening passengers is simply to talk to them. A 2014 study found that asking open-ended questions—known as the Controlled Cognitive Engagement method (CCE)—is 20 times more effective than trying to monitor based on behavior. For example, an agent might ask a passenger where they're traveling before prodding them with a random question like where they went to college and what they majored in, then watch for signs of panic. "If you're a regular passenger, you're just chatting about the thing you know the best—yourself," says researcher Thomas Ormerod, PhD, head of the School of Psychology at the University of Sussex in England. "It shouldn't feel like an interrogation." In the study, officers using conversation-based screening caught 66% of deceptive passengers, compared to just 3% who used behavior-based screening.

Your Fat Friend Doesn't Feel Fat

Your Fat Friend

Your Fat Friend blogs anonymously about issues related to body positivity on the site www.yourfatfriend.com. The blogger's work appears on sites such as Upworthy, Vox, and Medium. This post appeared on Medium on April 25, 2016.

"I feel fat."

I struggle to find my breath, and then my voice. Sometimes I don't bother, because it feels so fruitless to tell you how it feels when you say that you feel fat. You ask me if I know what you mean, and I genuinely don't. I have never felt fat.

I don't feel fat. I am fat.

You feel fat for good reason. You lost ten pounds and a dress size—down to an eight!—only to go on a date with a guy who told you he wasn't attracted to "thick girls." Your coworker can't stop talking about Dr. Oz and green coffee extract, cortisol and belly fat. As a child, your grandmother told you that if you just drank mustard, you could make yourself vomit, and you'd never need to put on another pound. *You can eat whatever you want!* You follow all the rules your mother told you about—no horizontal stripes, only wear black, nothing too tight, no cap sleeves—because "you can always stand to look slimmer." Sometimes you even buy *Woman's World* or *Ladies' Home Journal*, with their ridiculous crash diets. They never work, but what if this one does?

The whole world is telling you you're not thin enough. Get skinnier, but not too skinny. Work out, but don't show your muscle tone. Whole industries have been built on the wrongness of your body, on the certainty that if you just tried harder, if you just wanted it enough, your body would metamorphose into someone else's. That structure must stand, and your dissatisfaction with your body is its foundation. Your body must remain an urgent question, forever open to painful, public debate. You must stay hungry, always hungry, never satisfied. You must remain in pursuit.

I hear those messages, too. They're delivered differently, and the fact of my body demands a different desperation. My body does not qualify me for precariousness. Mine is not a story of vigilance, but of redemption. My body is not a question, but a foregone conclusion. My body is a lost cause.

Because of the size and shape of my body, you and I have different experiences. Compliments about my appearance are always harsh, chased with pity or advice, some small reminder that I am shirking my duty to have a more expected body. I am defying the mandate to be universally desirable.

Street harassment is different, too. I am as likely to hear insults shouted from the window of a passing car as I am to be catcalled. Unwanted sexual attention looks different, men's entitlement supercharged by the expectation of desperation. They act with certainty that any fat woman will be flattered by even the most violent demands. I do not balk as readily you do, with the confidence of a woman who is regularly reminded of her beauty. I have learned my place.

Being fat is never as simple as a feeling. And feeling fat is rarely about the shape or size of a body.

Feeling fat is a shorthand. You say it when you feel unattractive, slovenly, lazy, dissatisfied and unsatisfying. My body becomes your shorthand for your shortcomings.

Feeling fat is a way to bond. It is contagious, driving a never-ending race to the bottom. It announces a contest that's impossible to win: who can vocalize the cruelest feelings about their own body? It's a performance that forges connections in the fire of self-loathing.

As a woman, that self-loathing isn't new. As a fat person, it's not novel—it's dangerous. It's a reminder of all the ways my body has failed, all the times I've been rejected, all the hurt and pain and harm that's been caused. It is never a feeling, always an impossible, isolating truth.

And *feeling fat* is counter to your politics. It assumes terrible things about beauty standards, and makes demands of women's bodies that you never would. It elicits a deep shame, not just about what we look like, but about *who we are*—a shame that you'd never intentionally make anyone feel.

Still, you say it.

I grew up queer and came out young. In middle school, my classmates would play *smear the queer*, insist that unacceptable or ridiculous behavior was *so gay*. Socially powerful boys would call less popular boys *fags*. These words all stung me then as I'm sure they sting you now. Because we know—we all know—that using someone else's experience or identity as an insult is hurtful, unacceptable, foul. It was prevalent then, but its ubiquity didn't make it right.

But *feeling fat* is uniquely insidious because it's not externalized. *Feeling fat* is a weapon designed only to use on ourselves. It's a compulsory display of the ways we've learned to hate ourselves after years, decades, generations of self-hate being required of us. It's a public performance of dissatisfaction, and our only audience is ourselves. It is a theater of war.

Still, somehow, fat people are always collateral.

Fat people are casualties of this friendly fire because our needs are so rarely considered. Countless thin friends have told me they "feel fat" because it doesn't even cross their mind that their feelings might impact me. After all, they're just feelings, right? And people are only temporarily fat, since we're all duty-bound to lose weight at all costs. If I don't lose weight, then my experience needn't be considered. Who needs to account for the feelings of the lifelong fatass?

You and I both live in a world where hating fat people isn't just common, it's mandatory. The difference is that my body is the target of all that vitriol, quarantine and fear.

In amongst all of that, I have made the unpopular and essential decision not to hate myself. Family, friends, neighbors, colleagues, doctors, magazines and television shows make me feel terrible enough as it is. I have spent years making an overflowing hope chest. I have carefully collected trinkets and rations, thinspiration and too-small clothing—supplies for the life I'll only be allowed when I'm thin.

Now, after years of methodical and mandatory self-loathing, I have decided to stop waiting. I have decided that my life is worth living now, as I am. At size 26, I will date, I will travel, I will love, I will wear bright colors, I will swim and run. I will give myself the sustenance of moments of joy, even in a world that tells me my body affords me only shame.

So every day, I wake up and decide to take on the herculean task of learning to accept my body. Some days I get as far as indifference. On brighter days, I can see glints of love for my maligned skin. That love glimmers far away, a hint of a sunrise after a long and brutal night.

After all that hard work, *feeling fat* is a reminder of all the terrible things my body represents. It reminds me of how exhausting it is to defend my self-worth every day, how much energy it takes to exist in public, to be seen. It's enough to fend off the constant stream of explicit messages about what my body ought to be without hearing friends deal with the tragic fate of *feeling like they have the body I do.*

You are a fantastic friend and a thoughtful person. You deeply value respect, fairness and dignity, and you go to great lengths to live out those values. You are also the product of a world that teaches all of us to take up the mantle of hating ourselves. When you do that, it undercuts your tenderest self, the sweetest parts of you. It cuts you off from the values you hold dearest. And your dissatisfaction with your own body puts such distance between the two of us.

Loving yourself is an extraordinary act of compassion, dear friend. You wouldn't tolerate hatred of your friends, you[r] family, your community—anyone else. Call up the strength and courage to love yourself like that. It is as urgent for my subsistence as it is for yours.

Just once, let us be the causes we live for.

Want Better Journalism? Boost News Literacy.

Dean Miller

Dean Miller is the former director for the Center for News Literacy at Stony Brook University. The longtime journalist wrote this commentary for the January 14, 2010, edition of The Christian Science Monitor.

Citizens armed with the power of discernment will do more to rescue journalism than any dozen panels of veteran editors ruminating about their golden years in power and musing about better business models.

Could you tune out the news for a full 48 hours? I mean a total blackout: No text-message news updates. No e-mail with news in it. No newspapers. No magazines. No weather channel. No ESPN and certainly no CBS News, Fox News, or CNN. No radio. No websites that include news. No news reports on planes, atop gas pumps, or from screens in the back of taxicabs.

You'd even have to walk away from conversations about the news and leave the room if someone turns on a news show.

That's a real homework assignment we give students on their first day of class in a News Literacy course invented at Long Island's Stony Brook University.

It sounds easy enough—especially to the many students who enter the course saying they don't follow the news.

But after just two days, students report an amazing discovery: They have to work really hard to avoid it.

And with that fresh insight—that they are in fact passively being fed news all the time—these undergraduates are ready for a semester of hard work.

There's a lesson here for all of us who worry about the quality of journalism today: Citizens armed with the power of discernment will do more to rescue journalism than any dozen panels of veteran editors ruminating about their golden years in power and musing about better business models.

Unfortunately, most Millennial Generation students have been deprived of a good civics class. They're bombarded with 100,000 words' worth of information a day, yet they are unsure how government works or even who is in charge, and they don't know how to find trustworthy news in the torrent of information that besets them.

That's where the News Literacy curriculum comes in. It aims to sharpen their critical thinking skills, reteach the history of America's fourth estate, and start students on the lifetime search for reliable information.

This is a course an old-school journalist can teach spectacularly well, it turns out. At Stony Brook, Syracuse University, and a growing number of other campuses across America, the lectures and many of the small group classes in News Literacy are taught by journalists, recovering and active. The course gets consistently high marks from students, who say these are skills they'll use all their lives.

Since there's an overabundance of pontificating former editors offering their successors unwanted advice on how to rescue the news by fighting the future, I offer aging journalists this alternative:

Come work among the consumers for a while. It is amazing what you unlearn when you teach a course like this one, in which citizens come of age and decide how to run the world better than you did.

This isn't about reaching out to journalism majors. It's about preparing all students for full citizenship, which is why News Literacy enrolls students from all majors.

Many in my course are the first person in their family to attend college. Many come from multilingual homes. Most are on financial aid. All of them are digital natives.

In this course, they write up to two papers a week on their way to a firm grasp on verification, independence, and accountability as the distinguishing characteristics of journalism.

They write briefs and argue the treason/free speech case arising from fourth estate decisions to expose controversial executive branch actions in wartime.

To plumb the bias all readers bring to news coverage, students participate online in an ongoing Harvard University research study called Project Implicit, which measures their potential prejudices. They study cognitive dissonance—how people tend to dismiss ideas or facts that contradict their beliefs—and the natural quest for validation. They become expert at dissecting faulty accusations of media bias and at constructing meaningful examples of actual bias in news coverage.

Finally, they dissect specific stories using those ideas, plus a welter of classical lessons about rhetoric, evidence, and shoe-leather sourcing.

From that first news blackout, they progress to active deconstruction of the news in search of specific answers: Should I get the H1N1 vaccine? Will healthcare reform serve my family's needs? Can I trust a news organization that routinely airs unverified assertions?

Some cop a cynical pose. But more students push past black-and-white judgment into an inquiring mode: How much weight should I give this specific news item; what other information should I go seek; as an online "author," what is my responsibility before I forward a salacious e-mail or post a rumor on my blog?

Once students learn to seek truth instead of accept truth, they are well on their way to the kind of power the Founders abundantly reserved for American citizens.

Journalism's elders have a great deal to offer to students in this course. It permits a little pontification, but also requires professors to listen and learn how news gets used by busy strivers who have strong civic impulses and little patience for self-important news figures.

It's all about that sovereign individual, the news consumer, learning enough skills to gather reliable information and strike out on their own. This is the legacy we offer journalism's elders: stop wringing your hands. Teach what you know about the value of stubborn civic facts. Your guesses about a profitable new business model for news aren't worth much, but a generation of savvy news consumers is worth a great deal.

Rhetoric

Address to the Nation on the September 11th Attacks

Immediately after the terrorist attacks on September 11, 2001, a number of speeches were given to reassure the American people and to rally them around a common cause. This speech was President Bush's formal address to the nation, which established the language and content for many that followed. This version of the text was published by CNN the day it was given.

(CNN)—The text of President Bush's address Tuesday night, after terrorist attacks on New York and Washington:

Good evening.

Today, our fellow citizens, our way of life, our very freedom came under attack in a series of deliberate and deadly terrorist acts.

The victims were in airplanes or in their offices—secretaries, businessmen and women, military and federal workers. Moms and dads. Friends and neighbors.

Thousands of lives were suddenly ended by evil, despicable acts of terror.

The pictures of airplanes flying into buildings, fires burning, huge structures collapsing, have filled us with disbelief, terrible sadness and a quiet, unyielding anger.

These acts of mass murder were intended to frighten our nation into chaos and retreat. But they have failed. Our country is strong. A great people has been moved to defend a great nation.

Terrorist attacks can shake the foundations of our biggest buildings, but they cannot touch the foundation of America. These acts shatter steel, but they cannot dent the steel of American resolve.

America was targeted for attack because we're the brightest beacon for freedom and opportunity in the world. And no one will keep that light from shining.

Today, our nation saw evil, the very worst of human nature, and we responded with the best of America, with the daring of our rescue workers, with the caring for strangers and neighbors who came to give blood and help in any way they could.

Immediately following the first attack, I implemented our government's emergency response plans. Our military is powerful, and it's prepared. Our emergency teams are working in New York City and Washington, D.C., to help with local rescue efforts.

Our first priority is to get help to those who have been injured and to take every precaution to protect our citizens at home and around the world from further attacks.

The functions of our government continue without interruption. Federal agencies in Washington which had to be evacuated today are reopening for essential personnel tonight and will be open for business tomorrow.

Our financial institutions remain strong, and the American economy will be open for business as well.

The search is underway for those who are behind these evil acts. I've directed the full resources for our intelligence and law enforcement communities to find those responsible and bring them to justice. We will make no distinction between the terrorists who committed these acts and those who harbor them.

I appreciate so very much the members of Congress who have joined me in strongly condemning these attacks. And on behalf of the American people, I thank the many world leaders who have called to offer their condolences and assistance.

America and our friends and allies join with all those who want peace and security in the world and we stand together to win the war against terrorism.

Tonight I ask for your prayers for all those who grieve, for the children whose worlds have been shattered, for all whose sense of safety and security has been threatened. And I pray they will be comforted by a power greater than any of us spoken through the ages in Psalm 23: "Even though I walk through the valley of the shadow of death, I fear no evil, for You are with me."

This is a day when all Americans from every walk of life unite in our resolve for justice and peace. America has stood down enemies before, and we will do so this time.

None of us will ever forget this day, yet we go forward to defend freedom and all that is good and just in our world.

Thank you. Good night and God bless America.

Text of President Obama's Speech on the Death of bin Laden

As was the case with the 9/11 attacks, the death of Osama bin Laden was the cause of many speeches to the American public. This speech, delivered on May 1, 2011, was President Obama's public announcement of the event and outlines the history leading up to the SEAL team assault credited with killing bin Laden. This version of the text was posted on *The Daily Kos* by Susan Gardner shortly after it was delivered.

Good evening. Tonight, I can report to the American people and to the world that the United States has conducted an operation that killed Osama bin Laden, the leader of al Qaeda, and a terrorist who's responsible for the murder of thousands of innocent men, women, and children.

It was nearly 10 years ago that a bright September day was darkened by the worst attack on the American people in our history. The images of 9/11 are seared into our national memory—hijacked planes cutting through a cloudless September sky; the Twin Towers collapsing to the ground; black smoke billowing up from the Pentagon; the wreckage of Flight 93 in Shanksville, Pennsylvania, where the actions of heroic citizens saved even more heartbreak and destruction.

And yet we know that the worst images are those that were unseen to the world. The empty seat at the dinner table. Children who were forced to grow up without their mother or their father. Parents who would never know the feeling of their child's embrace. Nearly 3,000 citizens taken from us, leaving a gaping hole in our hearts.

On September 11, 2001, in our time of grief, the American people came together. We offered our neighbors a hand, and we offered the wounded our blood. We reaffirmed our ties to each other, and our love of community and country. On that day, no matter where we came from, what God we prayed to, or what race or ethnicity we were, we were united as one American family.

We were also united in our resolve to protect our nation and to bring those who committed this vicious attack to justice. We quickly learned that the 9/11 attacks were carried out by al Qaeda—an organization headed by Osama bin Laden, which had openly declared war on the United States and was committed to killing innocents in our country and around the globe. And so we went to war against al Qaeda to protect our citizens, our friends, and our allies.

Over the last 10 years, thanks to the tireless and heroic work of our military and our counterterrorism professionals, we've made great strides in that effort. We've disrupted terrorist attacks and strengthened our homeland defense. In Afghanistan, we removed the Taliban government, which had given bin Laden and al Qaeda safe haven and support. And around the globe, we worked with our friends and allies to capture or kill scores of al Qaeda terrorists, including several who were a part of the 9/11 plot.

Yet Osama bin Laden avoided capture and escaped across the Afghan border into Pakistan. Meanwhile, al Qaeda continued to operate from along that border and operate through its affiliates across the world.

And so shortly after taking office, I directed Leon Panetta, the director of the CIA, to make the killing or capture of bin Laden the top priority of our war against al Qaeda, even as we continued our broader efforts to disrupt, dismantle, and defeat his network.

Then, last August, after years of painstaking work by our intelligence community, I was briefed on a possible lead to bin Laden. It was far from certain, and it took many months to run this thread to ground. I met repeatedly with my national security team as we developed more information about the possibility that we had located bin Laden hiding within a compound deep inside of Pakistan. And finally, last week, I determined that we had enough intelligence to take action, and authorized an operation to get Osama bin Laden and bring him to justice.

Today, at my direction, the United States launched a targeted operation against that compound in Abbottabad, Pakistan. A small team of Americans carried out the operation with extraordinary courage and capability. No Americans were harmed. They took care to avoid civilian casualties. After a firefight, they killed Osama bin Laden and took custody of his body.

For over two decades, bin Laden has been al Qaeda's leader and symbol, and has continued to plot attacks against our country and our friends and allies. The death of bin Laden marks the most significant achievement to date in our nation's effort to defeat al Qaeda.

Yet his death does not mark the end of our effort. There's no doubt that al Qaeda will continue to pursue attacks against us. We must—and we will—remain vigilant at home and abroad.

As we do, we must also reaffirm that the United States is not—and never will be—at war with Islam. I've made clear, just as President Bush did shortly after 9/11, that our war is not against Islam. Bin Laden was not a Muslim leader; he was a mass murderer of Muslims. Indeed, al Qaeda has slaughtered scores of Muslims in many countries, including our own. So his demise should be welcomed by all who believe in peace and human dignity.

Over the years, I've repeatedly made clear that we would take action within Pakistan if we knew where bin Laden was. That is what we've done. But it's important to note that our counterterrorism cooperation with Pakistan helped lead us to bin Laden and the compound where he was hiding. Indeed, bin Laden had declared war against Pakistan as well, and ordered attacks against the Pakistani people.

Tonight, I called President Zardari, and my team has also spoken with their Pakistani counterparts. They agree that this is a good and historic day for both of our nations. And going forward, it is essential that Pakistan continue to join us in the fight against al Qaeda and its affiliates.

The American people did not choose this fight. It came to our shores, and started with the senseless slaughter of our citizens. After nearly 10 years of service, struggle, and sacrifice, we know well the costs of war. These efforts weigh on me every time I, as Commander-in-Chief, have to sign a letter to a family that has lost a loved one, or look into the eyes of a service member who's been gravely wounded.

So Americans understand the costs of war. Yet as a country, we will never tolerate our security being threatened, nor stand idly by when our people have been killed. We will be relentless in defense of our citizens and our friends and allies. We will be true to the values that make us who we are. And on nights like this one, we can say to those families who have lost loved ones to al Qaeda's terror: Justice has been done.

Tonight, we give thanks to the countless intelligence and counterterrorism professionals who've worked tirelessly to achieve this outcome. The American people do not see their work, nor know their names. But tonight, they feel the satisfaction of their work and the result of their pursuit of justice.

We give thanks for the men who carried out this operation, for they exemplify the professionalism, patriotism, and unparalleled courage of those who serve our country. And they are part of a generation that has borne the heaviest share of the burden since that September day.

Finally, let me say to the families who lost loved ones on 9/11 that we have never forgotten your loss, nor wavered in our commitment to see that we do whatever it takes to prevent another attack on our shores.

And tonight, let us think back to the sense of unity that prevailed on 9/11. I know that it has, at times, frayed. Yet today's achievement is a testament to the greatness of our country and the determination of the American people.

The cause of securing our country is not complete. But tonight, we are once again reminded that America can do whatever we set our mind to. That is the story of our history, whether it's the pursuit of prosperity for our people, or the struggle for equality for all our citizens; our commitment to stand up for our values abroad, and our sacrifices to make the world a safer place.

Let us remember that we can do these things not just because of wealth or power, but because of who we are: one nation, under God, indivisible, with liberty and justice for all.

Thank you. May God bless you. And may God bless the United States of America.

The Art of Controversy

Ambrose Bierce

Ambrose Bierce (1842-1914?) was an American essayist, journalist, satirist, and the author of a number of short stories including "An Occurrence at Owl Creek Bridge." He disappeared in 1913 while in Mexico to observe the Mexican Revolution. This version of his essay was originally published in 1899.

I

One who has not lived a life of controversy, yet has some knowledge of its laws and methods, would, I think, find a difficulty in conceiving the infantile ignorance of the race in general as to what constitutes argument, evidence and proof. Even lawyers and judges, whose profession it is to consider evidence, to sift it and pass upon it, are but little wiser in that way than others when the matter in hand is philosophy, or religion, or something outside the written law. Concerning these high themes, I have heard from the lips of hoary benchers so idiotic argument based on so meaningless evidence as made me shudder at the thought of being tried before them on an indictment charging me with having swallowed a neighbor's step-ladder. Yet doubtless in a matter of mere law these venerable babes would deliver judgment that would be roughly reasonable and approximately right. The theologian, on the contrary, is never so irrational as in his own trade; for, whatever religion may be, theology is a thing of unreason altogether, an edifice of assumptions and dreams, a superstructure without a substructure, an invention of the devil. It is to religion what law is to justice, what etiquette is to courtesy, astrology to astronomy, alchemy to chemistry and medicine to hygiene. The theologian cannot reason, for persons who can reason do not go in for theology. Its name refutes it: theology means discourse of God, concerning whom some of its expounders say that he has no existence and all the others that he cannot be known.

I set out to show the folly of men who think they think—to give a few typical examples of what they are pleased to call "evidence" supporting their views. I shall take them from the work of a man of far more than the average intelligence dealing with the doctrine of immortality. He is a believer and thinks it possible that immortal human souls are on an endless journey from star to star, inhabiting them in turn. And he "proves" it thus:

"No one thinks of space without knowing that it can be traversed; consequently the conception of space implies the ability to traverse it."

But how far? He could as cogently say: "No one thinks of the ocean without knowing that it can be swum in; consequently the conception of ocean implies the ability to swim from New York to Liverpool." Here is another precious bit of testimony:

"The fact that man can conceive the idea of space without beginning or end implies that man is on a journey without beginning or end. In fact, it is strong evidence of the immortality of man."

Good—now observe the possibilities in that kind of "reasoning." The fact that a pig can conceive the idea of a turnip implies that the pig is climbing a tree bearing turnips—which is strong evidence that the pig is a fish. In each of the gentleman's *dicta* the first part no more "implies" what follows than it implies a weeping baboon on a crimson iceberg.

Of the same unearthly sort are two more of this innocent's deliveries:

"The fact that we do not remember our former lives is no proof of our never having existed. We would remember them if we had accomplished something worth remembering."

Note the unconscious *petitio principii* involved in the first "our" and the pure assumption in the second sentence.

"We all know that character, traits and habits are as distinct in young children as in adults. This shows that if we had no preexistence all men would have the same character and traits and appearance, and would be turned out on the same model."

As apples are, for example, or pebbles, or cats. Unfortunately we do not "all" know, nor does any of us know, nor is it true, that young children have as much individuality as adults. And if we did all know it, or if any of us knew it, or if it were true, neither the fact itself nor the knowledge of it would "show" any such thing as that the differences could be produced by pre-existence only. They might be due to the will of God, or to some agency that no man has ever thought about, or has thought about but has not known to have that effect. In point of fact, we know that such peculiarities of character and disposition as a young child has are not brought from a former life across a gulf whose brinks are death and birth, but are endowments from the lives of others here. They are not individual, but hereditary—not vestigial, but ancestral.

The kind of "argument" here illustrated by horrible example is not peculiar to religious nor doctrinal themes, but characterizes men's reasoning in general. It is the rule everywhere—in oral discussion, in books, in newspapers. Assertions that mean nothing, testimony that is not evidence, facts having no relation to the matter in hand, and (everywhere and always) the sickening *non sequitur*: the conclusion that has nothing to do with the premises. I know not if there is another life, but if there is I do hope that to obtain it all will have to pass a rigid examination in logic and the art of not being a fool.

II

In an unfriendly controversy it is Important to remember that the public, in most cases, neither cares for the outcome of the fray, nor will remember its incidents. The controversialist should therefore confine his efforts and powers to accomplishment of two main purposes: 1—entertainment of the reader; 2—personal gratification. For the first of these objects no rules can be given; the good writer will entertain and the bad one will not, no matter what is the subject. The second is accomplishable (a) by guarding your self-respect; (b) by destroying your adversary's self-respect; (c) by making him respect you, against his will, as much as you respect yourself; (d) by provoking him into the blunder of permitting you to despise him. It follows that any falsification, prevarication, dodging, misrepresentation or other cheating on the part of one antagonist is a distinct advantage to the other, and by him devoutly to be wished. The public cares nothing for it, and if deceived will forget the deception; but he never forgets. I would no more willingly let my opponent find a flaw in my truth, honesty and frankness than in fencing I would let him beat down my guard. Of that part of victory which consists in respecting yourself and making your adversary respect you you can be always sure if you are worthy of respect; of that part which consists in despising him and making him despise himself you are not sure; that depends on his skill. He may be a very despicable person yet so cunning of fence that is to say, so frank and honest in writing that you will not find out his unworth. Remember that what you want is not so much to disclose his meanness to the reader (who cares nothing about it) as to make him disclose it to your private discernment. That is the whole gospel of controversial strategy.

You are one of two gladiators in the arena: your first duty is to amuse the multitude. But as the multitude is not going to remember very long after leaving the show who was victorious, it is not worthwhile to take any hurts for a merely visible advantage. So fight as to prove to yourself and to your adversary that you are the abler swordsman—that is the more honorable man. Victory in that is important· for it is lasting and is enjoyed ever afterward when you see or think of the vanquished. If in the battle I get a foul stroke, that is a distinct gain, for I never by any possibility forget that the man who delivered it is a foul man. That is what I wanted to think him, and the very thing which he should most strenuously have striven to prevent my knowing. I may meet him the street, at the club, any place where I cannot help; under whatever circumstances he becomes present to my consciousness I find a fresh delight in recalling my moral superiority and in despising him anew. Is it not strange, then, that ninety-nine disputants in a hundred deliberately and in cold blood concede to their antagonists this supreme and decisive advantage in pursuit of one which is merely illusory? Their faults are, first of course, lack of character; second, lack of sense. They are like an enraged mob engaged in hostilities without having taken the trouble to know something of the art of war. Happily for them, if they are defeated they do not know it: they have not even the sense to ascribe their sufferings to their wounds.

Chief Red Cloud on Indian Rights

Chief Red Cloud

Red Cloud (1822-1909) was the chief of the Teton Sioux (Oglala Lakota). He led a successful campaign against westward expansion of the United States, popularly known as Red Cloud's War, from 1866-1868 but was instrumental in helping his people adjust to reservation life after signing the Treaty of Ft. Laramie in 1868. This speech was delivered at a reception in his honor at Cooper Union in New York on 16 July, 1870, while he was on a tour of the East Coast to bolster support for Native American rights. Despite being a vocal critic of the US federal government and its Indian Agencies for the rest of his life, Red Cloud opposed further wars which would be detrimental to his people.

My brethren and my friends who are here before me this day, God Almighty has made us all, and He is here to bless what I have to say to you today. The Good Spirit made us both. He gave you lands and He gave us lands; He gave us these lands; you came in here, and we respected you as brothers. God Almighty made you but made you all white and clothed you; when He made us He made us with red skins and poor; now you have come.

When you first came we were very many, and you were few; now you are many, and we are getting very few, and we are poor. You do not know who appears before you today to speak. I am a representative of the original American race, the first people of this continent. We are good and not bad. The reports that you hear concerning us are all on one side. We are always well-disposed to them. You are here told that we are traders and thieves, and it is not so. We have given you nearly all our lands, and if we had any more land to give we would be very glad to give it. We have nothing more. We are driven into a very little land, and we want you now, as our dear friends, to help us with the government of the United States.

The Great Father made us poor and ignorant—made you rich and wise and more skillful in these things that we know nothing about. The Great Father, the Good Father in Heaven, made you all to eat tame food—made us to eat wild food—gives us the wild food. You ask anybody who has gone through our country to California; ask those who have settled there and in Utah, and you will find that we have treated them always well. You have children; we have children. You want to raise your children and make them happy and prosperous; we want to raise and make them happy and prosperous. We ask you to help us to do it.

At the mouth of the Horse Creek, in 1852, the Great Father made a treaty with us by which we agreed to let all that country open for fifty-five years for the transit of those who were going through. We kept this treaty; we never treated any man wrong; we never committed any murder or depredation until afterward the troops were sent into that country, and the troops killed our people and ill-treated them, and thus war and trouble arose; but before the troops were sent there we were quiet and peaceable, and there was no disturbance. Since that time there have been various goods sent from time to time to us, the only ones that ever reached us, and then after they reached us (very soon after) the government took them away. You, as good men, ought to help us to these goods.

Colonel Fitzpatrick of the government said we must all go to farm, and some of the people went to Fort Laramie and were badly treated. I only want to do that which is peaceful, and the Great Fathers know it, and also the Great Father who made us both. I came to Washington to see the Great Father in order to have peace and in order to have peace continue. That is all we want, and that is the reason why we are here now.

In 1868 men came out and brought papers. We are ignorant and do not read papers, and they did not tell us right what was in these papers. We wanted them to take away their forts, leave our country, would not make war, and give our traders something. They said we had bound ourselves to trade on the Missouri, and we said, no, we did not want that. The interpreters deceived us. When I went to Washington I saw the Great Father. The Great Father showed me what the treaties were; he showed me all these points and showed me that the interpreters had deceived me and did not let me know what the right side of the treaty was. All I want is right and justice....I represent the Sioux Nation; they will be governed by what I say and what I represent....

Look at me. I am poor and naked, but I am the Chief of the Nation. We do not want riches, we do not ask for riches, but we want our children properly trained and brought up. We look to you for your sympathy. Our riches will ... do us no good; we cannot take away into the other world anything we have—we want to have love and peace....We would like to know why commissioners are sent out there to do nothing but rob [us] and get the riches of this world away from us?

I was brought up among the traders and those who came out there in those early times. I had a good time for they treated us nicely and well. They taught me how to wear clothes and use tobacco, and to use firearms and ammunition, and all went on very well until the Great Father sent out another kind of men—men who drank whisky. He sent out whisky-men, men who drank and quarreled, men who were so bad that he could not keep them at home, and so he sent them out there. I have sent a great many words to the Great Father, but I don't know that they ever reach the Great Father. They were drowned on the way, therefore I was a little offended with it. The words I told the Great Father lately would never come to him, so I thought I would come and tell you myself.

And I am going to leave you today, and I am going back to my home. I want to tell the people that we cannot trust his agents and superintendents. I don't want strange people that we know nothing about. I am very glad that you belong to us. I am very glad that we have come here and found you and that we can understand one another. I don't want any more such men sent out there, who are so poor that when they come out there their first thoughts are how they can fill their own pockets.

We want preserves in our reserves. We want honest men, and we want you to help to keep us in the lands that belong to us so that we may not be a prey to those who are viciously disposed. I am going back home. I am very glad that you have listened to me, and I wish you goodbye and give you an affectionate farewell.

The Tyranny of Principles

Stephen Toulmin

Stephen Toulmin (1922 -2009) was a British philosopher whose work focused on moral reasoning and argument. The emphasis in his work on ethics, and their practical application can be seen in his model for argument (discussed in this book). Born in England and taking his degree from Cambridge, Toulmin taught for most of his life in the United States, including appointments at the University of Chicago, Columbia, Dartmouth, and Stanford. This essay originally appeared in *The Hastings Center Report* in 1981 and demonstrates the ways in which Toulmin applied moral logic to argument and analysis.

If this were a sermon (and perhaps it is), its text would be the quotation attributed to H.L. Mencken that hangs in the staff lounge at The Hastings Center:

> For every human problem, there is a solution that is simple, neat, and wrong.[1]

Oversimplification is a temptation to which moral philosophers are not immune, despite all their admirable intellectual care and seriousness; and the abstract generalizations of theoretical ethics are, I shall argue, no substitute for a sound tradition in practical ethics.

These days, public debates about ethical issues oscillate between, on the one hand, a narrow dogmatism that confines itself to unqualified general assertions dressed up as "matters of principle" and, on the other, a shallow relativism that evades all firm stands by suggesting that we choose our "value systems" as freely as we choose our clothes. Both approaches suffer from the same excess of generality. The rise of anthropology and the other human sciences in the early twentieth century encouraged a healthy sense of social and cultural differences; but this was uncritically taken as implying an end to all objectivity in practical ethics. The subsequent reassertion of ethical objectivity has led, in turn, to an insistence on the absoluteness of moral principles that is not balanced by a feeling for the complex problems of discrimination that arise when such principles are applied to particular real-life cases. So, the relativists have tended to overinterpret the need for discrimination in ethics, discretion in public administration, and equity in law, as a license for general personal subjectivity. The absolutists have responded by denying all real scope for personal judgment in ethics, insisting instead on

---

1 President Jimmy Carter used this quotation in a speech and attributed it to H.L. Mencken. However, the Humanities Section of the Enoch Pratt Library in Baltimore has been unable to locate it in Mencken's works.

strict construction in the law, on unfeeling consistency in public administration, and—above all—on the "inerrancy" of moral principles.

I propose to concentrate my attention on this last phenomenon—the revival of a tyrannical absolutism in recent discussions about social and personal ethics. I find it reflected in attitudes toward politics, public affairs, and the administration of justice, as much as toward questions of "ethics" in a narrower and more personal sense. My main purpose will be to ask: What is it about our present situation that inclines us to move in that direction? By way of reply, I shall argue that, in all large industrialized societies and cultures—regardless of their economic and political systems—ethics, law, and public administration have recently undergone similar historical transformations, so that all three fields are exposed to the same kinds of pressures, face common difficulties, and share in the same resulting public distrust. And I shall try to show what we can learn about those shared problems, and about the responses that they call for, by studying the common origins of our basic ethical, legal, and political ideas. All my central examples will be concerned with the same general topic: the nature, scope, and force of "rules" and "principles" in ethics and in law. Three personal experiences helped to bring these problems into focus for me.

Three Personal Experiences

Human Subjects Research. For several years in the mid-1970s, I worked as a staff member with the National Commission for the Protection of Human Subjects of Biomedical and Behavioral Research, which was established by the U.S. Congress, with the task of reporting and making recommendations about the ethics of using human subjects in medical and psychological research. Eleven commissioners—five of them scientists, the remaining six lawyers, theologians, and other nonscientists—were instructed to make recommendations about publicly financed human experimentation: in particular, to determine under what conditions subjects belonging to certain vulnerable groups (such as young children and prisoners) could participate in such research without moral objection.[2]

Before the Commission began work, many onlookers assumed that its discussions would degenerate into a Babel of rival opinions. One worldly commentator remarked in the *New England Journal of Medicine*, "Now (I suppose) we shall see matters of eternal principle decided by a six to five vote."[3] But things did not work out that way. In practice, the commissioners were never split along the line between scientists and nonscientists. In almost every case they came close to agreement even about quite detailed recommendations—at least for so long as their discussions proceeded taxonomically, taking one difficult class of cases at a time and comparing it in detail with other clearer and easier classes of cases.

---

2   The work of the U.S. National Commission for the Protection of Human Subjects of Biomedical and Behavioral Research will be discussed more fully in a paper to be published in a forthcoming Hastings Center volume on the "closure" of technical and scientific discussions.
3   So, at any rate, current legend reports. On the other hand, having worked through the files of the *Journal* for 1974-75 without finding any article or editorial on the subject, I am inclined to suspect that this may have been a casual remark by the late Dr. Franz Ingelfinger, the distinguished editor of the periodical.

Even when the Commission's recommendations were not unanimous, the discussions in no way resembled Babel: the commissioners were never in any doubt what it was that they were *not quite unanimous about*. Babel set in only afterwards. When the eleven individual commissioners asked themselves what "principles" underlay and supposedly justified their adhesion to the consensus, each of them answered in his or her own way: the Catholics appealed to Catholic principles, the humanists to humanist principles, and so on. They could agree; they could agree what they were agreeing about; but, apparently, they could not agree why they agreed about it.

This experience prompted me to wonder what this final "appeal to principles" really achieved. Certainly it did not add any weight or certitude to the commissioners' specific ethical recommendations, for example, about the kind of consent procedures required in biomedical research using five-year-old children. They were, quite evidently, surer about these shared, particular judgments than they were about the discordant general principles on which, in theory, their practical judgments were based. If anything, the appeal to principles undermined the recommendations by suggesting to onlookers that there was more disharmony than ever showed up in the commissioners' actual discussions. So, by the end of my tenure with the Commission I had begun to suspect that the point of "appealing to principles" was something quite else: not to give particular ethical judgments a more solid foundation, but rather to square the collective ethical conclusions of the Commission as a whole with each individual commissioner's other *non*ethical commitments. So (it seemed to me) the principles of Catholic ethics tell us more about Catholicism than they do about ethics, the principles of Jewish or humanist ethics more about Judaism or humanism than about ethics. Such principles serve less as foundations, adding intellectual strength or force to particular moral opinions, than they do as corridors or curtain walls linking the moral perceptions of all reflective human beings, with other, more general positions—theological, philosophical, ideological, or *Weltanschaulich*.

Abortion. The years of the National Commission's work were also years during which the morality of abortion became a matter of public controversy. In fact, the U.S. Congress established the Commission in the backwash of the Supreme Court's ruling on the legality of abortion, following a public dispute about research on the human fetus. And before long the public debate about abortion acquired some of the same puzzling features as the proceedings of the Commission itself. On the one hand, there were those who could discuss the morality of abortion temperately and with discrimination, acknowledging that here, as in other agonizing human situations, conflicting considerations are involved and that a just, if sometimes painful, balance has to be struck between different rights and claims, interests and responsibilities.[4] That temperate approach underlay traditional common law doctrines about abortion before the first statutory restrictions were enacted in the years around 1825. It was also the approach adopted by the U.S. Supreme Court in the classic case, *Roe v. Wade*; and, most important, it was the approach clearly

---

4   Daniel Callahan, *Abortion: Law, Choice and Morality* (New York: Macmillan, 1970); John T. Noonan, Jr., ed., *The Morality of Abortion: Legal and Historical Perspectives* (Cambridge, Mass.: Harvard University Press, 1970).

spelled out by Thomas Aquinas, whose position was close to that of the common law and the Supreme Court. (He acknowledged that the balance of moral considerations necessarily tilts in different directions at different stages in a woman's pregnancy, with crucial changes beginning around the time of "quickening."[5]) On the other hand, much of the public rhetoric increasingly came to turn on "matters of principle." As a result, the abortion debate became less temperate, less discriminating, and above all less resolvable. Too often, in subsequent years, the issue has boiled down to pure head-butting: an embryo's unqualified "right to life" being pitted against a woman's equally unqualified "right to choose." Those who have insisted on dealing with the issue at the level of high theory thus guarantee that the only possible practical outcome is deadlock.

Social Welfare Benefits. My perplexities about the force and value of "rules" and "principles" were further sharpened as the result of a television news magazine program about a handicapped young woman who had difficulties with the local Social Security office. Her Social Security payments were not sufficient to cover her rent and food, so she started an answering service, which she operated through the telephone at her bedside. The income from this service—though itself less than a living wage—made all the difference to her. When the local Social Security office heard about this extra income, however, they reduced her benefits accordingly; in addition, they ordered her to repay some of the money she had been receiving. (Apparently, they regarded her as a case of "welfare fraud.") The television reporter added two final statements. Since the report had been filmed, he told us, the young woman, in despair, had taken her own life. To this he added his personal comment that "there should be a *rule* to prevent this kind of thing from happening."

Notice that the reporter did not say, "The local office should be given discretion to waive, or at least bend, the existing rules in hard cases." What he said was, "There should be an *additional* rule to prevent such inequities in the future." Justice, he evidently believed, can be ensured only by establishing an adequate system of rules, and injustice can be prevented only by adding more rules.

Hence, the questions that arise from these experiences: What force and function do rules or principles truly possess, either in law or in ethics? What social and historical circumstances make it most natural and appropriate to discuss legal and ethical issues in the language of "rules" and "principles"? Why are our own contemporary legal and ethical discussions so preoccupied with rules and principles? And to what extent would we do better to look for justice and morality in other directions?

Rules in Roman Law

Far from playing an indispensable part in either law or ethics, "rules" have only a limited and conditional role. The current vogue for rules and principles is the outcome of certain powerful factors in recent social history; but these factors have always been balanced against counterweights. Justice has always required both law and equity, while morality has always demanded both fairness and discrimination.

---

5   Thomas Aquinas, *Commentarium Libro Tertio Sententiarum*, D.3, Q.5, A.2, Solutio.

When this essential duality is ignored, reliance on unchallengeable principles can generate, or become the instrument of, its own subtle kind of tyranny.

My reading soon led me back to Peter Stein's *Regulae Juris*, which traces the development of the concept of a "rule" in Roman law from its beginnings to the modern era.[6] His account of the earliest phases of Roman law was for me the most striking part. For the first three hundred years of Roman history, the legal system made no explicit use of the concept of rules. The College of Pontiffs acted as the city's judges, and individual pontiffs gave their adjudications on the cases submitted to them. But they were not required to cite any general rules as justifications for their decisions. Indeed, they were not required to give reasons at all. Their task was not to argue, but rather to pontificate.

How was this possible? How can any system of law operate in the absence of rules, reasons, and all the associated apparatus of binding force and precedent? Indeed, in such a situation can we say a true system of law exists at all? Those questions require us to consider the historical and anthropological circumstances of early Rome. Initially Rome was a small and relatively homogeneous community, whose members shared a correspondingly homogeneous tradition of ideas about justice and fairness, property and propriety, a tradition having more in common with Sir Henry Maine's ideas about traditional "customary law" than with the "positive law" of John Austin's *Province of Jurisprudence Determined*.[7] In any such community the functions of adjudication tend to be more arbitral than regulatory. Like labor arbitrators today, the judges will not be as sharply bound by precedent as contemporary high court judges. So the disputes that the pontiffs adjudicated were typically ones about which the traditional consensus was ambiguous; the balance of rights and obligations between the parties required the judgment call of a trusted and disinterested arbitrator. In these marginal cases all that the arbitrator may be able to say is, "Having taken all the circumstances into account, I find that on this particular occasion it would, all in all, be more reasonable to tilt the scale to A rather than to B. "This ruling will rest, not on the application of general legal rules, but rather on the exercise of judicial discrimination in assessing the balance of particulars. Initially, "pontificating" did not mean laying down the law in a dogmatic manner. Rather, it meant resolving marginal disputes by an equitable arbitration, and the pontiffs had the trust of their fellow citizens in doing so.

This state of affairs did not last. Long before the first Imperial codification, Roman law began to develop the full apparatus of "rules" with which we ourselves are familiar. Stein suggests that five sets of factors contributed to this new reliance on *regulae*.[8] First, as the city grew, the case load increased beyond what the pontiffs themselves could manage. Junior judges, who did not possess the same implicit trust as the pontiffs, were brought in to resolve disputes; so the consistency of their rulings had to be "regularized." Second, with the rise of lawyering as a profession, law schools were set up and *regulae* were articulated for the purpose of teaching the

---

6   Peter Stein, *Regulae Juris* (Edinburgh: Edinburgh University Press, 1966), pp. 4-10.

7   Lloyd A. Fallers, *Law without Precedent* (Chicago: University of Chicago Press, 1969): see also the classical discussion by Sir Henry Maine in *Lectures on the Early History of Institutions* (1914).

8   Stein, pp. 26ff, 80-82, 124-27.

law. Discretion, which had rested earlier on the personal characters of the pontiffs themselves and which is not so easy to teach, began to be displaced by formal rules and more teachable argumentative skills. Third, Rome acquired an empire, and foreign peoples came under the city's authority. Their systems of customary law had to be put into harmony with the Roman system, and this could be done only by establishing a concordance between the "rules" of different systems. Fourth, the empire itself developed a bureaucracy, which could not operate except on the basis of rules. Finally, the intellectual discussion of law was pursued in the context of Greek philosophy. Although Cicero, for example, was a practicing attorney, he was also a philosophical scholar with a professional interest in the Stoic doctrine of the *logos*, or "universal reason."

What followed the resulting proliferation of rules and laws is common knowledge. First, a functional differentiation grew up between two kinds of issues. On the one hand, there were issues that could be decided by applying *general* rules or laws, on the basis of the maxim that like cases should be treated alike. On the other hand, there were issues that called for discretion, with an eye to the *particular* features of each case, in accordance with the maxim that significantly different cases should be treated differently. This functional differentiation became the ancestor of our own distinction between legal and equitable jurisdiction. Second, the Emperor Constantine decided as a matter of imperial policy to bring equitable jurisdiction under his personal control by reserving the equitable function to his own personal court and chancellor. Out in the public arena, judges were given the menial task of applying general rules with only the minimum of discretion. Once legal proceedings were exhausted, the aggrieved citizen could appeal to the Emperor as *parens patriae* ("father of the fatherland") or the benevolent exercise of clemency or equity. Politically, this division of labor certainly did the Emperor no harm; but it also sowed the first seeds of public suspicion that the Law is one thing, Justice another.[9]

Carried over into the modern English-speaking world, the resulting division between courts of law and courts of equity is familiar to readers of Charles Dickens. And although during the twentieth century most Anglo-American jurisdictions have merged legal and equitable functions in the same courts,[10] it is still widely the case that equitable remedies can be sought only in cases where legal remedies are unavailable or unworkable—so that in this respect the dead hand of Constantine still rules us from the grave.

The Ethics of Strangers

Life in late-twentieth-century industrial societies clearly has more in common with life in Imperial Rome than it has with the Rome of Horatius at the Bridge or with Mrs. Gaskell's *Cranford*. Our cities are vast, our populations are mixed and fragmented, our public administrations bureaucratic, our jurisdictions (both

9   For the subsequent influence of this division on the Anglo-American legal tradition, see (e.g.) John H. Baker, *An Introduction to English Legal History* (Toronto and London: Butterworths, 1979).

10   Politically speaking, of course, the decline of monarchical sovereignty made the formal division of law from equity less functional; so it is no surprise that the nineteenth century saw its abolition both in the constitutional monarchy of England and also in the republican United States.

domestic and foreign) are many and varied. As a result, the moral consensus and civic trust on which the pontificate of early Rome depended for its general respect and efficacy often appear to be no more than a beguiling dream. The way we live now, people have come to value uniformity above responsiveness, to focus on law at the expense of equity, and to confuse "the rule of law" with a law of rules. Yet the balance between law and equity still needs to be struck, even if new ways need to be found that answer our new needs. From this point on, I shall work my way toward the question: how, in our actual situation, can that balance best be redressed?

In law, in ethics, and in public administration alike, there is nowadays a similar preoccupation with general principles and a similar distrust of individual discretion. In the administration of social services, the demand for equality of treatment makes us unwilling to permit administrators to "temper the wind to the shorn lamb"—that strikes us as unfair, and therefore unjust.[11] (The equation of justice with fairness is thus a two-edged sword.) In the professions, a widespread fear that professionals are taking unfair advantage of their fiduciary positions has contributed to the recent wave of malpractice suits. In the courts, judges are given less and less room to exercise discretion, and many lawyers view juries as no more trustworthy than judges; the more they are both kept in line by clear rules, or so it seems, the better.[12] As for public discussions of ethics, the recognition of genuine moral complexities, conflicts, and tragedies, that can be dealt with only on a case-by-case basis, is simply unfashionable. Victory in public argument goes, rather, to the person with the more imposing principle. Above all, many people involved in the current debate seem to have forgotten what the term "equity" actually means. They assume that it is just a literary synonym for "equality."[13] So, a demand for the uniform application of public policies leads to a submerging of the discretionary by the rigorous, the equitable by the equal. Faced with judicial injustices, we react like the television reporter, declaring, "There ought to be a law against it," even where it would be more appropriate to say, "In this particular case, the law is making an ass of itself." The same applies to the operation of our bureaucracies, and to the emphasis on principles in moral judgments.

In all three fields, we need to be reminded that equity requires not the imposition of uniformity or equality on all relevant cases, but rather reasonableness or responsiveness (*epieikeia*) in applying general rules to individual cases.[14] Equity

---

11   John Rawls, *A Theory of Justice* (Cambridge, Mass.: Harvard University Press, 1971) is only the most recent systematic exposition of this position, which has become something of a philosophical commonplace, at any rate since Kant raised the issue of "universalizability" in the late eighteenth century.

12   See, e.g., Kenneth C. Davis, *Discretionary Justice* (Urbana, Ill., Univ. of Illinois Press, 1969); Ralph A. Newman, *Equity and Law* (Dobbs Ferry, NY: Oceana, 1961); and particularly Ralph A. Newman, ed., *Equity in the World's Legal Systems* (Brussels: Bruylant, 1973).

13   This seems to be true even of so perceptive an author as Herbert Kaufman, in his ingenious tract, *Red Tape: its Origins, Uses and Abuses* (Washington, D.C.: Brookings Institution, 1977), pp. 76-77: "Quite apart from protective attitudes toward specific programs, general concern for uniform application of policy militates against wholesale devolution. Not that uniformity automatically assures equity or equality of treatment..."

14   The *locus classicus* for the discussion of the notion of *epieikeia* (or "equity") is Aristotle's *Nicomachean Ethics*, esp. 1136b30-1137b32. See also Max Hamburger's useful discussion in *Morals*

means doing justice with discretion around, in the interstices of, and in areas of conflict between our laws, rules, principles, and other general formulas. It means being responsive to the limits of all such formulas, to the special circumstances in which one can properly make exceptions, and to the trade-offs required where different formulas conflict. The degree to which such marginal judgments can be regularized or routinized remains limited today, just as it was in early Rome. Faced with the task of balancing the equities of different parties, a judge today may well be guided by previous precedents; but these precedents only illuminate broad maxims, they do not invoke formal rules.[15] Likewise, professional practice may be described in cut-and-dried terms as a matter of "routine and accepted" procedures only in the artificial context of a malpractice suit. In the actual exercise of his profession, a surgeon, say, may sometimes simply have to use his or her own best judgment in deciding how to proceed conscientiously. Finally, in ethics, moral wisdom is exercised not by those who stick by a single principle come what may, absolutely and without exception, but rather by those who understand that, in the long run, no principle—however absolute—can avoid running up against another equally ab-solute principle; and by those who have the experience and discrimination needed to balance conflicting considerations in the most humane way.[16]

By looking at the effects of changing social conditions and modes of life on our ethical perceptions, I believe we can best hit on the clues that will permit us to unravel this whole tangle of problems. A century ago in *Anna Karenina* Leo Tolstoy expressed a view which, though in my opinion exaggerated, is none the less illuminating. During his lifetime Tolstoy lived to see the abolition of serfdom, the introduction of railways, the movement of population away from the country to the cities, and the consequent emergence of modern city life; and he continued to have deep reservations about the possibility of living a truly moral life in a modern city. As he saw matters, genuinely "moral" relations can exist only between people who live, work, and associate together: inside a family, between intimates and associates, within a neighborhood. The natural limit to any person's moral universe, for Tolstoy, is the distance he or she can walk, or at most ride. By taking the train, a moral agent leaves the sphere of truly moral actions for a world of strangers, toward whom he or she has few real obligations and with whom dealings can be only casual or commercial. Whenever the moral pressures and demands become too strong to bear, Tolstoy has Anna go down to the railway station and take a train somewhere, anywhere. The final irony of Tolstoy's own painful life was that he finally broke away from his home and family, only to die in the local stationmaster's office.[17] Matters of state policy and the like, in Tolstoy's eyes, lay

---

and Law: the Growth of Aristotle's Legal Theory (New Haven: Yale University Press, 1951).

15   Henry L. McClintock, *Handbook of the Principles of Equity*, 2nd ed. (St. Paul, Minn.: West, 1948) pp.52-54; John N. Pomeroy, *A Treatise on Equity Jurisprudence* (San Francisco: Bancroft Whitney, 1918-19), secs 360-63.

16   Hence Aristotle's emphasis on the need for a person of sound ethical judgment to be an *anthropos megalopsychos*.

17   This image of the steam locomotive had a powerful hold on Tolstoy's imagination: it recurs, for example, in *War and Peace*, where he compares the ineluctable processes of history to the movements of the pistons and cranks of a railway engine, as a way of discrediting the assumption that "world historical figures" like Napoleon can exercise any effective freedom of action in the political realm.

quite outside the realm of ethics. Through the figure of Constantin Levin, he made clear his skepticism about all attempts either to turn ethics into a matter of theory or to make political reform an instrument of virtue.[18]

What Tolstoy rightly emphasized is the sharp difference that exists between our moral relations with our families, intimates, and immediate neighbors or associates, and our moral relations with complete strangers. In dealing with our children, friends, and immediate colleagues, we both expect to—and are expected to—make allowances for their individual personalities and tastes, and we do our best to time our actions according to our perception of their current moods and plans. In dealing with the bus driver, the sales clerk in a department store, the hotel barber, and other such casual contacts, there may be no basis for making these allowances, and so no chance of doing so. In these transient encounters, our moral obligations are limited and chiefly negative—for example, to avoid acting offensively or violently. So, in the ethics of strangers, respect for rules is all, and the opportunities for discretion are few. In the ethics of intimacy, discretion is all, and the relevance of strict rules is minimal.[19] For Tolstoy, of course, only the ethics of intimacy was properly called "ethics" at all—that is why I described his view as exaggerated. But in this respect the ethics of John Rawls is equally exaggerated, though in the opposite direction. In our relations with casual acquaintances and unidentified fellow citizens, absolute impartiality may be a prime moral demand; but among intimates a certain discreet partiality is, surely, only equitable, and certainly not unethical. So a system of ethics that rests its principles on "the veil of ignorance" may well be "fair," but it will also be—essentially—an ethics for relations between strangers.[20]

The Stresses of Lawsuits

Seeing how Tolstoy felt about his own time, what would he have thought about the life we lead today? The effects of the railways, in blurring the boundary between the moral world of the immediate community and the neutral world beyond, have been only multiplied by the private car, which breaks that boundary down almost completely. Living in a high-rise apartment building, taking the car from its underground garage to the supermarket and back, the modern city dweller may sometimes wonder whether he has any neighbors at all. For many of us, the sphere of intimacy has shrunk to the nuclear family, and this has placed an immense strain on family relations. Living in a world of comparative strangers, we find ourselves short on civic trust and increasingly estranged from our professional advisors. We are less inclined to give judges and bureaucrats room to use their discretion,

---

18   This is the central theme of the closing book of *Anna*, in which Tolstoy documents his own disillusion with social and political ethics through the character of Constantin Levin.
19   Notice how Aristotle treats the notion of *philia* as complementary to that of "equity." As he sees, the nature of the moral claims that arise within any situation depend on how closely the parties are related: indeed, it might be better to translate *philia* by some such term as "relationship" instead of the customary translation, "friendship," since his arguments intended to be analytical rather than edifying.
20   Rawls, *Theory of Justice*.

and more determined to obtain equal (if not always equitable) treatment. In a world of complete strangers, indeed, equality would be about the only virtue left.

Do not misunderstand my position. I am not taking a nostalgia trip back to the Good Old Days. The world of neighborliness and forced intimacy, of both geographical and social immobility, had its vices as well as its virtues. Jane Austen's caricature of Lady Catherine de Burgh in *Pride and Prejudice* reminds us that purchasing equity by submitting to gross condescension can make its price too dear:

> God bless the Squire and his relations,
> and keep us in our proper stations.

Any biography of Tolstoy reminds us that his world, too, had a darker side. Those who are seduced by his admiration for the moral wisdom of the newly emancipated peasantry will find an antidote in Frederick Douglass's memoirs of slave life on the Maryland shore. Nor am I deploring apartment buildings and private cars. People usually have reasons for living as they do, and attacking modernity in the name of the morality of an earlier time is an act of desperation, like building the Berlin Wall. No, my questions only: If we accept the modern world as it is—apartment buildings, private cars, and all—how can we strike the central balance between the ethics of intimates and the ethics of strangers, between uniformity of treatment and administrative discretion, and between equity and law, in ways that answer our contemporary needs?

To begin with the law: current public stereotypes focus on the shortcomings of the adversary process, but what first needs to be explained is just where the adversary system has gone astray, and in what fields of law we should be most concerned to replace it. That should not be hard to do. Given that we handle our moral relations with intimates and associates differently from our moral relations with strangers, is not some similar differentiation appropriate between our legal relations with strangers, on the one hand, and with intimates, associates, and close family members on the other?

Even in the United States, the homeland of the adversary system, at least two types of disputes—labor-management conflicts and the renegotiation of commercial contracts—are dealt with by using arbitration or conciliation rather than confrontation.[21] That is no accident. In a criminal prosecution or a routine civil damage suit arising out of a car collision, the parties are normally complete strangers before the proceedings and have no stake in one another's future, so no harm is done if they walk out of the court vowing never to set eyes on each other again. By contrast, the parties to a labor grievance will normally wish to continue working together after the adjudication, while the disputants in a commercial arbitration may well retain or resume business dealings with one another despite the present disagreement. In cases of these kinds, the psychological stresses of the adversary system can be quite destructive: by the time an enthusiastic litigating

---

21   In United States labor law practice, arbitrators are guided by the published decisions of previous arbitrations, but not bound by them, since their own decisions normally turn on an estimate of the exact personal and group relations between the workers and managers involved in the particular dispute. Indeed, in Switzerland—here, as elsewhere, an extreme case—the results of labor arbitrations are not even published, on the ground that they are a "purely private matter" as between the immediate parties.

attorney has done his bit, further labor relations or commercial dealings may be psychologically impossible. So in appraising different kinds of court proceedings, we need to consider how particular types of judicial episodes fit into the larger life histories of the individuals who are parties to them, and what impact the form of proceedings can have on those life histories.

A lawsuit that pits the full power of the state against a criminal defendant is one thing: in that context, Monroe Freedman may be right to underline the merits of the adversary mode, and the positive obligations of zealous defense advocacy.[22] A civil suit that pits colleagues, next-door neighbors, or family members against each other is another thing: in that context resort to adversary proceedings may only make a bad situation worse. So, reasonably enough, the main locus of dissatisfaction with the adversary system is those areas of human life in which the psychological outcomes are most damaging: family law, for example. By the time that the father, mother, and children involved in a custody dispute have all been zealously represented in court, the bad feelings from which the suit originally sprang may well have become irremediable. It is just such areas as family law that other nations (such as West Germany) have chosen to handle by arbitration rather than litigation, in chambers rather than in open court, so providing much more room for discretion.

I am suggesting, then, that a system of law consisting wholly of rules would treat all the parties coming before it in the ways appropriate to strangers. By contrast, in legal issues that arise between parties who wish to continue as close associates on an intimate or familiar level, the demands of equality and rule conformity lose their central place. There, above all, the differences between the desires, personalities, hopes, capacities, and ambitions of the parties most need to be taken into account; and only an adjudicator with authority to interpret existing rules, precedents, and maxims in the light of, and in response to, those differences will be in a position to respect the equities of all the parties involved.

Reviving the Friendly Society

In public administration, especially in the field of social services, the crucial historical changes were more recent, yet they appear much harder to reverse. Two centuries ago most of what we now call the social services—then known, collectively, as "charity"—were still dispensed through the churches. Local ministers of religion were generally trusted to perform this duty equitably and conscientiously; and in deciding to give more to (say) Mrs. Smith than Mrs. Jones, they were not strictly answerable to any supervisor, still less bound by a book of rules. (As with the Squirearchy, of course, this arrangement had its own abuses: the Rev. Mr. Collins could be as overbearing in his own way as Lady Catherine de Burgh.) Even a hundred years ago many such charitable functions were still carried on by private organizations, like those in Britain which were charmingly known as "friendly societies." But by this time things were beginning to change.

---

22 Monroe Freedman, *Lawyers' Ethics in an Adversary System* (Indianapolis: Bobbs Merrill, 1975). In this connection, current Chinese attempts to turn criminal proceedings into a species of chummy conciliation between the defendant and his fellow citizens can too easily serve to conceal tyranny behind a mask of paternalistic goodwill.

A friendly clergyman is one thing, but a friendly *society* is more of an anomaly: in due course irregularities in the administration of those organizations—like those in some trade union pension funds today—provoked government supervision, and a Registrar of Friendly Societies was appointed to keep an eye on them.

From that point on, the delivery of social services has become ever more routinized, centralized, and subject to bureaucratic routine. It should not take horror stories, like that of the handicapped young woman's answering service, to make us think again about the whole project of delivering human services through a bureaucracy: one only has to read Max Weber. The imperatives of bureaucratic administration require determinate procedures and full accountability; while a helping hand, whether known by the name of "charity" or "social services," can be truly equitable only if it is exercised with discretion, on the basis of substantive and informed judgments about need rather than formal rules of entitlement.

What might be done, then, to counter the rigors of bureaucracy in this field? Or should late-twentieth-century societies look for other ways of lending a collective hand to those in need? In an exemplary apologia for bureaucracy, Herbert Kaufman of the Brookings Institution has put his finger on many of the key points.[23] If we find public administration today complex, unresponsive, and procedure-bound, he argues that this is almost entirely our own fault. These defects are direct consequences of the demands that we ourselves have placed on our public servants in a situation increasingly marked by diversity, democracy, and distrust. Since we are unwilling to grant discretion to civil servants or fear that it will be abused, we leave ourselves with no measure for judging administrators' performance other than *equality*. As Kaufman remarks, "If people in one region discover that they are treated differently from people in other regions under the same program, they are apt to be resentful and uncooperative."[24]

Hence there arises a "general concern for uniform application of policy," which can be guaranteed only by making the rulebook even more inflexible. Yet is our demand for equality and uniformity really so unqualified that we are determined to purchase it at any price? If we were certain that our own insistence on absolute fairness made the social services dehumanizing and dehumanized, might we not consider opting for other, more *equitable* procedures even though their outcomes might be less *equal*?

Alternatively, perhaps we should reconsider the wholesale nationalization of charity that began in the early twentieth century. Plenty of uncorrupt private pension funds still operate alongside governmental retirement and old-age pension schemes, and a few communally based systems of welfare and charity remain trusted just because their accountability is to a particular community. Among the Ismailis, for instance, the world-wide branch of Islam of which the Aga Khan is the head, tithing is still the rule, and no promising high school graduate misses the chance of going to college merely because he comes from a poor family. Despite governmental programs, that is no longer true of the United States. So perhaps we have let ourselves become too skeptical too soon about the friendliness of "friendly societies," and we should take more seriously the possibility of reviving social

23   Kaufman, *Red Tape*.
24   Ibid., p. 77.

instruments with local roots, which do not need to insist on rigidly rule-governed procedures. That is of course a large "perhaps." The social changes that led to the nationalization of charity are powerful and longstanding, and thus far they have shown little sign of weakening. Given a choice, people may prefer to continue putting up with bureaucratic forms and procedures that they can grumble at with impunity if in this way they can avoid putting themselves at the mercy of social or communal relationships that they may find onerous.

Frail Hopes and Slender Foundations

In the field of ethics, all these difficulties are magnified. There I have one firm intellectual conviction, and one somewhat frailer hope on the social level.

In a 1932 poem Robert Frost wrote:

Don't join too many gangs. Join few if any.
Join the United States, and join the family.
But not much in between, unless a college.[25]

Frost, in his curmudgeonly way, captures that hostility toward communal ties and restraints which, since Tolstoy's day, has continued to undermine our "intermediate institutions" or "mediating structures." Toward the nuclear family and the nation, people do indeed still feel some natural loyalty; "but not much in between, unless a college." During the last thirty years, even the nation-state has lost much of its mystique, leaving the family exposed to stresses that it can hardly support. It is my frail social hope that we may find some new ways of shaping other intermediate institutions toward which we can develop a fuller loyalty and commitment: associations larger than the nuclear family, but not so large that they defeat in advance the initial presumption that our fellow members are trustworthy. For it is only in that context, I suspect, that the ethics of discretion and intimacy can regain the ground it has lost to the ethics of rules and strangers.

Where might we look for the beginnings of such associations? Traditionally their loci were determined by religious and ethnic ties, and these are still sometimes used constructively to extend the range of people's moral sympathies beyond the immediate household. But we scarcely need to look as far as Ulster or Lebanon to see the other side of that particular coin. Membership in schools and colleges has some of the same power, as Frost grudgingly admits, though is a power that tends to operate exclusively rather than generously. The great ethical hope of the Marxists was that "working-class solidarity" would, in effect, create a vast and cohesive extended family within which the dispossessed would find release from psychological as well as from political and economic oppression. But by now, alas, the evidence of history seems to show that awareness of shared injuries sets different groups against one another quite as often as it unites them. For some of us, the bonds of professional association are as powerful as any. The physicians of Tarrytown or the attorneys of Hyde Park probably have a close understanding of, feeling for, and even trust in one another; and despite all other reservations about

---

25   Robert Frost, "Build Soil—a Political Pastoral," in *Complete Poems of Robert Frost* (New York: Holt, Rinehart & Winston, 1949), pp. 421-32, at p. 430.

my fellow academics, I do still have a certain implicit trust in their professional responsibility and integrity. So each year, without any serious anxiety, I vote for colleagues whom I have never even met to serve on the boards that manage my pension funds. If it were proved that those elected representatives had been milking the premiums and salting them away in a Swiss bank, that revelation would shake up my moral universe more radically than any dishonesty among public figures on the national level.

True, these are frail hopes and provide only slender foundations to build on. Yet, in the realm of ethics, frail hopes and slender foundations may be what we should learn to live with as much better than nothing. And that brings me to the intellectual point about which I am much more confident. If the cult of absolute principles is so attractive today, that is a sign that we still find it impossible to break with the "quest for certainty" that John Dewey tried so hard to discredit.[26] Not that we needed Dewey to point out the shortcomings of absolutism. Aristotle himself had insisted that there are no "essences" in the realm of ethics, and so no basis for any rigorous "theory" of ethics. Practical reasoning in ethics, as elsewhere, is a matter of judgment, of weighing different considerations against one another, never a matter of formal theoretical deduction from strict or self-evident axioms. It is a task less for the clever arguer than for the *anthropos megalopsychos*, the "large-spirited human being."[27]

It was not for nothing, then, that the members of the National Commission for the Protection of Human Subjects were able to agree about the ethical issues for just so long as they discussed those issues taxonomically. In doing so they were reviving the older, Aristotelian procedures of the casuists and rabbinical scholars, who understood all along that in ethics, as in law, the best we can achieve in practices for good-hearted, clear-headed people to triangulate their way across the complex terrain of moral life and problems. So, starting from the paradigmatic cases that we do understand—what in the simplest situations harm is, and fairness, and cruelty, and generosity—we must simply work our way, one step at a time, to the more complex and perplexing cases in which extremely delicate balances may have to be struck. For example, we must decide on just what conditions, if any, it would be acceptable to inject a sample group of five-year-old children with an experimental vaccine from which countless other children should benefit even though the risks fall on those few individuals alone. Ethical argumentation thus makes most effective progress if we think of the "common morality" in the same way as we think about the common law:[28] if, for instance, we develop our perception of moral issues by the same kind of progressive triangulation that has extended

---

26   John Dewey, *The Quest for Certainty* (New York: Putnam, 1929).

27   Aristotle's "large spirited person"—commonly but wrongly translated as "great souled man," ignoring the care with which the Greeks differentiated between *anthropoi* (human beings) and *andres* (men)—is the final hero of the *Nicomachean Ethics*: the key feature of such a person was, for him, the ability to act on behalf of a friend from an understanding of that friend's own needs, wishes, and interests.

28   We are indebted to Alan Donagan for reintroducing the idea of the "common morality" into philosophical ethics, in his book, *The Theory of Morality* (Chicago: University of Chicago Press, 1977).

common law doctrines of tort into the areas, first of negligence and later of strict liability.[29]

Meanwhile, we must remain on guard against the moral enthusiasts. In their determination to nail their principles to the mast, they succeed only in blinding themselves to the equities embodied in real-life situations and problems. Their willingness to legislate morality threatens to transform the most painful and intimate moral quandaries into adversarial confrontations between strangers. To take one example, by reintroducing uncompromising legal restraints to enjoin all procedures of abortion whatever, they are pitting a woman against her own newly implanted zygote in some ghastly parody of a landlord-tenant dispute. This harsh inflexibility sets the present day moral enthusiasts in sharp contrast to Aristotle's *anthropoi megalopsychoi*, and recalls Tolstoy's portrait of Alexei Karenin's associate, the Countess Ivanovna, who in theory was a supporter of all fashionable good causes but in practice was ready to act harshly and unforgivingly.

When Pascal attacked the Jesuit casuists for being too ready to make allowances in favor of penitents who were rich or highborn, he no doubt had a point.[30] But when he used this point as a reason for completely rejecting the case method in ethics, he set the bad example that is so often followed today: assuming that we must withdraw discretion entirely when it is abused and impose rigid rules in its place, instead of inquiring how we could adjust matters so that necessary discretion would continue to be exercised in an equitable and discriminating manner. I vote without hesitation against Pascal and for the Jesuits and the Talmudic scholars. We do not need to go as far as Tolstoy and claim that an ethics modeled on law rather than on equity is no ethics at all. But we do need to recognize that a morality based entirely on general rules and principles is tyrannical and disproportioned, and that only those who make equitable allowances for subtle individual differences have a proper feeling for the deeper demands of ethics. In practice the casuists may occasionally have been lax; but they grasped the essential, Aristotelian point about applied ethics: it cannot get along on a diet of general principles alone. It requires a detailed taxonomy of particular, detailed types of cases and situations. So, even in practice, the faults of the casuists—such as they were—were faults on the right side.

---

29   Edward H. Levi, *Introduction to Legal Reasoning* (Chicago: University of Chicago Press, 1948).
30   Pascal's *Lettres Provinciales* were originally published in 1656-57, during the trial of his friend Antoine Arnauld, whose Jansenist associations made him a target for the Jesuits. Pascal's journalistic success with these letters did a great deal, by itself, to bring the tradition of "case reasoning" in ethics into discredit: so much so that the art of casuistics has subsequently been known by the name of "casuistry"—a word which the *Oxford English Dictionary* first records as having been used by Alexander Pope in 1725, and whose very form, as the dictionary makes clear, is dyslogistic. (It belongs to the same family of English words as "popery," "wizardry" and "sophistry," all of which refer to the *disreputable* employment of the arts in question.

Philosophy

The Allegory of the Cave

Plato

Plato (ca. 429 B.C. - ca. 348 B.C.) was a classical philosopher and rhetorician. After being a student of the Greek philosopher Socrates, Plato started a school called the Academy in which he instructed young Greek males, using a method called "the Socratic dialogue" in which he asked questions to lead students step-by-step to the answer. "The Allegory of the Cave" is from Plato's utopian political treatise, *The Republic.*

And now, I said, let me show in a figure how far our nature is enlightened or unenlightened:—Behold! human beings living in an underground den, which has a mouth open towards the light and reaching all along the den; here they have been from their childhood, and have their legs and necks chained so that they cannot move, and can only see before them, being prevented by the chains from turning round their heads. Above and behind them a fire is blazing at a distance, and between the fire and the prisoners there is a raised way; and you will see, if you look, a low wall built along the way, like the screen which marionette players have in front of them, over which they show the puppets.

I see.

And do you see, I said, men passing along the wall carrying all sorts of vessels, and statues and figures of animals made of wood and stone and various materials, which appear over the wall? Some of them are talking, others silent.

You have shown me a strange image, and they are strange prisoners.

Like ourselves, I replied; and they see only their own shadows, or the shadows of one another, which the fire throws on the opposite wall of the cave?

True, he said; how could they see anything but the shadows if they were never allowed to move their heads?

And of the objects which are being carried in like manner they would only see the shadows?

Yes, he said.

And if they were able to converse with one another, would they not suppose that they were naming what was actually before them?

Very true.

And suppose further that the prison had an echo which came from the other side, would they not be sure to fancy when one of the passers-by spoke that the voice which they heard came from the passing shadow?

No question, he replied.

To them, I said, the truth would be literally nothing but the shadows of the images.

That is certain.

And now look again, and see what will naturally follow if the prisoners are released and disabused of their error. At first, when any of them is liberated and compelled suddenly to stand up and turn his neck round and walk and look towards the light, he will suffer sharp pains; the glare will distress him, and he will be unable to see the realities of which in his former state he had seen the shadows; and then conceive someone saying to him, that what he saw before was an illusion, but that now, when he is approaching nearer to being and his eye is turned towards more real existence, he has a clearer vision—what will be his reply? And you may further imagine that his instructor is pointing to the objects as they pass and requiring him to name them,—will he not be perplexed? Will he not fancy that the shadows which he formerly saw are truer than the objects which are now shown to him?

Far truer.

And if he is compelled to look straight at the light, will he not have a pain in his eyes which will make him turn away to take refuge in the objects of vision which he can see, and which he will conceive to be in reality clearer than the things which are now being shown to him?

True, he said.

And suppose once more, that he is reluctantly dragged up a steep and rugged ascent, and held fast until he is forced into the presence of the sun himself, is he not likely to be pained and irritated? When he approaches the light his eyes will be dazzled, and he will not be able to see anything at all of what are now called realities.

Not all in a moment, he said.

He will require to grow accustomed to the sight of the upper world. And first he will see the shadows best, next the reflections of men and other objects in the water, and then the objects themselves; then he will gaze upon the light of the moon and the stars and the spangled heaven; and he will see the sky and the stars by night better than the sun or the light of the sun by day?

Certainly.

Last of all he will be able to see the sun, and not mere reflections of him in the water, but he will see him in his own proper place, and not in another; and he will contemplate him as he is.

Certainly.

He will then proceed to argue that this is he who gives the season and the years, and is the guardian of all that is in the visible world, and in a certain way the cause of all things which he and his fellows have been accustomed to behold?

Clearly, he said, he would first see the sun and then reason about him.

And when he remembered his old habitation, and the wisdom of the den and his fellow-prisoners, do you not suppose that he would felicitate himself on the change, and pity them?

Certainly, he would.

And if they were in the habit of conferring honors among themselves on those who were quickest to observe the passing shadows and to remark which of them went before, and which followed after, and which were together; and who were therefore best able to draw conclusions as to the future, do you think that he would care for such honors and glories, or envy the possessors of them? Would he not say with Homer, Better to be the poor servant of a poor master, and to endure anything, rather than think as they do and live after their manner? Yes, he said, I think that he would rather suffer anything than entertain these false notions and live in this miserable manner.

Imagine once more, I said, such a one coming suddenly out of the sun to be replaced in his old situation; would he not be certain to have his eyes full of darkness?

To be sure, he said.

And if there were a contest, and he had to compete in measuring the shadows with the prisoners who had never moved out of the den, while his sight was still weak, and before his eyes had become steady (and the time which would be needed to acquire this new habit of sight might be very considerable), would he not be ridiculous? Men would say of him that up he went and down he came without his eyes; and that it was better not even to think of ascending; and if any one tried to lose another and lead him up to the light, let them only catch the offender, and they would put him to death.

No question, he said.

The entire allegory, I said, you may now append, dear Glaucon, to the previous argument; the prison house is the world of sight, the light of the fire is the sun, and you will not misapprehend me if you interpret the journey upwards to be the ascent of the soul into the intellectual world according to my poor belief, which, at your desire, I have expressed—whether rightly or wrongly God knows. But, whether true or false, my opinion is that in the world of knowledge the idea of good appears last of all, and is seen only with an effort; and, when seen, is also inferred to be the universal author of all things beautiful and right, parent of light and of the lord of light in this visible world, and the immediate source of reason and truth in the intellectual; and that this is the power upon which he who would act rationally either in public or private life must have his eye fixed.

I agree, he said, as far as I am able to understand you.

Moreover, I said, you must not wonder that those who attain to this beatific vision are unwilling to descend to human affairs; for their souls are ever hastening into the upper world where they desire to dwell; which desire of theirs is very natural, if our allegory may be trusted.

Yes, very natural.

And is there anything surprising in one who passes from divine contemplations to the evil state of man, misbehaving himself in a ridiculous manner; if, while his eyes are blinking and before he has become accustomed to the surrounding darkness, he is compelled to fight in courts of law, or in other places, about the images or the shadows of images of justice, and is endeavoring to meet the conceptions of those who have never yet seen absolute justice?

Anything but surprising, he replied.

Anyone who has common sense will remember that the bewilderments of the eyes are of two kinds, and arise from two causes, either from coming out of the light or from going into the light, which is true of the mind's eye, quite as much as of the bodily eye; and he who remembers this when he sees anyone whose vision is perplexed and weak, will not be too ready to laugh; he will first ask whether that soul of man has come out of the brighter life, and is unable to see because unaccustomed to the dark, or having turned from darkness to the day is dazzled by excess of light. And he will count the one happy in his condition and state of being, and he will pity the other; or, if he have a mind to laugh at the soul which comes from below into the light, there will be more reason in this than in the laugh which greets him who returns from above out of the light into the den.

That, he said, is a very just distinction.

But then, if I am right, certain professors of education must be wrong when they say that they can put a knowledge into the soul which was not there before, like sight into blind eyes.

They undoubtedly say this, he replied.

Whereas, our argument shows that the power and capacity of learning exists in the soul already; and that just as the eye was unable to turn from darkness to light without the whole body, so too the instrument of knowledge can only by the movement of the whole soul be turned from the world of becoming into that of being, and learn by degrees to endure the sight of being, and of the brightest and best of being, or in other words, of the good.

Very true.

And must there not be some art which will effect conversion in the easiest and quickest manner; not implanting the faculty of sight, for that exists already, but has been turned in the wrong direction, and is looking away from the truth?

Yes, he said, such an art may be presumed.

And whereas the other so-called virtues of the soul seem to be akin to bodily qualities, for even when they are not originally innate they can be implanted later by habit and exercise, the virtue of wisdom more than anything else contains a divine element which always remains, and by this conversion is rendered useful and profitable; or, on the other hand, hurtful and useless. Did you never observe the narrow intelligence flashing from the keen eye of a clever rogue—how eager he is, how clearly his paltry soul sees the way to his end, he is the reverse of blind, but his keen eyesight is forced into the service of evil, and he is mischievous in proportion to his cleverness?

Very true, he said.

But what if there had been a circumcision of such natures in the days of their youth; and they had been severed from those sensual pleasures, such as eating and drinking, which, like leaden weights, were attached to them at their birth, and which drag them down and turn the vision of their souls upon the things that are below—if, I say, they had been released from these impediments and turned in the opposite direction, the very same faculty in them would have seen the truth as keenly as they see what their eyes are turned to now.

Very likely.

Yes, I said; and there is another thing which is likely, or rather a necessary inference from what has preceded, that neither the uneducated and uninformed of the truth, nor yet those who never make an end of their education, will be able ministers of State; not the former, because they have no single aim of duty which is the rule of all their actions, private as well as public; nor the latter, because they will not act at all except upon compulsion, fancying that they are already dwelling apart in the islands of the blessed.

Very true, he replied.

Then, I said, the business of us who are founders of the State will be to compel the best minds to attain that knowledge which we have already shown to be the greatest of all—they must continue to ascend until they arrive at the good; but when they have ascended and seen enough we must not allow them to do as they do now.

What do you mean?

I mean that they remain in the upper world: but this must not be allowed; they must be made to descend again among the prisoners in the den, and partake of their labors and honors, whether they are worth having or not.

But is not this unjust? He said; ought we to give them a worse life, when they have a better?

You have again forgotten, my friend, I said, the intention of the legislator, who did not aim at making any one class in the State happy above the rest; the happiness was to be in the whole State, and he held the citizens together by persuasion and necessity, making them benefactors of the State, and therefore benefactors of one another; to this end he created them, not to please themselves, but to be his instruments in binding up the State.

True, he said, I had forgotten.

Observe, Glaucon, that there will be no injustice in compelling our philosophers to have a care and providence of others; we shall explain to them that in other States, men of their class are not obliged to share in the toils of politics: and this is reasonable, for they grow up at their own sweet will, and the government would rather not have them. Being self-taught, they cannot be expected to show any gratitude for a culture which they have never received. But we have brought you into the world to be rulers of the hive, kings of yourselves and of the other citizens, and have educated you far better and more perfectly than they have been educated, and you are better able to share in the double duty. Wherefore each of you, when his turn comes, must go down to the general underground abode, and get the habit of seeing in the dark. When you have acquired the habit, you will see ten thousand times better than the inhabitants of the den, and you will know what the several images are, and what they represent, because you have seen the beautiful and just and good in their truth. And thus our State which is also yours will be a reality, and not a dream only, and will be administered in a spirit unlike that of other States, in which men fight with one another about shadows only and are distracted in the struggle for power, which in their eyes is a great good. Whereas the truth is that the State in which the rulers are most reluctant to govern is always the best and most quietly governed, and the State in which they are most eager, the worst.

Quite true, he replied.

And will our pupils, when they hear this, refuse to take their turn at the toils of State, when they are allowed to spend the greater part of their time with one another in the heavenly light?

Impossible, he answered; for they are just men, and the commands which we impose upon them are just; there can be no doubt that every one of them will take office as a stern necessity, and not after the fashion of our present rulers of State.

Yes, my friend, I said; and there lies the point. You must contrive for your future rulers another and a better life than that of a rule; and then you may have a well ordered State; for only in the State which offers this, will they rule who are truly rich, not in silver and gold, but in virtue and wisdom, which are the true blessings of life. Whereas if they go to the administration of public affairs, poor and hungering after their own private advantage, thinking that hence they are to snatch the chief good, order there can never be; for they will be fighting about office, and the civil and domestic broils which thus arise will be the ruin of the rulers themselves and of the whole State.

Most true, he replied.

And the only life which looks down upon the life of political ambition is that of true philosophy. Do you know of any other?

Indeed, I do not, he said.

Diogenes and Alexander

Gilbert Highet

Gilbert Highet (1906–1978) was a Professor of Greek and Latin, an author, a radio commentator, and translator. He was born on June 22, 1906 in Glasgow, Scotland and died in 1978. He attended Glasgow University and received his M.A. from the school in 1929. He later attended Oxford University, receiving a B.A. in 1932 and an M.A. in 1936. He immigrated to the U.S. in 1937. In World War II, he served in the British Army, but returned to the U.S. and became a naturalized citizen in 1951. He was employed by Columbia University in New York as a Professor of Greek and Latin from 1938 to 1950, an Anthon Professor of Latin Language and Literature from 1950 to 1972, and as a professor emeritus from 1972 to 1978. He acted as the chairman of the department of Greek and Latin between the years of 1965 and 1972. He also acted as a commentator on the radio program "People, Places, and Books," which aired on 300 radio stations in the United States and Canada from 1952 to 1959. In his work, he popularized intellectual topics but was criticized by other academics for his nonacademic treatment of literature.

Lying on the bare earth, shoeless, bearded, half-naked, he looked like a beggar or a lunatic. I was one, but not the other. He had opened his eyes with the sun at dawn, scratched, done his business like a dog at the roadside, washed at the public fountain, begged a piece of breakfast bread and a few olives, eaten them squatting on the ground, and washed them down with a few handfuls of water scooped from the spring. (Long ago he had owned a rough wooden cup, but he threw it away when he saw a boy drinking out of his hollowed hands.) Having no work to go to and no family to provide for, he was free. As the market place filed up with shoppers and merchants and gossipers and sharpers and slaves and foreigners, he had strolled through it for an hour or two. Everybody knew him, or knew of him. They would throw sharp questions at him and get sharper answers. Sometimes they threw jeers, and got jibes; sometimes bits of food, and got scant thanks; sometimes a mischievous pebble, and got a shower of stones and abuse. They were not quite sure whether he was mad or not. He knew they were mad, each in a different way; they amused him. Now he was back at his home.

It was not a house, not even a squatter's hut. He thought everybody lived far too elaborately, expensively, anxiously. What good is a house? No one needs privacy; natural acts are not shameful; we all do the same things, and need not hide them. No one needs beds and chairs and such furniture: the animals live healthy lives and sleep on the ground. All we require, since nature did not dress us properly, is one garment to keep us warm, and some shelter from rain and wind. So he had one blanket—to dress him in the daytime and cover him at night—and he slept in a cask. His name was Diogenes. He was the founder of the creed called Cynicism (the word means "doggishness"); he spent much of his life in the rich, lazy, corrupt Greek city of Corinth, mocking and satirizing its people, and occasionally converting one of them.

His home was not a barrel made of wood: too expensive. It was a storage jar made of earthenware, something like a modern fuel tank—no doubt discarded because a break had made it useless. He was not the first to inhabit such a thing: the refugees driven into Athens by the Spartan invasion had been forced to sleep in casks. But he was the first whoever did so by choice, out of principle.

Diogenes was not a degenerate or a maniac. He was a philosopher who wrote plays and poems and essays expounding his doctrine; he talked to those who cared to listen; he had pupils who admired him. But he taught chiefly by example. All should live naturally, he said, for what is natural is normal and cannot possibly be evil or shameful. Live without conventions, which are artificial and false; escape complexities and superfluities and extravagances: only so can you live a free life. The rich man believes he possesses his big house with its many rooms and its elaborate furniture, his pictures and his expensive clothes, his horses and his servants and his bank accounts. He does not. He depends on them, he worries about them, he spends most of his life's energy looking after them; the thought of losing them makes him sick with anxiety. They possess him. He is their slave. In order to procure quantity of false, perishable goods he has sold the only true, lasting good, his own independence.

There have been many men who grew tired of human society with its complications, and went away to live simply—on a small farm, in a quiet village, in a hermit's cave, or in the darkness of anonymity. Not so Diogenes. He was not a recluse, or a stylite, or a beatnik. He was a missionary. His life's aim was clear to him: it was "to restamp the currency." (He and his father had once been convicted for counterfeiting, long before he turned to philosophy, and this phrase was Diogenes' bold, unembarrassed joke on the subject.) To restamp the currency: to take the clean metal of human life, to erase the old false conventional markings, and to imprint it with its true values.

The other great philosophers of the fourth century before Christ taught mainly their own private pupils. In the shady groves and cool sanctuaries of the Academy, Plato discoursed to a chosen few on the unreality of this contingent existence. Aristotle, among the books and instruments and specimens and archives and research workers of his Lyceum, pursued investigations and gave lectures that were rightly named esoteric "for those within the walls." But for Diogenes, laboratory and specimens and lecture halls and pupils were all to be found in a crowd of ordinary people. Therefore he chose to live in Athens or in the rich city of Corinth, where travelers from all over the Mediterranean world constantly came and went. And by design he publicly behaved in such ways as to show people what real life was. He would constantly take up their spiritual coin, ring it on a stone, and laugh at its false superscription.

He thought most people were only half-alive, most men only half-men. At bright noonday he walked through the market place carrying a lighted lamp and inspecting the face of everyone he met. They asked him why. Diogenes answered, "I am trying to find a man."

To a gentleman whose servant was putting on his shoes for him, Diogenes said, "You won't be really happy until he wipes your nose for you: that will come after you lose the use of your hands."

Once there was a war scare so serious that it stirred even the lazy, profit-happy Corinthians. They began to drill, clean their weapons, and rebuild their neglected fortifications. Diogenes took his old cask and began to roll it up and down, back and forward. "When you are all so busy," he said, "I felt I ought to do something!"

And so he lived—like a dog, some said, because he cared nothing for privacy and other human conventions, and because he showed his teeth and barked at those whom he disliked. Now he was lying in the sunlight, as contented as a dog on the warm ground, happier (he himself used to toast) than the Shah of Persia. Although he knew he was going to have an important visitor, he would not move.

The little square began to fill with people. Page boys elegantly dressed, spearmen speaking a rough foreign dialect, discreet secretaries, hard-browed officers, suave diplomats, they all gradually formed a circle centered on Diogenes. He looked them over as a sober man looks at a crowd of tottering drunks, and shook his head. He knew who they were. They were the attendants of the conqueror of Greece, the servants of Alexander, the Macedonian king, who was visiting his newly subdued realm.

Only twenty, Alexander was far older and wiser than his years. Like all Macedonians he loved drinking, but he could usually handle it; and toward women he was nobly restrained and chivalrous. Like all Macedonians he loved fighting; he was a magnificent commander, but he was not merely a military automaton. He could think. At thirteen he had become a pupil of the greatest mind in Greece, Aristotle. No exact record of his schooling survives. It is clear, though, that

Aristotle took the passionate, half-barbarous boy and gave him the best of Greek culture. He taught Alexander poetry: the young prince slept with the Iliad under his pillow and longed to emulate Achilles, who brought the mighty power of Asia to ruin. He taught him philosophy, in particular the shapes and uses of political power: a few years later Alexander was to create a supranational empire that was not merely a power system but a vehicle for the exchange of Greek and Middle Eastern cultures.

Aristotle taught him the principles of scientific research: during his invasion of the Persian domains Alexander took with him a large corps of scientists, and shipped hundreds of zoological specimens back to Greece for study. Indeed, it was from Aristotle that Alexander learned to seek out everything strange which might be instructive. Jugglers and stunt artists and virtuosos of the absurd he dismissed with a shrug but on reaching India he was to spend hours discussing the problems of life and death with naked Hindu mystics, and later to see one demonstrate Yoga self-command by burning himself impassively to death.

Now, Alexander was in Corinth to take command of the League of Greek States which, after conquering them, his father Philip had created as a disguise for the New Macedonian Order. He was welcomed and honored and flattered. He was the man of the hour, of the century: he was unanimously appointed commander-in-chief of a new expedition against old, rich, corrupt Asia. Nearly everyone crowded to Corinth in order to congratulate him, to seek employment with him, even simply to see him: soldiers and statesmen, artists and merchants, poets and philosophers. He received their compliments graciously. Only Diogenes, although he lived in Corinth, did not visit the new monarch. With that generosity which Aristotle had taught him was a quality of the truly magnanimous man, Alexander determined to call upon Diogenes. Surely Diogenes, the God-born, would acknowledge the conqueror's power by some gift of hoarded wisdom.

With his handsome face, his fiery glance, his strong supple body, his purple and gold cloak, and his air of destiny, he moved through the parting crowd, toward the Dog's kennel. When a king approaches, all rise in respect. Diogenes did not rise, he merely sat up on one elbow. When a monarch enters a precinct, all greet him with a bow or an acclamation. Diogenes said nothing.

There was a silence. Some years later Alexander speared his best friend to the wall, for objecting to the exaggerated honors paid to His Majesty; but now he was still young and civil. He spoke first, with a kindly greeting. Looking at the poor broken cask, the single ragged garment, and the rough figure lying on the ground, he said: "Is there anything I can do for you, Diogenes?"

"Yes," said the Dog. "Stand to one side. You're blocking the sunlight."

There was silence, not the ominous silence preceding a burst of fury, but a hush of amazement. Slowly, Alexander turned away. A titter broke out from the elegant Greeks, who were already beginning to make jokes about the Cur that looked at the King. The Macedonian officers, after deciding that Diogenes was not worth the trouble of kicking, were starting to guffaw and nudge one another. Alexander was still silent.

To those nearest him he said quietly. "If I were not Alexander, I should be Diogenes." They took it as a paradox, designed to close the awkward little scene with a polite curtain line. But Alexander meant it. He understood Cynicism as the others could not. Later he took one of Diogenes' pupils with him to India as a philosophical interpreter (it was he who spoke to the naked saddhus). He was what Diogenes called himself, a cosmopolités, "citizen of the world." Like Diogenes, he admired the heroic figure of Hercules, the mighty conqueror who labors to help mankind while all others toil and sweat only for themselves. He knew that of all men then alive in the world only Alexander the conqueror and Diogenes the beggar were truly free.

The Four Idols

Francis Bacon

Francis Bacon (1561-1626) was an English philosopher, politician, and author. During his life he served as the Keeper of the Great Seal, a position his father had held, Attorney General, and Lord Chancellor of England. After being removed from political life following a scandal, he devoted the remainder of his life to scientific inquiry. Interested in education, the natural sciences, and social issues, many of Bacon's work contribute to the foundations of what is now called the scientific method, grounding arguments in observable fact and moving forward logically to explore the larger processes and ideas. His more literary and philosophical works, such as the essay below, evolved from his application of the deductive model of logic he championed to the kinds of personal and philosophical essays made popular by Michel de Montaigne. In rejecting de Montaigne's introspective approach, Bacon created the modern genre of the essay as it is now understood. This essay was originally printed in the 1620 edition of Bacon's *Novum Organum* (*New Organ for Gaining Knowledge*).

38. The idols and false notions which are now in possession of the human understanding, and have taken deep root therein, not only so beset men's minds that truth can hardly find entrance, but even after entrance is obtained, they will again in the very instauration of the sciences meet and trouble us, unless men being forewarned of the danger fortify themselves as far as may be against their assaults.

39. There are four classes of Idols which beset men's minds. To these for distinction's sake I have assigned names, calling the first class *Idols of the Tribe*; the second, *Idols of the Cave*; the third, *Idols of the Market Place*; the fourth, *Idols of the Theater*.

40. The formation of ideas and axioms by true induction is no doubt the proper remedy to be applied for the keeping off and clearing away of idols. To point them out, however, is of great use; for the doctrine of Idols is to the interpretation of nature what the doctrine of the refutation of sophisms is to common logic.

41. The Idols of the Tribe have their foundation in human nature itself, and in the tribe or race of men. For it is a false assertion that the sense of man is the measure of things. On the contrary, all perceptions as well of the sense as of the mind are according to the measure of the individual and not according to the measure of the universe. And the human understanding is like a false mirror, which, receiving rays irregularly, distorts and discolors the nature of things by mingling its own nature with it.

42. The Idols of the Cave are the idols of the individual man. For everyone (besides the errors common to human nature in general) has a cave or den of his own, which refracts and discolors the light of nature, owing either to his own proper and peculiar nature; or to his education and conversation with others; or to the reading of books, and the authority of those whom he esteems and admires; or to the differences of impressions, accordingly as they take place in a mind preoccupied and predisposed or in a mind indifferent and settled; or the like. So that the spirit of man (according as it is meted out to different individuals) is in fact a thing variable and full of perturbation, and governed as it were by chance. Whence it was well observed by Heraclitus that men look for sciences in their own lesser worlds, and not in the greater or common world.

43. There are also Idols formed by the intercourse and association of men with each other, which I call Idols of the Market Place, on account of the commerce and consort of men there. For it is by discourse that men associate, and words are imposed according to the apprehension of the vulgar. And therefore the ill and unfit choice of words wonderfully obstructs the understanding. Nor do the definitions or explanations wherewith in some things learned men are wont to guard and defend themselves, by any means set the matter right. But words plainly force and overrule the understanding, and throw all into confusion, and lead men away into numberless empty controversies and idle fancies.

44. Lastly, there are Idols which have immigrated into men's minds from the various dogmas of philosophies, and also from wrong laws of demonstration. These I call Idols of the Theater, because in my judgment all the received systems are but so many stage plays, representing worlds of their own creation after an unreal and scenic fashion. Nor is it only of the systems now in vogue, or only of the ancient sects and philosophies, that I speak; for many more plays of the same kind may yet be composed and in like artificial manner set forth; seeing that errors the most widely different have nevertheless causes for the most part alike. Neither again do I mean this only of entire systems, but also of many principles and axioms in science, which by tradition, credulity, and negligence have come to be received.

But of these several kinds of Idols I must speak more largely and exactly, that the understanding may be duly cautioned.

45. The human understanding is of its own nature prone to suppose the existence of more order and regularity in the world than it finds. And though there be many things in nature which are singular and unmatched, yet it devises for them parallels and conjugates and relatives which do not exist. Hence the fiction that all celestial bodies move in perfect circles, spirals and dragons being (except in name) utterly rejected. Hence too the element of fire with its orb is brought in, to make up the square with the other three which the sense perceives. Hence also the ratio of

density of the so-called elements is arbitrarily fixed at ten to one. And so on of other dreams. And these fancies affect not dogmas only, but simple notions also.

46. The human understanding when it has once adopted an opinion (either as being the received opinion or as being agreeable to itself) draws all things else to support and agree with it. And though there be a greater number and weight of instances to be found on the other side, yet these it either neglects and despises, or else by some distinction sets aside and rejects, in order that by this great and pernicious predetermination the authority of its former conclusions may remain inviolate. And therefore it was a good answer that was made by one who, when they showed him hanging in a temple a picture of those who had paid their vows as having escaped shipwreck, and would have him say whether he did not now acknowledge the power of the gods—"Aye," asked he again, "but where are they painted that were drowned after their vows?" And such is the way of all superstition, whether in astrology, dreams, omens, divine judgments, or the like; wherein men, having a delight in such vanities, mark the events where they are fulfilled, but where they fail, though this happen much oftener, neglect and pass them by. But with far more subtlety does this mischief insinuate itself into philosophy and the sciences; in which the first conclusion colors and brings into conformity with itself all that come after, though far sounder and better. Besides, independently of that delight and vanity which I have described, it is the peculiar and perpetual error of the human intellect to be more moved and excited by affirmatives than by negatives; whereas it ought properly to hold itself indifferently disposed toward both alike. Indeed, in the establishment of any true axiom, the negative instance is the more forcible of the two.

47. The human understanding is moved by those things most which strike and enter the mind simultaneously and suddenly, and so fill the imagination; and then it feigns and supposes all other things to be somehow, though it cannot see how, similar to those few things by which it is surrounded. But for that going to and fro to remote and heterogeneous instances by which axioms are tried as in the fire, the intellect is altogether slow and unfit, unless it be forced thereto by severe laws and overruling authority.

48. The human understanding is unquiet; it cannot stop or rest, and still presses onward, but in vain. Therefore it is that we cannot conceive of any end or limit to the world, but always as of necessity it occurs to us that there is something beyond. Neither, again, can it be conceived how eternity has flowed down to the present day, for that distinction which is commonly received of infinity in time past and in time to come can by no means hold; for it would thence follow that one infinity is greater than another, and that infinity is wasting away and tending to become finite. The like subtlety arises touching the infinite divisibility of lines, from the same inability of thought to stop. But this inability interferes more mischievously in the discovery of causes; for although the most general principles in nature ought to be held merely positive, as they are discovered, and cannot with truth be referred to a cause, nevertheless the human understanding being unable to rest still seeks something prior in the order of nature. And then it is that in struggling toward that which is further off it falls back upon that which is nearer at hand, namely, on final causes, which have relation clearly to the nature of man rather than to the

nature of the universe; and from this source have strangely defiled philosophy. But he is no less an unskilled and shallow philosopher who seeks causes of that which is most general, than he who in things subordinate and subaltern omits to do so.

49. The human understanding is no dry light, but receives an infusion from the will and affections; whence proceed sciences which may be called "sciences as one would." For what a man had rather were true he more readily believes. Therefore he rejects difficult things from impatience of research; sober things, because they narrow hope; the deeper things of nature, from superstition; the light of experience, from arrogance and pride, lest his mind should seem to be occupied with things mean and transitory; things not commonly believed, out of deference to the opinion of the vulgar. Numberless, in short, are the ways, and sometimes imperceptible, in which the affections color and infect the understanding.

50. But by far the greatest hindrance and aberration of the human understanding proceeds from the dullness, incompetency, and deceptions of the senses; in that things which strike the sense outweigh things which do not immediately strike it, though they be more important. Hence it is that speculation commonly ceases where sight ceases; insomuch that of things invisible there is little or no observation. Hence all the working of the spirits enclosed in tangible bodies lies hid and unobserved of men. So also all the more subtle changes of form in the parts of coarser substances (which they commonly call alteration, though it is in truth local motion through exceedingly small spaces) is in like manner unobserved. And yet unless these two things just mentioned be searched out and brought to light, nothing great can be achieved in nature, as far as the production of works is concerned. So again the essential nature of our common air, and of all bodies less dense than air (which are very many), is almost unknown. For the sense by itself is a thing infirm and erring; neither can instruments for enlarging or sharpening the senses do much; but all the truer kind of interpretation of nature is effected by instances and experiments fit and apposite; wherein the sense decides touching the experiment only, and the experiment touching the point in nature and the thing itself.

51. The human understanding is of its own nature prone to abstractions and gives a substance and reality to things which are fleeting. But to resolve nature into abstractions is less to our purpose than to dissect her into parts; as did the school of Democritus, which went further into nature than the rest. Matter rather than forms should be the object of our attention, its configurations and changes of configuration, and simple action, and law of action or motion; for forms are figments of the human mind, unless you will call those laws of action forms.

52. Such then are the idols which I call *Idols of the Tribe*, and which take their rise either from the homogeneity of the substance of the human spirit, or from its preoccupation, or from its narrowness, or from its restless motion, or from an infusion of the affections, or from the incompetency of the senses, or from the mode of impression.

53. The *Idols of the Cave* take their rise in the peculiar constitution, mental or bodily, of each individual; and also in education, habit, and accident. Of this kind there is a great number and variety. But I will instance those the pointing out of which contains the most important caution, and which have most effect in disturbing the clearness of the understanding.

54. Men become attached to certain particular sciences and speculations, either because they fancy themselves the authors and inventors thereof, or because they have bestowed the greatest pains upon them and become most habituated to them. But men of this kind, if they betake themselves to philosophy and contemplation of a general character, distort and color them in obedience to their former fancies; a thing especially to be noticed in Aristotle, who made his natural philosophy a mere bond servant to his logic, thereby rendering it contentious and well-nigh useless. The race of chemists, again out of a few experiments of the furnace, have built up a fantastic philosophy, framed with reference to a few things; and Gilbert also, after he had employed himself most laboriously in the study and observation of the loadstone, proceeded at once to construct an entire system in accordance with his favorite subject.

55. There is one principal and as it were radical distinction between different minds, in respect of philosophy and the sciences, which is this: that some minds are stronger and apter to mark the differences of things, others to mark their resemblances. The steady and acute mind can fix its contemplations and dwell and fasten on the subtlest distinctions; the lofty and discursive mind recognizes and puts together the finest and most general resemblances. Both kinds, however, easily err in excess, by catching the one at gradations, the other at shadows.

56. There are found some minds given to an extreme admiration of antiquity, others to an extreme love and appetite for novelty; but few so duly tempered that they can hold the mean, neither carping at what has been well laid down by the ancients, nor despising what is well introduced by the moderns. This, however, turns to the great injury of the sciences and philosophy, since these affectations of antiquity and novelty are the humors of partisans rather than judgments; and truth is to be sought for not in the felicity of any age, which is an unstable thing, but in the light of nature and experience, which is eternal. These factions therefore must be abjured, and care must be taken that the intellect be not hurried by them into assent.

57. Contemplations of nature and of bodies in their simple form break up and distract the understanding, while contemplations of nature and bodies in their composition and configuration overpower and dissolve the understanding, a distinction well seen in the school of Leucippus and Democritus as compared with the other philosophies. For that school is so busied with the particles that it hardly attends to the structure, while the others are so lost in admiration of the structure that they do not penetrate to the simplicity of nature. These kinds of contemplation should therefore be alternated and taken by turns, so that the understanding may be rendered at once penetrating and comprehensive, and the inconveniences above mentioned, with the idols which proceed from them, may be avoided.

58. Let such then be our provision and contemplative prudence for keeping off and dislodging the *Idols of the Cave*, which grow for the most part either out of the predominance of a favorite subject, or out of an excessive tendency to compare or to distinguish, or out of partiality for particular ages, or out of the largeness or minuteness of the objects contemplated. And generally let every student of nature take this as a rule: that whatever his mind seizes and dwells upon with peculiar satisfaction is to be held in suspicion, and that so much the more care is to be taken in dealing with such questions to keep the understanding even and clear.

59. But the *Idols of the Market Place* are the most troublesome of all—idols which have crept into the understanding through the alliances of words and names. For men believe that their reason governs words; but it is also true that words react on the understanding; and this it is that has rendered philosophy and the sciences sophistical and inactive. Now words, being commonly framed and applied according to the capacity of the vulgar, follow those lines of division which are most obvious to the vulgar understanding. And whenever an understanding of greater acuteness or a more diligent observation would alter those lines to suit the true divisions of nature, words stand in the way and resist the change. Whence it comes to pass that the high and formal discussions of learned men end oftentimes in disputes about words and names; with which (according to the use and wisdom of the mathematicians) it would be more prudent to begin, and so by means of definitions reduce them to order. Yet even definitions cannot cure this evil in dealing with natural and material things, since the definitions themselves consist of words, and those words beget others. So that it is necessary to recur to individual instances, and those in due series and order, as I shall say presently when I come to the method and scheme for the formation of notions and axioms.

60. The idols imposed by words on the understanding are of two kinds. They are either names of things which do not exist (for as there are things left unnamed through lack of observation, so likewise are there names which result from fantastic suppositions and to which nothing in reality corresponds), or they are names of things which exist, but yet confused and ill-defined, and hastily and irregularly derived from realities. Of the former kind are Fortune, the Prime Mover, Planetary Orbits, Element of Fire, and like fictions which owe their origin to false and idle theories. And this class of idols is more easily expelled, because to get rid of them it is only necessary that all theories should be steadily rejected and dismissed as obsolete.

But the other class, which springs out of a faulty and unskillful abstraction, is intricate and deeply rooted. Let us take for example such a word as *humid* and see how far the several things which the word is used to signify agree with each other, and we shall find the word *humid* to be nothing else than a mark loosely and confusedly applied to denote a variety of actions which will not bear to be reduced to any constant meaning. For it both signifies that which easily spreads itself round any other body; and that which in itself is indeterminate and cannot solidize; and that which readily yields in every direction; and that which easily divides and scatters itself; and that which easily unites and collects itself; and that which readily flows and is put in motion; and that which readily clings to another body and wets it; and that which is easily reduced to a liquid, or being solid easily melts. Accordingly, when you come to apply the word, if you take it in one sense, flame is humid; if in another, air is not humid; if in another, fine dust is humid; if in another, glass is humid. So that it is easy to see that the notion is taken by abstraction only from water and common and ordinary liquids, without any due verification.

There are, however, in words certain degrees of distortion and error. One of the least faulty kinds is that of names of substances, especially of lowest species and well-deduced (for the notion of *chalk* and of *mud* is good, of *earth* bad); a more faulty kind is that of actions, as *to generate, to corrupt, to alter*; the most faulty is of qualities (except such as are the immediate objects of the sense) as *heavy, light, rare, dense*, and the like. Yet in all these cases some notions are of necessity a little better than others, in proportion to the greater variety of subjects that fall within the range of the human sense.

61. But the *Idols of the Theater* are not innate, nor do they steal into the understanding secretly, but are plainly impressed and received into the mind from the playbooks of philosophical systems and the perverted rules of demonstration. To attempt refutations in this case would be merely inconsistent with what I have already said, for since we agree neither upon principles nor upon demonstrations there is no place for argument. And this is so far well, inasmuch as it leaves the honor of the ancients untouched. For they are no wise disparaged—the question between them and me being only as to the way. For as the saying is, the lame man who keeps the right road outstrips the runner who takes a wrong one. Nay, it is obvious that when a man runs the wrong way, the more active and swift he is, the further he will go astray.

But the course I propose for the discovery of sciences is such as leaves but little to the acuteness and strength of wits, but places all wits and understandings nearly on a level. For as in the drawing of a straight line or a perfect circle, much depends on the steadiness and practice of the hand, if it be done by aim of hand only, but if with the aid of rule or compass, little or nothing; so is it exactly with my plan. But though particular confutations would be of no avail, yet touching the sects and general divisions of such systems I must say something; something also touching the external signs which show that they are unsound; and finally something touching the causes of such great infelicity and of such lasting and general agreement in error; that so the access to truth may be made less difficult, and the human understanding may the more willingly submit to its purgation and dismiss its idols.

62. Idols of the Theater, or of Systems, are many, and there can be and perhaps will be yet many more. For were it not that now for many ages men's minds have been busied with religion and theology; and were it not that civil governments, especially monarchies, have been averse to such novelties, even in matters speculative; so that men labor therein to the peril and harming of their fortunes—not only unrewarded, but exposed also to contempt and envy—doubtless there would have arisen many other philosophical sects like those which in great variety flourished once among the Greeks. For as on the phenomena of the heavens many hypotheses may be constructed, so likewise (and more also) many various dogmas may be set up and established on the phenomena of philosophy. And in the plays of this philosophical theater you may observe the same thing which is found in the theater of the poets, that stories invented for the stage are more compact and elegant, and more as one would wish them to be, than true stories out of history.

In general, however, there is taken for the material of philosophy either a great deal out of a few things, or a very little out of many things; so that on both sides philosophy is based on too narrow a foundation of experiment and natural history, and decides on the authority of too few cases. For the Rational School of philosophers snatches from experience a variety of common instances, neither duly ascertained nor diligently examined and weighed, and leaves all the rest to meditation and agitation of wit.

There is also another class of philosophers who, having bestowed much diligent and careful labor on a few experiments, have thence made bold to educe and construct systems, wresting all other facts in a strange fashion to conformity therewith.

And there is yet a third class, consisting of those who out of faith and veneration mix their philosophy with theology and traditions; among whom the vanity of some has gone so far aside as to seek the origin of sciences among spirits and genii. So that this parent stock of errors—this false philosophy—is of three kinds: the Sophistical, the Empirical, and the Superstitious.

63. The most conspicuous example of the first class was Aristotle, who corrupted natural philosophy by his logic: fashioning the world out of categories; assigning to the human soul, the noblest of substances, a genus from words of the second intention; doing the business of density and rarity (which is to make bodies of greater or less dimensions, that is, occupy greater or less spaces), by the frigid distinction of act and power; asserting that single bodies have each a single and proper motion, and that if they participate in any other, then this results from an external cause; and imposing countless other arbitrary restrictions on the nature of things; being always more solicitous to provide an answer to the question and affirm something positive in words, than about the inner truth of things; a failing best shown when his philosophy is compared with other systems of note among the Greeks. For the *homoeomera* of Anaxagoras; the Atoms of Leucippus and Democritus; the Heaven and Earth of Parmenides; the Strife and Friendship of Empedocles; Heraclitus' doctrine how bodies are resolved into the indifferent nature of fire, and remolded into solids, have all of them some taste of the natural philosopher—some savor of the nature of things, and experience, and bodies; whereas in the physics of Aristotle you hear hardly anything but the words of logic, which in his metaphysics also, under a more imposing name, and more forsooth as a realist than a nominalist, he has handled over again. Nor let any weight be given to the fact that in his books on animals and his problems, and other of his treatises, there is frequent dealing with experiments. For he had come to his conclusion before; he did not consult experience, as he should have done, for the purpose of framing his decisions and axioms, but having first determined the question according to his will, he then resorts to experience, and bending her into conformity with his placets, leads her about like a captive in a procession. So that even on this count he is more guilty than his modern followers, the schoolmen, who have abandoned experience altogether.

64. But the Empirical school of philosophy gives birth to dogmas more deformed and monstrous than the Sophistical or Rational school. For it has its foundations not in the light of common notions (which though it be a faint and superficial light, is yet in a manner universal, and has reference to many things), but in the narrowness and darkness of a few experiments. To those therefore who are daily busied with these experiments and have infected their imagination with them, such a philosophy seems probable and all but certain; to all men else incredible and vain. Of this there is a notable instance in the alchemists and their

dogmas, though it is hardly to be found elsewhere in these times, except perhaps in the philosophy of Gilbert. Nevertheless, with regard to philosophies of this kind there is one caution not to be omitted; for I foresee that if ever men are roused by my admonitions to betake themselves seriously to experiment and bid farewell to sophistical doctrines, then indeed through the premature hurry of the understanding to leap or fly to universals and principles of things, great danger may be apprehended from philosophies of this kind, against which evil we ought even now to prepare.

65. But the corruption of philosophy by superstition and an admixture of theology is far more widely spread, and does the greatest harm, whether to entire systems or to their parts. For the human understanding is obnoxious to the influence of the imagination no less than to the influence of common notions. For the contentious and sophistical kind of philosophy ensnares the understanding; but this kind, being fanciful and tumid and half poetical, misleads it more by flattery. For there is in man an ambition of the understanding, no less than of the will, especially in high and lofty spirits.

Of this kind we have among the Greeks a striking example in Pythagoras, though he united with it a coarser and more cumbrous superstition; another in Plato and his school, more dangerous and subtle. It shows itself likewise in parts of other philosophies, in the introduction of abstract forms and final causes and first causes, with the omission in most cases of causes intermediate, and the like. Upon this point the greatest caution should be used. For nothing is so mischievous as the apotheosis of error; and it is a very plague of the understanding for vanity to become the object of veneration. Yet in this vanity some of the moderns have with extreme levity indulged so far as to attempt to found a system of natural philosophy on the first chapter of Genesis, on the book of Job, and other parts of the sacred writings, seeking for the dead among the living; which also makes the inhibition and repression of it the more important, because from this unwholesome mixture of things human and divine there arises not only a fantastic philosophy but also a heretical religion. Very meet it is therefore that we be sober-minded, and give to faith that only which is faith's.

Aristotle: *Nicomachean Ethics*, excerpts

Aristotle

Aristotle (384–322 BC) was a classical Greek philosopher and scientist. His work is considered foundational to much of Western philosophy and helped shape many of the philosophical debates from the early medieval period to today. A student of Plato, Aristotle later became the tutor of Alexander the Great before founding his own school, the Lyceum. A prolific writer and debater, it is commonly thought that less than a third of what Aristotle wrote has survived. While much of his work that has survived focus on scientific thought, a number of his philosophical texts (especially those focused on ethics and law) have also survived. The excerpt below from his *Nicomachean Ethics* represents some of the core elements of Aristotle's philosophy which remain influential today.

Every art and every inquiry, and similarly every action and pursuit, is thought to aim at some good; and for this reason the good has rightly been declared to be that at which all things aim. But a certain difference is found among ends; some are activities, others are products apart from the activities that produce them. Where there are ends apart from the actions, it is the nature of the products to be better than the activities. Now, as there are many actions, arts, and sciences, their ends also are many; the end of the medical art is health, that of shipbuilding a vessel, that of strategy victory, that of economics wealth. But where such arts fall under a single capacity—as bridle-making and the other arts concerned with the equipment of horses fall under the art of riding, and this and every military action under strategy, in the same way other arts fall under yet others—in all of these the ends of the master arts are to be preferred to all the subordinate ends; for it is for the sake of the former that the latter are pursued. It makes no difference whether the activities themselves are the ends of the actions, or something else apart from the activities, as in the case of the sciences just mentioned.

If, then, there is some end of the things we do, which we desire for its own sake (everything else being desired for the sake of this), and if we do not choose everything for the sake of something else (for at that rate the process would go on to infinity, so that our desire would be empty and vain), clearly this must be the good and the chief good. Will not the knowledge of it, then, have a great influence on life? Shall we not, like archers who have a mark to aim at, be more likely to hit upon what is right? If so, we must try, in outline at least, to determine what it is, and of which of the sciences or capacities it is the object. It would seem to belong to the most authoritative art and that which is most truly the master art. And politics appears to be of this nature; for it is this that ordains which of the sciences should be studied in a state, and which each class of citizens should learn and up to what point they should learn them; and we see even the most highly esteemed of capacities to fall under this, e.g. strategy, economics, rhetoric; now, since politics uses the rest of the sciences, and since, again, it legislates as to what we are to do and what we are to abstain from, the end of this science must include those of the others, so that this end must be the good for man. For even if the end is the same for a single man and for a state, that of the state seems at all events something greater and more complete whether to attain or to preserve; though it is worth while to attain the end merely for one man, it is finer and more godlike to attain it for a nation or for city-states. These, then, are the ends at which our inquiry aims, since it is political science, in one sense of that term.

Our discussion will be adequate if it has as much clearness as the subject-matter admits of, for precision is not to be sought for alike in all discussions, any more than in all the products of the crafts. Now fine and just actions, which political science investigates, admit of much variety and fluctuation of opinion, so that they may be thought to exist only by convention, and not by nature. And goods also give rise to a similar fluctuation because they bring harm to many people; for before now men have been undone by reason of their wealth, and others by reason of their courage. We must be content, then, in speaking of such subjects and with such premises to indicate the truth roughly and in outline, and in speaking about things which are only for the most part true and with premises of the same kind to reach conclusions that are no better. In the same spirit, therefore, should each type of statement be received; for it is the mark of an educated man to look for precision in each class of things just so far as the nature of the subject admits; it is evidently equally foolish to accept probable reasoning from a mathematician and to demand from a rhetorician scientific proofs.

Now each man judges well the things he knows, and of these he is a good judge. And so the man who has been educated in a subject is a good judge of that subject, and the man who has received an all-round education is a good judge in general. Hence a young man is not a proper hearer of lectures on political science; for he is inexperienced in the actions that occur in life, but its discussions start from these and are about these; and, further, since he tends to follow his passions, his study will be vain and unprofitable, because the end aimed at is not knowledge but action. And it makes no difference whether he is young in years or youthful in character; the defect does not depend on time, but on his living, and pursuing each successive object, as passion directs. For to such persons, as to the incontinent, knowledge brings no profit; but to those who desire and act in accordance with a rational principle knowledge about such matters will be of great benefit.

****

Let us again return to the good we are seeking, and ask what it can be. It seems different in different actions and arts; it is different in medicine, in strategy, and in the other arts likewise. What then is the good of each? Surely that for whose sake everything else is done. In medicine this is health, in strategy victory, in architecture a house, in any other sphere something else, and in every action and pursuit the end; for it is for the sake of this that all men do whatever else they do. Therefore, if there is an end for all that we do, this will be the good achievable by action, and if there are more than one, these will be the goods achievable by action.

So the argument has by a different course reached the same point; but we must try to state this even more clearly. Since there are evidently more than one end, and we choose some of these (e.g. wealth, flutes, and in general instruments) for the sake of something else, clearly not all ends are final ends; but the chief good is evidently something final. Therefore, if there is only one final end, this will be what we are seeking, and if there are more than one, the most final of these will be what we are seeking. Now we call that which is in itself worthy of pursuit more final than that which is worthy of pursuit for the sake of something else, and that which is never desirable for the sake of something else more final than the things that are desirable both in themselves and for the sake of that other thing, and therefore we call final without qualification that which is always desirable in itself and never for the sake of something else.

Now such a thing happiness, above all else, is held to be; for this we choose always for self and never for the sake of something else, but honour, pleasure, reason, and every virtue we choose indeed for themselves (for if nothing resulted from them we should still choose each of them), but we choose them also for the sake of happiness, judging that by means of them we shall be happy. Happiness, on the other hand, no one chooses for the sake of these, nor, in general, for anything other than itself.

From the point of view of self-sufficiency the same result seems to follow; for the final good is thought to be self-sufficient. Now by self-sufficient we do not mean that which is sufficient for a man by himself, for one who lives a solitary life, but also for parents, children, wife, and in general for his friends and fellow citizens, since man is born for citizenship. But some limit must be set to this; for if we extend our requirement to ancestors and descendants and friends' friends we are in for an infinite series. Let us examine this question, however, on another occasion; the self-sufficient we now define as that which when isolated makes life desirable and lacking in nothing; and such we think happiness to be; and further we think it most desirable of all things, without being counted as one good thing among others—if it were so counted it would clearly be made more desirable by the addition of even the least of goods; for that which is added becomes an excess of goods, and of goods the greater is always more desirable. Happiness, then, is something final and self-sufficient, and is the end of action.

Presumably, however, to say that happiness is the chief good seems a platitude, and a clearer account of what it is still desired. This might perhaps be given, if we could first ascertain the function of man. For just as for a flute-player, a sculptor, or an artist, and, in general, for all things that have a function or activity, the good and the 'well' is thought to reside in the function, so would it seem to be for man, if he has a function. Have the carpenter, then, and the tanner certain functions or activities, and has man none? Is he born without a function? Or as eye, hand, foot, and in general each of the parts evidently has a function, may one lay it down that man similarly has a function apart from all these? What then can this be? Life seems to be common even to plants, but we are seeking what is peculiar to man. Let us exclude, therefore, the life of nutrition and growth. Next there would be a life of perception, but it also seems to be common even to the horse, the ox, and every animal. There remains, then, an active life of the element that has a rational principle; of this, one part has such a principle in the sense of being obedient to one, the other in the sense of possessing one and exercising thought. And, as 'life of the rational element' also has two meanings, we must state that life in the sense of activity is what we mean; for this seems to be the more proper sense of the term. Now if the function of man is an activity of soul which follows or implies a rational principle, and if we say 'so-and-so-and 'a good so-and-so' have a function which is the same in kind, e.g. a lyre, and a good lyre-player, and so without qualification in all cases, eminence in respect of goodness being idded to the name of the function (for the function of a lyre-player is to play the lyre, and that of a good lyre-player is to do so well): if this is the case, and we state the function of man to be a certain kind of life, and this to be an activity or actions of the soul implying a rational principle, and the function of a good man to be the good and noble performance of these, and if any action is well performed when it is performed in accordance with the appropriate excellence: if this is the case, human good turns out to be activity of soul in accordance with virtue, and if there are more than one virtue, in accordance with the best and most complete.

But we must add 'in a complete life.' For one swallow does not make a summer, nor does one day; and so too one day, or a short time, does not make a man blessed and happy.

Let this serve as an outline of the good; for we must presumably first sketch it roughly, and then later fill in the details.

****

Must no one at all, then, be called happy while he lives; must we, as Solon says, see the end? Even if we are to lay down this doctrine, is it also the case that a man is happy when he is dead? Or is not this quite absurd, especially for us who say that happiness is an activity? But if we do not call the dead man happy, and if Solon does not mean this, but that one can then safely call a man blessed as being at last beyond evils and misfortunes, this also affords matter for discussion; for both evil and good are thought to exist for a dead man, as much as for one who is alive but not aware of them; e.g. honours and dishonours and the good or bad fortunes of children and in general of descendants. And this also presents a problem; for though a man has lived happily up to old age and has had a death worthy of his life, many reverses may befall his descendants—some of them may be good and attain the life they deserve, while with others the opposite may be the case; and clearly too the degrees of relationship between them and their ancestors may vary indefinitely. It would be odd, then, if the dead man were to share in these changes and become at one time happy, at another wretched; while it would also be odd if the fortunes of the descendants did not for some time have some effect on the happiness of their ancestors.

But we must return to our first difficulty; for perhaps by a consideration of it our present problem might be solved. Now if we must see the end and only then call a man happy, not as being happy but as having been so before, surely this is a paradox, that when he is happy the attribute that belongs to him is not to be truly predicated of him because we do not wish to call living men happy, on account of the changes that may befall them, and because we have assumed happiness to be something permanent and by no means easily changed, while a single man may suffer many turns of fortune's wheel. For clearly if we were to keep pace with his fortunes, we should often call the same man happy and again wretched, making the happy man out to be chameleon and insecurely based. Or is this keeping pace with his fortunes quite wrong? Success or failure in life does not depend on these, but human life, as we said, needs these as mere additions, while virtuous activities or their opposites are what constitute happiness or the reverse.

The question we have now discussed confirms our definition. For no function of man has so much permanence as virtuous activities (these are thought to be more durable even than knowledge of the sciences), and of these themselves the most valuable are more durable because those who are happy spend their life most readily and most continuously in these; for this seems to be the reason why we do not forget them. The attribute in question, then, will belong to the happy man, and he will be happy throughout his life; for always, or by preference to everything else, he will be engaged in virtuous action and contemplation, and he will bear the chances of life most nobly and altogether decorously, if he is 'truly good' and 'foursquare beyond reproach'.

Now many events happen by chance, and events differing in importance; small pieces of good fortune or of its opposite clearly do not weigh down the scales of life one way or the other, but a multitude of great events if they turn out well will make life happier (for not only are they themselves such as to add beauty to life, but the way a man deals with them may be noble and good), while if they turn out ill they crush and maim happiness; for they both bring pain with them and hinder many activities. Yet even in these nobility shines through, when a man bears with resignation many great misfortunes, not through insensibility to pain but through nobility and greatness of soul.

If activities are, as we said, what gives life its character, no happy man can become miserable; for he will never do the acts that are hateful and mean. For the man who is truly good and wise, we think, bears all the chances life becomingly and always makes the best of circumstances, as a good general makes the best military use of the army at his command and a good shoemaker makes the best shoes out of the hides that are given him; and so with all other craftsmen. And if this is the case, the happy man can never become miserable; though he will not reach blessedness, if he meet with fortunes like those of Priam.

Nor, again, is he many-coloured and changeable; for neither will he be moved from his happy state easily or by any ordinary misadventures, but only by many great ones, nor, if he has had many great misadventures, will he recover his happiness in a short time, but if at all, only in a long and complete one in which he has attained many splendid successes.

When then should we not say that he is happy who is active in accordance with complete virtue and is sufficiently equipped with external goods, not for some chance period but throughout a complete life? Or must we add 'and who is destined to live thus and die as befits his life'? Certainly the future is obscure to us, while happiness, we claim, is an end and something in every way final. If so, we shall call happy those among living men in whom these conditions are, and are to be, fulfilled—but happy men. So much for these questions.

The University

The Idea of the University

John Henry, Cardinal Newman

John Henry, Cardinal Newman, (1801-1890) began his career an Anglican priest, poet, and theologian before converting to Catholicism and eventually being created as a Cardinal of the Catholic Church. Newman's political and social connections, as well as his wide range of writings, made him a popular and controversial figure in Victorian England. His actions strengthened the Catholic Church in England and he eventually helped to found the Catholic University of Ireland (now University College Dublin), the largest university in Ireland today. Newman was an advocate for education at all levels, and the excerpt below comes from his *The Idea of the University*, written while he was the rector of the Catholic University of Ireland in 1854, in which he argues the role education should serve in a moral and practical sense.

Discourse V.

A University may be considered with reference either to its Students or to its Studies; and the principle, that all Knowledge is a whole and the separate Sciences parts of one, which I have hitherto been using in behalf of its studies, is equally important when we direct our attention to its students. Now then I turn to the students, and shall consider the education which, by virtue of this principle, a University will give them; and thus I shall be introduced, Gentlemen, to the second question, which I proposed to discuss, viz, whether and in what sense its teaching, viewed relatively to the taught, carries the attribute of Utility along with it.

1.

I have said that all branches of knowledge are connected together, because the subject-matter of knowledge is intimately united in itself, as being the acts and the work of the Creator. Hence it is that the Sciences, into which our knowledge may be said to be cast, have multiplied bearings one on another, and an internal sympathy, and admit, or rather demand, comparison and adjustment. They complete, correct, balance each other. This consideration, if well-founded, must be taken into account, not only as regards the attainment of truth, which is their common [100] end, but as regards the influence which they exercise upon those whose education consists in the study of them. I have said already, that to give undue prominence to one is to be unjust to another; to neglect or supersede these is to divert those from their proper object. It is to unsettle the boundary lines between science and science, to disturb their action, to destroy the harmony which binds them together. Such a proceeding will have a corresponding effect when introduced into a place of education. There is no science but tells a different tale, when viewed as a portion of a whole, from what it is likely to suggest when taken by itself, without the safeguard, as I may call it, of others…

It is a great point then to enlarge the range of studies which a University professes, even for the sake of the students; and, though they cannot pursue every subject which is open to them, they will be the gainers by living among those and under those who represent the whole circle. This I conceive to be the advantage of a seat of universal learning, considered as a place of education. An assemblage of learned men, zealous for their own sciences, and rivals of each other, are brought, by familiar intercourse and for the sake of intellectual peace, to adjust together the claims and relations of their respective subjects of investigation. They learn to respect, to consult, to aid each other. Thus is created a pure and clear atmosphere of thought, which the student also breathes, though in his own case he only pursues a few sciences out of the multitude. He profits by an intellectual tradition, which is independent of particular teachers, which guides him in his choice of subjects, and duly interprets for him those which he chooses. He apprehends the great outlines of knowledge, the principles on which it rests, the scale of its parts, its lights and its shades, its great points and its little, as he otherwise cannot apprehend them. Hence it is that his education is called "Liberal."

2.

Cautious and practical thinkers, I say, will ask of me, what, after all, is the gain of this Philosophy, of which I make such account, and from which I promise so much. Even supposing it to enable us to exercise the degree of trust exactly due to every science respectively, and to estimate precisely the value of every truth which is anywhere to be found, how are we better for this master view of things, which I have been extolling? Does it not reverse the principle of the division of labour? will practical objects be obtained better or worse by its cultivation? to what then does it lead? where does it end? what does it do? how does it profit? what does it promise? Particular sciences are respectively the basis of definite arts, which carry on to results tangible and beneficial the truths which are the subjects of the knowledge attained; what is the Art of this science of sciences? what is the fruit of such a Philosophy? what are we proposing to effect, what inducements do we hold out to the Catholic community, when we set about the enterprise of founding a University?

I am asked what is the end of University Education, and of the Liberal or Philosophical Knowledge which I conceive it to impart: I answer, that what I have already said has been sufficient to show that it has a very tangible, real, and sufficient end, though the end cannot be divided from that knowledge itself. Knowledge is capable of being its own end. Such is the constitution of the human mind, that any kind of knowledge, if it be really such, is its own reward. And if this is true of all knowledge, it is true also of that special Philosophy, which I have made to consist in a comprehensive view of truth in all its branches, of the relations of science to science, of their mutual bearings, and their respective values. What the worth of such an acquirement is, compared with other objects which we seek,—wealth or power or honour or the conveniences and comforts of life, I do not profess here to discuss; but I would maintain, and mean to show, that it is an object, in its own nature so really and undeniably good, as to be the compensation of a great deal of thought in the compassing, and a great deal of trouble in the attaining.

Now, when I say that Knowledge is, not merely a means to something beyond it, or the preliminary of certain arts into which it naturally resolves, but an end sufficient to rest in and to pursue for its own sake, surely I am uttering no paradox, for I am stating what is both intelligible in itself, and has ever been the common judgment of philosophers and the ordinary feeling of mankind. That further advantages accrue to us and redound to others by its possession, over and above what it is in itself, I am very far indeed from denying; but, independent of these, we are satisfying a direct need of our nature in its very acquisition; and, whereas our nature, unlike that of the inferior creation, does not at once reach its perfection, but depends, in order to it, on a number of external aids and appliances, Knowledge, as one of the principal of these, is valuable for what its very presence in us does for us after the manner of a habit, even though it be turned to no further account, nor subserve any direct end.

6.

Now bear with me, Gentlemen, if what I am about to say, has at first sight a fanciful appearance. Philosophy, then, or Science, is related to Knowledge in this way:— Knowledge is called by the name of Science or Philosophy, when it is acted upon, informed, or if I may use a strong figure, impregnated by Reason. Reason is the principle of that intrinsic fecundity of Knowledge, which, to those who possess it, is its especial value, and which dispenses with the necessity of their looking abroad for any end to rest upon external to itself. Knowledge, indeed, when thus exalted into a scientific form, is also power; not only is it excellent [112] in itself, but whatever such excellence may be, it is something more, it has a result beyond itself. Doubtless; but that is a further consideration, with which I am not concerned. I only say that, prior to its being a power, it is a good; that it is, not only an instrument, but an end. I know well it may resolve itself into an art, and terminate in a mechanical process, and in tangible fruit; but it also may fall back upon that Reason which informs it, and resolve itself into Philosophy. In one case it is called Useful Knowledge, in the other Liberal. The same person may cultivate it in both ways at once; but this again is a matter foreign to my subject; here I do but say that there are two ways of using Knowledge, and in matter of fact those who use it in one way are not likely to use it in the other, or at least in a very limited measure. You see, then, here are two methods of Education; the end of the one is to be philosophical, of the other to be mechanical; the one rises towards general ideas, the other is exhausted upon what is particular and external. Let me not be thought to deny the necessity, or to decry the benefit, of such attention to what is particular and practical, as belongs to the useful or mechanical arts; life could not go on without them; we owe our daily welfare to them; their exercise is the duty of the many, and we owe to the many a debt of gratitude for fulfilling that duty.

I only say that Knowledge, in proportion as it tends more and more to be particular, ceases to be Knowledge. It is a question whether Knowledge can in any proper sense be predicated of the brute creation; without pretending to metaphysical exactness of phraseology, which would be unsuitable to an occasion like this,

I say, it seems to me improper to call that passive sensation, or perception of things, which brutes seem to possess, by the name of Knowledge. When I speak of Knowledge, I mean something intellectual, something which grasps what it perceives through the senses; something which takes a view of things; which sees more than the senses convey; which reasons upon what it sees, and while it sees; which invests it with an idea. It expresses itself, not in a mere enunciation, but by an enthymeme: it is of the nature of science from the first, and in this consists its dignity. The principle of real dignity in Knowledge, its worth, its desirableness, considered irrespectively of its results, is this germ within it of a scientific or a philosophical process. This is how it comes to be an end in itself; this is why it admits of being called Liberal. Not to know the relative disposition of things is the state of slaves or children; to have mapped out the Universe is the boast, or at least the ambition, of Philosophy.

Moreover, such knowledge is not a mere extrinsic or accidental advantage, which is ours to-day and another's to-morrow, which may be got up from a book, and easily forgotten again, which we can command or communicate at our pleasure, which we can borrow for the occasion, carry about in our hand, and take into the market; it is an acquired illumination, it is a habit, a personal possession, and an inward endowment. And this is the reason, why it is more correct, as well as more usual, to speak of a University as a place of education, than of instruction, though, when knowledge is concerned, instruction would at first sight have seemed the more appropriate word. We are instructed, for instance, in manual exercises, in the fine and useful arts, in trades, and in ways of business; for these are methods, which have little or no effect on the mind itself…But education is a higher word; it implies an action upon our mental nature, and the formation of a character; it is something individual and permanent, and is commonly spoken of in connection with religion and virtue. When, then, we speak of the communication of Knowledge as being Education, we thereby really imply that that Knowledge is a state or condition of mind; and since cultivation of mind is surely worth seeking for its own sake, we are thus brought once more to the conclusion, which the word "Liberal" and the word "Philosophy" have already suggested, that there is a Knowledge, which is desirable, though nothing come of it, as being of itself a treasure, and a sufficient remuneration of years of labour.

9.

Useful Knowledge then, I grant, has done its work; and Liberal Knowledge as certainly has not done its work,—that is, supposing, as the objectors assume, its direct end, like Religious Knowledge, is to make men better; but this I will not for an instant allow, and, unless I allow it, those objectors have said nothing to the purpose. I admit, rather I maintain, what they have been urging, for I consider Knowledge to have its end in itself. For all its friends, or its enemies, may say, I insist upon it, that it is as real a mistake to burden it with virtue or religion as with the mechanical arts. Its direct business is not to steel the soul against temptation or to console it in affliction, any more than to set the loom in motion, or to direct the steam carriage; be it ever so much the means or the condition of both material and moral advancement, still, taken by and in itself, it as little mends our hearts as it improves our temporal circumstances. And if its eulogists claim for it such a power, they commit the very same kind of encroachment on a province not their own as the political economist who should maintain that his science educated him for casuistry or diplomacy. Knowledge is one thing, virtue is another; good sense is not conscience, refinement is not humility, nor is largeness and justness of view faith. Philosophy, however enlightened, however profound, gives no command over the passions, no influential motives, no vivifying principles. ...

Surely we are not driven to theories of this kind, in order to vindicate the value and dignity of Liberal Knowledge. Surely the real grounds on which its pretensions rest are not so very subtle or abstruse, so very strange or improbable. Surely it is very intelligible to say, and that is what I say here, that Liberal Education, viewed in itself, is simply the cultivation of the intellect, as such, and its object is nothing more or less than intellectual excellence. Every thing has its own perfection, be it higher or lower in the scale of things; and the perfection of one is not the perfection of another. Things animate, inanimate, visible, invisible, all are good in their kind, and have a *best* of themselves, which is an object of pursuit. Why do you take such pains with your garden or your park? You see to your walks and turf and shrubberies; to your trees and drives; not as if you meant to make an orchard of the one, or corn or pasture land of the other, but because there is a special beauty in all that is goodly in wood, water, plain, and slope, brought all together by art into one shape, and grouped into one whole. Your cities are beautiful, your palaces, your public buildings, your territorial mansions, your churches; and their beauty leads to nothing beyond itself. There is a physical beauty and a moral: there is a beauty of person, there is a beauty of our moral being, which is natural virtue; and in like manner there is a beauty, there is a perfection, of the intellect. There is an ideal perfection in these various subject-matters, towards which individual instances are seen to rise, and which are the standards for all instances whatever.

Discourse VI.

Knowledge Viewed In Relation To Learning.

1.

I have called the perfection or virtue of the intellect by the name of philosophy, philosophical knowledge, enlargement of mind, or illumination; terms which are not uncommonly given to it by writers of this day: but, whatever name we bestow on it, it is, I believe, as a matter of history, the business of a University to make this intellectual culture its direct scope, or to employ itself in the education of the intellect,—just as the work of a Hospital lies in healing the sick or wounded, of a Riding or Fencing School, or of a Gymnasium, in exercising the limbs, of an Almshouse, in aiding and solacing the old, of an Orphanage, in protecting innocence, of a Penitentiary, in restoring the guilty. I say, a University, taken in its bare idea, … has this object and this mission; it contemplates neither moral impression nor mechanical production; it professes to exercise the mind neither in art nor in duty; its function is intellectual culture; here it may leave its scholars, and it has done its work when it has done as much as this. It educates the intellect to reason well in all matters, to reach out towards truth, and to grasp it.

3.

I suppose the *primâ-facie* view which the public at large would take of a University, considering it as a place of Education, is nothing more or less than a place for acquiring a great deal of knowledge on a great many subjects. Memory is one of the first developed of the mental faculties; a boy's business when he goes to school is to learn, that is, to store up things in his memory. For some years his intellect is little more than an instrument for taking in facts, or a receptacle for storing them: he welcomes them as fast as they come to him; he lives on what is without; he has his eyes ever about him; he has a lively susceptibility of impressions; he imbibes information of every kind; and little does he make his own in a true sense of the word, living rather upon his neighbours all around him. …

The same notion possesses the public mind, when it passes on from the thought of a school to that of a University: and with the best of reasons so far as this, that there is no true culture without acquirements, and that philosophy presupposes knowledge. It requires a great deal of reading, or a wide range of information, to warrant us in putting forth our opinions on any serious subject; and without such learning the most original mind may be able indeed to dazzle, to amuse, to refute, to perplex, but not to come to any useful result or any trustworthy conclusion. There are indeed persons who profess a different view of the matter, and even act upon it. Every now and then you will find a person of vigorous or fertile mind, who relies upon his own resources, despises all former authors, and gives the world, with the utmost fearlessness, his views upon religion, or history, or any other popular subject. And his works may sell for a while; he may get a name in his day; but this will be all. His readers are sure to find on the long run that his doctrines are mere theories, and not the expression of facts, that they are chaff instead of bread, and then his popularity drops as suddenly as it rose.

Knowledge then is the indispensable condition of expansion of mind, and the instrument of attaining to it; this cannot be denied, it is ever to be insisted on; I begin with it as a first principle; however, the very truth of it carries men too far, and confirms to them the notion that it is the whole of the matter. A narrow mind is thought to be that which contains little knowledge; and an enlarged mind, that which holds a great deal; and what seems to put the matter beyond dispute is, the fact of the great number of studies which are pursued in a University, by its very profession. Lectures are given on every kind of subject; examinations are held; prizes awarded. There are moral, metaphysical, physical Professors; Professors of languages, of history, of mathematics, of experimental science. Lists of questions are published, wonderful for their range and depth, variety and difficulty; treatises are written, which carry upon their very face the evidence of extensive reading or multifarious information; what then is wanting for mental culture to a person of large reading and scientific attainments? what is grasp of mind but acquirement? where shall philosophical repose be found, but in the consciousness and enjoyment of large intellectual possessions?

And yet this notion is, I conceive, a mistake, and my present business is to show that it is one, and that the end of a Liberal Education is not mere knowledge, or knowledge considered in its *matter*; and I shall best attain my object, by actually setting down some cases, which will be generally granted to be instances of the process of enlightenment or enlargement of mind, and others which are not, and thus, by the comparison, you will be able to judge for yourselves, Gentlemen, whether Knowledge, that is, acquirement, is after all the real principle of the enlargement, or whether that principle is not rather something beyond it.

8.

Education is a high word; it is the preparation for knowledge, and it is the imparting of knowledge in proportion to that preparation. We require intellectual eyes to know withal, as bodily eyes for sight. We need both objects and organs intellectual; we cannot gain them without setting about it; we cannot gain them in our sleep, or by hap-hazard. The best telescope does not dispense with eyes; the printing press or the lecture room will assist us greatly, but we must be true to ourselves, we must be parties in the work. A University is, according to the usual designation, an Alma Mater, knowing her children one by one, not a foundry, or a mint, or a treadmill.

Beyond the Utilitarian University[1]

Brian Easton

Brian Easton (born 1943) is an economist based in New Zealand. As the author, co-author, or editor for more than 30 books, including *Globalisation and the Wealth of Nations* (2007) and serving as a contributing editor for the *Listener* for thirty years, his subjects include education, fiscal policy, global politics, and social stability. His economic work has led to his induction into the Royal Statistical Society, the Royal Society of New Zealand, and he has held teaching posts at Georgetown and Harvard in addition to several universities in New Zealand. This essay was originally a paper delivered at the Forum on the Future of Universities at the University of Canterbury in 1999.

It is better to be Socrates dissatisfied than a pig satisfied; better to be Socrates dissatisfied than a fool satisfied. And if the fool, or the pig, are of a different

---

1   This is a revised version of paper presented to the Forum on the Future of Universities, University of Canterbury, 17 November 1999. Because the address was to a university audience, little attention is paid to the needs of polytechnics/ institutes of technology. However the principles discussed here are broadly relevant to them too, providing it is remembered that a vocational training needs an educational context. The author was invited to submit the revised paper to the journal by the Editor, so as to reach a wider audience than those participating in the 1999 forum.

opinion, it is because they only know their own side of the question. The other party to the comparisons knows both sides.[2]

The Idea of a University[3]

John Stuart Mill's quotation which heads this article is profoundly subversive, not only because Mill was challenging the utilitarianism of his father James Mill and his mentor Jeremy Bentham by suggesting there was a hierarchy of utilities, but also because it provides a critique of today's educational policies.

The subversion of the conventional economics has been extended by Amartya Sen, awarded an economics prize in honour of Alfred Nobel. He acknowledges the continuing importance of utilitarianism in public policy, but argues for an alternative approach, in which the possibility of choice—of opportunities—is given a separate role from what he (and Adam Smith) called "opulence"—the abundance of material things. The pig or the fool may be happy, but in their satisfaction they have no choice: no knowledge of the possibilities that lie beyond their current satiation.[4]

The pre-Mills utilitarianism which emphasises material production and consumption, without any distinction of quality, continues to dominate much of New Zealand public policy, including that to the tertiary sector. The 1988 *Report on Post Compulsory Education and Training in New Zealand* nicely captured the emphasis when it said that 'distinctions between education and training should be avoided'.[5] It may not be a distinction which pigs and fools make, but philosophers such as Mill and Sen—and anyone with a decent education—would.

The result of the failure to recognise the distinction is evident in the subsequent evolution of the New Zealand tertiary sector, which has focussed on the development of vocational skills for the accumulation of wealth to satisfy pigs and fools. Any educational role has become subservient, and is danger of being eliminated.

This issue is not a new one. One hundred and fifty years ago John Henry (Cardinal) Newman in his great advocacy of liberal education in *The Idea of a University*, poured scorn upon advocates of the utilitarian university:

> '[T]hey insist that Education should be confined to some particular and narrow end, and issue some definite work, which can be weighed and measured. They argue as if everything, as well as every person, had its price; and that where there has been great outlay, they have a right to expect a return in kind. This they call making Education and Instruction `useful', and `Utility' becomes their watchword. With a fundamental principle of this nature, they very naturally go on to ask, what there is to show for the expense of a University; what is the real

2   J.S. Mill (1863) 'Utilitarianism', page 260 of M. Warnock, (ed.) *Utilitarianism*, Collins, London, Fontana Library Edition, 1962.
3   Much of the broad analysis in this presentation is developed in my *The Commercialisation of New Zealand* (Auckland University Press, 1997), and *The Whimpering of the State: Policy After MMP* (Auckland University Press, 1999).
4   A. Sen (1999) *Development as Freedom*, Knopf, New York, p. 58.
5   G.R. Hawke (1989) *Report on Post Compulsory Education and Training in New Zealand*, Government Printer, Wellington.

worth in the market of the article called `Liberal Education,' on the supposition that it does not teach us definitely how to advance our manufactures, or improve our lands, or to better our civil economy; or again, if it does not at once make this man a lawyer, that an engineer, and that a surgeon, or at least if it does not lead to discoveries in chemistry, astronomy, geology, magnetism, and science of every kind.'[6]

James Fitzgerald had similar fears. In his 1852 inaugural address as Canterbury's first provincial superintendent he warned:

'There is something to my mind awful in the prospect of the great mass of the community rapidly increasing in wealth and power without that moral refinement which fits them to enjoy the one or that intellectual cultivation which enables them to use the other.'[7]

Yet, with a few minor changes the course the two were objecting to could summarize public policy for much of the 1990s, in which the function of universities is to provide the skills and the technologies for economic growth.

The universities—in part—and many university teachers seized upon the vocational objective for their institution, usually without realising that given today's conventional wisdom of how economic growth occurs, its logic was a policy framework in which universities are business enterprises responding to the vocational aspirations of paying students in a competitive market environment.

Fitzgerald's and Newman's broader objective for universities of cultivating the intellect, does not mean that universities should have nothing to do with economic growth. To the contrary, there are a number of principled and practical reasons it should.

First, as Sen makes very clear, while opulence is not the same thing as choice, greater opulence can in some circumstances give greater choice. He advocates a strategy of developing material wealth and choice, not an either or.

Second, universities are enormous users of the material output of the economy, and they cannot idly stand by consuming such quantities without contributing to their production.

Third, universities can contribute to increased material prosperity, as well as to opportunity and the intellect. If they do not, some other institutions will take over that role, and the universities will be diminished and unable to pursue their other objectives very well either. The dominance of the French *Ecoles* as a case in point.

Fourth, the economy is one of the central features of the human condition, and inevitably the universities will want to be involved with it in all its various manifestations.

So while Newman believed in liberal education, the university he developed had faculties of engineering, law and medicine as well as arts and science. The implication is that he thought it was possible for a university to have liberal objectives

---

6   J.H. Newman, *The Idea of a University* (1853) This edition Oxford, 1976, edited with introduction and notes by I.T. Kerr. p.125.

7   J. Hight & C.R. Strauble (ed) (1957-1971) *A History of Canterbury*, Whitcombe and Tombs, Christchurch.

without compromising their contribution to opulence. But how to organise such a university system?

The Objectives of a University

It is fundamental to a liberal society that there is no simple objective for a university or, indeed, for many other social institutions. The notion that a university's performance can be solely characterised by a financial bottom line (or the state of its balance sheet) is flawed. This fallacy was taken to the absurd limit by the Scott-Smelt report, which seemed to think each university was a property company owned by the central government.[8]

Certainly the physical assets of a university are substantial, valuable in market terms, and evident. But as my *The Commercialisation of New Zealand* demonstrates, they are only a small part of the totality of the assets which make up a university, for the market value of the faculty and student interests far exceeding any property interest. Perhaps universities should separate out their property interests into a company, but that would be to quarantine an obsession with physical assets from the central activities of a university.

What should really matter to a university is its reputation: its standing in the world of international scholarship, of the community in which it serves, among its alumni their friends and employers. Reputation is intangible but as Cassio says to Iago 'Reputation! O, I have lost my reputation! I have lost the immortal part of myself, and what remains is bestial.' (*Othello*: II, iii)

Because it is a multi-dimensional objective assessing reputation is not easy. But that does not justify identifying an easily indicator and setting that as the indicator. It is too reminiscent of the drunk looking under a lamppost for his keys lost in the dark, because he could see there.

It makes far more sense to someone associated with a university to ask at the end of the day, have I added to my university's reputation (and among whom have I added to the reputation), rather than what have I done for the bottom line of the institution's statement of economic performance. That does not mean that they should be unaware of the bottom line. But it is a means to an end, not as the Scott-Smelt report would seem to have it, and end in itself.

While ultimately the reputation of a university is assessed in the public area an institution needs trustees or guardians of its reputation? In the first instance it has to be the faculty, with the authority embodied in an academic body such as a professorial board or senate.

But their internal assessment needs to be monitored by a group from the wider community who are the ultimate assessors of reputation. There is no single interest group. The Scott-Smelt report, with its obsession of universities as property companies, advocated a Council consisting of business people appointed by the government. Not only would that give oppressive authoritarian powers to the central government, but it failed to recognize the diversity of the university

---

8 G.C. Scott and S. Smelt (1995) Ownership of Universities, New Zealand Vice-chancellor's Committee, Wellington.

objectives. The typical Council with its representatives of staff and students, the Court of Convocation, the local community (including its Maori dimension) and secondary schools, economic sectoral interests, is a sensible attempt to reflect the diversity.

One might also add academics with international reputations who are based offshore or in other domestic institutions, since they are some of the most important judges of each university's reputation. Given the difficult of their regular attendance this might suggest two tiers: a large Court that met once a year to review the university's performance, and elect a much smaller Council which met monthly and ran the affairs of the university as is the current practice. (Of course such a Council may need to co-opt to cover gaps in expertise.) The emphasis in the Court—and to a lesser extent the Council—should be on representativeness of all the diverse interest universities have. Appointees to the Court by the government may be appropriate, but should be very much a minority. The government needs to have some confidence in the inherent democracy of a widely representative Court.

Public Funding for Universities

The funding of each university needs to be as diverse as possible, although given that New Zealand has not a tradition of private foundations and charities, the majority will come from various public sources—and, possibly, student fees. The public funding needs to be diverse and protected from direct political interference. In the 1990s, following the abolition of the University Grants Committee, this simple principle was ignored. University teaching was directly funded by parliament (with any research funding increasingly separated out).

Initially, and consistent with the PCET report philosophy, the approach to funding was to treat all courses as if they were vocational, with little assessment of quality of even the vocational component. The quantum was broadly in proportion to the perceived length of the course. The result was to penalise institutions which favoured longer high quality courses with an educational component—most obviously the universities. As Newman remarked 'They measure knowledge by bulk, as it lies in a rude block, without symmetry, without design.'[9]

International comparison of cohort attainment show New Zealand is strong on certificates (although this does not take into consideration that many of them are of little worth) but it is below the OECD average on degrees—which is exactly what one would predict if the focus is on 'bulk'.

The principle of an intermediary between government and the institutions was reintroduced in 2000 with the Tertiary Education Commission. While it has begun to address the absurdity of the previous funding arrangements, the Commission seems trapped by its obligations towards primarily vocational courses. It is difficult to separate out educational and vocational—although unlike the PCET report—we should try. It may be a useful test is course length, with no government funding for short courses, and an increasing proportion as the course lengthens. A practical consideration is that longer courses are relatively cheaper to monitor for quality.

---

9 *Op. cit.* p.135

That fifteen years after the PCET report, the issues are still not properly resolved indicates just how pernicious the report's philosophy has been. New Zealand universities continue to be dogged by the weakness identified by the 1925 (Reichel-Tate) Royal Commission Universities which concluded they 'offer[ed] unrivalled facilities for gaining university degrees but…[are] less successful in providing a university education'.[10]

The Performance Based Research Fund (PBRF) evaluation concluded that around 40 percent of university staff were research inactive. Whatever the exact meaning of the higher grades, and acknowledging that some of the research inactive staff were involved on valuable non-teaching activities which did not constitute research under the PBRF, one is left with the uneasy feeling that a good proportion of university staff are nowhere near the frontier of their subject or profession and may not even care. Reichel and Tate would not have been surprised. More surprising is that in the mid 1990s, most university departments underwent external performance reviews, which gave no indication of a widespread problem which the 40 percent figure suggests. It can't be merely a matter of funding, for there would have been little difference in the ranking between universities and departments. The fact is that many departments have no culture of research or of academic and professional excellence.

From this perspective, PBRF funding—that is separate funding based on research performance—may be welcomed. But it only indirectly addresses the problem of the quality of the courses. Today universities are focussing on improving their PBRF indicators. This is understandable given that there is funding attached. But the way the game is scored shapes the way it is played, and the PBRF is subverting the central issues of degrees rather than education. The smartest thing the Tertiary Education Commission could do would be to abandon revising the PBRF, and introduce new funding measures which focus on the central issue. It needs to be imaginative. Why not include making a grant in terms of the library facilities each university has.

Any funding needs to be more stable and long term, too. The current weakness is captured by the conclusion of the White Paper, *Tertiary Education in New Zealand*, that 'funding for up to three years may be allocated to encourage strategically-focussed research portfolios rather than short-term projects.' Three years for a research project is short term in academic—although not necessarily business—terms. Year-to-year funding for teaching is equally short sighted.

The Student Contribution to Funding Universities

One of the major funding sources of a utilitarian university is fees from students. They are justified because their courses are seen a primarily vocational, with no benefit other than the higher income the student will eventually end up with as a result of the course. We can dispute over what part of the total costs of a university are for teaching, and just what proportion students should pay—all very utilitarian.

---

10   H.R. Reichal (1925) *Report of Royal Commission on University Education in New Zealand*, Govt Printer, Wellington, p. 11.

However, I want to ask a more fundamental question. If the utilitarian model has no distinction between education and training, why should students not also pay for their secondary school education, or their primary school education, or even pre-school education? This was not a question the PCET committee addressed, but I take it their answer would have been that it was all a matter of time and political strategy.

In contrast surely in a liberal democracy there is the principle that New Zealand children have an educational entitlement (which encompasses a vocational element too). It is best articulated in Peter Fraser's famous statement drafted by Clarence Beeby:

> "The government's objective, broadly expressed, is that every person, whatever her or his level of academic ability, whether he or she be rich or poor, whether he or she live in country or town, has a right, as a citizen, to a free education of the kind for which her or she is best fitted, and to the fullest extent of her or his powers."[11]

This entitlement—(broadly) free access to educational opportunity—is a part of the core of a modern society together with civil rights, a reasonable standard of living, health care, and access to a safe and sustainable physical and social environment. (Plus, Sen would add, genuine choice for life paths which is what the entitlement is about.)

The extent of these entitlements reflects the overall national circumstances. They will be less extensive in a poorer country than a rich one. A very poor country might only be able to supply an entitlement of primary education, a rich country will include tertiary education in its entitlement.

Where does New Zealand fit on this spectrum? From the 1960s—the Parry Report is the marker—the tertiary educational entitlement was broadened as more students—notably women and from minorities— came up to university and as polytechnics/ institutes of technology became more available. However since the early 1990s that entitlement is being steadily diminished. Are we no longer a rich country and can only offer educational entitlements to the end of secondary school?

The issue is further complicated by students making sacrifices to obtain a tertiary qualification. Even if all their fees and subsistence are paid by others, they could still have a higher material standard of living by working. However, they are not—in general—going to have all tuition and living costs paid by the state. That may have been possible when only a minority continued after school but in the age of mass education that is no longer practical. So how are we going to share the cost burden between student and state?

Any convincing answer requires a systematic review, which will take up more space than is available here. The review could be a private sector or a public sector one. Key to its success will be a membership of people with open minds rather than representing interest groups who already have taken positions (a common New Zealand failure). The committee needs to avoid being stacked with utilitarians, like the PCET committee was. Ideally the membership should have the liberality

---

11   *AJHR*, 1939, E.1, pp.2-3, with amendments suggested by C.E. Beeby, *The Biography of an Idea: Beeby on Education* (NZER, 1992), p.189.

and vision that universities praise, but sadly do not always deliver. They also need to be acutely aware of the fiscal constrains the nation faces.

My inclinations—but I could be persuadable otherwise by such a committee—are that all New Zealand citizens should be eligible for a tertiary entitlement of (say) three years of post secondary school education and vocational training, the cost of which—including subsistence—would be paid largely by the state. After that I would be willing to countenance full cost charging, because by that stage most courses are getting vocational or professional (although there may be exceptions to ensure there is an adequate proportion of cultural minorities in programs where culture matters). But there could be provision for an extra year's entitlement for an extra year of liberal education, enabling a student to do an honours year in arts or pure science. Obviously defining such courses is difficult, but the option of treating everything as 'vocational' is worse. A liberal society gives some preference to a liberal education.

Courses which were fully funded would have to be systematically identified. Relying on student choice to assess quality does not work—and distorts the systems towards degrees (often of poor quality) over education. As already explained, I would be inclined to exclude all short term courses—except remedial language, mathematics and such like which would be run by the secondary system—although students would be allowed student loans to pay any fees.

This counsel of perfection is probably too expensive, given New Zealand's unwillingness to raise tax rates (and other pressing public expenditure demands) and the numbers of today's generations (together with past ones catching up) requiring tertiary qualifications. That probably means student allowances which are more generous to the poorest, student fees, and student loans to cover the deficit. But the aim should be to phase them out over time in favour of a more generous entitlement.

The current system of student loans involves financial instruments—technically, liabilities contingent on future income—which are manifestly inefficient, as is evident by the lack of understanding of them in the public discussion. How to reform them without a budget blowout is not easy. I would give some priority to government write-offs where the graduate was doing socially valuable, if poorly paid, work such as working for NGOs, or was located in regions which were not near—and therefore directly benefiting from—a university or similar organisation with a high educational content.

The Organisation of a University

Since 1989, public policy has tried to force universities into a business mode of operation. The approach is ultimately flawed, unless the objective is purely utilitarian. This has an important implication for vice-chancellors, who under the 1989 legislation were set up as chief executives of quasi-businesses. Whatever the law says, the practice has to be of the Vice Chancellor as primus inter pares—the first among the equals. If reputation is the simplest way of thinking about a university's objectives, that reputation rests with the faculty—the college of academics. The Vice Chancellor heads the college. On the other hand, individual faculty members are going to have to take more responsibility for the resources they utilize. This is not a problem unique to the universities—for instance in the medical profession is increasingly facing the challenge of being resource managers. It is partly a question of efficiency, but it is also one of autonomy for if the medics do not take resources into consideration when the make clinical decisions, they will find non-medics increasingly taking the medical decisions for them. The same applies to academics.

This devolution of resource management closer to academic units has been going on over the last few years. Sadly it has not reflected an academic philosophy of empowering staff to take greater responsibility for their contribution to the university reputation, but a desperate decentralisation by central university administration to cope with the limited resources.

As already mentioned, teaching is having to operate on a shorter cycle as its resource allocation becomes increasingly at the whim of students. That could mean that eventually the teaching process becomes very flexible, with only temporary teachers hired for six or twelve months, with the only permanent university staff being the administration. This will do little for research, scholarship or reputation. The alternative possibility is that there will be increased restriction of entry into courses, so that the teaching process is stable. But students would have no guarantees of activating their entitlements wherever they chose.

I shall not be surprised if the tertiary system evolves to a mix of the two approaches. Students would start off with open entry into general courses where it is possible to vary scale without compromising teaching standards and for which there is little concomitant scholarship or research. Further on there would be restricted entry for advanced courses, access being dependent upon attainment in the open entry courses. We are already familiar with the case to intermediates to professional courses, but it may become more widespread. We may even have universities designating colleges—including polytechnics or other tertiary education providers—to teach the open entry courses, because the culture of the different teaching may become so divergent.

Direct competitive pressures for students only aggravate the instability of student demand, with a concomitant deterioration of the effectiveness of the supply side. The 1990s policy framework encouraged competition. This has been abandoned in recent years, but there is still a need to encourage co-operation, especially where there are very specialist resources. The most specialist resources will frequently be teachers in particular fields. The logic is to share them between institutions, not to make inferior appointments, while under-working top specialists.

There is no simple answer to maintaining quality standards, which underpin reputation. During the 1990s there was a move towards bench-marking but that seems to have come to a halt. Could the Tertiary Education Commission provide funding incentives for regular bench-marking, typically against overseas universities or departments? Done systematically and sensitively that is likely to give better outcomes than the PBRF exercise.

Epilogue

There has always been a tendency for New Zealand universities to be utilitarian reflecting the practicality of New Zealand life and a lack of prominence of the intellectual. However, the 1990s saw much greater pressure to make utilitarian vocational trainers of New Zealand's universities. There has been some blunting of those pressures in recent years, but there is little sense of an alternative vision.

Because the modern mass university cannot isolate itself from the international, national, and local society in which it exists, any change to the policy framework—a reduction in its utilitarianism—will be of benefit to the wider society too, not least in its promotion of liberal democracy, of choice and opportunity, and of the value of the intellect.

John Henry Newman and the Modern University

David Roberts

> **David Roberts** is the Dean of Faculty at Birmingham City University and taught at Bristol, Oxford, and Worchester before being named as the inaugural John Henry Newman Chair at Newman University College in 2008. His research focuses on seventeenth and eighteenth-century literature, and he has written five books on the subject in addition to being published in top journals, but also includes social history and educational philosophy. The short essay below was written in response to his appointment to the John Henry Newman Chair at Newman University College, Birmingham.

In 2008, Newman University College in Birmingham decided to celebrate its fortieth anniversary in a very unusual way: not with a plaque or even a party but by creating a very unusual job. The brief for the John Henry Newman Chair was as wide-ranging as it is unorthodox. It involves helping to develop research in the arts and humanities, to work with local and national partners on educational projects and—here's where the man himself really enters the equation—to contribute to public debate about higher education in the context of Newman's own thinking, most famously expressed in the lecture series first published in 1852 *The Idea of a University Defined and Illustrated*. In the world of modern universities, awash with targets, PR speak and bureaucracy, nothing could be more timely. After many years of running a large department in a huge urban university, I accepted the offer to become the first John Henry Newman Professor with a mixture of pride, humility, pleasure and relief.

Why is *The Idea of a University* such an important text for our times? Largely because it gives us the best definitions of a term many of us treasure, and which is in danger of falling into disrepute. When Newman defined 'liberal education' he set out a network of ideas about people, knowledge and intellectual communities that are increasingly under threat as more universities resemble, in his ringing words, foundries, mints and treadmills. Not for Newman a system in which universities are in a state of constant paranoia about the whims of government; only if they are configured as self-governing communities can they fulfil their essential purpose of being a genuine 'Alma Mater, knowing her children one by one'. In his fine 1996 Yale edition of *The Idea of a University*, Frank M. Turner throws down the gauntlet for Vice Chancellors who think they can ignore this canonical work: 'At their peril those concerned with modern university life—students, faculty, trustees, alumni and parents—may ignore Newman's volume, but if they read it and think seriously about it, whether in agreement or disagreement, they cannot remain indifferent to what he wrote—unless they are fundamentally indifferent to higher education to begin with.'

We shouldn't infer that reading Newman is easy for the modern student or Vice Chancellor. Turner's a fine gauntlet to throw down when his edition includes five modern scholarly essays detailing all the excuses there are for remaining indifferent to Newman. 'Virtually every circumstance surrounding the conception, the character and the contents of *The Idea of a University*,' Turner writes in one of them, 'apparently works against its ongoing claims to relevance.' It's easy—correct, facile—to show why. At the time Newman was an Oxonian exiled to Dublin and among the questions that did not concern him were public funding, government regulation, assessment, research, female students, careers advice, cultural relativism, widening participation, the internet, not to mention the possibility that compulsory theology might not be the best way to up your UCAS applications or top the league table for student satisfaction. Even in the 1850s, Turner points out, Newman was globally speaking 'in an academic time warp', since in 1862 the Morrill Act would pave the way for non-religious, research-based US universities such as Johns Hopkins and Cornell.

Even the table of contents for *The Idea of a University* may be enough to persuade secular readers that taking up Turner's gauntlet and actually reading the book will not do much for their understanding of universities today. Of its nine chapters or 'discourses', one defines theology as a branch of knowledge, another two the relation between theology and broader knowledge, and a further two the relation between knowledge and religious belief and institutions—not, on the face of it, the stuff of mission statements for any educational establishment except a seminary.

Turner's gauntlet lies there all the same. Canonical texts are by definition not slaves to their contexts, and to object that Newman couldn't imagine the internet or junior colleges is no better than accusing Shakespeare of being an incompetent aviator. *The Idea of a University* has a stubborn core of interest for today's 'students, faculty, trustees, alumni and parents' and it is largely to be found in Discourses 5 and 6 ('Knowledge Its Own End' and 'Knowledge in Relation to Learning'). For indifference to the questions they raise there really is no excuse.

To take one example among many, the opening of Discourse 5 marks the point where Newman moves from 'Studies' to 'Students', from the curriculum to its benefit for individuals. Although Newman's idea of the curriculum has little to do with ours, the fact that he raises it as a primary concern for universities and their students presents a challenge since the student, not the subject, is the explicit focus of today's dominant discourse of higher education. Students are choosers in a market and through individual development portfolios and checklists of skills we make them, systematically, the objects of their own attention. With the exception of professionally accredited courses we try to give them what we think they want or can cope with, in whatever combinations we can manage. It is harder than ever before to design a course around the principles of a subject and to fail students because they can't prove they understand them. In learning outcomes, mere 'knowledge' is a dirty word; among criteria for a bare pass, a 'fragmentary' grasp of the subject will do.

It follows that university mission statements rarely mention the idea of the curriculum except to signify that desirable quality, up-to-dateness. An unintentionally hilarious example is drawn from the website of an institution that is 'striving to become a world-class regional university' by having a curriculum 'refreshed by running streams of insights, expertise and creativity', qualities that didn't extend to the drafting of its mission statement. Instead, there is a pervasive appeal to a 'whole person' composed of tolerant social attitudes and the desire to 'make a difference'.

Radically in the current circumstances, Discourse 5 of *The Idea of a University* argues both that the 'whole person' emerges through knowledge and that knowledge is modified in the process: 'the drift and meaning of a branch of knowledge varies with the company in which it is introduced to the student'—not an easy idea to square with any apparatus of common learning outcomes and criteria. It is no contradiction to say that knowledge is also 'an intellectual tradition ... independent of particular teachers', since it is there for any student to engage with and be guided by. The object is not, in the usual misunderstanding, to acquire knowledge 'for its own sake', but what Newman calls 'habits of mind', defined as 'freedom, equitableness, calmness, moderation and wisdom'.

If those habits stick, they can't be reduced to an 'accidental advantage ... which we can borrow for the occasion, carry about in our hand, and take to the market'; not just a set of skills with a price tag. Newman has in mind the far richer transformation of learning that makes it, for each and every student, 'an acquired illumination' and 'an inward endowment'. Those phrases remind us that he was above all else a religious thinker but they also invite comparison with the miserably impoverished, instrumental way in which universities often characterize a process that for every student should be made not just of skills, or compliance, or even tolerance. For if we are not to be fundamentally indifferent to higher education, we should learn again to conceive of it as Newman did: in the double sense of the term, a process of wonder.

The Higher Education of Women

Anna Julia Cooper

Anna Julia Cooper (1858-1964) was an influential African-American educator and writer from the early twentieth century. She received her PhD from the Sorbonne in 1924 and was an educator in Washington, DC, for much of her career. This essay, "The Higher Education of Women," is an excerpt from *A Voice from the South* (1892), a canonical text in black feminism.

In the very first year of our century, the year 1801, there appeared in Paris, a book by Silvain Marechal, entitled "Shall Woman Learn the Alphabet." The book proposes a law prohibiting the alphabet to women, and quotes authorities weighty and various, to prove that the woman who knows the alphabet has already lost part of her womanliness. The author declares that woman can use the alphabet only as Moliere predicted they would, in spelling out the verb *amo*; that they have no occasion to peruse Ovid's *Ars Amoris*, since that is already the ground and limit of their intuitive furnishing; that Madame Guion would have been far more adorable had she remained a beautiful ignoramus as nature made her; that Ruth, Naomi, the Spartan woman, the Amazons, Penelope, Andromache, Lucretia, Joan of Arc, Petrarch's Laura, the daughters of Charlemagne, could not spell their names; while Sappho, Aspasia, Madame de Maintenon, and Madame de Stael could read altogether too well for their good; finally, that if women were once permitted to read Sophocles and work with logarithms, or to nibble at any side of the apple of knowledge, there would be an end forever to their sewing on buttons and embroidering slippers.

Please remember this book was published at the *beginning* of the Nineteenth Century. At the end of its first third, (in the year 1833) one solitary college in America decided to admit women within its sacred precincts, and organized what was called a "Ladies' Course" as well as the regular B. A. or Gentlemen's course.

It was felt to be an experiment—a rather dangerous experiment—and was adopted with fear and trembling by the good fathers, who looked as if they had been caught secretly mixing explosive compounds and were guiltily expecting every moment to see the foundations under them shaken and rent and their fair superstructure shattered into fragments.

But the girls came, and there was no upheaval. They performed their tasks modestly and intelligently. Once in a while one or two, were found choosing the gentlemen's course. Still no collapse; and the dear, careful, scrupulous, frightened old professors were just getting their hearts out of their throats and preparing to draw one good free breath, when they found they would have to change the names of those courses; for there were as many ladies in the gentlemen's course as in the ladies', and a distinctively Ladies' Course, inferior in scope and aim to the regular classical course, did not and could not exist.

Other colleges gradually fell into line, and to-day there are one hundred and ninety-eight colleges for women, and two hundred and seven coeducational colleges and universities in the United States alone offering the degree of B. A. to women, and sending out yearly into the arteries of this nation a warm, rich flood of strong, brave, active, energetic, well-equipped, thoughtful women—women quick to see and eager to help the needs of this needy world—women who can think as well as feel, and who feel none the less because they think—women who are none the less tender and true for the parchment scroll they bear in their hands—women who have given a, deeper, richer, nobler and grander meaning to the word "womanly" than any one-sided masculine definition could [e]ver have suggested or inspired—women whom the world has long waited for in pain and anguish till there should be at last added to its forces and allowed to permeate its thought the complement of that masculine influence which has dominated it for fourteen centuries.

Since the idea of order and subordination succumbed to barbarian brawn and brutality in the fifth century, the civilized world has been like a child brought up by his father. It has needed the great mother heart to teach it to be pitiful, to love mercy, to succor the weak and care for the lowly.

Whence came this apotheosis of greed and cruelty? Whence this sneaking admiration we all have for bullies and prize-fighters? Whence the self-congratulation of "dominant" races, as if "dominant" meant "righteous" and carried with it a title to inherit the earth? Whence the scorn of so-called weak or unwarlike races and individuals, and the very comfortable assurance that it is their manifest destiny to be wiped out as vermin before this advancing civilization? As if the possession of the Christian graces of meekness, non-resistance and forgiveness, were incompatible with a civilization professedly based on Christianity, the religion of love! Just listen to this little bit of Barbarian brag: "As for Far Orientals, they are not of those who will survive. Artistic attractive people that they are, their civilization is like their own tree flowers, beautiful blossoms destined never to bear fruit. If these people continue in their old course, their earthly career is closed. Just as surely as morning passes into afternoon, so surely are these races of the Far East, if unchanged, destined to disappear before the advancing nations of the West. Vanish, they will, off the face of the earth, and leave our planet the eventual possession of the dwellers where the day declines. Unless their newly imported ideas really take root, it is from this whole world that Japanese and Koreans, as well as Chinese, will inevitably be excluded. Their Nirvana is already being realized; already, it has wrapped Far Eastern Asia in its winding sheet."—*Soul of the Far East—P. Lowell.*

Delightful reflection for "the dwellers where day declines." A spectacle to make the gods laugh, truly, to see the scion of an upstart race by one sweep of his generalizing pen consigning to annihilation one-third the inhabitants of the globe—a people whose civilization was hoary headed before the parent elements that begot his race had advanced beyond nebulosity.

How like Longfellow's Iagoo, we Westerners are, to be sure! In the few hundred years, we have had to strut across our allotted territory and bask in the afternoon sun, we imagine we have exhausted the possibilities of humanity. Verily, we are the people, and after us there is none other. Our God is power; strength, our standard of excellence, inherited from barbarian ancestors through a long line of male progenitors, the Law Salic permitting no feminine modifications.

Says one, "The Chinaman is not popular with us, and we do not like the Negro. It is not that the eyes of the one are set bias, and the other is dark-skinned; but the Chinaman, the Negro is weak—*and Anglo Saxons don't like weakness.*"

The world of thought under the predominant man-influence, unmollified and unrestrained by its complementary force, would become like Daniel's fourth beast: "dreadful and terrible, and *strong* exceedingly;" "it had great iron teeth; it devoured and brake in pieces, and stamped the residue with the feet of it;" and the most independent of us find ourselves ready at times to fall down and worship this incarnation of power.

Mrs. Mary A. Livermore, a woman whom I can mention only to admire, came near shaking my faith a few weeks ago in my theory of the thinking woman's mission to put in the tender and sympathetic chord in nature's grand symphony, and counteract, or better, harmonize the diapason of more strength and might.

She was dwelling on the Anglo-Saxon genius for power and his contempt for weakness, and described a scene in San Francisco which she had witnessed.

The incorrigible animal known as the American small-boy, had pounced upon a simple, unoffending Chinaman, who was taking home his work, and had emptied the beautifully laundried contents of his basket into the ditch. "And," said she, "when that great man stood there and blubbered before that crowd of lawless urchins, to any one of whom he might have taught a lesson with his two fists, *I didn't much care.*"

This is said like a man! It grates harshly. It smacks of the worship of the beast. It is contempt for weakness, and taken out of its setting it seems to contradict my theory. It either shows that one of the highest exponents of the Higher Education can be at times untrue to the instincts I have ascribed to the thinking woman and to the contribution she is to add to the civilized world, or else the influence she wields upon our civilization may be potent without being necessarily and always direct and conscious. The latter is the case. Her voice may strike a false note, but her whole being is musical with the vibrations of human suffering. Her tongue may parrot over the cold conceits that some man has taught her, but her heart is aglow with sympathy and loving kindness, and she cannot be true to her real self without giving out these elements into the forces of the world.

No one is in any danger of imagining Mark Antony "a plain blunt man," nor Cassius a sincere one—whatever the speeches they may make.

As individuals, we are constantly and inevitably, whether we are conscious of it or not, giving out our real selves into our several little worlds, inexorably adding our own true ray to the flood of starlight, quite independently of our professions and our masquerading; and so in the world of thought, the influence of thinking woman far transcends her feeble declamation and may seem at times even opposed to it.

A visitor in Oberlin once said to the lady principal, "Have you no rabble in Oberlin? How is it I see no police here, and yet the streets are as quiet and orderly as if there were an officer of the law standing on every corner."

Mrs. Johnston replied, "Oh, yes; there are vicious persons in Oberlin just as in other towns—*but our girls are our police.*"

With from five to ten hundred pure-minded young women threading the streets of the village every evening unattended, vice must slink away, like frost before the rising sun and yet I venture to say there was not one in a hundred of those girls who would not have run from a street brawl as she would from a mouse, and who would not have declared she could never stand the sight of blood and pistols.

There is, then, a real and special influence of woman. An influence subtle and often involuntary, an influence so intimately interwoven in, so intricately interpenetrated by the masculine influence of the time that it is often difficult to extricate the delicate meshes and analyze and identify the closely clinging fibers. And yet, without this influence—so long as woman sat with bandaged eyes and manacled hands, fast bound in the clamps of ignorance and inaction, the world of thought moved in its orbit like the revolutions of the moon; with one face (the man's face) always out, so that the spectator could not distinguish whether it was disc or sphere.

Now I claim that it is the prevalence of the Higher Education among women, the making it a common everyday affair for women to reason and think and express their thought, the training and stimulus which enable and encourage women to administer to the world the bread it needs as well as the sugar it cries for; in short it is the transmitting the potential forces of her soul into dynamic factors that has given symmetry and completeness to the world's agencies. So only could it be consummated that Mercy, the lesson she teaches, and Truth, the task man has set himself, should meet together: that righteousness, or *rightness*, man's ideal,—and *peace*, its necessary 'other half,' should kiss each other.

We must thank the general enlightenment and independence of woman (which we may now regard as a *fait accompli*) that both these forces are now at work in the world, and it is fair to demand from them for the twentieth century a higher type of civilization than any attained in the nineteenth. Religion, science, art, economics, have all needed the feminine flavor; and literature, the expression of what is permanent and best in all of these, may be gauged at any time to measure the strength of the feminine ingredient. You will not find theology consigning infants to lakes of unquenchable fire long after women have had a chance to grasp, master, and wield its dogmas. You will not find science annihilating personality from the government of the Universe and making of God an ungovernable, unintelligible, blind, often destructive physical force; you will not find jurisprudence formulating as an axiom the absurdity that man and wife are one, and that one the man—that the married woman may not hold or bequeath her own property save as subject to her husband's direction; you will not find political economists declaring that the only possible adjustment between laborers and capitalists is that of selfishness and rapacity—that each must get all he can and keep all that he gets, while the world cries *laissez faire* and the lawyers explain, "it is the beautiful working of the law of supply and demand;" in fine, you will not find the law of love shut out from the affairs of men after the feminine half of the world's truth is completed.

Nay, put your ear now close to the pulse of the time. What is the key-note of the literature of these days? What is the banner cry of all the activities of the last half decade?" What is the dominant seventh which is to add richness and tone to the final cadences of this century and lead by a grand modulation into the triumphant harmonies of the next? Is it not compassion for the poor and unfortunate, and, as Bellamy has expressed it, "indignant outcry against the failure of the social machinery as it is, to ameliorate the miseries of men!" Even Christianity is being brought to the bar of humanity and tried by the standard of its ability to alleviate the world's suffering and lighten and brighten its woe. What else can be the meaning of Matthew Arnold's saddening protest, "We cannot do without Christianity," cried he, "and we cannot endure it as it is."

When went there by an age, when so much time and thought, so much money and labor were given to God's poor and God's invalids, the lowly and unlovely, the sinning as well as the suffering—homes for inebriates and homes for lunatics, shelter for the aged and shelter for babes, hospitals for the sick, props and braces for the falling, reformatory prisons and prison reformatories, all show that a "mothering" influence from some source is leavening the nation.

Now please understand me. I do not ask you to admit that these benefactions and virtues are the exclusive possession of women, or even that women are their chief and only advocates. It may be a man who formulates and makes them vocal. It may be, and often is, a man who weeps over the wrongs and struggles for the amelioration: but that man has imbibed those impulses from a mother rather than from a father and is simply materializing and giving back to the world in tangible form the ideal love and tenderness, devotion and care that have cherished and nourished the helpless period of his own existence.

All I claim is that there is a feminine as well as a masculine side to truth; that these are related not as inferior and superior, not as better and worse, not as weaker and stronger, but as complements—complements in one necessary and symmetric whole. That as the man is more noble in reason, so the woman is more quick in sympathy. That as he is indefatigable in pursuit of abstract truth, so is she in caring for the interests by the way—striving tenderly and lovingly that not one of the least of these 'little ones' should perish. That while we not unfrequently see women who reason, we say, with the coolness and precision of a man, and men as considerate of helplessness as a woman, still there is a general consensus of mankind that the one trait is essentially masculine and the other as peculiarly feminine. That both are needed to be worked into the training of children, in order that our boys may supplement their virility by tenderness and sensibility, and our girls may round out their gentleness by strength and self-reliance. That, as both are alike necessary in giving symmetry to the individual, so a nation or a race will degenerate into mere emotionalism on the one hand, or bullyism on the other, if dominated by either exclusively; lastly, and most emphatically, that the feminine factor can have its proper effect only through woman's development and education so that she may fitly and intelligently stamp her force on the forces of her day, and add her modicum to the riches of the world's thought.

"For woman's cause is man's: they rise or sink
Together, dwarfed or godlike, bond or free:
For she that out of Lethe scales with man

The shining steps of nature, shares with man
His nights, his days, moves with him to one goal.
If she be small, slight-natured, miserable,
How shall men grow?

* * *

Let, her make herself her own
To give or keep, to live and learn and be
All that not harms distinctive womanhood.
For woman is not undeveloped man
But diverse: could we make her as the man
Sweet love were slain; his dearest bond is this,
Not like to like, but like in difference.
Yet in the long years liker must they grow;
The man be more of woman, she of man;
He gain in sweetness and in moral height,
Nor lose the wrestling thews that throw the world;
She mental breadth, nor fail in childward care,
Nor lose the childlike in the larger mind;
Till at the last she set herself to man,
Like perfect music unto noble words."

Now you will argue, perhaps, and rightly, that higher education for women is not a modern idea, and that, if that is the means of setting free and invigorating the long desired feminine force in the world, it has already had a trial and should, in the past, have produced some of these glowing effects. Sappho, the bright, sweet singer of Lesbos, "the violet-crowned, pure, sweetly smiling Sappho" as Alcaeus calls her, chanted her lyrics and poured forth her soul nearly six centuries before Christ, in notes as full and free, as passionate and eloquent as did ever Archilochus or Anacreon.

Aspasia, that earliest queen of the drawing-room, a century later ministered to the intellectual entertainment of Socrates and the leading wits and philosophers of her time. Indeed, to her is attributed, by the best critics, the authorship of one of the most noted speeches ever delivered by Pericles.

Later on, during the Renaissance period, women were professors in mathematics, physics, metaphysics, and the classic languages in Bologna, Pavia, Padua, and Brescia. Olympia Fulvia Morata, of Ferrara, a most interesting character, whose magnificent library was destroyed in 1553 in the invasion of Schweinfurt by Albert of Brandenburg, had acquired a most extensive education. It is said that this wonderful girl gave lectures on classical subjects in her sixteenth year, and had even before that written several very remarkable Greek and Latin poems, and what is also to the point, she married a professor at Heidelberg, and became a *help-meet for him.*

It is true then that the higher education for women—in fact, the highest that the world has ever witnessed—belongs to the past; but we must remember that it was possible, down to the middle of our own century, only to a select few; and that the fashions and traditions of the times were before that all against it. There were not only no stimuli to encourage women to make the most of their powers and to welcome their development as a helpful agency in the progress of civilization, but their little aspirations, when they had any, were chilled and snubbed in embryo, and any attempt at thought was received as a monstrous usurpation of man's prerogative.

Lessing declared that "the woman who thinks is like the man who puts on rouge—ridiculous;" and Voltaire in his coarse, flippant way used to say, "Ideas are like beards—women and boys have none." Dr. Maginn remarked, "We like to hear a few words of sense from a woman sometimes, as we do from a parrot—they are so unexpected!" and even the pious Fenelon taught that virgin delicacy is almost as incompatible with learning as with vice.

That the average woman retired before these shafts of wit and ridicule and even gloried in her ignorance is not surprising. The Abbe Choisi, it is said, praised the Duchesse de Fontanges as being pretty as an angel and silly as a goose, and all the young ladies of the court strove to make up in folly what they lacked in charms. The ideal of the day was that "women must be pretty, dress prettily, flirt prettily, and not be too well informed;" that it was the *summum bonum* of her earthly hopes to have, as Thackeray puts it, "all the fellows battling to dance with her;" that she had no God-given destiny, no soul with unquenchable longings and inexhaustible possibilities—no work of her own to do and give to the world—no absolute and inherent value, no duty to self, transcending all pleasure-giving that may be demanded of a mere toy; but that her value was purely a relative one and to be estimated as are the fine arts—by the pleasure they give. "Woman, wine and song," as "the world's best gifts to man," were linked together in praise with as little thought of the first saying, "What doest thou," as that the wine and the song should declare, "We must be about our Father's business."

Men believed, or pretended to believe, that the great law of self development was obligatory on their half of the human family only; that while it was the chief end of man to glorify God and put his five talents to the exchangers, gaining thereby other five, it was, or ought to be, the sole end of woman to glorify man and wrap her one decently away in a napkin, retiring into "Hezekiah Smith's lady during her natural life and Hezekiah Smith's relict on her tombstone;" that higher education was incompatible with the shape of the female cerebrum, and that even if it could be acquired it must inevitably unsex woman destroying the lisping, clinging, tenderly helpless, and beautifully dependent creatures whom men would so heroically think for and so gallantly fight for, and giving in their stead a formidable race of blue stockings with corkscrew ringlets and other sinister propensities.

But these are eighteenth century ideas.

We have seen how the pendulum has swung across our present century. The men of our time have asked with Emerson, "that woman only show us how she can best be served;" and woman has replied: the chance of the seedling and of the animalcule is all I ask—the chance for growth and self development, the permission to be true to the aspirations of my soul without incurring the blight of your censure and ridicule.

"Audetque viris concurrere virgo."

In soul-culture woman at last dares to contend with men, and we may cite Grant Allen (who certainly cannot be suspected of advocating the unsexing of woman) as an example of the broadening effect of this contest on the ideas at least of the men of the day. He says, in his *Plain Words on the Woman Question*, recently published:

"The position of woman was not [in the] past [a] position which could bear the test of nineteenth-century scrutiny. Their education was inadequate, their social status was humiliating, their political power was nil, their practical and personal grievances were innumerable; above all, their relations to the family—to their husbands, their children, their friends, their property—was simply insupportable."

And again:

"As a body we 'Advanced men' are, I think, prepared to reconsider, and to reconsider fundamentally, without prejudice or misconception, the entire question of the relation [between] the sexes. We are ready to make any modifications in those relations which will satisfy the woman's just aspiration for personal independence, for intellectual and moral development, for physical culture, for political activity, and for a voice in the arrangement of her own affairs, both domestic and national."

Now this is magnanimous enough, surely; and quite a step from eighteenth century preaching, is it not? The higher education of Woman has certainly developed the men; —let us see what it has done for the women.

Matthew Arnold during his last visit to America in '82 or '83, lectured before a certain co-educational college in the West. After the lecture he remarked, with some surprise, to a lady professor, that the young women in his audience, he noticed, paid as close attention as the men, *all the way through*. This led, of course, to a spirited discussion of the higher education for women, during which he said to his enthusiastic interlocutor, eyeing her philosophically through his English eyeglass: "But—eh—don't you think it—eh—spoils their *chawnces*, you know!"

Now, as to the result to women, this is the most serious argument ever used against the higher education. If it interferes with marriage, classical training has a grave objection to weigh and answer.

For I agree with Mr. Allen at least on this one point, that there must be marrying and giving in marriage even till the end of time.

I grant you that intellectual development, with the self-reliance and capacity for earning a livelihood which it gives, renders woman less dependent on the marriage relation for physical support (which, by the way, does not always accompany it). Neither is she compelled to look to sexual love as the one sensation capable of giving tone and relish, movement and vim to the life she leads. Her horizon is extended. Her sympathies are broadened and deepened and multiplied. She is in closer touch with nature. Not a bud that opens, not a dew drop, not a ray of light, not a cloud-burst or a thunderbolt, but adds to the expansiveness and zest of her soul. And if the sun of an absorbing passion be gone down, still 'tis night that brings the stars. She has remaining the mellow, less obtrusive, but none the less enchanting and inspiring light of friendship, and into its charmed circle she may gather the best the world has known. She can commune with Socrates about the *daimon* he knew and to which she too can bear witness; she can revel in the majesty of Dante, the sweetness of Virgil, the simplicity of Homer, the strength of Milton. She can listen to the pulsing heart throbs of passionate Sappho's encaged soul, as she beats her bruised wings against her prison bars and struggles to flutter out into Heaven's æther, and the fires of her own soul cry back as she listens. "Yes; Sappho, I know it all; I know it all." Here, at last, can be communion without suspicion; friendship, without misunderstanding; love without jealousy.

We must admit then that Byron's picture, whether a thing of beauty or not, has faded from the canvas of to-day.

> "Man's love," he wrote, "is of man's life a thing apart,
> 'Tis woman's whole existence.
> Man may range the court, camp, church, the vessel and the mart,
> Sword, gown, gain, glory offer in exchange.
> Pride, fame, ambition, to fill up his heart—
> And few there are whom these cannot estrange.
> Men have all these resources, we *but one*—
> *To love again and be again undone.*"

This may have been true when written. *It is not true to-day.* The old, subjective, stagnant, indolent and wretched life for woman has gone. She has as many resources as men, as many activities beckon her on. As large possibilities swell and inspire her heart.

Now, then, does it destroy or diminish her capacity for loving?

Her standards have undoubtedly gone up. The necessity of speculating in 'chawnces' has probably shifted. The question is not now with the woman "How shall I so cramp, stunt, simplify and nullify myself as to make me el[i]gible to the honor of being swallowed up into some little man?" but the problem, I trow, now rests with the man as to how he can so develop his God-given powers as to reach the ideal of a generation of women who demand the noblest, grandest, and best achievements of which he is capable; and this surely is the only fair and natural adjustment of the chances. Nature never meant that the ideals and standards of the world should be dwarfing and minimizing ones, and the men should thank us for requiring of them the richest fruits which they can grow. If it makes them work, all the better for them.

As to the adaptability of the educated woman to the marriage relation, I shall simply quote from that excellent symposium of learned women that appeared recently under Mrs. Armstrong's signature in answer to the "Plain Words" of Mr. Allen, already referred to. "Admitting no longer any question as to their intellectual equality with the men whom they meet, with the simplicity of conscious strength, they take their place beside the men who challenge them, and fearlessly face the result of their actions. They deny that their education in any way unfits them for the duty of wifehood and maternity or primarily renders these conditions any less attractive to them than to the domestic type of woman. On the contrary, they hold that their knowledge of physiology makes them better mothers and housekeepers; their knowledge of chemistry makes them better cooks; while from their training in other natural sciences and in mathematics, they obtain an accuracy and fair-mindedness which is of great value to them in dealing with their children or employees."

So much for their willingness. Now the apple may be good for food and pleasant to the eyes, and a fruit to be desired to make one wise. Nay, it may even assure you that it has no aversion whatever to being tasted. Still, if you do not like the flavor all these recommendations are nothing. Is the intellectual woman *desirable* in the matrimonial market?

This I cannot answer. I confess my ignorance. I am no judge of such things. I have been told that strong-minded women could be, when they thought it worth their while, quite endurable, and, judging from the number of female names I find in college catalogues among the alumnae with double patronymics, I surmise that quite a number of men are willing to put up with them.

Now I would that my task ended here. Having shown that a great want of the world in the past has been a feminine force; that that force can have its full effect only through the untrammeled development of woman; that such development, while it gives her to the world and to civilization, does not necessarily remove her from the home and fireside; finally, that while past centuries have witnessed sporadic instances of this higher growth, still it was reserved for the latter half of the nineteenth century to render it common and general enough to be effective; I might close with a glowing prediction of what the twentieth century may expect from this heritage of twin forces—the masculine battered and toil-worn as a grim veteran after centuries of warfare, but still strong, active, and vigorous, ready to help with his hard-won experience the young recruit rejoicing in her newly found freedom, who so confidently places her hand in his with mutual pledges to redeem the ages.

> "And so, the twain upon the skirts of Time,
>   Sit side by side, full-summed in all their powers,
>   Dispensing harvest, sowing the To-be,
>   Self-reverent each and reverencing each."

Fain would I follow them, but duty is nearer home. The high ground of generalities is alluring but my pen is devoted to a special cause: and with a view to further enlightenment on the achievements of the century for THE HIGHER EDUCATION OF COLORED WOMEN, I wrote a few days ago to the colleges which admit women and asked how many-colored women had completed the B. A. course in each during its entire history. These are the figures returned: Fisk leads the way with twelve; Oberlin next with five; Wilberforce, four; Ann Arbor and Wellesley three each, Livingstone two, Atlanta one, Howard, as yet, none.

I then asked the principal of the Washington High School how many out of a large number of female graduates from his school had chosen to go forward and take a collegiate course. He replied that but one had ever done so, and she was then in Cornell.

*Graduated from Scientific Course, June 1890, the first colored woman to graduate from Cornell.

Others ask questions too, sometimes, and I was asked a few years ago by a white friend, "How is it that the men of your race seem to outstrip the women in mental attainment?" "Oh," I said, "so far as it is true, the men, I suppose, from the life they lead, gain more by contact; and so far, as it is only apparent, I think the women are more quiet. They don't feel called to mount a barrel and harangue by the hour every time they imagine they have produced an idea."

But I am sure there is another reason which I did not at that time see fit to give. The atmosphere, the standards, the requirements of our little world do not afford any special stimulus to female development.

It seems hardly a gracious thing to say, but it strikes me as true, that while our men seem thoroughly abreast of the times on almost every other subject, when they strike the woman question they drop back into sixteenth century logic. They leave nothing to be desired generally in regard to gallantry and chivalry, but they actually do not seem sometimes to have outgrown that old contemporary of chivalry—the idea that women may stand on pedestals or live in doll houses, (if they happen to have them) but they must not furrow their brows with thought or attempt to help men tug at the great questions of the world. I fear the majority of colored men do not yet think it worth while that women aspire to higher education. Not many will subscribe to the "advanced" ideas of Grant Allen already quoted. The three R's, a little music and a good deal of dancing, a first rate dress-maker and a bottle of magnolia balm, are quite enough generally to render charming any woman possessed of tact and the capacity for worshipping masculinity.

My readers will pardon my illustrating my point and also giving a reason for the fear that is in me, by a little bit of personal experience. When a child I was put into a school near home that professed to be normal and collegiate, i.e., to prepare teachers for colored youth, furnish candidates for the ministry, and offer collegiate training for those who should be ready for it. Well, I found after a while that I had a good deal of time on my hands. I had devoured what was put before me, and, like Oliver Twist, was looking around to ask for more. I constantly felt (as I suppose many an ambitious girl has felt) a thumping from within unanswered by any beckoning from without. Class after class was organized for these ministerial candidates (many of them men who had been preaching before I was born). Into every one of these classes I was expected to go, with the sole intent, I thought at the time, of enabling the dear old principal, as he looked from the vacant countenances of his sleepy old class over to where I sat, to get off his solitary pun—his never-failing pleasantry, especially in hot weather—which was, as he called out "Any one!" to the effect that "*any* one" then meant "*Annie* one."

Finally, a Greek class was to be formed. My inspiring preceptor informed me that Greek had never been taught in the school, but that he was going to form a class *for the candidates for the ministry*, and if I liked I might join it. I replied—humbly I hope, as became a female of the human species—that I would like very much to study Greek, and that I was thankful for the opportunity, and so it went on. A boy, however meager his equipment and shallow his pretentions, had only to declare a floating intention to study theology and he could get all the support, encouragement and stimulus he needed, be absolved from work and invested beforehand with all the dignity of his far away office. While a self-supporting girl had to struggle on by teaching in the summer and working after school hours to keep up with her board bills, and actually to fight her way against positive discouragements to the higher education; till one such girl one day flared out and told the principal "the only mission opening before a girl in his school was to marry one of those candidates." He said he didn't know but it was. And when at last that same girl announced her desire and intention to go to college it was received with about the same incredulity and dismay as if a brass button on one of those candidate's coats had propounded a new method for squaring the circle or trisecting the arc.

Now this is not fancy. It is a simple unvarnished photograph, and what I believe was not in those days exceptional in colored schools, and I ask the men and women who are teachers and co-workers for the highest interests of the race, that they give the girls a chance! We might as well expect to grow trees from leaves as hope to build up a civilization or a manhood without taking into consideration our women and the home life made by them, which must be the root and ground of the whole matter. Let us insist then on special encouragement for the education of our women and special care in their training. Let our girls feel that we expect something more of them than that they merely look pretty and appear well in society. Teach them that there is a race with special needs which they and only they can help; that the world needs and is already asking for their trained, efficient forces. Finally, if there is an ambitious girl with pluck and brain to take the higher education, encourage her to make the most of it. Let there be the same flourish of trumpets and clapping of hands as when a boy announces his determination to enter the lists; and then, as you know that she is physically the weaker of the two, don't stand from under and leave her to buffet the waves alone. Let her know that your heart is following her, that your hand, though she sees it not, is ready to support her. To be plain, I mean let money be raised and scholarships be founded in our colleges and universities for self-supporting, worthy young women, to offset and balance the aid that can always be found for boys who will take theology.

The earnest well trained Christian young woman, as a teacher, as a home-maker, as wife, mother, or silent influence even, is as potent a missionary agency among our people as is the theologian; and I claim that at the present stage of our development in the South she is even more important and necessary.

Let us then, here and now, recognize this force and resolve to make the most of it—not the boys less, but the girls more.

Being Educated

Sara Corbett

Sara Corbett is a contributing writer for the *New York Times Magazine* who
frequently writes about literacy, culture, and related topics. This version of her
essay originally appeared in the September 15, 2010 edition of the magazine.

One morning last winter I watched a middle-school teacher named Al Doyle give
a lesson, though not your typical lesson. This was New York City, a noncharter
public school in an old building on a nondescript street near Gramercy Park,
inside an ordinary room that looked a lot like all the other rooms around it, with
fluorescent lights and linoleum floors and steam-driven radiators that hissed and
clanked endlessly.

Doyle was, at 54, a veteran teacher and had logged 32 years in schools all over
Manhattan, where he primarily taught art and computer graphics. In the school,
which was called Quest to Learn, he was teaching a class, Sports for the Mind,
which every student attended three times a week. It was described in a jargony
flourish on the school's Web site as "a primary space of practice attuned to new
media literacies, which are multimodal and multicultural, operating as they do
within specific contexts for specific purposes." What it was, really, was a class in
technology and game design.

The lesson that day was on enemy movement, and the enemy was a dastardly
collection of spiky-headed robots roving inside a computer game. The students—a
pack of about 20 boisterous sixth graders—were meant to observe how the robots
moved, then chart any patterns they saw on pieces of graph paper. Later in the
class period, working on laptops, they would design their own games. For the
moment, though, they were spectators.

Doyle, who is thin and gray-haired with a neatly trimmed goatee, sat at a
desk in the center of the room, his eyeglasses perched low on his nose, his fingers
frenetically tapping the keyboard of a MacBook. The laptop was connected to a
wall-mounted interactive whiteboard, giving the students who were sprawled on
the floor in front of it an excellent view of his computer screen. Which was a good
thing, because at least as they saw it, Doyle was going to die an embarrassing death
without their help. Doyle had 60 seconds to steer a little bubble-shaped sprite—a
toddling avatar dressed in a royal blue cape and matching helmet—through a two-

dimensional maze without bumping into the proliferating robots. In order to win, he would need to gobble up some number of yellow reward points, Pac-Man style.

"Go right! Go right! Go right!" the students were shouting. "Now down, down, down, downdowndown!" A few had lifted themselves onto their knees and were pounding invisible keyboards in front of them. "Whoa!" they yelled in unison, some of them instinctively ducking as Doyle's sprite narrowly avoided a patrolling enemy.

Beauchamp, a round-faced boy wearing a dark sweatshirt, watched Doyle backtrack to snap up more points and calmly offered a piece of advice. "That extra movement cost you some precious time, Al," he said, sounding almost professorial. "There are more points up there than what you need to finish."

"How much time do I have?" Doyle asked.

"Nineteen seconds."

"Thanks," said Doyle, his eyes not leaving the screen. He added, "See, us older people, we don't have the peripheral vision to check the time because we didn't grow up with these games."

For a few seconds, it was quiet. Doyle pinged through a row of reward points and then, hitting a little cul-de-sac in the maze, he paused. His avatar's tiny yellow feet pedaled uselessly against a wall. The students began to yowl. A girl named Shianne pressed her hand to her forehead in faux anguish.

"Go! Go! Turn around. Don't slow down. What are you *waiting for*?" someone called out.

"How much time do I have left?"

"Thirteen seconds!"

Doyle smiled. "All the time in the world," he said, before taking his sprite on a deliberate detour to get even more reward points. The move, like a premature touchdown dance, put his students in agony.

"To the goal! To the goal! Al, run to the goal!"

And as the clock wound down and the students hollered and the steam radiator in the corner let out another long hiss, Doyle's little blue self rounded a final corner, waited out a passing robot and charged into the goal at the end of the maze with less than two seconds to spare. This caused a microriot in the classroom. Cheers erupted. Fists pumped. A few kids lay back on the floor as if knocked out by the drama. Several made notes on their graph paper. Doyle leaned back in his chair. Had he taught anything? Had they learned anything? It depended, really, on how you wanted to think about teaching and learning.

What if teachers gave up the vestiges of their educational past, threw away the worksheets, burned the canon and reconfigured the foundation upon which a century of learning has been built? What if we blurred the lines between academic subjects and reimagined the typical American classroom so that, at least in theory, it came to resemble a typical American living room or a child's bedroom or even a child's pocket, circa 2010—if, in other words, the slipstream of broadband and always-on technology that fuels our world became the source and organizing principle of our children's learning? What if, instead of seeing school the way we've known it, we saw it for what our children dreamed it might be: a big, delicious video game?

It is a radical proposition, sure. But during an era in which just about everything is downloadable and remixable, when children are frequently more digitally savvy than the adults around them, it's perhaps not so crazy to think that schools—or at least one school, anyway—might try to remix our assumptions about how to reach and educate those children. What makes Quest to Learn unique is not so much that it has been loaded with laptops or even that it bills itself expressly as a home for "digital kids," but rather that it is the brainchild of a professional game designer named Katie Salen. Salen, like many people interested in education, has spent a lot of time thinking about whether there is a way to make learning feel simultaneously more relevant to students and more connected to the world beyond school. And the answer, as she sees it, lies in games.

Quest to Learn is organized specifically around the idea that digital games are central to the lives of today's children and also increasingly, as their speed and capability grow, powerful tools for intellectual exploration. Salen, a professor of design and technology at Parsons the New School for Design, also directs a research-based organization called Institute of Play, which examines the connections between games and learning. Working with Robert Torres, a learning scientist who is a former school principal, and a small team of curriculum and game designers, Salen spent two years planning Quest to Learn in conjunction with the education-reform group New Visions for Public Schools. Her work was financed by a research grant from the MacArthur Foundation, which is pouring $50 million into exploring the possibilities of digital media and learning in a variety of settings nationwide. The school was approved by New York City's schools chancellor, Joel Klein, as one of a handful of "demonstration sites" for innovative technology-based instructional methods and is part of a larger effort on the city's part to create and experiment with new models for schools.

Quest to Learn is now beginning its second year, with about 145 sixth and seventh graders, all of whom were admitted by a districtwide lottery. (The intention is to add a grade level each year until it is a 6th-through-12th-grade school; Quest to Learn recently relocated to a larger but equally unmodern building in Chelsea.) Operating on a public-school budget but powered by additional grants from the MacArthur Foundation and the Bill and Melinda Gates Foundation, among others, it is a well-financed and carefully watched educational experiment concerning children, video games and the thrumming, largely unexplored, force field between them.

Salen and Torres are at the forefront of a small but increasingly influential group of education specialists who believe that going to school can and should be more like playing a game, which is to say it could be made more participatory, more immersive and also, well, fun. Nearly every aspect of life at Quest to Learn is thus designed to be gamelike, even when it doesn't involve using a computer. Students don't receive grades but rather achieve levels of expertise, denoted on their report cards as "pre-novice," "novice," "apprentice," "senior" and "master." They are enlisted to do things like defeat villains and lend a hand to struggling aliens, mostly by working in groups to overcome multifaceted challenges, all created by a collection of behind-the-scenes game designers. The principles are similar to those used in problem-based learning, a more established educational method in which students collaborate to tackle broad, open-ended problems, with a teacher providing guidance though not necessarily a lot of instruction. But at Quest to Learn, the problems have been expertly aerated with fantasy.

Once it has been worked over by game designers, a lesson doesn't look like a lesson anymore. It is now a quest. And while students at the school are put through the usual rigors of studying pre-algebra, basic physics, ancient civilizations and writing, they do it inside interdisciplinary classes with names like Codeworlds—a hybrid of math and English class—where the quests blend skills from different subject areas. Students have been called upon to balance the budget and brainstorm business ideas for an imaginary community called Creepytown, for example, and to design architectural blueprints for a village of bumbling little creatures called the Troggles. There are elements of the school's curriculum that look familiar— nightly independent reading assignments, weekly reading-comprehension packets and plenty of work with pencils and paper—and others that don't. Quest to Learn students record podcasts, film and edit videos, play video games, blog avidly and occasionally receive video messages from aliens.

They also spend significant time building their own games. Sometimes they design board games using cardboard and markers and ungodly amounts of tape. Most of the time, though, they invent games for the computer. Salen's theory goes like this: building a game—even the kind of simple game a sixth grader might build—is equivalent to building a miniworld, a dynamic system governed by a set of rules, complete with challenges, obstacles and goals. At its best, game design can be an interdisciplinary exercise involving math, writing, art, computer programming, deductive reasoning and critical thinking skills. If children can build, play and understand games that work, it's possible that someday they will understand and design systems that work. And the world is full of complicated systems.

Does this educational approach actually work? And is it something that can, or should, find its way into schools in other parts of the country? As we fret about the perils of multitasking and digital distraction in adult life, the question arises: should a school provide practice with or relief from those things? It is still too early to say. But the introduction of Quest to Learn is tied to a continuing and sometimes heated national dialogue about what skills today's learners most need to prepare them for success in a rapidly evolving, digitally mediated world. There is, at least, growing support for experimentation: in March, Arne Duncan, the Secretary of Education, released a draft National Educational Technology Plan that reads a bit like a manifesto for change, proposing among other things that the full force of technology be leveraged to meet "aggressive goals" and "grand" challenges, including increasing the percentage of the population that graduates from college to 60 percent from 39 percent in the next 10 years. What it takes to get there, the report suggests, is a "new kind of R.& D. for education" that encourages bold ideas and "high risk/high gain" endeavors—possibly even a school built around aliens, villains and video games.

Salen is 43, reddish-haired, hyperorganized and a quirky dresser. Some would consider her an unlikely prophet when it comes to education. Among Quest to Learn students, she is clearly beloved. Unlike most authority figures they know, she is a gifted player of Guitar Hero and has been spotted playing her Nintendo DSi on the subway. Until a few years ago she knew little about educational pedagogy and was instead immersed in doing things like converting an ice-cream truck into a mobile karaoke unit that traveled around San Jose, Calif., with a man dressed as a squirrel dispensing free frozen treats and encouraging city residents to pick up a microphone and belt out tunes. This was a community-building sort of game—or as Salen describes it, "an interactive play-based experience"—as was the race she helped design in Minneapolis and St. Paul, in which randomly organized groups of people carried 25-foot-high inflatable playing pieces modeled after those used in the board game Sorry through the streets of the cities.

A game, as Salen sees it, is really just a "designed experience," in which a participant is motivated to achieve a goal while operating inside a prescribed system of boundaries and rules. In this way, school itself is one giant designed experience. It could be viewed, in fact, as the biggest and most important game any child will ever play. To this end, Quest to Learn has three full-time game designers supporting the work of the school's 11 teachers—a ratio that reflects a trend more familiar to the business world, where designers and design-thinking have ascended to new and voguish heights.

Salen, like many designers, views things in terms of their ideal potential and also the physical space they occupy. She is thus less apt to refer to a school as "school" but rather as a "learning space" or a "discovery space" or sometimes as a "possibility space." She and her colleagues are wrapped up in the idea that technology is doing for learning what it has done for pretty much every other aspect of living, which is to say that it has dismantled the walls between spaces. As anyone who has ever checked e-mail from a bathroom stall or browsed eBay from a chairlift can attest, what once occurred in just one space now happens in practically every space. This has revolutionized design, media, most workplaces and especially the lives of children, who routinely tap into vast social and information pools outside school. Yet, generally speaking, it has hardly touched public education.

The traditional school structure strikes Salen as "weird." "You go to a math class, and that is the only place math is happening, and you are supposed to learn math just in that one space," she told me one day, sitting in the small room at the school that served as Quest to Learn's operational headquarters. She was dressed in a purple skirt with a hot pink scarf knotted around her neck. "There's been this assumption that school is the only place that learning is happening, that everything a kid is supposed to know is delivered between 8 a.m. and 3 p.m., and it happens in the confines of a building," she said. "But the fact is that kids are doing a lot of interesting learning outside of school. We acknowledge that, and we are trying to bring that into their learning here."

Waiting in the hallway line to go into Sports for the Mind class one day last winter, I met a boy named Kai Goree. He was dressed in a red T-shirt, jeans and sneakers. He had a puckish mouth, vivid brown eyes and short dark hair, pieces of which had been dyed in vibrant shingles of blue and green, not unlike what you might expect to find on the roof of a fairy-tale house.

Kai was 11. He sometimes got into trouble with teachers for talking too much. In the next 10 minutes, as we wandered into class and found seats and waited for everybody else to settle in, plus a few minutes beyond that, Kai relayed the following bits of information: he lived with his parents and older brother in an apartment on East 56th Street. He was a huge fan of professional wrestling. At home he sometimes filmed and edited his own wrestling-news commentaries or demonstrated wrestling moves on a giant plush gorilla he had named Green Gangsta. Then he put them on YouTube, where he had several personal channels. At home, his family had a "very awesome big computer." He also had an Android phone, but at that point was lusting after a Flip camera and a MacBook as well. He preferred OS X, but his dad, alas, was "a die-hard Windows fan," so the prospects for a Mac were unclear. If I was interested, I could follow him on Twitter. (Sample post from Kai: "I AM SO ANGRY. My mom is not letting me get a coolatta from dunkin donuts…") He used to have a blog, but it took too much time so he dropped it.

What he cared about most was games. "Games and games and games," he said. He had been playing games since he was about 18 months old, when his mother, who is a college professor, introduced him to a computer game called Reader Rabbit, intended to teach literacy skills. Like many of his friends, as he grew, he migrated from educational computer games to hand-held games to the Xbox 360.

At the start of middle school, Kai was almost a full decade into his digital life. This might have put him slightly ahead of his peers, but also, arguably, it made him more like the sixth grader of the near future. Research shows that, on average, children who have access to computers have mastered pointing and clicking with a mouse by the time they are 3½. They are also, thanks in part to mobile-phone apps, playing more games earlier in life. According to research by the Joan Ganz Cooney Center, an arm of the Sesame Workshop that explores the educational potential of interactive media, 60 percent of the top-selling iPhone apps on the education store are made for toddlers and preschoolers.

In the evenings, once he met the requirements for parental face time and homework, Kai could be found riding an armored dune buggy around a post-apocalyptic African landscape, blasting his machine gun at squads of alien jackals (Halo 3) or catching and juking for a touchdown (Madden NFL 09) or maybe adding wikki wikki scratches to a Jay-Z tune (DJ Hero). Sometimes he fired up the family Wii and did virtually assisted yoga. I came to learn that Kai could dissect, analyze and recommend video games with the acuity of a French sommelier. He was waiting anxiously, he said, to hear back from "some people at Lucas" who may or may not use him to beta test a multiplayer Star Wars game that wasn't yet on the market.

Kai's passion for games was unusual, but only a little. Earlier this year, the Kaiser Family Foundation released the results of a national survey in which 60 percent of children 8 to 18 reported that a typical day included playing games on hand-held or console devices. Their average daily investment was about two hours. According to Kaiser's data, the percentage of children playing digital games has increased by more than 50 percent in the last 10 years, and the amount of time they spend playing games has almost doubled. This follows research showing that the more time children spend playing video games, the less time they spend on homework. For educators, it's a sorry equation and one that mirrors a larger paradox when it comes to the divergent and often competing paths of children and their schools.

Even as technology spending in K-12 public education has risen steadily in the last 20 years, student performance—as measured by test results—has improved only incrementally. Meanwhile, children are proving to be wildly adaptive when it comes to using media outside school. They are fervently making YouTube videos, piloting avatars through complex game scenarios, sampling music, lighting up social networks and inventing or retooling (or purists would say, bludgeoning) language so that it better suits the text-messaging pay plan on their cellphones, only to show up to school to find cellphones outlawed, Internet access filtered and computers partitioned off from the rest of the classroom—at least in many cases. Michael H. Levine, who directs the Joan Ganz Cooney Center, acknowledges the conundrum. While there may be sound reasons behind limiting things like Internet browsing and social networking at school, he says, it does little to teach students how to live in the 21st century. It also may contribute to a broader relevancy issue. A 2006 study financed by the Bill and Melinda Gates Foundation set out to examine the reasons that almost a third of American public-high-school students fail to graduate with their class. Researchers surveyed high-school dropouts in 25 cities, suburbs and small towns across the country, where they were told again and again that school was boring. The final report recommended, among other things, that educators take steps to "make school more relevant and engaging."

One way to do this, according to Levine, would be to stop looking so critically at the way children use media and to start exploring how that energy might best be harnessed to help drive them academically. "Kids are literally wearing digital media," he says. "It's present everywhere in their lives, except for in the learning environment." A game-based approach like that used at Quest to Learn shows a lot of promise, he says, in part because it capitalizes on something kids already love. He is careful to note that there will be "huge challenges" in bringing the idea to schools nationally. Clearly, not every community is going to have the money for interactive whiteboards, laptops and PlayStation consoles. Someone will also need to figure out how to train teachers, develop curriculums, establish assessment measures and decide to what extent the focus on systems thinking and design skills used in game-based learning should be tied to common standards—and win over parents. "Odds are it will take a long time," Levine says. "But I don't know what the alternative is. My view of it is that we will never get to the holy land in terms of educational performance unless we do something about the engagement factor."

Often, watching the students and teachers at Quest to Learn, I was struck by how enviably resource-rich the school was, with its game designers and curriculum specialists and a full-time technologist wheeling carts of netbooks up and down the hallway. Salen recently told me that she is hoping to find a corner of the school where she can set up Rock Band—a video game in which users play drums, guitar and bass—"for teachers to unwind around." The school functioned with the intensity of a high-stakes start-up. It was clear the staff members worked long hours. Still, if Quest to Learn was a "possibility space"—a sort of laboratory for the future of learning—you could also see how those possibilities might feel entirely out of reach to an educator working in a more typically cash-strapped, understaffed school.

Yet with the federal government focusing more on innovation, and given the deep pockets of similarly focused corporate foundations, it may be feasible to implement game-based learning, even modestly, into more schools. But not before it has been proved to work. Quest to Learn students who took federally mandated standardized tests last spring scored on average no better and no worse than other sixth graders in their district, according to Elisa Aragon, the school's executive director. Valerie Shute, an assessment specialist in the educational psychology and learning systems department at Florida State University, is working on a MacArthur-financed effort to develop and test new assessment measures for Quest to Learn, which are meant to look at progress in areas like systems thinking, teamwork and time management. The federal government is likewise sponsoring an overhaul of standardized tests to be introduced in the 2014-2015 school year, with added emphasis on "higher order" thinking and problem-solving skills.

Quest to Learn's most innovative piece of technology was set up in a corner of one classroom, looking something like an extremely wired stage set. This was the school's $18,000 Smallab, which stands for "situated multimedia art learning lab," a system now being used in a handful of schools and museums around the country. Created by a team led by David Birchfield, a media artist at Arizona State University, it is a 3-D learning environment, or in designspeak, a "hybrid physical-digital space."

In Smallab sessions, students hold wands and Sputnik-like orbs whose movements are picked up by 12 scaffold-mounted motion-capture cameras and have an immediate effect inside the game space, which is beamed from a nearby computer onto the floor via overhead projector. It is a little bit like playing a multiplayer Wii game while standing inside the game instead of in front of it. Students can thus learn chemical titration by pushing king-size molecules around the virtual space. They can study geology by building and shifting digital layers of sediment and fossils on the classroom floor or explore complementary and supplementary angles by racing the clock to move a giant virtual protractor around the floor.

As new as the Smallab concept is, it is already showing promise when it comes to improving learning results: Birchfield and his colleagues say that in a small 2009 study, they found that at-risk ninth graders in earth sciences scored consistently and significantly higher on content-area tests when they had also done Smallab exercises. A second study compared the Smallab approach with traditional hands-on lab experimentation, with the group that used mixed-reality again showing greater retention and mastery. As it is more generally with games, the cognitive elements at work are not entirely understood, but they are of great interest to a growing number of learning scientists. Did the students learn more using digital mixed-reality because the process was more physical than hearing a classroom lecture or performing a lab experiment? Because it was more collaborative or more visual? Or was it simply because it seemed novel and more fun?

Here are some differences between Kai and me: Kai hates Justin Bieber whereas I only dislike him. Kai sends and receives about 50 text messages a day. My average is about 4. My idea of leisure involves wandering aimlessly and anonymously through the local bookstore whereas Kai—"not a fan of books"—can be found hanging around the Apple Store on Fifth Avenue, where he is on a first-name basis with employees. When I am sick with a cold, I sit at home flipping through magazines and not really wanting to be seen by anyone. When Kai is sick with a cold, he sits at home and makes YouTube videos. ("If I sneeze during this video," he tells the camera, "don't yell at me.") We also feel very differently, it turns out, about the game Halo. Kai sees it as having amazing graphics and a great story line and violence, "but only against aliens," he says. I see it mostly as violent.

One night at Kai's apartment, we turned on the Xbox and played Halo 3 as teammates. He played the role of Master Chief, the ultimate superwarrior, and I was a friendly alien who liked to fight. It started like this: I sat on the couch, and Kai sat on the floor in front of the TV. He said, "You get the machine gun, and I'll drive the car." I'm not really sure what happened after that. I would call it a nine-minute-long, jackhammering bloodbath, in which we (me poorly, Kai deftly) killed a lot of bad aliens until my lack of experience almost cost our team the game, and—a little sweaty and yes, totally excited—I handed my controller off to Kai's 14-year-old brother, Sam.

It was, for me, a reminder of how confusing it can be to think about video games and schools in the same frame. Not only has excessive gaming—much like excessive TV watching—been associated with obesity and depression, but playing violent games has been linked in some studies to an increase in aggressive behavior. Advocates of game-based learning concede that these games can be spectacularly gory, amoral and loud, even when they are artful and complicated. They like to point out that the majority of games sold commercially are not particularly violent and are rated "E"—for "everyone."

And then this: Brain researchers have found that playing first-person shooter games like Call of Duty does seem to have some neurological benefits, including improving peripheral vision and the ability to focus attention. The playing of shooter games has also been shown to enhance something called visual-spatial thinking—for example, the ability to rotate objects in one's mind—which, it turns out, is a cognitive building block for understanding concepts in science and engineering. Women, who tend to score lower when tested for visual-spatial skills, apparently gain more from virtual machine-gun outings than men: a 2007 study done at the University of Toronto showed that women who played just 10 hours of an action-oriented video game (Medal of Honor: Pacific Assault) not only improved their spatial attention and mental-rotation abilities more significantly than their male counterparts, but the game-play also appeared to substantially reduce any sex-related gaps in visual-spatial thinking abilities. Five months later, the effects still held. (Bad news for pacifists: a control group that played a stimulating but nonviolent 3-D video puzzle game showed no measurable improvement.)

Unsurprisingly, no one I spoke with who works in the field of games and learning says that first-person shooter games are the key to building future scientists and engineers. One topic under discussion is the broader question of "transfer," whether a skill developed by playing a game actually translates to improved abilities in other areas. They also note that we are only just beginning to tease apart the mechanisms that make game play so powerful. And inside those mechanisms, there is at least potential to advance our country's educational aims—if only we can sort out how we feel about games. Even the first family has sent mixed messages: President Obama has criticized video games for displacing family time and physical activity—urging parents, for example, to "turn off the TV, put away the video games and read to your child"—but he has also encouraged the development of new games to bolster the all-important science, technology, engineering and math (STEM) skills in young Americans. In March, Michelle Obama helped introduce a government-sponsored design contest to reward those who create mobile-phone games and apps to combat obesity, lamenting at a national Parent Teacher Association conference that "we know our kids spend way too much time with these games," but that at least the time could be spent more productively. The cognitive dissonance is likely familiar to any parent: she has also admitted, cheerfully, to owning a Wii.

When it comes to capturing and keeping the attention of children, game designers appear to be getting something right that schools, in many cases, are getting wrong. James Paul Gee, a professor of literacy studies at Arizona State University who grew interested in video games when his son began playing them years ago, has written several seminal books on the power of video games to inspire learning. He says that in working through the levels of a complex game, a person is decoding its "internal design grammar" and that this is a form of critical thinking. "A game is nothing but a set of problems to solve," Gee says. Its design often pushes players to explore, take risks, role-play and strategize—in other words putting a game's informational content to use. Gee has advocated for years that our definition of "literacy" needs to be widened to better suit the times. Where a book provides knowledge, Gee says, a good game can provide a learner with knowledge and also experience solving problems using that knowledge.

Slowly, this idea has won some unlikely converts. The retired Supreme Court Justice Sandra Day O'Connor recently introduced a Web site called iCivics, which features a series of interactive games meant to animate and revive the lost art of learning civics. "She was relatively hostile toward games," says Gee, who collaborated with her on the project, "and now she's a fan." E. O. Wilson, the renowned Harvard evolutionary biologist, has lauded digital games for their ability to immerse and challenge players in vivid, virtual environments. "I think games are the future in education," Wilson said in an interview with the game designer Will Wright last year. "We're going through a rapid transition now. We're about to leave print and textbooks behind."

In a speech given the day before the start of the 2009 G-20 economic summit, Eric Schmidt, the chief executive of Google, offered his own tacit approval, suggesting that playing video games, especially online multiplayer games, fosters collaboration, and that collaboration, in turn, fosters innovation—making it good training for a career in technology. "Everything in the future online is going to look like a multiplayer game," Schmidt said. "If I were 15 years old, that's what I'd be doing right now."

All this goes back to the debate over what constitutes "21st-century skills." How do schools manage to teach new media without letting go of old media? Is it possible to teach game design and still find time for "The Catcher in the Rye"?

One afternoon at Quest to Learn, I sat with Al Doyle in an empty office. Doyle had been teaching Sports for the Mind for only a few months—and at the end of the school year, he would end up leaving Quest to Learn to teach game design at a private school elsewhere in Manhattan—but the experience was causing him to think differently about what schools should be teaching. His students were building 3-D computer games and had also just finished a unit on podcasting. "Ten years ago, it would have taken a week to get kids to learn the difference between 'save' and 'save as,'" he said. "Now I show them GarageBand"—a digital audio sequencer produced by Apple—"and five minutes later they're recording and editing sound." Doyle made a point that others had also made: whatever digital fluidity his students possessed, it hadn't been taught to them, at least not by adults.

Here, perhaps, was a paradigm shift. As Doyle saw it, his role was moving from teaching toward facilitating, building upon learning being done outside school. He talked about all the wasted energy that goes into teaching things that students don't need so much anymore, thanks to the tools now available to them. Why memorize the 50 states and their capitals? Why, in the age of Google and pocket computers, memorize anything? "Handwriting?" Doyle said. "That's a 20th-century skill." Realizing this sounded radical, he amended his thought, saying that students should learn to write, but that keyboarding was far more important. He took aim at spelling, calling it "outmoded." Then he went back to podcasting, saying that after a student has written, revised, scripted and recorded a podcast, "it's just as valid as writing an essay."

I must have been wearing the shocked expression of an old-guard English major, because Doyle tried to put a finer point on it. "We feel like we're preparing these kids to be producers of media—whether they become graphic designers, video designers, journalists, publishers, communicators, bloggers, whatever," he said. "The goal is that they're comfortable expressing themselves in any media, whether it's video, audio, podcast, the written word, the spoken word or the animated feature." He added: "Game design is the platform that we can hook them into because this is where they live. Video games are more important to them than film, than broadcast television, than journalism. This is their medium. Games are this generation's rock and roll."

Spend time at a middle school—even a hyperinnovative one like Quest to Learn—and one thing becomes immediately apparent: Being a sixth grader is a timeless art. Kids chew gum when they're not supposed to. They ask for hugs from teachers when they need them. They get rowdy in gym class, dip Oreos in their chocolate-milk cartons at lunch, pick bits of food out of their braces and shout things like, "Hey, your epidermis is showing!" There is little they like to do quietly.

"I am *really sorry* it is taking you so long to sit in your chairs today," an aggrieved Doyle was calling over the din one morning at the start of class. In the brief quiet that followed, he announced that, connected to work they were doing on ancient architecture, each student was to design a game that took place inside either a labyrinth, a pyramid or a cave. This would happen using an online game-making platform called Gamestar Mechanic, which was developed by Katie Salen and a team and is soon to be sold commercially. The platform allows users to learn game-making skills without being versed in programming language.

A hand shot up. It was Ellisa, a diminutive girl who wore her hair in a giant ponytailed puff on one side of her head. "Al, can I do a game with a cave, a pyramid and a labyrinth?"

"Sorry, you may not."

Another hand. "What about a pyramid with a labyrinth inside of it?"

Doyle shook his head. "Just one," he said.

Sitting in front of laptops, the students started in on their game-building, each one beginning with a blank screen. They created borders, paths and obstacles by dragging and dropping small cubes from a menu. They chose an animated sprite to serve as a game's protagonist. They picked enemy sprites and set them marching in various patterns around the screen. They wrote the text that introduced the game and the text that flashed when a player reaches a new level. ("If the entrance to your cave is being guarded by a bear or a woolly mammoth," said Doyle, sounding teacherly, "you have to tell us it's a bear or a woolly mammoth.") They added a variety of rewards and punishments. If the game seemed too easy, they made it harder. If the game seemed too hard, they made it easier. Earlier that day, I watched a girl named Maya make a game. She created a labyrinth, changed all the colors, swapped enemies in and out, changed the background, changed the music and finally set the game's timer to 90 seconds. Then she played her game and finished it in 75. She adjusted the timer to 75 seconds and played again, this time losing. Finally, she set the timer at 80 and beat the game, but only just barely, at which point she declared the whole thing perfect.

The work appeared simple, but the challenge was evident. Twenty minutes in, the Sports for the Mind classroom was hushed but for the sound of keyboards being pounded and a faint arcadelike cacophony of poinging and bleeping over the syncopated pulse of game music. That night for homework, they would play one another's games and write up constructive critiques.

The gold standard in class, I was told by nearly every student I spoke with, was to create a game that was hard to beat but harder still to quit. Kai was sitting in one corner working on a game he named What the Cave. It was teeming with robot enemies. "The whole point," Kai said, "is you want your game to be hard, but you want it to be good." He studied his screen for a moment. Then using his mouse, he deftly deleted a row of enemies. "What you want," he said finally, "is good-hard."

The language of gamers is, when you begin to decipher it, the language of strivers. People who play video games speak enthusiastically about "leveling up" and are always shooting for the epic win. Getting to the end of even a supposedly simple video game can take 15 or more hours of play time, and it almost always involves failure—lots and lots of failure.

This concept is something that Will Wright, who is best known for designing the Sims game franchise and the 2008 evolution-related game Spore, refers to as "failure-based learning," in which failure is brief, surmountable, often exciting and therefore not scary. A well-built game is, in essence, a series of short-term feedback loops, delivering assessment in small, frequent doses. This in the end may be both more palatable and also more instructive to someone trying to learn.

According to Ntiedo Etuk, the chief executive of Tabula Digita, which designs computer games that are now being used in roughly 1,200 schools around the country, children who persist in playing a game are demonstrating a valuable educational ideal. "They play for five minutes and they lose," he says. "They play for 10 minutes and they lose. They'll go back and do it a hundred times. They'll fail until they win." He adds: "Failure in an academic environment is depressing. Failure in a video game is pleasant. It's completely aspirational."

It is also, says James Paul Gee, antithetical to the governing reality of today's public schools. "If you think about kids in school—especially in our testing regime— both the teacher and the student think that failure will lead to disaster," he says. "That's pretty much a guarantee that you'll never get to truly deep learning." Gee and others in the games-and-learning field have suggested that someday, if we choose to channel our resources into developing more and better games for use in classrooms, the games themselves could feasibly replace tests altogether. Students, by virtue of making it through the escalating levels of a game that teaches, say, the principles of quantum physics, will demonstrate their mastery simply by finishing the game. Or, as Gee says: "Think about it: if I make it through every level of Halo, do you really need to give me a test to see if I know everything it takes to get through every level of Halo?"

One day last spring, Jan Plass, a professor of educational communication and technology at New York University, and I were sitting in a classroom at the Urban Assembly Institute of Math and Science for Young Women, a girls-only public middle school in Brooklyn, where he and several graduate students were conducting research. Plass works at an organization called the Games for Learning Institute, directed by Ken Perlin, an N.Y.U. computer-science professor, that is dedicated to exploring the granular details of what makes games so mesmerizing and effective for learning.

We were watching a small group of sixth-to-eighth-grade girls play a relatively low-tech math game on a series of laptops. The girls played in pairs, solving equations to score points. All the while, the laptops' built-in cameras recorded their voices and faces, while an imbedded piece of software tracked their movements inside the game. What Plass and his research team were hoping to find inside this data—which was being collected at 12 New York schools—were answers about whether children learn more when playing individually or collaboratively. (In order to measure progress, researchers gave the students tests before and after the game playing.)

Two of the girls were talking and pointing at the screen. "They're spending time discussing how to solve the problem," Plass said in a low voice. "They might not solve as many problems. But the question for us is whether the conversation adds to the learning, versus if they spent their time on more practice. Does discourse result in deeper processing?"

A question like this is, of course, as old as Socrates and not at all limited to game-oriented learning. But given that digital games like those designed by Plass and his colleagues allow researchers to capture and examine a student's second-by-second decision-making, they offer what seem to be uniquely refined opportunities to peer into the cognitive process. What they are studying, Plass said, is the science behind focused engagement—a psychological phenomenon known as "flow."

Much of this work is still in its infancy. Neuroscientists have connected game play to the production of dopamine, a powerful neurotransmitter central to the brain's reward-seeking system and thought to drive motivation and memory processing (and more negatively, addictive behaviors)—all of which could have implications for how, when and what type of games should be used to advance children's learning. But as it is with just about everything involving teaching and learning, there are no simple answers. Games, for example, appear to trigger greater dopamine releases in men than women, which could mean that game-based learning is more effective with boys than girls. Or, says Plass, it could be a matter of design: ideally, games can be built in such a way that they adapt to the individual learning styles of their players.

Paul Howard-Jones, a neuroscientist who teaches in the graduate school of education at the University of Bristol in Britain and coordinates the NeuroEducational Research Network, says that dopamine sends a "ready to learn" signal to the brain, essentially priming it to receive new information pleasurably. His research has shown that children's engagement levels are higher when they are anticipating a reward but cannot predict whether they will get it—or, as Howard-Jones put it to me, "when you move from a conventional educational atmosphere to something that more resembles sport." He is careful to add that games are not meant to supplant teachers nor undermine the value of more traditional learning. "Children need to learn how to read a book," he says. "They need to learn how to ask questions." But as our understanding of both cognitive science and game design continues to advance, he says that game play will find a central place inside schools. "I think in 30 years' time," he says, "we will marvel that we ever tried to deliver a curriculum without gaming."

One day last winter, I watched students at Quest to Learn playing with a different sort of technological tool—a newly introduced online social network for the school that had been built by Salen and her team of designers and was open to students, staff members and parents. The network, called Being Me, looked like a starter Facebook. In the coming weeks, mostly through the school's wellness class, students would work on learning things like how to tag photos, update their status, credit the work of others, comment meaningfully on blog posts and navigate the complex politics of "friending." It was another effort on the school's part to look at the things kids are already doing—social networking, playing video games, tinkering with digital media—and try to help them do it with more thought and purpose, to recognize both their role and their influence inside a larger system.

Being Me had been online for just one day, but it was already zinging with activity, as most of the students seemed to have logged on overnight. Isabel posted a video of herself riding a horse. Clyde put up a survey querying everyone on whether PlayStation 3 was better than Xbox 360. Charles blogged about a new restaurant he tried. ("I had the Caprese pizza. The tomato had a lot of flavor.") Kai posted a video—now being watched by practically everyone in the class—of himself dressed in a pink wig and a red raincoat, pretending to be a girl he called "Heather." Comments began to pile up. "Cool beans," a girl sitting nearby wrote.

Then another from a boy named Nuridin: "Dude, stop making me die over here. LOL."

Seeing this as learning required a kind of leap—the same way it required a leap to watch students build digital mazes and load them with plinking cartoon sprites and imagine it might make them more successful as future adults—that it would possibly help them untangle and rebuild whatever broken systems we will have left for them. The electric pencil sharpener buzzed from a corner.

I watched a long-haired kid named Akahr pull up his profile on Being Me and spend a moment pondering what he would do for his first official status update. By design of the network, every status update began with the words "I am . . ." after which students could choose from an array of designated verbs and objects listed on drop-down menus. Most of the sixth graders were mixing and matching with a kind of frenzied abandon, playfully testing every last variation, posting their updates and waiting for a peal of laughter from somewhere in the classroom—a sign their status had been read. There was, "I am dancing Godzilla" and "I am hugging my bed." Akhar clicked on his menu and pondered his options. Around the classroom, there were students respecting eggs and creating soy sauce and reading glitter and looking for Paris. Was this learning or a distraction from learning? Serious or not serious? Or was it possible, somehow, that it was both? Word by word, Akahr made his choices: "I am . . . imagining . . . the future."

Take This Fish and Look at It

Samuel H. Scudder

Samuel Scudder (1837-1911) was an American entomologist and paleontologist. While most of his work focused on the fossil records of North America, he served as the first editor of *Science* magazine (which is still in print today) and as the General Secretary for the American Association for the Advancement of Science. His book on inductive reasoning, education, and the way the mind works, *The Student, the Fish, and Aggasiz*, was inspired by his work with renowned scientist Louis Aggasiz while a student at Harvard University. This essay comes from the third edition of that book (1879).

It was more than fifteen years ago that I entered the laboratory of Professor Agassiz, and told him I had enrolled my name in the Scientific School as a student of natural history. He asked me a few questions about my object in coming, my antecedents generally, the mode in which I afterwards proposed to use the knowledge I might acquire, and, finally, whether I wished to study any special branch. To the latter I replied that, while I wished to be well grounded in all departments of zoology, I proposed to devote myself specially to insects.

"When do you wish to begin?" he asked.

"Now," I replied.

This seemed to please him, and with an energetic "Very well!" he reached from a shelf a huge jar of specimens in yellow alcohol. "Take this fish," he said, "and look at it; we call it a haemulon; by and by I will ask what you have seen."

With that he left me, but in a moment returned with explicit instructions as to the care of the object entrusted to me.

"No man is fit to be a naturalist," said he, "who does not know how to take care of specimens."

I was to keep the fish before me in a tin tray, and occasionally moisten the surface with alcohol from the jar, always taking care to replace the stopper tightly. Those were not the days of ground-glass stoppers and elegantly shaped exhibition jars; all the old students will recall the huge neckless glass bottles with their leaky, wax-besmeared corks, half eaten by insects, and begrimed with cellar dust. Entomology was a cleaner science than ichthyology, but the example of the Professor, who had unhesitatingly plunged to the bottom of the jar to produce the fish, was infectious; and though this alcohol had a "very ancient and fishlike smell," I really dared not show any aversion within these sacred precincts, and treated the alcohol as though it were pure water. Still I was conscious of a passing feeling of disappointment, for gazing at a fish did not commend itself to an ardent entomologist. My friends at home, too, were annoyed when they discovered that no amount of eau-de-Cologne would drown the perfume which haunted me like a shadow.

In ten minutes I had seen all that could be seen in that fish, and started in search of the Professor—who had, however, left the Museum; and when I returned, after lingering over some of the odd animals stored in the upper apartment, my specimen was dry all over. I dashed the fluid over the fish as if to resuscitate the beast from a fainting fit, and looked with anxiety for a return of the normal sloppy appearance. This little excitement over, nothing was to be done but to return to a steadfast gaze at my mute companion. Half an hour passed—an hour—another hour; the fish began to look loathsome. I turned it over and around; looked it in the face—ghastly; from behind, beneath, above, sideways, at three-quarters' view—just as ghastly. I was in despair; at an early hour I concluded that lunch was necessary; so, with infinite relief, the fish was carefully replaced in the jar, and for an hour I was free.

On my return, I learned that Professor Agassiz had been at the Museum, but had gone, and would not return for several hours. My fellow students were too busy to be disturbed by continued conversation. Slowly I drew forth that hideous fish, and with a feeling of desperation again looked at it. I might not use a magnifying-glass; instruments of all kinds were interdicted. My two hands, my two eyes, and the fish: it seemed a most limited field. I pushed my finger down its throat to feel how sharp the teeth were. I began to count the scales in the different rows, until I was convinced that was nonsense. At last a happy thought struck me—I would draw the fish; and now with surprise I began to discover new features in the creature. Just then the Professor returned.

"That is right" said he; "a pencil is one of the best of eyes. I am glad to notice, too, that you keep your specimen wet, and your bottle corked."

With these encouraging words, he added:

"Well, what is it like?"

He listened attentively to my brief rehearsal of the structure of parts whose names were still unknown to me: the fringed gill—arches and movable operculum; the pores of the head, fleshy lips and lidless eyes; the lateral line, the spinous fins and forked tail; the compressed and arched body. When I finished, he waited as if expecting more, and then, with an air of disappointment:

"You have not looked very carefully; why," he continued more earnestly, "you haven't even seen one of the most conspicuous features of the animal, which is plainly before your eyes as the fish itself; look again, look again!" and he left me to my misery.

I was piqued; I was mortified. Still more of that wretched fish! But now I set myself to my task with a will, and discovered one new thing after another, until I saw how just the Professor's criticism had been. The afternoon passed quickly; and when, towards its close, the Professor inquired:

"Do you see it yet?"

"No," I replied, "I am certain I do not, but I see how little I saw before."

"That is next best," said he, earnestly, "but I won't hear you now; put away your fish and go home; perhaps you will be ready with a better answer in the morning. I will examine you before you look at the fish."

This was disconcerting. Not only must I think of my fish all night, studying, without the object before me, what this unknown but most visible feature might be; but also, without reviewing my discoveries, I must give an exact account of them the next day. I had a bad memory; so I walked home by Charles River in a distracted state, with my two perplexities.

The cordial greeting from the Professor the next morning was reassuring; here was a man who seemed to be quite as anxious as I that I should see for myself what he saw.

"Do you perhaps mean," I asked, "that the fish has symmetrical sides with paired organs?"

His thoroughly pleased "Of course! Of course!" repaid the wakeful hours of the previous night. After he had discoursed most happily and enthusiastically—as he always did—upon the importance of this point, I ventured to ask what I should do next.

"Oh, look at your fish!" he said, and left me again to my own devices. In a little more than an hour he returned, and heard my new catalogue.

"That is good, that is good!" he repeated; "but that is not all; go on"; and so for three long days he placed that fish before my eyes, forbidding me to look at anything else, or to use any artificial aid. "Look, look, look," was his repeated injunction.

This was the best entomological lesson I ever had—a lesson whose influence has extended to the details of every subsequent study; a legacy the Professor had left to me, as he has left it to so many others, of inestimable value, which we could not buy, with which we cannot part.

A year afterward, some of us were amusing ourselves with chalking outlandish beasts on the Museum blackboard. We drew prancing starfishes; frogs in mortal combat; hydra-headed worms; stately crawfishes, standing on their tails, bearing aloft umbrellas; and grotesque fishes with gaping mouths and staring eyes. The Professor came in shortly after, and was as amused as any at our experiments. He looked at the fishes.

"Haemulons, every one of them," he said; "Mr._____drew them."

True; and to this day, if I attempt a fish, I can draw nothing but haemulons.

The fourth day, a second fish of the same group was placed beside the first, and I was bidden to point out the resemblances and differences between the two; another and another followed, until the entire family lay before me, and a whole legion of jars covered the table and surrounding shelves; the odor had become a pleasant perfume; and even now, the sight of an old, six-inch, worm-eaten cork brings fragrant memories.

The whole group of haemulons was thus brought in review; and, whether engaged upon the dissection of the internal organs, the preparation and examination of the bony framework, or the description of the various parts, Agassiz's training in the method of observing facts and their orderly arrangement was ever accompanied by the urgent exhortation not to be content with them.

"Facts are stupid things," he would say, "until brought into connection with some general law."

What Does It Mean to Be Well-Educated?

Alfie Kohn

Alfie Kohn is an American author, lecturer, and teacher who has written twelve books, which focus on education, parenting, and human behavior. Having taught at the high school and university level, he is extremely familiar with the course of education in America in the last twenty years. *Time Magazine* describes him as one of the most vocal critics of the current fixation on grades and test scores in education. This essay originally appeared on his website in 2003.

No one should offer pronouncements about what it means to be well-educated without meeting my ex-wife. When I met her, she was at Harvard, putting the finishing touches on her doctoral dissertation in anthropology. A year later, having spent her entire life in school, she decided to do the only logical thing . . . and apply to medical school. She subsequently became a successful practicing physician. However, she will freeze up if you ask her what 8 times 7 is, because she never learned the multiplication table. And forget about grammar ("Me and him went over her house today" is fairly typical) or literature ("Who's Faulkner?").

So what do you make of this paradox? Is she a walking indictment of the system that let her get so far—29 years of schooling, not counting medical residency—

without acquiring the basics of English and math? Or does she offer an invitation to rethink what it means to be well-educated since what she lacks didn't prevent her from becoming a high-functioning, multiply credentialed, professionally successful individual?

Of course, if those features describe what it means to be well-educated, then there is no dilemma to be resolved. She fits the bill. The problem arises only if your definition includes a list of facts and skills that one must have but that she lacks. In that case, though, my wife is not alone. Thanks to the Internet, which allows writers and researchers to circulate rough drafts of their manuscripts, I've come to realize just how many truly brilliant people cannot spell or punctuate. Their insights and discoveries may be changing the shape of their respective fields, but they can't use an apostrophe correctly to save their lives.

Or what about me (he suddenly inquired, relinquishing his comfortable perch from which issue all those judgments of other people)? I could embarrass myself pretty quickly by listing the number of classic works of literature I've never read. And I can multiply reasonably well, but everything mathematical I was taught after first-year algebra (and even some of that) is completely gone. How well-educated am I?

*

The issue is sufficiently complex that questions are easier to formulate than answers. So let's at least be sure we're asking the right questions and framing them well.

1. The Point of Schooling: Rather than attempting to define what it means to be well-educated, should we instead be asking about the *purposes of education*? The latter formulation invites us to look beyond academic goals. For example, Nel Noddings, professor emerita at Stanford University, urges us to reject "the deadly notion that the schools' first priority should be intellectual development" and contends that "the main aim of education should be to produce competent, caring, loving, and lovable people." Alternatively, we might wade into the dispute between those who see education as a means to creating or sustaining a democratic society and those who believe its primary role is economic, amounting to an "investment" in future workers and, ultimately, corporate profits. In short, perhaps the question "How do we know if education has been successful?" shouldn't be posed until we have asked what it's supposed to be successful at.

2. Evaluating People vs. Their Education: Does the phrase *well-educated* refer to a quality of the schooling you received, or to something about you? Does it denote what you were taught, or what you learned (and remember)? If the term applies to what you now know and can do, you could be poorly educated despite having received a top-notch education. However, if the term refers to the quality of your schooling, then we'd have to conclude that a lot of "well-educated" people sat through lessons that barely registered, or at least are hazy to the point of irrelevance a few years later.

3. An Absence of Consensus: Is it even possible to agree on a *single definition* of what every high school student should know or be able to do in order to be considered well-educated? Is such a definition expected to remain invariant across cultures (with a single standard for the U.S. and Somalia, for example), or even across subcultures (South-Central Los Angeles and Scarsdale; a Louisiana fishing community, the upper East side of Manhattan, and Pennsylvania Dutch country)? How about across historical eras: would anyone seriously argue that our criteria for "well-educated" today are exactly the same as those used a century ago—or that they should be?

To cast a skeptical eye on such claims is not necessarily to suggest that the term is purely relativistic: you like vanilla, I like chocolate; you favor knowledge about poetry, I prefer familiarity with the Gettysburg Address. Some criteria are more defensible than others. Nevertheless, we have to acknowledge a striking absence of consensus about what the term ought to mean. Furthermore, any consensus that does develop is ineluctably rooted in time and place. It is misleading and even dangerous to justify our own pedagogical values by pretending they are grounded in some objective, transcendent Truth, as though the quality of being well-educated is a Platonic form waiting to be discovered.

4. Some Poor Definitions: Should we instead try to stipulate which answers *don't* make sense? I'd argue that certain attributes are either insufficient (possessing them isn't enough to make one well-educated) or unnecessary (one can be well-educated without possessing them)—or both. Let us therefore consider ruling out:

Seat time. Merely sitting in classrooms for x hours doesn't make one well-educated.

Job skills. It would be a mistake to reduce schooling to vocational preparation, if only because we can easily imagine graduates who are well-prepared for the workplace (or at least for some workplaces) but whom we would not regard as well-educated. In any case, pressure to redesign secondary education so as to suit the demands of employers reflects little more than the financial interests—and the political power—of these corporations.

Test scores. To a disconcerting extent, high scores on standardized tests signify a facility with taking standardized tests. Most teachers can instantly name students who are talented thinkers but who just don't do well on these exams—as well as students whose scores seem to overestimate their intellectual gifts. Indeed, researchers have found a statistically significant correlation between high scores on a range of standardized tests and a shallow approach to learning. In any case, no single test is sufficiently valid, reliable, or meaningful that it can be treated as a marker for academic success.

Memorization of a bunch o' facts. Familiarity with a list of words, names, books, and ideas is a uniquely poor way to judge who is well-educated. As the philosopher Alfred North Whitehead observed long ago, "A merely well-informed man is the most useless bore on God's earth. . . . Scraps of information" are only worth something if they are put to use, or at least "thrown into fresh combinations."

Look more carefully at the superficially plausible claim that you must be familiar with, say, *King Lear* in order to be considered well-educated. To be sure, it's a classic meditation on mortality, greed, belated understanding, and other important themes. But *how* familiar with it must you be? Is it enough that you can name its author, or that you know it's a play? Do you have to be able to recite the basic plot? What if you read it once but barely remember it now?

If you don't like that example, pick another one. How much do you have to know about neutrinos, or the Boxer rebellion, or the side-angle-side theorem? If deep understanding is required, then (a) very few people could be considered well-educated (which raises serious doubts about the reasonableness of such a definition), and (b) the number of items about which anyone could have that level of knowledge is sharply limited because time is finite. On the other hand, how can we justify a cocktail-party level of familiarity with all these items—reminiscent of Woody Allen's summary of *War and Peace* after taking a speed-reading course: "It's about Russia." What sense does it make to say that one person is well-educated for having a single sentence's worth of knowledge about the Progressive Era or photosynthesis, while someone who has to look it up is not?

Knowing a lot of stuff may seem harmless, albeit insufficient, but the problem is that efforts to shape schooling around this goal, dressed up with pretentious labels like "cultural literacy," have the effect of taking time away from more meaningful objectives, such as knowing how to think. If the Bunch o' Facts model proves a poor foundation on which to decide who is properly educated, it makes no sense to peel off items from such a list and assign clusters of them to students at each grade level. It is as poor a basis for designing curriculum as it is for judging the success of schooling.

The number of people who do, in fact, confuse the possession of a storehouse of knowledge with being "smart"—the latter being a disconcertingly common designation for those who fare well on quiz shows—is testament to the naïve appeal that such a model holds. But there are also political implications to be considered here. To emphasize the importance of absorbing a pile of information is to support a larger worldview that sees the primary purpose of education as reproducing our current culture. It is probably not a coincidence that a Core Knowledge model wins rave reviews from Phyllis Schlafly's Eagle Forum (and other conservative Christian groups) as well as from the likes of *Investor's Business Daily*. To be sure, not every individual who favors this approach is a right-winger, but defining the notion of educational mastery in terms of the number of facts one can recall is well-suited to the task of preserving the status quo. By contrast, consider Dewey's suggestion that an educated person is one who has "gained the power of reflective attention, the power to hold problems, questions, before the mind." Without this capability, he added, "the mind remains at the mercy of custom and external suggestions."

5. Mandating a Single Definition: *Who gets to decide* what it means to be well-educated? Even assuming that you and I agree to include one criterion and exclude another, that doesn't mean our definition should be imposed with the force of law—taking the form, for example, of requirements for a high school diploma. There are other considerations, such as the real suffering imposed on individuals who aren't permitted to graduate from high school, the egregious disparities in resources and opportunities available in different neighborhoods, and so on.

More to the point, the fact that so many of us *don't* agree suggests that a national (or, better yet, international) conversation should continue, that one definition may never fit all, and, therefore, that we should leave it up to local communities to decide who gets to graduate. But that is not what has happened. In about half the states, people sitting atop Mount Olympus have decreed that anyone who doesn't pass a certain standardized test will be denied a diploma and, by implication, classified as inadequately educated. This example of accountability gone haywire violates not only common sense but the consensus of educational measurement specialists. And the consequences are entirely predictable: no high school graduation for a disproportionate number of students of color, from low-income neighborhoods, with learning disabilities, attending vocational schools, or not yet fluent in English.

Less obviously, the idea of making diplomas contingent on passing an exam answers by default the question of what it means to be well- (or sufficiently) educated: Rather than grappling with the messy issues involved, we simply declare that standardized tests will tell us the answer. This is disturbing not merely because of the inherent limits of the tests, but also because teaching becomes distorted when passing those tests becomes the paramount goal. Students arguably receive an inferior education when pressure is applied to raise their test scores, which means that high school exit exams may actually *lower* standards.

Beyond proclaiming "Pass this standardized test or you don't graduate," most states now issue long lists of curriculum standards, containing hundreds of facts, skills, and subskills that all students are expected to master at a given grade level and for a given subject. These standards are not guidelines but mandates (to which teachers are supposed to "align" their instruction). In effect, a Core Knowledge model, with its implication of students as interchangeable receptacles into which knowledge is poured, has become the law of the land in many places. Surely even defenders of this approach can appreciate the difference between *arguing* in its behalf and *requiring* that every school adopt it.

6. The Good School: Finally, instead of asking what it means to be well-educated, perhaps we should inquire into the *qualities* of a school likely to offer a good education. I've offered my own answer to that question at book length, as have other contributors to this issue. As I see it, the best sort of schooling is organized around problems, projects, and questions—as opposed to facts, skills, and disciplines. Knowledge is acquired, of course, but in a context and for a purpose. The emphasis is not only on depth rather than breadth, but also on discovering ideas rather than on covering a prescribed curriculum. Teachers are generalists first and specialists (in a given subject matter) second; they commonly collaborate to offer interdisciplinary courses that students play an active role in designing. All of this happens in small, democratic schools that are experienced as caring communities.

Notwithstanding the claims of traditionalists eager to offer—and then dismiss—a touchy-feely caricature of progressive education, a substantial body of evidence exists to support the effectiveness of each of these components as well as the benefits of using them in combination. By contrast, it isn't easy to find *any* data to justify the traditional (and still dominant) model of secondary education: large schools, short classes, huge student loads for each teacher, a fact-transmission kind of instruction that is the very antithesis of "student-centered," the virtual absence of any attempt to integrate diverse areas of study, the rating and ranking of students, and so on. Such a system acts as a powerful *obstacle* to good teaching, and it thwarts the best efforts of many talented educators on a daily basis.

Low-quality instruction can be assessed with low-quality tests, including homegrown quizzes and standardized exams designed to measure (with faux objectivity) the number of facts and skills crammed into short-term memory. The effects of high-quality instruction are trickier, but not impossible, to assess. The most promising model turns on the notion of "exhibitions" of learning, in which students reveal their understanding by means of in-depth projects, portfolios of assignments, and other demonstrations—a model pioneered by Ted Sizer, Deborah Meier, and others affiliated with the Coalition of Essential Schools. By now we're fortunate to have access not only to essays about how this might be done (such as Sizer's invaluable *Horace* series) but to books about schools that are actually doing it: *The Power of Their Ideas* by Meier, about Central Park East Secondary School in New York City; *Rethinking High School* by Harvey Daniels and his colleagues, about Best Practice High School in Chicago; and *One Kid at a Time* by Eliot Levine, about the Met in Providence, RI.

The assessments in such schools are based on meaningful standards of excellence, standards that may collectively offer the best answer to our original question simply because to meet those criteria is as good a way as any to show that one is well-educated. The Met School focuses on social reasoning, empirical reasoning, quantitative reasoning, communication, and personal qualities (such as responsibility, capacity for leadership, and self-awareness). Meier has emphasized the importance of developing five "habits of mind": the value of raising questions about *evidence* ("How do we know what we know?"), *point of view* ("Whose perspective does this represent?"), *connections* ("How is this related to that?"), *supposition* ("How might things have been otherwise?"), and *relevance* ("Why is this important?").

It's not only the ability to raise and answer those questions that matters, though, but also the disposition to do so. For that matter, any set of intellectual objectives, any description of what it means to think deeply and critically, should be accompanied by a reference to one's interest or intrinsic motivation to do such thinking. Dewey reminded us that the goal of education is more education. To be well-educated, then, is to have the desire as well as the means to make sure that learning never ends.

The Historian As Artist

Barbara Tuchman

Barbara Tuchman (1912-1989) was an American academic and historian whose work surveyed almost every major period of history. Her works are widely recognized for the human qualities she was able to impart to major historical figures. This skill at presenting familiar characters in new ways and with new insights earned her the Pulitzer Prize for General Non-Fiction twice (1963 and 1972) and her book on the 14th Century, *A Distant Mirror,* won the National Book Prize in History in 1980. This selection comes from *Practicing History,* a 1981 collection of essays focused on her experiences as a historian.

I would like to share some good news with you. I recently came back from skiing at Aspen, where on one occasion I shared the double-chair ski-lift with an advertising man from Chicago. He told me he was in charge of all copy for his firm in all media: TV, radio, and the printed word. On the strength of this he assured me—and I quote—that "Writing is coming back, *books* are coming back." I cannot tell you how pleased I was, and I knew you would be too.

Now that we know that the future is safe for writing, I want to talk about a particular kind of writer—the historian—not just as historian but as artist; that is, as a creative writer on the same level as the poet or novelist. What follows will sound less immodest if you will take the word "artist" in the way I think of it, not as form of praise but as a category, like clerk or laborer or actor.

Why is it generally assumed that in writing, the creative process is the exclusive property of poets and novelists? I would like to suggest that the thought applied by the historian to his subject matter can be no less creative than the imagination applied by the novelist to his. And when it comes to writing as an art, is Gibbon necessarily less of an artist in words than, let us say, Dickens? Or Winston Churchill less so than William Faulkner or Sinclair Lewis?

George Macaulay Trevelyan, the late professor of modern history at Cambridge and the great champion of literary as opposed to scientific history, said in a famous essay on his muse that ideally history should be the exposition of facts about the past, "in their full emotional and intellectual value to a wide public by the difficult art of literature." Notice "wide public." Trevelyan always stressed writing for the general reader as opposed to writing just for fellow scholars because he knew that when you write for the public you have to be *clear* and you have to be *interesting* and these are the two criteria which make for good writing. He had no patience with the idea that only imaginative writing is literature. Novels, he pointed out, if they are bad enough, are *not* literature, while even pamphlets, if they are good enough, and he cites those by Milton, Swift, and Burke, are.

The "difficult art of literature" is well said. Trevelyan was a dirt farmer in that field and he knew. I may as well admit now that I have always *felt* like an artist when I work on a book but I did not think I ought to say so until someone else said it first (it's like waiting to be proposed to). Now that an occasional reviewer here and there had made the observation, I feel I can talk about it. I see no reason why the word should always be confined to writers of fiction and poetry while the rest of us are lumped together under that despicable term "Nonfiction"—as if we were some sort of remainder. I do not feel like a Non-something; I feel quite specific. I wish I could think of a name in place of "Nonfiction." In the hope of finding an antonym I looked up "Fiction" in Webster and found it defined as opposed to "Fact, Truth and Reality." I thought for a while of adopting FTR, standing for

Fact, Truth, and Reality, as my new term, but it is awkward to use. "Writers of Reality" is the nearest I can come to what I want, but I cannot very well call us "Realtors" because that had been pre-empted—although as a matter of fact I would like to. "Real Estate," when you come to think of it, is a very fine phrase and it is exactly the sphere that writers of nonfiction deal in: The real estate of man, of human conduct. I wish we could get it back from the dealers in land. Then the categories could be poets, novelists, and realtors.

I should add that I do not entirely go along with Webster's statement that fiction is what is distinct from fact, truth, and reality because good fiction (as opposed to junk), even if it has nothing to with fact, is usually *founded* on reality and *perceives* truths—often more truly than some historians. It is exactly this quality of perceiving truth, extracting it from irrelevant surroundings and conveying it to the reader or the viewer of a picture, which distinguishes the artist. What the artist has is an *extra* vision and an *inner* vision plus the ability to express it. He supplies a view or an understanding that the viewer or reader would not have gained without the aid of the artist's creative vision. This is what Monet does in one of those shimmering rivers reflecting poplars, or El Greco in the stormy sky over Toledo, or Jane Austen compressing a whole society into Mr. and Mrs. Bennet, Lady Catherine, and Mr. Darcy. We realtors, at least those of us who aspire to write literature, do the same thing. Lytton Strachey perceived a truth about Queen Victoria and the Eminent Victorians, and the style and form which he created to portray what he saw have changed the whole approach to biography since his time. Rachel Carson perceived truth about the seashore or the silent spring, Thoreau about Walden Pond, De Tocqueville and James Cryce about America, Gibbon about Rome, Karl Marx about Capital, Carlyle about the French Revolution. Their work is based on study, observation, and accumulation of fact, but does anyone suppose that these realtors did not make use of their imagination? Certainly they did; that is what gave them their extra vision.

Trevelyan wrote that the best historian was he who combined knowledge of the evidence with "the largest intellect, the warmest human sympathy and the highest imaginative powers." The last two qualities are no different than those necessary to a great novelist. They are a necessary part of the historian's equipment because they are what enable him to *understand* the evidence he had accumulated. Imagination stretches the available facts—extrapolates from them, so to speak, thus often supplying an otherwise missing answer to the "Why" of what happened. Sympathy is essential to the understanding of motive. Without sympathy and imagination the historian can copy figures from a tax roll forever—or count them by computer as they do nowadays—but he will never know or be able to portray the people who paid the taxes.

When I say that I felt like an artist, I mean that I constantly found myself perceiving a historical truth (at least, what *I* believe to be truth) by seizing upon a suggestion; then, after careful gathering of the evidence, conveying it in turn to the reader, not by piling up a list of all the facts I have collected, which the way of the Ph.D., but by exercising the artist's privilege of selection.

Actually the idea for *The Proud Tower* evolved in that way from a number of such perceptions. The initial impulse was a line I quoted in *The Guns of August* from Belgian Socialist poet Emile Verhaeren. After a lifetime as a pacifist dedicated to the social and humanitarian ideas which were then believed to erase national lines, he found himself filled with hatred of the German invader and disillusioned in all he had formerly believed in. And yet, as he wrote, "Since it seems to me that in this state of hatred my conscience becomes diminished, I dedicate these pages, with emotion, to the man I used to be."

I was deeply moved by this. His confession seemed to me so poignant, so evocative of a time and mood, that I decided to try to retrieve that vanished era. It led to the last chapter in *The Proud Tower* on the Socialists, to Jaures as the authentic Socialist, to his prophetic lines, "I summon the living, I mourn the dead," and to his assassination as the perfect and dramatically right ending for the book, both chronologically and symbolically.

Then there was Lord Ribblesdale. I owe this to *American Heritage*, which back in October 1961 published a piece on Sargent and Whistler with a handsome reproduction of the Ribblesdale portrait. In Sargent's painting Ribblesdale stared out upon the world, as I later wrote in *The Proud Tower*, "in an attitude of such natural arrogance, elegance and self-confidence as no man of a later day would ever achieve." Here too was a vanished era which came together in my mind with Verhaeren's line, "the man I used to be"—like two globules of mercury making a single mass. From that came the idea for the book. Ribblesdale, of course, was the suggestion that ultimately became the opening chapter on the Patricians. This is the reward of the artist's eye: It always leads you to the right thing.

As I see it, there are three parts to the creative process: first, the extra vision with which the artist perceives a truth and conveys it by suggestion. Second, medium of expression: language for writers, paint for painters, clay or stone for sculptors, sound expressed in musical notes for composers. Third, design or structure.

When it comes to language, nothing is more satisfying than to write a good sentence. It is no fun to write lumpishly, dully, to compose prose the reader must plod through like wet sand. But it is a pleasure to achieve, if one can, a clear running prose that is simple yet full of surprises. This does not just happen. It requires skill, hard work, a good ear, and continued practice, as much as it takes Heifetz to play the violin. The goals, as I have said, are clarity, interest, and aesthetic pleasure. On the first of these I would like to quote Macaulay, a great historian and great writer, who once wrote to a friend, "How little the all important art of making meaning pellucid is studied now! Hardly any popular writer except myself thinks of it."

As to structure, my own form is narrative, which is not every historian's, I may say—Indeed, it is rather looked down on now by advanced academics, but I don't mind because no one could possibly persuade me that telling a story is not the most desirable thing a writer can do. Narrative history is neither as simple nor as straightforward as it might seem. It requires arrangement, composition, panning just like a painting—Rembrandt's "Night Watch," for example. He did not fit in all those figures with certain ones in the foreground and other in back and the light falling on them just so, without much trial and error and innumerable preliminary sketches. It is the same with writing history. Although the finished result may look to the reader natural and inevitable, as if the author had only to follow the sequence of events, it is not that easy. Sometimes, to catch attention, the crucial event and the causative circumstance have to be reversed in order—the event first and the cause afterwards, as in *The Zimmermann Telegram*. One must juggle with time.

In *The Proud Tower*, for instance, the two English chapters were originally conceived as one. I divided them and placed them well apart in order to give a feeling of progression, of forward chronological movement to the book. The story of the anarchists with their ideas and deeds set in counterpoint to each other was a problem in arrangement. The middle section of the Hague chapter on the Paris Exposition of 1900 was originally planned as a separate short center-piece, marking the turn of the century, until I saw it as a bridge linking the two Hague conferences, where it now seems to belong.

Structure is chiefly a problem of selection, an agonizing business because there is always more material than one can use or fit into a story. The problem is how and what to select out of all that happened without, by the very process of selection, giving an over- or under-emphasis which violates truth. One cannot put in everything: The result would be a shapeless mass. The job is to achieve a narrative line without straying from the essential facts or leaving out any essential facts and without twisting the material to suit one's convenience. To do so is a temptation, but if you do it with history you invariably get tripped up by later events. I have been tempted once or twice and I know.

The most difficult task of selection I had was in the Dreyfus chapter. To try to skip over the facts about the *bordereau* and the handwriting and the forgeries—all the elements of the Case as distinct from the Affair—in order to focus instead on what happened to France and yet at the same time give the reader enough background information to enable him to understand what was going on, nearly drove me to despair. My writing slowed down to a trickle until one dreadful day when I went to my study at nine and stayed there all day in a blank coma until five, when I emerged without having written a single word. Anyone who is a writer will know how frightening that was. You feel you have come to the end of your powers; you will not finish the book; you may never write again.

There are other problems of structure peculiar to writing history: how to explain background and yet keep the story moving; how to create suspense and sustain interest in a narrative of which the outcome (like who won the war) is, to put it mildly, known. If anyone thinks this does not take creative writing, I can only say, try it.

Mr. Capote's *In Cold Blood*, for example, which deals with real life as does mine, is notable for conscious design. One can see him planning, arranging, composing his material until he achieves his perfectly balanced structure. That is art, although the hand is too obtrusive and the design too contrived to qualify as history. His method of investigation, moreover, is hardly so new as he thinks. He is merely applying to contemporary material what historians have been doing for years. Herodotus started it more than two thousand years ago, walking all over Asia Minor asking questions. Francis Parkman went to live among the Indians: hunted, traveled, and ate with them so that his pages would be steeped in understanding; E. A. Freeman, before he wrote *The Norman Conquest*, visited every spot the Conqueror had set foot on. New to these techniques, Mr. Capote is perhaps naively impressed by them. He uses them in a deliberate effort to raise what might be called "creative" journalism to the level of literature. A great company from Herodotus to Trevelyan have been doing the same with history for quite some time.

How To Make it in College, Now that You're Here

Brian O'Keeney

Comparatively little is known about Brian O'Keeney outside of this essay. After appearing in John Langan's *College Writing Skills* in 1985, it has been widely anthologized for its simple and direct approach to problems which many college students encounter. It is possible Langan himself is the author of the essay using a pseudonym, as the essay was never published before its appearance in his book.

Today is your first day on campus. You were a high school senior three months ago. Or maybe you've been at home with your children for the last ten years. Or maybe you work full-time and you're coming to school to start the process that leads to a better job. Whatever your background is, you're probably not too concerned today with staying in college. After all, you just got over the hurdle (and the paperwork) of applying to this place and organizing your life so that you could attend. And today, you're confused and tired. Everything is a hassle, from finding the classrooms to standing in line at the bookstore. But read my advice anyway. And if you don't read it today, save this article. You might want to look at it a little further down the road.

By the way, if this isn't your first day, don't skip this article. Maybe you haven't been doing as well in your studies as you'd hoped. Or perhaps you've had problems juggling your work schedule, your class schedule, and your social life. If so, read on. You're about to get the inside story on making it in college. Based on my own experience as a final-year student, and on dozens of interviews with successful students, I've worked out the no-fail system for coping with college. These are the inside tips every student needs to do well in school. I've put myself in your place, and I'm going to answer the questions that will cross (or have already crossed) your mind during your stay here.

What's the Secret to Getting Good Grades?

It all comes down to getting those grades, doesn't it? After all, you came here for some reason, and you're going to need passing grades to get the credits or degree you want. Many of us never did much studying in high school; most of the learning we did took place in the classroom. College, however, is a lot different. You're really on your own when it comes to passing courses. In fact, sometimes you'll feel as if nobody cares if you make it or not. Therefore, you've got to figure out a study system that gets results. Sooner or later, you'll be alone with those books. After that, you'll be sitting in a classroom with an exam sheet on your desk. Whether you stare at that exam with a queasy stomach, or whip through it fairly confidently, depends on your study techniques. Most of the successful students I talked to agreed that the following eight study tips deliver solid results:

1. *Set up a study place.* Those students you see "studying" in the cafeteria or game room aren't learning much. You just can't learn when you're distracted by people and noise. Even the library can be a bad place to study if you constantly find yourself watching the clouds outside or the students walking through the stacks. It takes guts to sit, alone, in a quiet place in order to study. But you have to do it. Find a room at home or a spot in the library that's relatively quiet—and boring. When you sit there, you won't have much to do except study.

2. *Get into a study frame of mind.* When you sit down, do it with the attitude that you're really going to get this studying done. You're not going to doodle on your notebook or make a list for the supermarket. Decide that you're going to study and learn now, so that you can move on to more interesting things as soon as possible.

3. *Give yourself rewards.* If you sweat out a block of study time, and do a good job on it, treat yourself. You deserve it. You can "psych" yourself up for studying by promising to reward yourself afterwards. A present for yourself can be anything from a favorite TV show to a relaxing bath to a dish of double-chocolate ice cream.

4. *Skim the textbook first.* Lots of students sit down with an assignment like "read chapter five, pages 125-150" and do just that. They turn to page 125 and start to read. After a while, they find that they have no idea what they just read. For the last ten minutes, they've been thinking about their five-year-old or what they're going to eat for dinner. Eventually, they plod through all the pages but don't remember much afterwards. In order to prevent this problem, skim the textbook chapter first. This means: look at the title, the subtitles, the headings, the pictures, the first and last paragraphs. Try to find out what the person who wrote the book had in mind when he or she organized the chapter. What was important enough to set off as a title or in bold type? After skimming, you should be able to explain to yourself what the main points of the chapter are. Unless you're the kind of person who would step into an empty elevator shaft without looking first, you'll soon discover the value of skimming.

5. *Take notes on what you're studying.* This sounds like a hassle, but it works. Go back over the material after you've read it, and jot down key words and phrases in the margins. When you review the chapter for a test, you'll have handy little things like "definition of rationalization" or "example of regression" in the margins. If the material is especially tough, organize a separate sheet of notes. Write down definitions, examples, lists, and main ideas. The idea is to have a single sheet that boils the entire chapter down to a digestible lump.

6. *Review after you've read and taken notes.* Some people swear that talking to yourself works. Tell yourself about the most important points in the chapter. Once you've said them out loud, they seem to stick better in your mind. If you can't talk to yourself about the material after reading it, that's a sure sign you don't really know it.

7. *Give up.* This may sound contradictory, but give up when you've had enough. You should try to make it through at least an hour, though. Ten minutes here and there are useless. When your head starts to pound and your eyes develop spidery red lines, quit. Rest for a bit with a short nap and go back later. *Take the college skills course if you need it.* Don't hesitate or feel embarrassed about enrolling in a study skills course. Many students say they wouldn't have made it without one.

How Can I Keep Up with All My Responsibilities Without Going Crazy?

You've got a class schedule. You're supposed to study. You've got a family. You've got a husband, wife, boyfriend, child. You've got a job. How are you possibly going to cover all the bases in your life and maintain your sanity? This is one of the toughest problems students face. Even if they start the semester with the best of intentions, they eventually find themselves tearing their hair out trying to do everything they're supposed to do. Believe it or not, though, it is possible to meet all your responsibilities. And you don't have to turn into a hermit or give up your loved ones to do it.

The secret here is to organize your time. But don't just sit around half the semester planning to get everything together soon. Before you know it, you'll be confronted with midterms, papers, family, and work all at once. Don't let yourself reach that breaking point. Instead, try these three tactics:

1. *Prepare a monthly calendar:* Get one of those calendars with big blocks around the dates. Give yourself an overview of the whole term by marking down the due dates for papers and projects. Circle test and exam days. This way those days don't sneak up on you unexpectedly.

2. *Make up a study schedule:* Sit down during the first few days of this semester and make up a sheet listing the days and hours of the week. Fill in your work and class hours first. Then try to block out some study hours. It's better to study a little every day than to create a huge once-or-twice-a-week marathon session. Schedule study hours for your hardest classes for the times when you feel most energetic. For example, I battled my tax law textbook in the mornings; when I looked at it after 7:00 P.M. I may as well have been reading Chinese. The usual proportion, by the way, is one hour of study time for every class hour. In case you're one of those people who get carried away, remember to leave blocks of free time, too. You won't be any good to yourself or anyone else if you don't relax and pack in the studying once in a while.

3. *Use "to-do" lists:* This is the secret that single-handedly got me through college. Once a week (or every day if you want to), write a list of what you have to do. Write down everything from "write English paper" to "buy cold cuts for

lunches." The best thing about a "to-do" list is that it seems to tame all those stray "I have to" thoughts that nag at your mind. After you finish something on the list, cross it off. Don't be compulsive about finishing everything; you're not Superman or Wonder Woman. Get the important things done first. The secondary things you don't finish can simply be moved to your next "to-do" list.

What Can I Do If Personal Problems Get in the Way of My Studies?

One student, Roger, told me this story:

Everything was going okay for me until the middle of the spring semester. I went through a terrible time when I broke up with my girlfriend and started seeing her best friend. I was trying to deal with my ex-girlfriend's hurt and anger, my new girlfriend's guilt, and my own worries and anxieties at the same time. In addition to this, my mother was sick and on a medication that made her really irritable. I hated to go home because the atmosphere was so uncomfortable. Soon, I started missing classes because I couldn't deal with the academic pressures as well as my own personal problems. It seemed easier to hang around my girlfriend's apartment than to face all my problems at home and at school.

Another student, Marian, told me:

I'd been married for eight years and the relationship wasn't going too well. I saw the handwriting on the wall, and I decided to prepare for the future. I enrolled in college because I knew I'd need a decent job to support myself. Well, my husband had a fit because I was going to school. We were arguing a lot anyway, and he made it almost impossible for me to study at home. I think he was angry and almost jealous because I was drawing away from him. It got so bad that I thought about quitting college for a while. I wasn't getting any support at home and it was just too hard to go on.

Personal troubles like these are overwhelming when you're going through them. School seems like the least important thing in your life. The two students above are perfect examples of this. But if you think about it, quitting or failing school would be the worst thing for these two students. Roger's problems, at least with his girlfriends, would simmer down eventually, and then he'd regret having left school

Marian had to finish college if she wanted to be able to live independently. Sometimes, you've just got to hang tough.

But what do you do while you're trying to live through a lousy time? First of all, do something difficult. Ask yourself, honestly, if you're exaggerating small problems as an excuse to avoid classes and studying. It takes strength to admit this, but there's no sense in kidding yourself. If your problems are serious, and real, try to make some human contacts at school. Lots of students hide inside a miserable shell made of their own troubles and feel isolated and lonely. Believe me, there are plenty of students with problems. Not everyone is getting A's and having a fabulous social and home life at the same time. As you go through the term, you'll pick up some vibrations about the students in your classes. Perhaps someone strikes you as a compatible person. Why not speak to that person after class? Share a cup of coffee in the cafeteria or walk to the parking lot together. You're not looking for a best friend or the love of your life. You just want to build a little network of support for yourself. Sharing your difficulties, questions, and complaints with a friendly person on campus can make a world of difference in how you feel.

Finally, if your problems are overwhelming, get some professional help. Why do you think colleges spend countless dollars on counseling departments and campus psychiatric services? More than ever, students all over the country are taking advantage of the help offered by support groups and therapy sessions. There's no shame attached to asking for help, either. In fact, almost 40 percent of college students (according to one survey) will use counseling services during their time in school. Just walk into a student center or counseling office and ask for an appointment. You wouldn't think twice about asking a dentist to help you get rid of your toothache. Counselors are paid—and want—to help you with your problems.

Why Do Some People Make It and Some People Drop Out?

Anyone who spends at least one semester in college notices that some students give up on their classes. The person who sits behind you in accounting, for example, begins to miss a lot of class meetings and eventually vanishes. Or another student comes to class without the assignment, doodles in his notebook during the lecture, and leaves during the break. What's the difference between students like this and the ones who succeed in school? My survey may be non-scientific, but everyone I asked said the same thing: attitude. A positive attitude is the key to everything else—good study habits, smart time scheduling, and coping with personal difficulties.

What does "a positive attitude" mean? Well, for one thing, it means not acting like a zombie. It means not only showing up for your classes, but also doing something while you're there. Really listen. Take notes. Ask a question if you want to. Don't just walk into a class, put your mind in neutral, and drift away to never-never land.

Having a positive attitude goes deeper than this, though. It means being mature about college as an institution. Too many students approach college classes like six-year-olds who expect first grade to be as much fun as *Sesame Street*. First grade, as we all know, isn't as much fun as *Sesame Street*. And college classes can sometimes be downright dull and boring. If you let a boring class discourage you so much that you want to leave school, you'll lose in the long run. Look at your priorities. You want a degree, or a certificate, or a career. If you have to, you can make it through a less-than-interesting class in order to achieve what you want. Get whatever you can out of every class. But if you simply can't stand a certain class, be determined to fulfill its requirements and be done with it once and for all.

After the initial high of starting school, you have to settle in for the long haul. If you follow the advice here, you'll be prepared to face the academic crunch. You'll also live through the semester without giving up your family, your job, or Monday Night Football. Finally, going to college can be an exciting time. As you learn things, the world truly becomes a more interesting place.

Literature

The Partly Cloudy Patriot

CREATIVE NONFICTION

Sarah Vowell

Sarah Vowell (1969–): Born in Muskogee, OK, Sarah Vowell eventually found herself earning a B.A. degree in Modern Languages and Literatures from Montana State University (1993) and an M.A. in Art History in 1996 from the Art Institute of Chicago. Sarah is a social commentator, journalist, essayist and author. Her works include *Wordy Shipmates* (2008), and *Assassination Vacation* (2005). Sarah has also been published in several publications as *The New York Times, SF Weekly*, and the *Village Voice*.

In the summer of 2000, I went to see the Mel Gibson blockbuster *The Patriot*. I enjoyed that movie. Watching a story line like that is always a relief. Of course the British must be expelled, just as the Confederates must surrender, Hitler must be crushed, and yee-haw when the Red Sea swallows those slavemongering Egyptians. There were editorials about *The Patriot*, the kind that always accompany any historical film, written by professors who insist things nobody cares about, like Salieri wasn't that bad a sort or the fact that Roman gladiators maybe didn't have Australian accents. A little anachronism is part of the fun, and I don't mind if in real life General Cornwallis never lost a battle in the South as he does rather gloriously in the film. Isn't art supposed to improve on life?

Personally, I think there was more than enough historical accuracy in *The Patriot* to keep the spoilsports happy. Because I'm part spoilsport on my father's side, and I felt nagged with quandaries every few minutes during the nearly three hour film. American history is a quagmire, and the more one knows, the quaggier the mire gets. If you're paying attention during *The Patriot* and you know your history and you have a stake in that history, not to mention a conscience, the movie is not an entirely cartoonish march to glory. For example, Mel Gibson's character, Benjamin Martin, is conflicted. He doesn't want to fight the British because he still feels bad about chopping up some Cherokee into little pieces during the French and Indian War. Since I'm a part-Cherokee person myself, Gibson lost a little of the sympathy I'd stored up for him because he'd been underrated in *Conspiracy Theory*. And did I mention his character lives in South Carolina? So by the end of the movie, you look at the youngest Mel junior bundled in his mother's arms and think, Mel just risked his life so that the kid's kids can rape their slaves and vote to be the first state to secede from the Union.

The Patriot did confirm that I owe George Washington an apology. I always liked George fine, though, I dismissed him as a mere soldier. I prefer the pen to the sword, so I've always been more of a Jeffersonhead. The words of the Declaration of Independence are so right and true that it seems like its poetry alone would have knocked King George III in the head. Like, he would have read this beloved passage, "We hold these Truths to be self-evident, that all Men are created equal, that they are endowed by their Creator with certain unalienable Rights—that among these are Life, Liberty, and the pursuit of Happiness," and thought the notion so just, and yet still so wonderfully whimsical, that he would have dethroned himself on the spot. But no, it took a grueling, six-year-long war to make independence a fact. I rarely remember this. In my ninety-five-cent copy of the Declaration of Independence and the Constitution, the two documents are separated by only a blank half page. I forget that there are eleven years between them, eleven years of war and the whole Articles of Confederation debacle. In my head, the two documents are like the A side and B side of the greatest single ever released that was recorded in one great drunken night, but no, there's a lot of bleeding life between them. Dead boys and dead Indians and Valley Forge.

Anyway, *The Patriot*. The best part of seeing it was standing in line for tickets. I remember how jarring it was to hear my fellow moviegoers say that word. "Two for *The Patriot* please." "One for *The Patriot* at 5:30." For years, I called it the P word, because it tended to make nice people flinch. For the better part of the 1990s, it seemed like the only Americans who publicly described themselves as patriots were scary militia types hiding out in the backwoods of Michigan and Montana, cleaning their guns. One of the few Americans still celebrating Patriot's Day—a nearly forgotten holiday on April 19 commemorating the Revolutionary War's first shots at Lexington and Concord—did so in 1995 by murdering 168 people in the federal building in Oklahoma City. In fact, the same week I saw *The Patriot*, I was out with some friends for dessert. When I asked a fellow named Andy why he had chosen a cupcake with a little American flag stuck in the frosting, I expected him to say that he was in a patriotic mood, but he didn't. He said that he was "feeling jingoistic."

Well, that was a long time ago. As I write this, it's December 2001 in New York City. The only words one hears more often than variations on *patriot* are "in the wake of," "in the aftermath of," and "since the events of September 11." We also use the word *we* more. Patriotism as a word and deed had made a comeback. At Halloween, costume shops did a brisk business in Uncle Sam and Betsy Ross getups. Teen pop bombshell Britney Spears took a breather during her live telecast from Vegas's MGM Grand to sit on a piano bench with her belly ring glinting in the spotlight and talk about "how proud I am of our nation right now." Chinese textile factories are working overtime to fill the consumer demand for American flags.

Immediately after the attack, seeing the flag all over the place was moving, endearing. So when the newspaper I subscribe to published a full-page, full-color flag to clip out and hang in the window, how come I couldn't? It took me a while to figure out why I guiltily slid the flag into the recycling bin instead of taping it up. The meaning had changed; or let's say it changed back. In the first day or two the flags were plastered everywhere, seeing them was heartening because they indicated that we're all in this sorrow together. The flags were purely emotional. Once we went to war, once the president announced that we were going to retaliate against the "evildoers," then the flag again represented what it usually represents, the government. I think that's when the flags started making me nervous. The true American patriot is by definition skeptical of the government. Skepticism of the government was actually one of the platforms that current figurehead of the government ran on. How many times in the campaign did President Bush proclaim of his opponent, the then vice president, "He trusts the federal government and I trust the people"? This deep suspicion of Washington is one of the most American emotions an American can have. So by the beginning of October, the ubiquity of the flag came to feel like peer pressure to always stand behind policies one might not necessarily agree with. And, like any normal citizen, I prefer to make up my mind about the issues of the day on a case by case basis at 3:00 A.M. when I wake up from my *Nightline*-inspired nightmares.

One Independence Day, when I was in college, I was living in a house with other students on a street that happened to be one of the main roads leading to the football stadium where the town's official Fourth of July fireworks festivities would be held. I looked out the window and noticed a little American flag stabbed in my yard. Then I walked outside and saw that all the yards in front of all the houses on the street had little flags waving above the grass. The flags, according to a tag, were underwritten by a local real estate agency and the Veterans of Foreign Wars. I marched into the house, yanked out the phone book, found the real estate office in the yellow pages, and phoned them up immediately, demanding that they come and take their fucking flag off my lawn, screaming into the phone, "The whole point of that goddamn flag is that people don't stick flags in my yard without asking me!" I felt like Jimmy Stewart in Mr. Smith Goes to Washington, but with profanity. A few minutes later, an elderly gentleman in a VFW cap, who probably lost his best friend liberating France or something, pulled up in a big car, grabbed the flag, and rolled his eyes as I stared at him through the window. Then I felt dramatic and dumb. Still, sometimes I think the true American flag has always been that one with the snake hissing "Don't Tread on Me."

The week of the attack on the World Trade Center and the Pentagon, I watched TV news all day and slept with the radio on. I found myself flipping channels hoping to see the FBI handcuff a terrorist on camera. What did happen, a lot, was that citizens or politicians or journalists would mention that they wonder what it will be like for Americans now to live with the constant threat of random, sudden death. I know a little bit about what that's like. I did grow up during the Cold War. Maybe it says something about my level of cheer that I found this notion comforting, to remember that all those years I was sure the world might blow up at any second, I somehow managed to graduate from high school and do my laundry and see Smokey Robinson live.

Things were bad in New York. I stopped being able to tell whether my eyes were teary all of the time from grief or from the dirty, smoky wind. Just when it seemed as if the dust had started to settle, then came the anthrax. I was on the phone with a friend who works in Rockefeller Center, and he had to hang up to be evacuated because a contaminated envelope had infected a person in the building;

an hour later, another friend in another building was sitting at his desk eating his lunch and men in sealed plastic disease-control space suits walked through his office, taking samples. Once delivering the mail became life-threatening, pedestrians trudging past the main post office on Eighth Avenue bowed their heads a little as they read the credo chiseled on the facade, "Neither snow, nor rain, nor heat, nor gloom of night stays these couriers from the swift completion of their appointed rounds."

During another war, across the river, in Newark, a writer turned soldier named Thomas Paine sat down by a campfire in September 1776 and wrote, "These are the times that try men's souls. The summer soldier and the sunshine patriot will, in this crisis, shrink from the service of their country; but he that stands it now, deserves the love and thanks of man and woman." In September and October, I liked to read that before I pulled the rubber band off the newspaper to find out what was being done to my country and what my country was doing back. I like the black and white of Paine's words. I know I'm no sunshine patriot. I wasn't shrinking, though, honestly; the most important service we mere mortal citizens were called upon to perform was to spend money, so I dutifully paid for Korean dinners and a new living room lamp. But still I longed for the morning that I could open up the paper and the only people in it who would irk me would be dead suicide bombers and retreating totalitarians on the other side of the world. Because that would be the morning I pulled that flag out of the recycling bin and taped it up in the window. And while I could shake my fists for sure at the terrorists on page one, buried domestic items could still make my stomach hurt—school prayer partisans taking advantage of the grief of children to circumvent the separation of church and state; the White House press secretary condemning a late-night talk show host for making a questionable remark about the U.S. military: "The reminder is to all Americans, that they need to watch what they say, watch what they do, and that this is not a time for remarks like that." Those are the sorts of never-ending qualms that have turned me into the partly cloudy patriot I long not to be.

When Paine wrote his pamphlet, which came to be called "The American Crisis," winter was coming, Washington's armies were in retreat, the Revolution was floundering. His words inspired soldiers and civilians alike to buck up and endure the war so that someday "not a place upon earth might be so happy as America."

Thing is, it worked. The British got kicked out. The trees got cleared. Time passed, laws passed and, five student loans later, I made a nice little life for myself. I can feel it with every passing year, how I'm that much farther away from the sacrifices of the cast-off Indians and Okie farmers I descend from. As recently as fifty years ago my grandmother was picking cotton with bleeding fingers. I think about her all the time while I'm getting overpaid to sit at a computer, eat Chinese takeout, and think things up in my pajamas. The half century separating my fingers, which are moisturized with cucumber lotion and type eighty words per minute, and her bloody digits is an ordinary Land of Opportunity parable, and don't think I don't appreciate it. I'm keenly aware of all the ways my life is easier and lighter, how lucky I am to have the time and energy to contemplate the truly important things—Bill Murray in *Groundhog Day*, the baked Alaska at Sardi's, the Dean Martin Christmas record, my growing collection of souvenir snowglobes. After all, what is happiness without cheap thrills? Reminds me of that passage in Philip Roth's novel American Pastoral when the middle-aged, prosperous grandson of immigrants marvels that his own daughter loathes the country enough to try to blow it up:

> Hate America? Why, he lived in America the way he lived inside his own skin. All the pleasures of his younger years were American pleasures, all that success and happiness had been American, and he need no longer keep his mouth shut about it just to defuse her ignorant hatred. The loneliness he would feel if he had to live in another country. Yes, everything that gave meaning to his accomplishments had been American. Everything he loved was here.

A few weeks after the United States started bombing Afghanistan and the Taliban were in retreat, I turned on the TV news and watched grinning Afghans in the streets of Kabul, allowed to play music for the first time in years. I pull a brain muscle when I try to fathom the rationale for outlawing all music all the time—not certain genres of music, not music with offensive lyrics played by the corrupters of youth, but any form of organized sound. Under Taliban rule, my whole life as an educated (well, at a state school), working with CD storage problems would have been null and void. I don't know what's more ridiculous, that people like that would deny a person like me the ability to earn a living using skills and knowledge I learned in school, or that they would deny me my unalienable right to chop garlic in time with the B-52's "Rock Lobster" as I cook dinner.

A few years back, a war correspondent friend of mine gave a speech about Bosnia to an international relations department at a famous Midwestern university. I went with him. After he finished, a group of hangers-on, all men except for me, stuck around to debate the finer points of the former Yugoslavia. The conversation was very detailed, including references to specific mayors of specific Croatian villages. It was like record collector geek talk, only about Bosnia. They were the record collectors of Bosnia. So they went on denouncing the various idiotic nationalist causes of various splinter groups, blaming nationalism itself for the genocidal war. And of course a racist nationalism is to blame. But the more they ranted, the more uncomfortable I became. They, many of them immigrants themselves, considered patriotic allegiance to be a sin, a divisive, villainous drive leading to exclusion, hate, and murder. I, theretofore silent, spoke up. This is what I said. I said that I had recently flown over Memphis, Tennessee. I said that the idea of Memphis, Tennessee, not to mention looking down at it, made me go all soft. Because I looked down at Memphis, Tennessee, and thought of all my heroes who had walked its streets. I thought of Sun Records, of the producer Sam Phillips. Sam Phillips, who once described the sort of person he recorded as "a person who had dreamed, and dreamed, and dreamed." A person like Elvis Presley, his funny bass player Bill Black, his guitarist Scotty Moore (we have the same birthday he and I). Jerry Lee Lewis. Carl Perkins. Hello, I'm Johnny Cash. I told the Bosnian record collectors that when I thought of the records of these Memphis men, when I looked out the window at the Mississippi mud and felt their names moistening my tongue what I felt, what I was proud to feel, was patriotic. I noticed one man staring at me. He said he was born in some something-istan I hadn't heard of.

Now that my globe is permanently turned to that part of the world, I realize he was talking about Tajikistan, the country bordering Afghanistan. The man looked me in the eye and delivered the following warning.

"Those," he said, of my accolades for Elvis and friends, "are the seeds of war."

I laughed and told him not to step on my blue suede shoes, but I got the feeling he wasn't joking.

Before September 11, the national events that have made the deepest impressions on me are, in chronological order: the 1976 Bicentennial, the Iran hostage crisis, Iran-Contra, the Los Angeles riots, the impeachment trial of President Clinton, and the 2000 presidential election. From those events, I learned the following: that the Declaration of Independence is full of truth and beauty; that some people in other parts of the world hate us because we're Americans; what a shredder is; that the rage for justice is so fierce people will set fire to their own neighborhoods when they don't get it; that Republicans hate Bill Clinton; and that the ideal of one man, one vote doesn't always come true. (In the U.S. Commission on Civil Right's report "Voting Irregularities in Florida During the 2000 Presidential Election," the testimony of Dr. Frederick Shotz of Broward County especially sticks out. A handicapped voter in a wheelchair, Dr. Shotz "had to use his upper body to lift himself up to get up the step in order for him to access his polling place. Once he was inside the polling place, he was not given a wheelchair accessible polling booth. Once again, he had to use his arms to left himself up to see the ballot and, while balancing on his arms, simultaneously attempt to cast his ballot.")

Looking over my list, I can't help but notice that only one of my formative experiences, the Bicentennial, came with balloons and cake. Being a little kid that year, visiting the Freedom Train with its dramatically lit facsimile of the Declaration, learning that I lived in the greatest, most fair and wise and lovely place on earth, made a big impression on me. I think it's one of the reasons I'm so fond of President Lincoln. Because he stared down the crap. More than anyone in the history of the country, he faced up to our most troubling contradiction—that a nation born in freedom would permit the enslavement of human beings—and never once stopped believing in the Declaration of Independence's ideals, never stopped trying to make them come true.

On a Sunday in November, I walked up to the New York Public Library to see the Emancipation Proclamation. On loan from the National Archives, the document was in town for three days. They put it in a glass case in a small, dark room. Being alone with old pieces of paper and one guard in an alcove at the library was nice and quiet. I stared at Abraham Lincoln's signature for a long time. I stood there, thinking what one is supposed to think: this is the paper he held in his hands and there is the ink that came from his pen, and when the ink dried the slaves were freed. Except look at the date, January 1, 1863. The words wouldn't come true for a couple of years, which, I'm guessing, is a long time when another person owns your body. But I love how Lincoln dated the document, noting that it was signed "in the year of our Lord one thousand eight hundred and sixty-three, and of the Independence of the United States of America the eighty-seventh." Four score and seven years before, is the wonderfully arrogant implication, something as miraculous as the virgin birth happened on this earth, and the calendar should reflect that.

The Emancipation Proclamation is a perfect American artifact to me—a good deed that made a lot of other Americans mad enough to kill. I think that's why the Civil War is my favorite American metaphor. I'm so much more comfortable when we're bickering with each other than when we have to link arms and fight a common enemy. But right after September 11, the TV was full of unity. Congressmen, political enemies from both houses of Congress, from both sides of the aisle, stood together on the Capitol steps and sang "God Bless America." At the memorial service at the National Cathedral, President and Mrs. Carter chatted like old friends with President and Mrs. Ford. Rudolph Giuliani, the mayor of New York, kissed his former opponent Senator Hillary Clinton on the cheek as the New York congressional delegation toured the World Trade Center disaster area.

In September, people across the country and all over the world—including, bless them, the Canadians, and they are born sick of us—were singing the American national anthem. And when I heard their voices I couldn't help but remember the last time I had sung that song. I was one of the hundreds of people standing in the mud on the Washington Mall on January 20 at the inauguration of George W. Bush. Everyone standing there in the cold rain had very strong feelings. It was either/or. Either you beamed through the ceremony with smiles of joy, or you wept through it with tears of rage. I admit, I was one of the people there who needed a hankie when it was over. At the end of the ceremony, it was time to sing the national anthem. Some of the dissenters refused to join in. Such was their anger at the country at that moment they couldn't find it in their hearts to sing. But I was standing there next to my friend Jack, and Jack and I put our hands over our hearts and sang that song loud. Because we love our country too. Because we wouldn't have been standing there, wouldn't have driven down to Washington just to burst into tears if we didn't care so very, very much about how this country is run.

When the anthem ended—land of the free, home of the brave—Jack and I walked to the other end of the Mall to the Lincoln Memorial to read Lincoln's Second Inaugural Address, the speech Lincoln gave at the end of the Civil War about how "we must bind up the nation's wounds." It seems so quaint to me now, after September, after CNN started doing hourly live remotes from St. Vincent's, my neighborhood hospital, that I would conceive of a wound as being peeved about who got to be president.

My ideal picture of citizenship will always be an argument, not a sing-along. I did not get it out of a civics textbook either. I got it from my parents. My mom and dad disagree with me about almost everything. I do not share their religion or their political affiliation. I get on their nerves sometimes. But, and this [is] the most important thing they taught me, so what? We love each other. My parents and I have been through so much and known each other for so long, share so many in-jokes and memories, our differences of opinion on everything from gun control to Robin Williams movies hardly matter at all. Plus, our disagreements make us appreciate the things we have in common all the more. When I call Republican Senator Orrin Hatch's office to say that I admire something he said about stem cell research, I am my parents' daughter. Because they have always enjoyed playing up the things we do have in common, like Dolly Parton or ibuprofen. Maybe sometimes, in quiet moments of reflection, my mom would prefer that I not burn eternally in the flames of hell when I die, but otherwise she wants me to follow my own heart.

I will say that, in September, atheism was a lonely creed. Not because atheists have no god to turn to, but because everyone else forgot about us. At a televised interfaith memorial service at Yankee Stadium on September 23, Muslim, Christian, Jewish, Sikh, and Hindu clerics spoke to their fellow worshippers. Placido Domingo sang "Ave Maria" for the mayor. I waited in vain for someone like me to stand up and say the only thing those of us who don't believe in god have to believe in is other people and that New York City is the best place there ever was for a godless person to practice her moral code. I think it has something to do with the crowded sidewalks and subways. Walking to and from the hardware store requires the push and pull of selfishness and selflessness, taking turns between getting out of someone's way and them getting out of yours. Waiting for a dog to move, helping a stroller up steps, protecting the eyes from runaway umbrellas. Walking in New York is a battle of the wills, a balance of aggression and kindness. I'm not saying it's always easy. The occasional "Watch where you're going, bitch" can, I admit, put a crimp in one's day. But I believe all that choreography has made me a better person. The other day, in the subway at 5:30, I was crammed into my sweaty, crabby fellow citizens, and I kept whispering under my breath "we the people, we the people" over and over again, reminding myself we're all in this together and they had as much right—exactly as much right—as I to be in the muggy underground on their way to wherever they were on their way to.

Once, headed uptown on the 9 train, I noticed a sign posted by the Metropolitan Transit Authority advising subway riders who might become ill in the train. The sign asked that the suddenly infirm inform another passenger or get out at the next stop and approach the stationmaster. Do not, repeat, do not pull the emergency brake, the sign said, as this will only delay aid. Which was all very logical, but for the following proclamation at the bottom of the sign, something along the lines of "If you are sick, you will not be left alone." This strikes me as not only kind, not only comforting, but the very epitome of civilization, good government, i.e., the crux of the societal impulse. Banding together, pooling our taxes, not just making trains, not just making trains that move underground, not just making trains that move underground with surprising efficiency at a fair price—but posting on said trains a notification of such surprising compassion and thoughtfulness, I found myself scanning the faces of my fellow passengers, hoping for fainting, obvious fevers, at the very least a sneeze so that I might offer a tissue.

A Modest Proposal: For Preventing the Children of Poor People in Ireland from Being a Burden to Their Parents or Country, and for Making Them Beneficial to the Public

SATIRE

Jonathan Swift

Jonathan Swift (1667–1745) was an essayist, satirist, novelist, and poet. This essay is a commentary on the treatment of the Irish by absentee English landlords and the exploitation of his country, mocking the treatment of the poor. It was originally published anonymously in 1729.

It is a melancholy object to those who walk through this great town or travel in the country, when they see the streets, the roads, and cabin doors, crowded with beggars of the female sex, followed by three, four, or six children, all in rags and importuning every passenger for an alms. These mothers, instead of being able to work for their honest livelihood, are forced to employ all their time in strolling to beg sustenance for their helpless infants: who as they grow up either turn thieves for want of work, or leave their dear native country to fight for the Pretender in Spain, or sell themselves to the Barbadoes.

I think it is agreed by all parties that this prodigious number of children in the arms, or on the backs, or at the heels of their mothers, and frequently of their fathers, is in the present deplorable state of the kingdom a very great additional grievance; and, therefore, whoever could find out a fair, cheap, and easy method of making these children sound, useful members of the commonwealth, would deserve so well of the public as to have his statue set up for a preserver of the nation.

But my intention is very far from being confined to provide only for the children of professed beggars; it is of a much greater extent, and shall take in the whole number of infants at a certain age who are born of parents in effect as little able to support them as those who demand our charity in the streets.

As to my own part, having turned my thoughts for many years upon this important subject, and maturely weighed the several schemes of other projectors, I have always found them grossly mistaken in the computation. It is true, a child just dropped from its dam may be supported by her milk for a solar year, with little other nourishment; at most not above the value of 2s., which the mother may certainly get, or the value in scraps, by her lawful occupation of begging; and it is exactly at one year old that I propose to provide for them in such a manner as instead of being a charge upon their parents or the parish, or wanting food and raiment for the rest of their lives, they shall on the contrary contribute to the feeding, and partly to the clothing, of many thousands.

There is likewise another great advantage in my scheme, that it will prevent those voluntary abortions, and that horrid practice of women murdering their bastard children, alas! too frequent among us! sacrificing the poor innocent babes I doubt more to avoid the expense than the shame, which would move tears and pity in the most savage and inhuman breast.

The number of souls in this kingdom being usually reckoned one million and a half, of these I calculate there may be about two hundred thousand couple whose wives are breeders; from which number I subtract thirty thousand couples who are able to maintain their own children, although I apprehend there cannot be so many, under the present distresses of the kingdom; but this being granted, there will remain an hundred and seventy thousand breeders. I again subtract fifty thousand for those women who miscarry, or whose children die by accident or disease within the year. There only remains one hundred and twenty thousand children of poor parents annually born. The question therefore is, how this number shall be reared and provided for, which, as I have already said, under the present situation of affairs, is utterly impossible by all the methods hitherto proposed. For we can neither employ them in handicraft or agriculture; we neither build houses (I mean in the country) nor cultivate land: they can very seldom pick up a livelihood by stealing, till they arrive at six years old, except where they are of towardly parts, although I confess they learn the rudiments much earlier, during which time, they can however be properly looked upon only as probationers, as I have been informed by a principal gentleman in the county of Cavan, who protested to me that he never knew above one or two instances under the age of six, even in a part of the kingdom so renowned for the quickest proficiency in that art.

I am assured by our merchants, that a boy or a girl before twelve years old is no salable commodity; and even when they come to this age they will not yield above three pounds, or three pounds and half-a-crown at most on the exchange; which cannot turn to account either to the parents or kingdom, the charge of nutriment and rags having been at least four times that value.

I shall now therefore humbly propose my own thoughts, which I hope will not be liable to the least objection.

I have been assured by a very knowing American of my acquaintance in London, that a young healthy child well nursed is at a year old a most delicious, nourishing, and wholesome food, whether stewed, roasted, baked, or boiled; and I make no doubt that it will equally serve in a fricassee or a ragout.

I do therefore humbly offer it to public consideration that of the hundred and twenty thousand children already computed, twenty thousand may be reserved for breed, whereof only one-fourth part to be males; which is more than we allow to sheep, black cattle or swine; and my reason is, that these children are seldom the fruits of marriage, a circumstance not much regarded by our savages, therefore one male will be sufficient to serve four females. That the remaining hundred thousand may, at a year old, be offered in the sale to the persons of quality and fortune through the kingdom; always advising the mother to let them suck plentifully in the last month, so as to render them plump and fat for a good table. A child will make two dishes at an entertainment for friends; and when the family dines alone, the fore or hind quarter will make a reasonable dish, and seasoned with a little pepper or salt will be very good boiled on the fourth day, especially in winter.

I have reckoned upon a medium that a child just born will weigh 12 pounds, and in a solar year, if tolerably nursed, increaseth to 28 pounds.

I grant this food will be somewhat dear, and therefore very proper for landlords, who, as they have already devoured most of the parents, seem to have the best title to the children.

Infant's flesh will be in season throughout the year, but more plentiful in March, and a little before and after; for we are told by a grave author, an eminent French physician, that fish being a prolific diet, there are more children born in Roman Catholic countries about nine months after Lent than at any other season; therefore, reckoning a year after Lent, the markets will be more glutted than usual, because the number of popish infants is at least three to one in this kingdom: and therefore it will have one other collateral advantage, by lessening the number of papists among us.

I have already computed the charge of nursing a beggar's child (in which list I reckon all cottagers, laborers, and four-fifths of the farmers) to be about two shillings per annum, rags included; and I believe no gentleman would repine to give ten shillings for the carcass of a good fat child, which, as I have said, will make four dishes of excellent nutritive meat, when he hath only some particular friend or his own family to dine with him. Thus the squire will learn to be a good landlord, and grow popular among his tenants; the mother will have eight shillings net profit, and be fit for work till she produces another child.

Those who are more thrifty (as I must confess the times require) may flay the carcass; the skin of which artificially dressed will make admirable gloves for ladies, and summer boots for fine gentlemen.

As to our city of Dublin, shambles may be appointed for this purpose in the most convenient parts of it, and butchers we may be assured will not be wanting; although I rather recommend buying the children alive, and dressing them hot from the knife, as we do roasting pigs.

A very worthy person, a true lover of his country, and whose virtues I highly esteem, was lately pleased in discoursing on this matter to offer a refinement upon my scheme. He said that many gentlemen of this kingdom, having of late destroyed their deer, he conceived that the want of venison might be well supplied by the bodies of young lads and maidens, not exceeding fourteen years of age nor under twelve; so great a number of both sexes in every country being now ready to starve for want of work and service; and these to be disposed of by their parents, if alive, or otherwise by their nearest relations. But with due deference to so excellent a friend and so deserving a patriot, I cannot be altogether in his sentiments; for as to the males, my American acquaintance assured me, from frequent experience, that their flesh was generally tough and lean, like that of our schoolboys by continual exercise, and their taste disagreeable; and to fatten them would not answer the charge. Then as to the females, it would, I think, with humble submission be a loss to the public, because they soon would become breeders themselves; and besides, it is not improbable that some scrupulous people might be apt to censure such a practice (although indeed very unjustly), as a little bordering upon cruelty; which, I confess, hath always been with me the strongest objection against any project, however so well intended.

But in order to justify my friend, he confessed that this expedient was put into his head by the famous Psalmanazar, a native of the island Formosa, who came from thence to London above twenty years ago, and in conversation told my friend, that in his country when any young person happened to be put to death, the executioner sold the carcass to persons of quality as a prime dainty; and that in his time the body of a plump girl of fifteen, who was crucified for an attempt to poison the emperor, was sold to his imperial majesty's prime minister of state, and other great mandarins of the court, in joints from the gibbet, at four hundred crowns. Neither indeed can I deny, that if the same use were made of several plump young girls in this town, who without one single groat to their fortunes cannot stir abroad without a chair, and appear at playhouse and assemblies in foreign fineries which they never will pay for, the kingdom would not be the worse.

Some persons of a desponding spirit are in great concern about that vast number of poor people, who are aged, diseased, or maimed, and I have been desired to employ my thoughts what course may be taken to ease the nation of so grievous an encumbrance. But I am not in the least pain upon that matter, because it is very well known that they are every day dying and rotting by cold and famine, and filth and vermin, as fast as can be reasonably expected. And as to the young laborers, they are now in as hopeful a condition; they cannot get work, and consequently pine away for want of nourishment, to a degree that if at any time they are accidentally hired to common labor, they have not strength to perform it; and thus the country and themselves are happily delivered from the evils to come.

I have too long digressed, and therefore shall return to my subject. I think the advantages by the proposal which I have made are obvious and many, as well as of the highest importance. For first, as I have already observed, it would greatly lessen the number of papists, with whom we are yearly overrun, being the principal breeders of the nation as well as our most dangerous enemies; and who stay at home on purpose with a design to deliver the kingdom to the Pretender, hoping to take their advantage by the absence of so many good protestants, who have chosen rather to leave their country than stay at home and pay tithes against their conscience to an episcopal curate.

Secondly, The poorer tenants will have something valuable of their own, which by law may be made liable to distress and help to pay their landlord's rent, their corn and cattle being already seized, and money a thing unknown.

Thirdly, Whereas the maintenance of an hundred thousand children, from two years old and upward, cannot be computed at less than ten shillings a-piece per annum, the nation's stock will be thereby increased fifty thousand pounds per annum, beside the profit of a new dish introduced to the tables of all gentlemen of fortune in the kingdom who have any refinement in taste. And the money will circulate among ourselves, the goods being entirely of our own growth and manufacture.

Fourthly, The constant breeders, beside the gain of eight shillings sterling per annum by the sale of their children, will be rid of the charge of maintaining them after the first year.

Fifthly, This food would likewise bring great custom to taverns; where the vintners will certainly be so prudent as to procure the best receipts for dressing it to perfection, and consequently have their houses frequented by all the fine gentlemen, who justly value themselves upon their knowledge in good eating: and a skilful cook, who understands how to oblige his guests, will contrive to make it as expensive as they please.

Sixthly, This would be a great inducement to marriage, which all wise nations have either encouraged by rewards or enforced by laws and penalties. It would increase the care and tenderness of mothers toward their children, when they were sure of a settlement for life to the poor babes, provided in some sort by the public, to their annual profit instead of expense. We should see an honest emulation among the married women, which of them could bring the fattest child to the market. Men would become as fond of their wives during the time of their pregnancy as they are now of their mares in foal, their cows in calf, their sows when they are ready to farrow; nor offer to beat or kick them (as is too frequent a practice) for fear of a miscarriage.

Many other advantages might be enumerated. For instance, the addition of some thousand carcasses in our exportation of barreled beef, the propagation of swine's flesh, and improvement in the art of making good bacon, so much wanted among us by the great destruction of pigs, too frequent at our tables; which are no way comparable in taste or magnificence to a well-grown, fat, yearling child, which roasted whole will make a considerable figure at a lord mayor's feast or any other public entertainment. But this and many others I omit, being studious of brevity.

Supposing that one thousand families in this city, would be constant customers for Infant's Flesh, besides others who might have it at merry meetings, particularly at weddings and christenings, I compute that Dublin would take off annually about twenty thousand carcasses, and the rest of the Kingdom (where probably they will be sold somewhat cheaper) the remaining eighty thousand.

I can think of no one objection, that will possibly be raised against this proposal, unless it should be urged, that the number of people will be thereby much lessened in the Kingdom. This I freely own, and 'twas indeed one principal design in offering it to the world. I desire the reader will observe, that I calculate my remedy for this one individual kingdom of Ireland, and for no other that ever was, is, or I think, ever can be upon Earth. Therefore let no man talk to me of other expedients: of taxing our absentees at five shillings a pound: of using neither clothes, nor household furniture, except what is of our own growth and manufacture: of utterly rejecting the materials and instruments that promote foreign luxury: of curing the expensiveness of pride, vanity, idleness, and gaming in our women: of introducing a vein of parsimony, prudence and temperance: of learning to love our country, wherein we differ even from Laplanders, and the inhabitants of Topinamboo: of quitting our animosities, and factions, nor act any longer like the Jews, who were murdering one another at the very moment their city was taken: of being a little cautious not to sell our country and consciences for nothing: of teaching our landlords to have at least one degree of mercy towards their tenants. Lastly, of putting a spirit of honesty, industry, and skill into our shop-keepers, who, if a resolution could now be taken to buy only our native goods, would immediately unite to cheat and exact upon us in the price, the measure and the goodness, nor could ever yet be brought to make one fair proposal of just dealing, though often and earnestly invited to it.

Therefore I repeat, let no man talk to me of these and the like expedients, till he hath at least some glimpse of hope, that there will ever be some hearty and sincere attempt to put them into practice.

But as to myself, having been wearied out for many years with offering vain, idle, visionary thoughts, and at length despairing of success, I fortunately fell upon this proposal, which as it is wholly new, so it hath something solid and real, of no expense and little trouble, full in our own power, and whereby we can incur no danger in disobliging England. For this kind of commodity will not bear exportation, the flesh being of too tender a consistence, to admit a long continuance in salt, although perhaps I could name a country, which would be glad to eat up our whole nation without it.

After all, I am not so violently bent upon my own opinion as to reject any offer proposed by wise men, which shall be found equally innocent, cheap, easy, and effectual. But before something of that kind shall be advanced in contradiction to my scheme, and offering a better, I desire the author or authors will be pleased maturely to consider two points. First, as things now stand, how they will be able to find food and raiment for an hundred thousand useless mouths and backs. And secondly, there being a round million of creatures in human figure throughout this kingdom, whose whole subsistence put into a common stock would leave them in debt two millions of pounds sterling, adding those who are beggars by profession to the bulk of farmers, cottagers, and laborers, with their wives and children who are beggars in effect: I desire those politicians who dislike my overture, and may perhaps be so bold as to attempt an answer, that they will first ask the parents of these mortals, whether they would not at this day think it a great happiness to have been sold for food, at a year old in the manner I prescribe, and thereby have avoided such a perpetual scene of misfortunes as they have since gone through by the oppression of landlords, the impossibility of paying rent without money or trade, the want of common sustenance, with neither house nor clothes to cover them from the inclemencies of the weather, and the most inevitable prospect of entailing the like or greater miseries upon their breed forever.

I profess, in the sincerity of my heart, that I have not the least personal interest in endeavoring to promote this necessary work, having no other motive than the public good of my country, by advancing our trade, providing for infants, relieving the poor, and giving some pleasure to the rich. I have no children by which I can propose to get a single penny; the youngest being nine years old, and my wife past child-bearing.

The Making of Harlem

JOURNALISM

James Weldon Johnson

James Weldon Johnson (1871-1938) was a political activist, author, educator, lawyer, and songwriter. Johnson served as the first African-American executive secretary for the National Association for the Advancement of Colored People (NAACP), holding that position for ten years (1920-1930). He was the first African-American professor at New York University, and later taught literature and creative writing at Fisk University in Nashville, Tennessee. For his literary works, Johnson is best known for writing and editing poetry, *The Autobiography of an Ex-Colored Man* (novel), and his autobiography *Along This Way*. This essay originally appeared in *Survey Graphic* magazine in 1925, documenting the height of the Harlem Renaissance in New York.

In the history of New York, the significance of the name Harlem has changed from Dutch to Irish to Jewish to Negro. Of these changes, the last has come most swiftly. Throughout colored America, from Massachusetts to Mississippi, and across the continent to Los Angeles and Seattle, its name, which as late as fifteen years ago had scarcely been heard, now stands for the Negro metropolis. Harlem is indeed the great Mecca for the sight-seer, the pleasure-seeker, the curious, the adventurous, the enterprising, the ambitious and the talented of the whole Negro world; for the lure of it has reached down to every island of the Caribbean Sea and has penetrated even into Africa.

In the make-up of New York, Harlem is not merely a Negro colony or community, it is a city within a city, the greatest Negro city in the world. It is not a slum or a fringe, it is located in the heart of Manhattan and occupies one of the most beautiful and healthful sections of the city. It is not a "quarter" of dilapidated tenements, but is made up of new-law apartments and handsome dwellings, with well-paved and well-lighted streets. It has its own churches, social and civic centers, shops, theatres and other places of amusement. And it contains more Negroes to the square mile than any other spot on earth. A stranger who rides up magnificent Seventh Avenue on a bus or in an automobile must be struck with surprise at the transformation which takes place after he crosses One Hundred and Twenty-fifth Street. Beginning there, the population suddenly darkens and he rides through twenty-five solid blocks where the passers-by, the shoppers, those sitting in restaurants, coming out of theatres, standing in doorways and looking out of windows are practically all Negroes; and then he emerges where the population as suddenly becomes white again. There is nothing just like it in any other city in the country, for there is no preparation for it; no change in the character of the houses and streets; no change, indeed, in the appearance of the people, except their color.

Negro Harlem is practically a development of the past decade, but the story behind it goes back a long way. There have always been colored people in New York. In the middle of the last century they lived in the vicinity of Lispenard, Broome and Spring Streets. When Washington Square and lower Fifth Avenue was the center of aristocratic life, the colored people, whose chief occupation was domestic service in the homes of the rich, lived in a fringe and were scattered in nests to the south, east and west of the square. As late as the '80s, the major part of the colored population lived in Sullivan, Thompson, Bleecker, Grove, Minnetta Lane and adjacent streets. It is curious to note that some of these nests still persist. In a number of the blocks of Greenwich Village and Little Italy may be found small groups of Negroes who have never lived in any other section of the city. By about 1890, the center of colored population had shifted to the upper Twenties and lower Thirties west of Sixth Avenue. Ten years later another considerable shift northward had been made to West Fifty-third Street.

The West Fifty-third Street settlement deserves some special mention because it ushered in a new phase of life among colored New Yorkers. Three rather well appointed hotels were opened in the street and they quickly became the centers of a sort of fashionable life that hitherto had not existed. On Sunday evenings these hotels served dinner to music and attracted crowds of well-dressed diners. One of these hotels, The Marshall, became famous as the headquarters of Negro talent. There gathered the actors, the musicians, the composers, the writers, the singers, dancers and vaudevillians. There one went to get a close-up of Williams and Walker, Cole and Johnson, Ernest Hogan, Will Marlon Cook, Jim Europe, Aida Overton, and of others equally and less known. Paul Laurence Dunbar was frequently there whenever he was in New York. Numbers of those who love to shine by the light reflected from celebrities were always to be found. The first modem jazz band ever heard in New York, or, perhaps anywhere, was organized at The Marshall. It was a playing-singing-dancing orchestra, making the first dominant use of banjos, saxophones, clarinets and trap drums in combination, and was called The Memphis Students. Jim Europe was a member of that band, and out of it grew the famous Clef Club, of which he was the noted leader, and which for a long time monopolized the business of "entertaining" private parties and furnishing music for the New dance craze. Also in the Clef Club was "Buddy" Gilmore who originated trap drumming as it is now practiced, and set hundreds of white men to juggling their sticks and doing acrobatic stunts while they manipulated a dozen other noise-making devices aside from their drums. A good many well-known white performers frequented The Marshall and for seven or eight years the place was one of the sights of New York.

Death of a Soldier

FICTION

Louisa May Alcott

Louisa May Alcott (1832-1888) is best known for her novels, *Little Women, Little Men,* and *Jo's Boys,* but is also remembered for her essays and her association with some of the great intellectuals of her time including Emerson, Thoreau, and Hawthorne. Her essays on her experiences as a nurse during the Civil War were published in several magazines at the time and were collected into *Hospital Sketches* (1863). This essay was first published in *Commonwealth Magazine* in 1862 and reprinted in the revised version of *Hospital Sketches* in 1869.

[A]s I went my rounds with Dr. P., I happened to ask which man in the room probably suffered most; and, to my great surprise, he glanced at John.

"Every breath he draws is like a stab; for the ball pierced the left lung, broke a rib, and did no end of damage here and there; so the poor lad can find neither forgetfulness nor ease, because he must lie on his wounded back or suffocate. It will be a hard struggle, and a long one, for he possesses great vitality; but even his temperate life can't save him; I wish it could."

"You don't mean he must die, Doctor?"

"Bless you, there's not the slightest hope for him; and you'd better tell him so before long; women have a way of doing such things comfortably, so I leave it to you. He won't last more than a day or two, at furthest."

I could have sat down on the spot and cried heartily, if I had not learned the wisdom of bottling up one's tears for leisure moments. Such an end seemed very hard for such a man, when half a dozen worn out, worthless bodies round him, were gathering up the remnants of wasted lives, to linger on for years perhaps, burdens to others, dally reproaches to themselves. The army needed men like John, earnest, brave, and faithful; fighting for liberty and justice with both heart and hand, true soldiers of the Lord. I could not give him up so soon, or think with any patience of so excellent a nature robbed of its fulfillment, and blundered into eternity by the rashness or stupidity of those at whose hands so many lives may be required. It was an easy thing for Dr. P. to say: "Tell him he must die," but a cruelly hard thing to do, and by no means as "comfortable" as he politely suggested. I had not the heart to do it then, and privately indulged the hope that some change for the better might take place, in spite of gloomy prophesies; so, rendering my task unnecessary.

A few minutes later, as I came in again, with fresh rollers, I saw John, sitting erect, with no one to support him, while the surgeon dressed his back. I had never hitherto seen it done; for, having simpler wounds to attend to, and knowing the fidelity of the attendant, I had left John to him, thinking it might be more agreeable and safe; for both strength and experience were needed in his case. I had forgotten that the strong man might long for the gentle tendance of a woman's hands, the sympathetic magnetism of a woman's presence, as well as the feebler souls about him. The Doctor's words caused me to reproach myself with neglect, not of any real duty perhaps, but of those little cares and kindnesses that solace homesick spirits, and make the heavy hours pass easier. John looked lonely and forsaken just then, as he sat with bent head, hands folded on his knee, and no outward sign of suffering, till, looking nearer, I saw great tears roll down and drop upon the floor. It was a new sight there; for, though I had seen many suffer, some swore, some groaned, most endured silently, but none wept. Yet it did not seem weak, only very touching, and straightway my fear vanished, my heart opened wide and took him in, as, gathering the bent head on my arms, as freely as if he had been a little child, I said, "Let me help you bear it, John."

Never, on any human countenance, have I seen so swift and beautiful a look of gratitude, surprise and comfort, as that which answered me more eloquently than the whispered—

"Thank you, ma'am, this is right good! This is what I wanted!"

"Then why not ask for it before?"

"I didn't like to be a trouble; you seemed so busy, and I could manage to get on alone."

"You shall not want it any more, John."

Nor did he; for now I understood the wistful look that sometimes followed me, as I went out, after a brief pause beside his bed, or merely a passing nod, while busied with those who seemed to need me more than he, because more urgent in their demands. Now I knew that to him, as to so many, I was the poor substitute for mother, wife, or sister, and in his eyes no stranger, but a friend who hitherto had seemed neglectful, for, in his modesty, he had never guessed the truth. This was changed now; and, through the tedious operation of probing, bathing, and dressing his wounds, he leaned against me, holding my hand fast, and, if pain wrung further tears from him, no one saw them fall but me. When he was laid down again, I hovered about him, in a remorseful state of mind that would not let me rest, till I had bathed his face, brushed his bonny brown hair, set all things smooth about him, and laid a knot of heath and heliotrope on his clean pillow. While doing this, he watched me with the satisfied expression I so I liked to see; and when I offered the little nosegay, held it carefully in his great hand, smoothed a ruffled leaf or two, surveyed and smelt it with an air of genuine delight, and lay contentedly regarding the glimmer of the sunshine on the green. Although the manliest man among my forty, he said, "Yes, ma'am," like a little boy; received suggestions for his comfort with the quick smile that brightened his whole face; and now and then, as I stood tidying the table by his bed, I felt him softly touch my gown, as if to assure himself that I was there. Anything more natural and frank I never saw, and found this brave John as bashful as brave, yet full of excellencies and fine aspirations, which, having no power to express themselves in words, seemed to have bloomed into his character and made him what he was.

Selected Sonnets

POETRY

William Shakespeare

William Shakespeare (1564-1616) is best known today as a playwright and actor, but also wrote long-form poetry and 154 sonnets. His sonnets, in particular, are important in understanding the evolution of poetry in English as his rhyme scheme (*abab cdcd efef gg*) has become the standard meter for the form and his use of blank verse iambics in his poetry and plays redefined what the language is capable of. The sonnets below are representative of his work as a whole and closed form poetry.

XVII

Who will believe my verse in time to come,
If it were fill'd with your most high deserts?
Though yet heaven knows it is but as a tomb
Which hides your life, and shows not half your parts.
If I could write the beauty of your eyes,
And in fresh numbers number all your graces,
The age to come would say 'This poet lies;
Such heavenly touches ne'er touch'd earthly faces.'
So should my papers, yellow'd with their age,
Be scorn'd, like old men of less truth than tongue,
And your true rights be term'd a poet's rage
And stretched metre of an antique song:
But were some child of yours alive that time,
You should live twice,—in it, and in my rhyme.

XXIII

As an unperfect actor on the stage,
Who with his fear is put beside his part,
Or some fierce thing replete with too much rage,
Whose strength's abundance weakens his own heart;
So I, for fear of trust, forget to say
The perfect ceremony of love's rite,
And in mine own love's strength seem to decay,
O'ercharg'd with burthen of mine own love's might.
O! let my looks be then the eloquence
And dumb presagers of my speaking breast,

Who plead for love, and look for recompense,
More than that tongue that more hath more express'd.
O! learn to read what silent love hath writ:
To hear with eyes belongs to love's fine wit.

LV

Not marble, nor the gilded monuments
Of princes, shall outlive this powerful rhyme;
But you shall shine more bright in these contents
Than unswept stone, besmear'd with sluttish time.
When wasteful war shall statues overturn,
And broils root out the work of masonry,
Nor Mars his sword, nor war's quick fire shall burn
The living record of your memory.
'Gainst death, and all-oblivious enmity
Shall you pace forth; your praise shall still find room
Even in the eyes of all posterity
That wear this world out to the ending doom.
So, till the judgment that yourself arise,
You live in this, and dwell in lovers' eyes.

CXXX

My mistress' eyes are nothing like the sun;
Coral is far more red, than her lips red:
If snow be white, why then her breasts are dun;
If hairs be wires, black wires grow on her head.
I have seen roses damask'd, red and white,
But no such roses see I in her cheeks;
And in some perfumes is there more delight
Than in the breath that from my mistress reeks.
I love to hear her speak, yet well I know
That music hath a far more pleasing sound:
I grant I never saw a goddess go,—
My mistress, when she walks, treads on the ground:
And yet by heaven, I think my love as rare,
As any she belied with false compare.

Acknowledgements